THE OAKWOOD LIBRARY OF RAILWAY HIS

The Leven & East of Fife Railway

by
Andrew Hajducki, Michael Jodeluk
& Alan Simpson

THE OAKWOOD PRESS

British Library Cataloguing in Publication Data
A Record for this book is available from the British Library
ISBN 978 0 85361 728 0
Typeset by Oakwood Graphics.
Repro by PKmediaworks, Cranborne, Dorset.
Printed by Berforts Information Press Ltd, Eynsham, Oxford.

Companions to this volume, published by the Oakwood Press
The St Andrews Railway (OL146, 2008, ISBN 978 0 85361 673 3)
The Anstruther & St Andrews Railway (OL149, 2009, ISBN 978 0 85361 687 0)

'J37' class 0-6-0 No. 64546 travels through Cameron Bridge with a westbound goods. *W.J.V. Anderson*

Title page: Watched by the summer tourists, Gresley 'J38' 0-6-0 No. 65911 heads across Largo viaduct with a train for Edinburgh. *G. Fairlie*

Front cover: 'D34' class 4-4-0 No. 62467 at St Monance station in May 1959. *G.H. Hunt/Colour-Rail.com/SC903*
Rear cover, top: 'B1' class 4-6-0 No. 61343 crosses Largo viaduct with the a Crail-Edinburgh train in June 1965. *GPC/Colour-Rail.com/SC639*
Rear cover, bottom: A Railway Clearing House map showing the route of the Leven & East of Fife Railway.

Published by The Oakwood Press (Usk), P.O. Box 13, Usk, Mon., NP15 1YS.
E-mail: sales@oakwoodpress.co.uk
Website: www.oakwoodpress.co.uk

Contents

Preface

This book recounts the history of the railway that once served the northern shores of the Firth of Forth and for a century or more faithfully carried coal, fish, farmers and tourists along the 20 or so miles of line between Thornton Junction and Anstruther. Built in stages, the Leven & East of Fife Railway (LEoFR) started life as a locally promoted link with the Edinburgh, Perth and Dundee (EP&D) main line and the expanding town of Leven and, within time, to the beautiful fishing ports and seaside villages of the East Neuk. Having fallen out with its larger neighbour the Leven Railway was forced, at short notice, to find its own locomotives and second-hand carriages to operate its trains and it did so successfully for a generation until, in 1877, it was acquired by the North British Railway (NBR). From then on it enjoyed a golden heyday that lasted until the war after which nationalization, the decline in coal, the desertion of the herring shoals and the increasing competition from road traffic brought this to an abrupt end. But although the Kilconquhar and Anstruther extensions have been long abandoned the original section remains intact and the recent resumption of coal traffic to Thornton is an indication that, one day, the line may once again see regular passenger trains running between Leven and Edinburgh after an absence of more than 40 years.

With the present authors' two previous volumes, *The St Andrews Railway* and *The Anstruther & St Andrews Railway*, their trilogy dealing with the Fife coastal railway line from Leuchars and Thornton is now complete. In compiling all three books the authors have endeavoured to give a full picture as they can of the social, financial and historical context of this interesting line. They hope that they have provided enjoyment not only to those who enjoy finding out more about Britain's vanished rural railway network but also to those whose interest is more in the affairs of the Kingdom of Fife in general and the beautiful East Neuk in particular; whether we have succeeded in these aims is for the reader to decide for him or her self. Once again we would welcome any comments via our publishers and would apologize for the seemingly inordinate delay in the appearance of this book and, using contemporary railway jargon, we regret any inconvenience caused by its late arrival.

Still to come at a future, but hopefully not too distant date, is our final volume on the railways of the area, *The East of Fife Central Railway (The Lochty Branch)* which will also cover the Lochty Private Railway and the Kingdom of Fife Preservation Society activities at their Kirkland Yard depot.

A.H., M.J. & A.S.
Edinburgh, Cellardyke, Stirling and Kirkcaldy
Midsummer's Day 2013

Chapter One

North of the Forth:
A Beggar's Mantle Fringed with Onions

'Sae many royal burghs yoken on end to end like ropes of ingans'
Sir Walter Scott, 'Rob Roy'

Beside the Firth

The Firth of Forth presents a formidable sea barrier to travellers journeying between Edinburgh and the once remote peninsula of Fife, a self-styled Kingdom whose inhabitants still regard themselves as being a race apart from the rest of Scotland. Proud of their birthright and individuality, Fifers still cherish their independence and, having twice fought off local government changes that threatened the very existence of their county, are determined that Fife will remain very recognisably Fife. An area of varied landscapes and changing fortunes, the eastern part of Fife consists of a generally low-lying area of carboniferous limestone and calciferous sandstone covered with an often-thin layer of soil which provided a hard living for its inhabitants while a rock-girt sandy shoreline caused King James VI to comment that Fife was like 'a beggar's mantle fringed with gold'. Along this coast are a number of small towns and harbours which gave the area its wealth in former times and the crow-stepped gables and red pantile roofs of its houses spoke of a once vigorous trade with Denmark and the Low Countries and of a flourishing fishing industry; indeed so important were these towns to the area that they were sometimes likened to a rope of pearls strung along the coast although Andrew Fairservice, a character in Walter Scott's *Rob Roy*, more prosaically spoke of them as being 'yoken on end to end like ropes of ingans', a pointed reference to the fine onions for which Fife was justly renowned.

Verdant Valleys

In describing the country through which the subject of this book was later to run, one has to begin with the course of the River Orr (otherwise Ore) which arises on the south-eastern slopes of the Cleish Hills on the borders of Fife and Kinross and, in the words of the late-Victorian *Ordnance Gazetteer of Scotland*, was described as 'a sluggish rivulet' whose 'banks are everywhere flat, though in places heavily wooded; its current is muddy and the trout, pike and perch of its waters afford but indifferent fishing'. Some 14 miles from the source of the Orr and four miles to the north of the 'Lang Toun' of Kirkcaldy the river was crossed by the Falkland Road (the present A92) at the appropriately named Orr Bridge and it was here that the small village of Thornton, the scene of coal workings owned by the Earl of Rothes and where an early Boulton and Watt beam engine was employed to keep the mines dry at the end of the 18th century. In 1848 Thornton became an intermediate station on the Edinburgh & Northern Railway's new main line from the Forth crossing at Burntisland to the cities of Perth and Dundee and a junction for the Dunfermline and Cowdenbeath line. Within time Thornton became an important railway centre where passengers changed trains for the East Fife and Methil branch lines as well as being the scene of an extensive wagon works, a motive power depot and, at a later date, a major marshalling yard to serve a large part of the ever-expanding Fife coalfield.

Parallel to the Ore runs the River Leven which issues from the south bank of the Loch of that name, a wide expanse of fresh water containing an island on which Mary Queen of Scots was once held prisoner. From the loch the river flowed eastwards close to Markinch, where the Edinburgh & Northern had another station and a tall viaduct spanning it beyond reaching, a mile or so beyond Milton of Balgonie, a confluence with the Orr at a point called 'The Meetings'. Then, still in a verdant valley, the Leven was crossed by the Kirkcaldy to St Andrews Road (the present A915) at Cameron Bridge, where the Haugh flax spinning mill had been established in 1794 and the distillery of that name in 1813, before travelling through what was an increasingly industrialized but still pretty landscape to reach the sea among a series of mudflats and silt deposits at the town of Leven.

Elegant and respectable

Leven was a settlement of relatively recent origin, a burgh of barony established in 1609 and established on the eastern bank of the river it was named after and lying within the ancient parish of Scoonie. By the end of the 18th century it was 'a handsome village which may soon become a place of considerable trade, having upwards of 1,200 inhabitants' while its harbour, rebuilt in the 1830s, was home to a number of coastal vessels and to two brigs which traded with America and here was the huge cotton spinning mill, the area's main employer. Leven was also the scene of a number of local industries which included flax spinning and linen manufacturing, fulling and bleaching works, cotton spinning, weaving, canvas making, a sawmill, a pottery, a brewery, salt pans, coal mines, an ochre mine, a brickworks and tile manufactory, bone milling and a foundry with associated imports of raw materials and exports of finished products via its harbour. Indeed local industry was such that a writer in the period when the railway had not long reached the town commented that 'perhaps no other town in Fifeshire possesses in so great degree the elements of future prosperity'. Fortunately, this industry did not detract from the natural beauties of the town and its situation for in 1827 one writer commented that 'the shops are more elegant and respectable in appearance than many of those of any other town of similar size in Fife, and perhaps in Scotland'. A decade later the local minister said that 'during the summer months, Leven is the resort of a number of respectable families from the interior, for the benefit of sea-bathing'.

Largo, village and bay

Eastwards from Leven the coastline follows the great arc of Largo Bay with a wide sandy shore backed by grassy links atop the ancient raised beach that, long before the arrival of the railway, were already an irresistible lure to golfers. Passing out of the parish of Scoonie into the neighbouring parish of Largo (from the Gaelic *Learg* meaning, appropriately, the sloping hill face) lies the prominent landmark of Largo Law, an isolated volcanic outcrop reaching a height above sea level of 958 feet. Passing by the estate of Lundin, with its group of impressive bronze-age megaliths erroneously thought by early antiquarians to be druidical in origin, lay two small settlements namely Emsdorf (named after a notable British victory in the Seven Years War) and Drummochie, situated on the west bank of the Keil Burn which reached the sea here after traversing a deep ravine or den created by the melting of post-glacial waters. To the north the main coast road crosses the burn at Lundin Mill, where flour was once milled and linen manufactured in a factory founded by the British Linen Company and then, on the higher ground to the north and east, is Kirkton of Largo, (better known nowadays as Upper Largo), described as 'a remarkably agreeable little village much resorted to as summer quarters'. This settlement was unusual in that it contained Scotland's oldest canal which was built by Sir Andrew Wood. Having served as an admiral under three Scottish kings and defeated the English fleet at Dunbar, Sir Andrew came to live in retirement in Largo in 1492 and, three years later, constructed a canal to run the quarter-mile between his residence and the parish kirk. The canal was provided so that Sir Andrew could be rowed in his barge to the church every Sunday 'in great state' and in 1521 he made his last journey to the kirk so as to be buried there; the canal subsequently fell in to disuse and there are now few visible signs to remind one of this strange venture. To the south of Kirkton of Largo, and joined to it by the twisting Serpentine Walk, lies the village of Seatown of Largo or Lower Largo. This small fishing village has a harbour and a cluster of houses and is best known for being the birthplace of Alexander Selkirk who was marooned on a remote island off Chile and whose exploits were recorded by Daniel Defoe as Robinson Crusoe. By the middle of the 19th century Lower Largo was a resort and ferry port, on account of the daily steam packet sailings to Newhaven (on the opposite side of the Forth, north of Edinburgh), and also provided a livelihood to 60 or so families through its piscatorial activities.

Lapwings, swans and a strange name

As the coastline continued eastwards towards Ruddon's Point its hinterland is a desolate area called the Drumeldrie or Dumbarnie Links 'a veritable rabbit warren and haunt of aquatic birds but the pee-weep is its most audible inhabitant; the melancholic cry its most memorable impression'. Here the Cocklemill Burn reaches the sea and a mile to the north of Elie lies St Ford ('sandy ford') and the small inland village of Kilconquhar, a settlement whose name indicated that it contained the church dedicated to Conchar or Conobar, an early Celtic saint. By a strange quirk of fate Kilconquhar was altered in the local dialect back to its original pronunciation of 'Kinneuchar' but its spelling remained untouched. The village, well off the main road, had some 200 inhabitants and was dominated by its church and loch, described as 'a beautiful fresh-water lake, wooded on three sides and very deep in places. Swans haunt it still'. In 1705 Colin Lindsay, the third earl of Crawford and Balcarres, began the building of a new village a mile to the north of Kilconquhar and situated on the Largo to Pittenweem inland road and, within time, Colinsburgh began to thrive at the expense of the older settlement which became a quiet rural backwater largely devoid of trade.

Earls, islands and rubies

From Kincraig Point and backed by the hill of the same name, one properly enters the East Neuk* and reaches the links upon which golf is played and where Robert Keddie's coal and iron works were situated. At the western end of Elie bay lies the burgh of Earlsferry, formerly the northern landfall of the pilgrim route to St Andrews from North Berwick. Given royal burgh status in 1582, Earlsferry ceased to flourish when its harbour and fishing fleet were destroyed by a great storm a couple of centuries later and its 'narrow township split longwise by a High Street and whose

* A term much used in this book. The East Neuk (meaning the east nook of that part of the county) is a term to describe the coastal area from Elie to Crail and Fife Ness and its hinterland northwards to Kingsbarns parish; the term 'East Neuk of Fife' is only used outwith Fife.

The harbour at Largo with fishing boats moored beside the Crusoe Hotel, 1905.
. *Alan Brotchie Collection*

Kilconquhar with its kirk and loch - this peaceful scene from the turn of the last century remains largely unchanged. *Alan Brotchie Collection*

houses know no law of alignment' was overtaken in importance by its neighbour, Elie. *Eiladh*, the boat passage possibly referring to the gap between the mainland and the island now joined to it by a causeway) was in Victorian times a quiet and unassuming village and the home to a number of small fishing boats and possessed a harbour from which grain and potatoes were exported. Already famed for its 'rubies', garnets of a brilliant lustre found in the aptly-named Ruby Bay, Elie had already assumed a position of being a favoured watering place and the arrival of the summer steam packet and the founding of the Earlsferry and Elie Golf Club in 1858, together with the subsequent improvement of its harbour, saw to the fact that 'the majority of the inhabitants appear to cultivate the genteel business of letting their houses in summer, and occupying them in winter'. It was clear that Elie would 'flourish more abundantly in that respect when its advantages became more known' and later became a favoured holiday resort for the bourgeoisie of Kelvinside and the Edinburgh New Town.

We live by the sea

At Elie Ness, marked by the lighthouse and folly-like Lady's Tower (built by Sir John Anstruther of Elie House to protect his wife's modesty when bathing), the coastline turns abruptly north-east and, being exposed to the gales that beset the ever-widening mouth of the firth, becomes rocky and inhospitable in nature. Passing the ancient sea-girt castles of Ardross and Newark, the next place of note is St Monance,* named after another early saint of Celtic origin and whose sturdy late-medieval church dedicated to him dominated the town. Aptly the punning Latin motto of the burgh, translated as 'we live by the sea' and so its inhabitants did. One commentator described the St Monance as a place where 'the houses tumble down the cliff to the little harbour and the children tumble down to the boats as soon as they can walk'. The harbour, a very good one partly natural and partly enclosed by substantial piers, was home to a number of fishing boats and smaller craft seeking crabs and lobsters and was the refuge when storms were brewing. In common with the other East Neuk fishing burghs the female population of St Monance was engaged in the curing and gutting of fish, the mending of nets and other occupations ancillary to the fishing. A number of other industries had also been found in the town such as the production of coal and iron ore and the panning of salt and an early waggonway had linked the pans, the coal pits and the harbour at neighbouring Pittenweem. But, by the time the railway reached the area, the only other industries still in existence in the town were fish curing and boat-building.† Known locally as 'the Holy City', St Monance was also unusual in that a number of non-conformist and evangelical sects were represented among its fishermen and their families and the religious zeal of its adherents were famed throughout the East Neuk.

* St Monans or St Monance? Both versions are still used and the former is still favoured by the Ordnance Survey but the latter was used by the railway between 1863 and 1875 and again from 1936 until closure with St Monans prevailing outwith these dates. A letter published in the *East of Fife Observer* in April 1893 comments that the station nameboard was altered from the original and 'the "ce" was half-obliterated and an "s" painted over it' so that the name could be read both ways. In these days of enamel, that is now impossible and the "ce" has given way to the "s" both at the station and in the timetables'. The local pronunciation of the name was the abbreviated 'S' Minnans'; the early settlement here was first known as 'Inverie'.

† Miller's boat-building yard continued in existence until it closed in 1996, by which time it was the oldest surviving boat yard in Scotland.

Coal, cod and a cave

The next pearl on the coastal string is Pittenweem whose name, denoting the 'place of the cave' derived from its noted topographical feature, namely the 7th century cliff dwelling of St Fillan. When the harbour was improved it became the centre of Scotland's largest trade in cod and the second largest trade in herring as well as having a flourishing import trade of timber, iron, linen, lace, silk, brandy, gin and spirits from France, the low countries and Scandinavia. The merchants 'lived chiefly on the shore adjacent to the harbour' in what was thought to be 'the most ancient part of the burgh' but trade declined at the time of the union and the town reached a nadir at the beginning of the 18th century when 'it gained an unenviable notoriety in the local histories of witch-hunting ... [when] wretched women perished miserably under the hands of a benighted mob of the burghers'. Pirrenweem's trade began to improve again and by the time the railway arrived the town again enjoyed the revenue from fishing and its ancillary trades and from the shipping of potatoes and grain and its harbour was home to a number of vessels and, like St Monance and Anstruther, the site of an open-air fish market when the boats came in.

Twa Ansters and one Sillerdyke

A mile to the east of Pittenweem lies the largest town in the East Neuk namely Anstruther (Gaelic *An Struthair*, 'the streams') which, in reality, was made up of two independent burghs divided by the Dreel Burn, namely Anstruther Wester and Anstruther Easter but usually referred to locally simply as 'Anster'. The western settlement was the smaller and had eventually assumed more of a residential character while the eastern settlement contained most of the industry, trade and commerce along with the harbour with its fleet of fishing boats and trading vessels and even a steam ship which connected the burgh with Elie, Largo and Newhaven. In time Anstruther surpassed its neighbours as the main fishing port and by 1839 contained 50 or more tradesmen domiciled there, including bakers, tailors, masons, blacksmiths, saddlers, shoemakers, wrights, butchers, a bookbinder and bookseller, two inns and 13 public houses which, as the local minister commented in *The New Statistical Account* was 'far too great a number for the wants of the inhabitants'. Adjacent to the town was Cellardyke (the 'siller dykes' being a reference to the herring on the rocky coastline) containing the harbour for Kilrenny and, despite being described as 'consisting of a long rambling street' it housed sea captains, fishing boat skippers, fishermen, coopers, fish gutters, salters, clothing manufacturers and others who drew their trade from the fishing. All of this justified Cellardyke's motto of *'semper tibi pendiat hamus'* or, in Scots, 'mae your hauk aye be in the watter'.* The three burghs eventually were united legally (but not necessarily in the hearts of their inhabitants) in 1929 and rejoiced in the longest council name in Scotland: 'The United Burgh of Kilrenny, Anstruther Easter and Anstruther Wester'.

Anstruther for Cellardyke, as its railway station became known from 1932 onwards, marks the end of our journey as it also marked the point where the Leven & East of Fife Railway terminated at an end-on junction with the Anstruther & St Andrews Railway whose tale is told in a companion volume.

---

* 'May your hook be always in the water'.

Anstruther from the west in an 1840 etching. *Authors' Collection*

The winter wayfarer

The railway may have come and gone within just over a century but the beauties of the East Neuk and its environs remain and in order to see and fully enjoy it the authors would agree with the sentiments expressed by John Geddie, in his celebrated book *The Fringes of Fife,* when he suggested making a one's pilgrimage to the area,

> when the last of the bathers and holidaymakers have fled with the leaves … for only then can one fully appreciate nature's handiwork and man's that is written along the margin of the Fife coast. The little burghs huddled under the shelter of cape and high ground, the red-tiled steep-ridged houses crowding together and turning their crow-stepped gables and forestairs to the street and groups of old tombstones and storm-stressed trees gathered round some fragment of ivied ruin; the Dutch looking kirk spire and the town-house steeple asserting themselves … much of this the summer wayfarer misses.

Leven harbour with trading vessels at the quayside in this 1860s view. *Alan Brotchie Collection*

A postcard view of Largo with a paddle steamer described as being now 'an infrequent visitor'. *Alan Brotchie Collection*

Chapter Two

A Great Channel of Communication: Steamboats, Coaches and Waggonways

'The great channel of communication is the sea'
New Statistical Account of Scotland: Parish of Elie

Speed Bonnie Boat

For those who lived on the coast of Fife the sea was always regarded as the principal means of communication with the outside world whether it was with the lands lying across the North Sea or the more immediate shores of Edinburgh or East Lothian. The voyage by boat was, however, often uninviting and even hazardous in the days of sail and the combination of tides, currents, irregular sailings, unpredictable winds, off-shore rocks and the comparatively high cost of a passage across the Forth did much to dissuade the casual traveller. The great improvement came when, in the opening decades of the 19th century, sail gave way to the auxiliary power of steam and the minister of Elie in his account of the parish in the *New Statistical Account* commented that steam had been 'the chief agent and nothing has done more for the opening-up of the coast of Fife than the application of it to sailing vessels'.

The impact of steam power could not be over-estimated it was said that, 'for a journey that less than 30 years ago occupied a whole day, or perhaps two or three, is now performed in two hours and a half and for a very trifling sum' thanks to the introduction of the paddle steamer which was peculiarly suitable for operation on the Forth. The traditional five-mile short crossing from Pettycur to the Newhaven was operated several times a day by the Forth and Midlothian Ferry Trustees and this remained a popular service later augmented by the railway ferry service between Burntisland and Granton. Further east a regular packet boat service served Kirkcaldy and the eastern part of the county was served by the Leven and Largo Steam Packet Company with a daily (twice daily in summer) 21-mile service from Largo to the new chain pier at Newhaven. This was later joined by the locally owned Anstruther and Leith Steam Ship Company with their regular service from Anstruther to Elie, Largo and Leith provided, from 1848, by their new paddle steamer *Xantio*. In addition to this run Anstruther, Pittenweem and Elie were also served by a twice-daily service from Dundee to Granton, a four times a week service from Aberdeen and a twice a week service from Montrose. As the railway network began to spread some of these services remained popular with traders but less popular with passengers although their tourist potential was beginning to be recognized and of the Anstruther to Leith service it was said that, 'A trip on board will give you a good idea of the coast scenery'. In 1855 the Anstruther vessels omitted the call at Largo and made the Pittenweem call only occasionally although in the following year the company introduced a new vessel *Forth* which continued the Anstruther to Elie and Leith run until well into the railway age. Surviving in summer with such gestures as advertised cheap day trips to Anstruther the service was eventually withdrawn in May 1875 having outlived the other regular ferry runs to the area.

Thereafter the passenger steam ship services to Elie and Largo, and occasionally to Anstruther, were intermittent and provided solely for the tourist trade. An attempt to run a commuter service from Largo in competition with the railway was started in 1886 and abandoned three years later and a daily ferry service from Elie was started in 1887 and abandoned at the end of the season in 1891 despite the protests of the inhabitants of that town. The tourist services survived until 1914 and despite a partial revival after World War I the age of the pleasure steamer to the East Neuk ports is virtually over.

Imports and exports

Goods were principally moved by sea both in coastal vessels and in brigs destined for overseas. In the case of Leven Harbour in the year 1835 exports to the value of £60,400 were shipped from there and were comprised of 500 tons of bone dust, £50 worth of bricks and tiles, 900 bales of linen cloth to the value of £18,000, 215 tons of cast-iron products (thought to be stoves and piping destined for Canada), 30 tons of pig-iron, 191 tons of ochre used as a pigment, £60 worth of oats, £780 worth of potatoes, whisky from the Cameron Bridge distillery valued at £15,000 and 440 tons of linen yarn valued at £20,240. Imports in the same year amounted in value to £43,190 and were made up of 566 tons of ground ash, pulverized bone to the value of £951, 205 quarters of wheat, 905 quarters of barley, 966 quarters of malt, 566 tons of coal, flax to the value of £17,850, 7,942 tons of hemp for rope-making, 272 tons of herring from elsewhere in Scotland, 400 tons of pig-iron, 40 tons of rape cake for cattle food, 1,322 tons of stone, 105 tons of slates and 6,513 tons of timber. This trade was handled by a total of 222 coasters and 15 foreign vessels. Largo and Elie dealt with exports of potatoes, grain and fish and imports of general household and domestic goods. The *Fifeshire Journal* in April 1858 reported that in Elie:

> Several pretty large vessels, principally English, are loading and unloading in our harbour at present. We have the *Pettrill* of Fleetwood, discharging seed potatoes, the *Star* of Faversham, a large brigantine, and the *Mary and Ann*, a schooner of Portsmouth, both loading potatoes. One vessel has left laden with iron stone from Grange coal works and another cargo lies on the pier ready for shipment.

Perhaps the trade at Pittenweem and Anstruther is best dealt with quoting the shipping arrivals at those ports in the period between 24th and 30th August, 1860:

ANSTRUTHER

Aug. 24 – *Agnes* of Leith (master: Mears) for herrings; *Phoenix* of Montrose (Strachen), do. 25 – *Isabella* of Dumfries (Knight) with barrels; *Catherine* of Pittenweem (Taylor) coal; *Trio* of Arbroath (Anderson) with barrels; *Java* of Anstruther (Nicol) with coal; *Barbara* of Anstruther (Baxter) with coal; *Blossom* of St Monans (Fyall) barrels; *Mary & Jean* of St Monans (Santh) barrels; 26 – *Happy Return* of Arbroath (Clark) barrels; *Volant* of Peterhead (Ferguson) for herrings; 27 – *Teaser* of Jersey (Johnstone) for herrings; 28 – *David Kay* of Pittenweem (Garvie) for herrings; *Amandus* of Prussia (Pommerach) do.;*Olive Branch* of Dublin (Cannon) do.; *Vixon* of Dublin (McCourt) do.; *Rover* of Dublin (Edwards) for do.; *Ann* of Berwick (Lough) for do., *Lark* of Dundee (Anderson) with salt; *Traveller* of Montrose (Ingles) for herrings; *Alert* of Fowey (Salt) with salt; *Isle of Arran* (Anderson) with barrels. 29 – *Gleaner* of Cardigan (Joins) for herrings.

PITTENWEEM

Aug. 25 – *S.S. Victor* of Leith with barrels and salt; 28 – *David Kay* (Garvie) from Stonehaven ballast; *Agnes* (Duffie) from Leith barrels and salt; *Mary Ann* (Welch) Leith, ballast; 29 – *Henry & Betsy* (Jones) Liverpool, salt; *Clipper* (Anderson) from Leith, barrels and salt; *Blossom* (Fyall) from Buckhaven, barrels and salt; *David Edwards* (Edwards) from Perth, barrels and salt, *Twins* (Malcolm) Leith, barrels and salt; *Mary Ann* (Welch) Leith ballast; *Steamer K* (McLaughton) Leith, barrels and salt. *SAILINGS FROM PITTENWEEM* Aug. 24 – *Agnes*, (Duffie) for Leith, herrings; Steamer *Victor*, Leith, herrings; 30 – *Brilliant* (Miller); Peterhead, herrings; *Steamer K* (McLaughton) Leith, herrings.

Plying the turnpikes

The introduction of toll gates and turnpike trusts in Fife meant that local roads were now kept in a reasonably good state of repair* so that a regular service of horse-drawn coaches was now a possibility and several daily routes were in consequence in operation. The stage coach *Balcarres* ran every Monday, Wednesday and Friday from Anstruther at 7.30 am to Pittenweem, Elie, Kilconquhar, Colinsburgh (where it stopped at the Plough Inn), Upper Largo, Leven, Cameron Bridge, Dysart, Kirkcaldy and the ferry terminus at Pettycur (later moved to Burntisland); it returned following the same route on Tuesday, Thursday and Saturday mornings arriving back at Anstruther at 3 pm. A daily service ran from Anstruther at 6.30 am (10 in winter) to Pittenweem and Elie to Lower Largo to connect with the packet boats to Newhaven and in summer two return journeys were completed daily to connect with the summer sailings. Leven was connected to Upper Largo and St Andrews by a (horse) bus service while Anstruther was also linked to St Andrews by a similar service and Elie to Ceres and Cupar were also so connected. Where the bus services were not paralleled by the railway these services survived but others were cut back when the railway arrived so that a Kilconquhar to Anstruther service was operated from 1857 and 1863. No comprehensive network of bus or coach services was ever planned in the horse-drawn period and it was not until after World War I when the motor bus finally arrived that East Fife gained a pattern of inter-connecting public services. Much of this network has now been lost and at the present time buses now connect the towns of the East Neuk in much the same way that they did in 1850, albeit with an increased frequency. Local goods services were operated by a number of different carters each operating in a defined area or on a particular route and special runs were undertaken when and if necessary – examples of Leven carters in 1860 were those who operated on a Leven, Kirkcaldy and Burntisland service (despite the rivalry of the railway) and three carters who operated in the Largo-Leven-Kirkcaldy area including David Lindsay of Kirkton of Largo who operated a twice-weekly service to Colinsburgh, St Monans, Pittenweem and Anstruther.

A waggonway for Leven

Prior to the coming of the railway there were a number of early waggonways in Scotland consisting of dedicated routes linking particular coal pits with local harbours and, as was often the case, with salt works containing pans filled with sea water under which coal fires were lit in order to heat the water to boiling point and cause the water to evaporate leaving the salt behind – an early example of full industrial integration. In the case of East Fife salt was not only a household necessity but was also required for the linen and textile industry and, more importantly, for the processing of fish where herrings were packed into barrels and 'cured' with salt to act as a preservative. The coal itself was carried in open waggons constructed of

* There were, however, criticisms of both the poorly kept surfaces and the tendency of local roads to flood – criticisms that are not unknown to the East Neuk motorist of the present time!

wood and hauled by a single horse over a dedicated formation on which wooden rails were laid. Where a gradient was involved the horse could be unhitched from the waggon and it then be allowed to travel under gravity with the horse walking alongside.

In Leven itself this precursor of the railway was first laid down in about 1760 to link the several small pits which existed on the eastern part of the Durie Estate owned by the Christie family with the salt pans which already existed on the shore. In 1783 a plan was drawn which showed the waggonway running to the No.11 pit with a branch southwards to No. 6 pit and extending at its full extent to some 1¼ miles in length. The *Statistical Account of Scotland* entry for Scoonie parish, published in 1791 mentions that there were seams of coal in the Durie estate which were of excellent quality and exported to Holland 'but that at present the coals now working are of inferior quality but answer for landsale [i.e. local usage] and furnish fuel for two or three salt pans which are very productive'. The waggonway did not apparently link up with Leven Harbour and seems to have gone out of use before 1835 when it was reported that no coal whatsoever was exported from Leven and indeed a small quantity was imported. Whether or not this was for the salt pans is not clear but by then the waggonway had been apparently 'shorn of its glory' and part of its route was later obstructed by the building of the Free Church, later the Town Hall, some 200 yards north of the shore.

In *Rambles in Scoonie and Weymss*, published in 1905, the author Andrew S. Cunningham, a local newspaper proprietor, stated that:

> Amongst all the changes that have been experienced in the Burgh of Leven in recent years, perhaps the most striking change of all is that which has been wrought on the old Waggonroad. The coals which were exported from Leven Harbour to Holland, Norway and the upper reaches of the Baltic were trundled down the old waggonroad in bogies. The bogies were drawn by horses on wooden rails and in the busy shipping season the crack of the driver's whip, the creaking of stiff wheels and the rattle of tail chains could be heard day and night. The sides of the waggonway have, for a considerable distance, been taken up by cottages of a modern type. Brambles and rose bushes grow in profusion on the slopes of the line to the north of the North British Railway. The waggonway is one of the finest walks in the district, so if the people of Leven have lost through the stoppage of the Sauchenbush and Siller Hole pits* they have gained in another by their having been permitted to ramble among the haunts of bush and birds without being troubled by the rattle of wagons and the noise which form the accessories of a colliery.

The coal pits were disused by the early 1830s but the adjacent Scoonie Colliery was re-opened by Charles Landale in 1854. The original salt pans and their associated windmill to pump water in to them ceased operation prior to 1840 although a later venture to process salt from imported rock salt was started on the same site by a Prestonpans man named Alexander Clark and subsequently run as Gerrards Salt works for many years. With the construction of the promenade the whole area was altered and no trace of the pans or windmill and of the waggonway south of Durie Street still exists but its line can be traced along aptly named Waggon Road up to Windygates Road. All traces have again disappeared north of this with housing developments obscuring the former Sauchenbush and Sillerhole pits and the line of the waggonway.

* The Sauchenbush was a small stair pit sunk to the east of Sillerhole Den and just to the south of Coldstream Farm on the Dangerfield Road between Leven and Cupar. The Sillerhole was on the Aithernie estate to the west of the Sillerhole Den.

The Leven Brickworks tramway

Another early industrial line situated in Leven was the Leven Brickworks tramway* which was opened in 1830 and travelled from a clay pit 150 yards west of the waggonway to the Cuttlehill Brick and Tile Works of Alex. White & Sons, a flourishing institution which, it is said, manufactured half of the bricks with which Leven was made. Presumably the rails were iron and no motive power was employed other than a horse stabled at Cuttlehill to take wagon-fulls of the raw material from the pit to the works. In 1856 the tramway was re-aligned after the East of Fife Railway was extended eastwards from the original Leven station and a flat crossing was made between the tramway and the railway, the latter being protected by warning signals. In 1883 the brickwork proprietors received compensation of £400 or so after they raised an action in the Court of Session against the North British Railway for damages occasioned by lost profits after the railway was relaid the previous year and the flat crossing negligently omitted so that the tramway could not be used.† A dispute then arose between the minister of Scoonie and White regarding the level of rental to be paid for the use of part of the Glebe lands in the period from Martinmas 1885 – White wished to pay a marginally increased rent while the minister demanded a much greater annual payment. After the latter successfully forced White to remove the tramway that ran through his land, clay from the pit could no longer being brought to the works resulting in closure of the tramway and the subsequent closure of the brick works which, it was claimed, were by then the oldest subsisting industry in the parish.#

The Newark Coal and Salt waggonway

Eastwards along the coast from Leven there existed another early waggonway which was once again built to serve coal and salt. Although there had been earlier small pits in the area around Pittenweem and St Monance under the control of the Earls of Kellie, it was not until 1771 that a concerted effort was set up to exploit commercially this coal in conjunction with the production of sea salt to take advantage of a severe shortage of that essential commodity used by the local fishing industry. In that year Sir John Anstruther of Elie House set up in partnership with John Fall, a grain merchant of Dunbar, in a venture called The Newark Coal and Salt Company with the twin aims of producing coal to heat the salt pans at St Philips, a third of a mile to the east of St Monance, and of transporting their surplus coal to Pittenweem Harbour for export. In order to carry out these aims the company constructed a total of 2½ miles of waggonway using wooden rails and horse-drawn waggons capable of holding more than two tons of coal each. The 'main' line commenced at the pithead at First Deep which was situated a little to the north of the present day Coal Farm and proceeded to the north-east crossing the Colinsburgh to Pittenweem Road (the present B942) close to where the railway had its Waterless bridge. Then turning in a more easterly direction it followed the trackbed of the later line until, reaching the future site of Pittenweem station, it swung to the south and entered the town by crossing James Street on the level. It proceeded down what is now a narrow lane called Waggon Road to cross Marygate and on entering the

* By 1830 the term 'tramway' had largely replaced 'waggonway' for such horse-drawn lines.
† *Alex. White & Sons v North British Railway*, reported in *East of Fife Record*, 27th October, 1882.
\# *Rev. Charles Durward v Alex. White & Sons*, reported in *The Fifeshire Advertiser* of 13th and 20th May, 1887 under the heading of 'Extraordinary Action at Leven'.

priory grounds ran through a shallow cutting on a downward gradient worked by gravity to emerge between numbers 5 and 7 East Shore and onto the central coal pier at Pittenweem harbour which had been constructed by Sir John to facilitate his exports. A branch line ran from the salt pans via a ramp in a north-easterly direction to the south of Pathead Cottage and across both the Elie to Anstruther road (A917) and the Colinsburgh Road to the west of their junction before heading north by the now-vanished Waterless Farm to join up with the main line. The route had been carefully chosen to avoid trespassing upon the land owned by Sir John's cousin, Sir Robert Anstruther of Balcaskie, an estate situated a mile to the north of Coal Farm and in a litigation raised by Sir Robert in 1785 Sir John was careful to state that the waggonway had been laid 'a way round to carefully avoid to touch or come near his ground'.

The fortunes of the waggonway varied with the price of salt and the ease with which coal could be extracted and although Fall went bankrupt in 1788 his shares were acquired by others. The whole venture ceased production in about 1814 when production of coal finally ceased. Long before this, in 1794, the waggonway went out of use although for many years its route remained untouched by Pittenweem council in case it would ever be needed again. With the removal of the tax on English rock salt panning was no longer economic and customs duties rendered the export of coal uneconomic unless it was sent by large vessels. In 1852 the coal field was offered for sale in the short-lived local paper *The Pittenweem Register* and it was subsequently surveyed by David Landale who operated the Scoonie Pits referred to earlier. Despite further interest in re-opening the mine workings nothing was heard of the scheme again despite the fact that the term 'Pittenweem coal' was in the 1850s still used on the continent as a by-word for good quality Scottish coal. In September 1889 workmen relaying a gas main at the junction of James Street and Waggon Road in Pittenweem were reported to have unearthed several of the sleepers of the old waggonway. The *East of Fife Record* marvelled that 'notwithstanding the length of time the rails have been underground they were in a wonderful good state of preservation'.

In 1890 a proposed Pittenweem Coal Company was mentioned in the local press and it was claimed that new pits to be opened up in the vicinity of Coal Farm and that 300 tons per day of coal 'is expected to yield a very handsome return to the shareholders'. No potential shareholders came forward and the plan was later abandoned. Sir John Anstruther 's at Pittenweem was demolished when the harbour was reconstructed in the first decade of the 20th century but a very comprehensive topographic and cartographic survey of the route of the waggonway has recently been carried out.* At the present time there are but few reminders of this early line other than in the street name, the cutting and the gap between the houses in East Shore in Pittenweem and the pits are remembered only in the name Coal Farm. However, in St Monance the salt pans are still evident in the recently restored windmill which once pumped the water in and the excavated pans themselves with the accompanying interpretive signs boards.

* See Lewis, Martin, Martin and Murdoch, *The Salt and Coal Industry at St Monans, Fife in the 18th and 19th Centuries*, Tayside & Fife Archeological Committee Monograph 2 (Glenrothes, 1999). The *East of Fife Record* of 20th March, 1891 showed a fairly accurate map of the supposed line of the Pittenweem waggonway from the salt pans, presumably drawn from local sources of knowledge.

Chapter Three

An Excellent Return:
The first East of Fife Railway 1845-1850

'The estimate of revenue ... shows an excellent return for the capital invested.'
East of Fife Railway Prospectus

Railway Mania

Apart from Leven itself there were numerous other potential attractions for those who wished to see a railway built to serve both that town and the settlements which lay to the east. On 31st June, 1845 the Edinburgh & Northern Railway Act was passed and construction began on what was later to form the present-day main line through Fife. Subsequently re-named the Edinburgh, Perth & Dundee Railway the line began at Burntisland which was served by a steamer packet service from Granton (connected by rail for the short distance to Edinburgh via the Scotland Street tunnel). From Burntisland the line ran along the coast to Kinghorn, Kirkcaldy and Dysart before heading inland to Thornton and Markinch to Ladybank where it forked and one line led through Newburgh to Perth and the other proceeded to Cupar, Leuchars and Tayport. Here it made a connection with another crossing to Broughty Ferry which was then to be connected by rail to Dundee, Arbroath, Montrose and Aberdeen - a direct (if one ignored the ferry passages) service linking the second, third and fourth most populous towns in Scotland.

There was, at this time, a great desire to promote a flood of new railway lines throughout the whole of Britain since every town thought that it deserved a direct link with both its neighbours and the emerging network of new trunk routes, actual and proposed. It was also a period of intense capital speculation and monies were being sought almost without recourse to whether or not any particular scheme was likely to be financially viable or attractive to the proposed shareholders. The bubble eventually burst in what was afterwards described as the period of 'Railway Mania' when the supply of easy money ran out and the get-rich-quickly merchants turned their energies elsewhere. Some of the proposed lines were built, others abandoned forever and some were merely postponed to another day and in this category the East of Fife Railway (EoFR) firmly fell.

The first East of Fife Railway

On 25th August, 1845, barely two months after the Edinburgh & Northern Bill received the Royal Assent, a Prospectus was issued for a new line to be provisionally entitled the East of Fife Railway. This informed the public that the new company was being formed 'with a view to extending the benefits of railway communication to the district lying to the South and Eastern coast of Fife from the Edinburgh and Northern Railway to the burgh of Anstruther Wester' and that the length of the line was to be 20 miles via either the valley of the Orr or the valley of the Leven 'as fixed by the engineer'. The Prospectus went on to state that,

> If along the Orr, it will leave the Edinburgh and Northern Railway near Thornton, and if by Leven at or near Markinch. In either case it will pass by, or near, to Cameron Bridge,

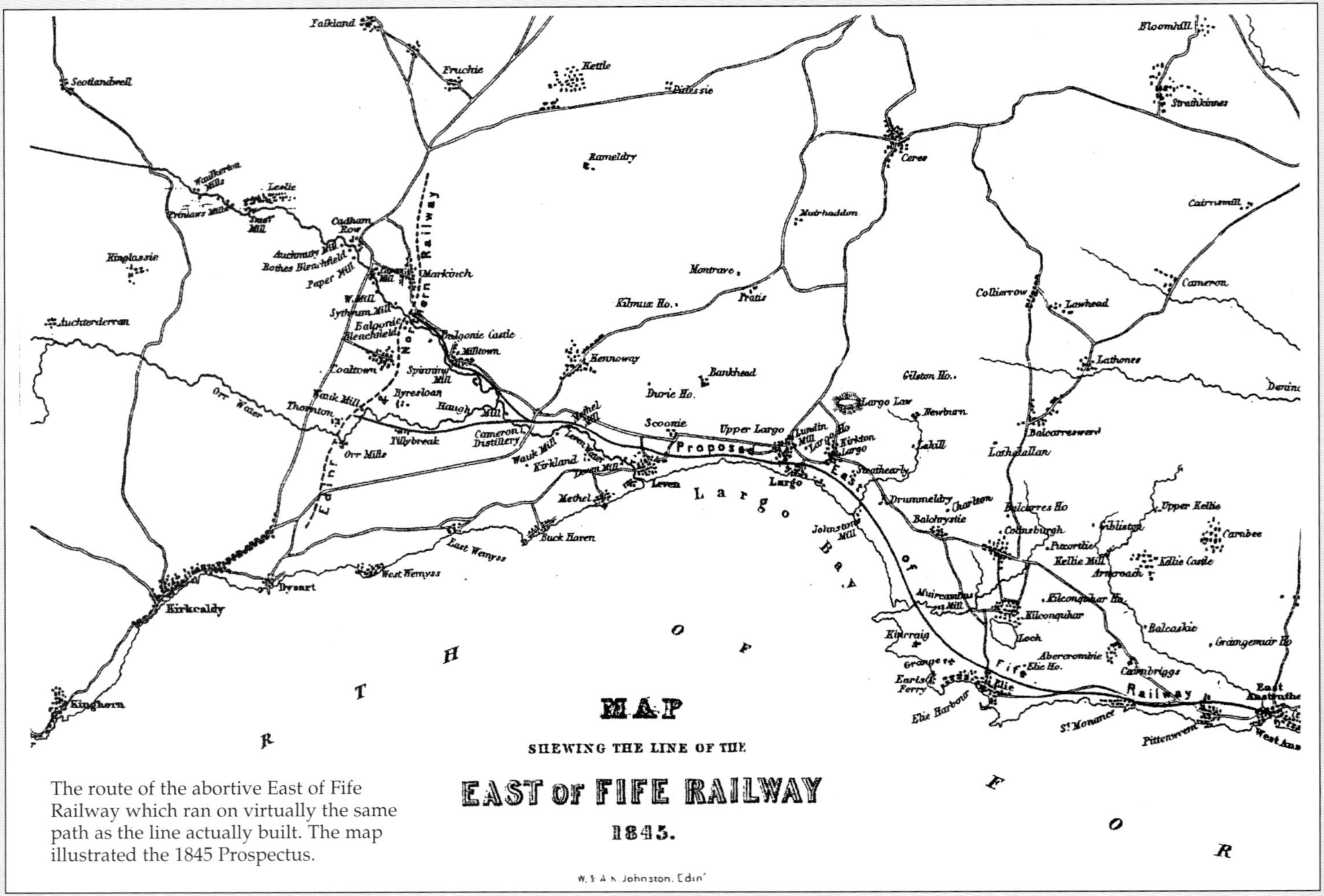

The route of the abortive East of Fife Railway which ran on virtually the same path as the line actually built. The map illustrated the 1845 Prospectus.

Kennoway, Leven, Largo, Kirkton of Largo, Newburn, Colinsburgh, Kilconquhar, Earls Ferry, Elie, St Monance, Pittenweem, and terminate at the Harbour of Anstruther. The whole of this district, and that of Kingsbarns and Crail, lying to the eastward, possesses the richest and most fertile soil in Fife, and from the situation of the burghs along the sea coast, it includes a very great proportion of the county.This railway will, by means of Lines sanctioned by Parliament, or for which Companies have been formed, and deposits on the stock paid, connect the above towns and district with Kirkcaldy, Kinghorn, Burntisland, Dunfermline, Perth, Cupar, Dundee, St Andrews and other important places.A general survey of the country has already been made, and it has been found that the works will not only be free from tunnelling or embanking, but of the easiest description. As the Line will run along sands lying between the different burghs above mentioned for a distance of nearly six miles, it will neither alter the features of the country nor require the purchase of valuable land which it will accommodate, and will thus be made at a comparatively small cost. The estimate of revenue, based upon the existing traffic, shows an excellent return for the capital invested.

The Prospectus then went on to comment on the present arrangements for travellers from the area, highlighting that the Edinburgh to Largo steamer sailings carried on average some 220 passengers a day and that there were regular services by sea from Elie and Anstruther and that feeder coach services linked the East Neuk towns to the ferries but added that (in recognition of the 12 or more feet of tidal rise and fall in this part of the Forth), 'The whole of this large passenger traffic by steam-boats being subjected to a tedious and often stormy sea-voyage, without the benefits of low-water piers, only requires the formation of a Railway to be at once diverted to that mode of conveyance, whereby the comfort of the low-water piers at Granton, Burntisland and Queensferry will also be gained'.

The Prospectus voiced the opinion that, 'the number of visitors attracted annually to the watering-places of Wemyss, Leven, Largo, and Elie is at present very great, and, with the advantages of a Railway, will be much increased' although whether they agreed with Sandy Sharp of Lower Largo who, in a letter printed in the *Pittenweem Register* of 24th June, 1848 was of the view that, 'the responsible portion of the inhabitants of Edinburgh and Leith' who visited the locality by steamship and were prone to be harassed by less desirable elements were to be made safe by him 'and in order to meet no obstruction from sturdybeggars, landloupers, rogues, vagabonds of any description, I have resolved to keep the coast clear of that description of vermin from Leven to Lundin Mill'. The Prospectus, however, envisaged no such 'vermin' and went on to state that:

The goods traffic will be no less considerable, and will be supplied by the extensive mills and works on the Line; and by the carriage of coals and lime to the burghs and district eastwards of Elie, where at present the carriage of the coals equals the prime cost. The conveyance of fat cattle and sheep to the Edinburgh and Glasgow markets will also form a large source of revenue; these and the agricultural produce of the district being presently conveyed by several sailing packets from the different ports under great disadvantages, and at very heavy charges. There will likewise be a large sum paid for the carriage of fish from the flourishing ports of Anstruther, Pittenweem, and St Monance to the Edinburgh and Glasgow markets, and to Dundee, Perth, and the inland districts, with which a very extensive trade, employing a large proportion of the population is at present carried on. Independent of the white fishing, which is carried on to a very great extent, there are during the herring fishing months no less than from 80 to 120 tons carried daily to the western and middle districts of the county, and to the markets of Dundee and Perth, almost the whole of which would pass over this Line of Railway. The numerous assurances of support received from the landowners, the principal of whom are upon the

Provisional Committee, leave no doubt of the successful issue of the application which will be made to Parliament for an Act of Incorporation in the next session. Indeed it is believed that no undertaking has been presented to Parliament for a length of time which has received more support from Landowners, and the promoters have reason to calculate on their unanimous concurrence. Powers will be sought in the Act to allow interest at £4 per cent per annum on all paid-up calls during the progress of the works, and the liability of the Shareholders will be limited to the amount of their subscriptions.

The published plans, which resulted from a detailed survey, show a line of some 19 miles extending from the Edinburgh & Northern line at Markinch and running via the valley of the Leven River to Cameron Bridge and Leven, with an alternative route from Thornton to Cameron Bridge via the Orr valley, and then, following the coastline of Largo Bay, via Largo, Elie, St Monance and Pittenweem to a terminus situated on reclaimed land adjacent to the West Pier at Anstruther. A short branch line to serve the Kirkland Works was also provided for.

The Fife Central Junction Railway

At or about the same time another railway scheme was being promoted by a concern that rather grandly described itself as the Fife Central Junction Railway and its published plans showed a line that began at Elie pier where it was to connect with separate ferry services over the eight miles of so of the Firth to connect up with branch lines to North Berwick and Yellowcraigs near Direlton. This was perhaps the proposed company's first major error in that there would have been little traffic interested in travelling over this route – indeed no regular passenger service by steamship had been (or indeed would ever be likely to be) provided between these points. The second error was that it was to connect up with a new main line to the south, the Scottish Grand Union Railway proposed to run via Haddington to Carlisle and Berwick despite the fact that the North British Railway had been authorized to run between Edinburgh and Berwick on a different route and construction was underway. On the north side of the Forth a short branch was to connect the harbour at Elie to the East of Fife Railway and then at Largo the new line was to run northwards to Ceres where it would join a loop line between Kettle and Dairsie on the Edinburgh & Northern. Needless to say neither of these lines ever saw the light of day although there were curious echoes of at least part of the proposals in the later plans for the East Fife Central Railway at the end of the century.

Hopes dashed

The promoters who formed the Provisional Committee of the East of Fife Railway were an interesting lot and included Sir Windham Carmichael Anstruther of Anstruther and Carmichael, Bart., Onesipherus Tyndal Bruce of Nuthill, the Fife County Convenor, Henry Raeburn of Stockbridge, Edinburgh (the son of Sir Henry Raeburn, the noted Scottish portrait painter), Robert Buchan of Balchristy, Manchester, the proprietors of the Kirkland mills, the Chief Magistrates of Pittenweem, Anstruther Easter and Anstruther Wester, and a number of local bankers, builders, merchants, fish curers, landowners and other worthies. The Interim Secretary was an Edinburgh solicitor, James Hill.

What, perhaps, was somewhat surprising was the fact that the proposed capital to be raised for the line amounted to a fairly staggering £250,000 to be made up of 10,000

£25 shares – an ambitious amount to be raised locally for a line which was only to be worked as a branch off the Edinburgh & Northern main line. On 16th July, 1846 the East of Fife Railway Act (9 & 10 Vict., cap. cxc) received the Royal Assent, providing for 'a line from the Edinburgh & Northern Railway at Markinch to Anstruther Easter, with a branch to the Kirkland Works near Leven', but in the financial crisis that followed the crash of the Railway Mania of 1845-1846 there was little hope of raising the capital required. The promoters, however, struggled on and on 22nd July, 1847 the East of Fife Railway (Markinch Deviation) Act (10 & 11 Vict., cap. ccxxiv) was passed, authorizing the construction of a deviation line at Markinch to improve the junction with the Edinburgh & Northern at that point and also to relieve the promoters from any obligation to build the alternative route via the valley of the Orr. Eventually, however, the promoters had to bow to the inevitable given that the scheme was viewed as an ambitious and over-costly project and the first East of Fife Railway was quietly abandoned, its name to be resurrected in a later and this time successful scheme. On 14th August, 1850 'An Act for the Dissolution of the East of Fife Railway Company and For the Abandonment of the Company' (13 & 14 Vict., cap. xcvii) was passed and, for the time being, the East of Fife Railway was no more.

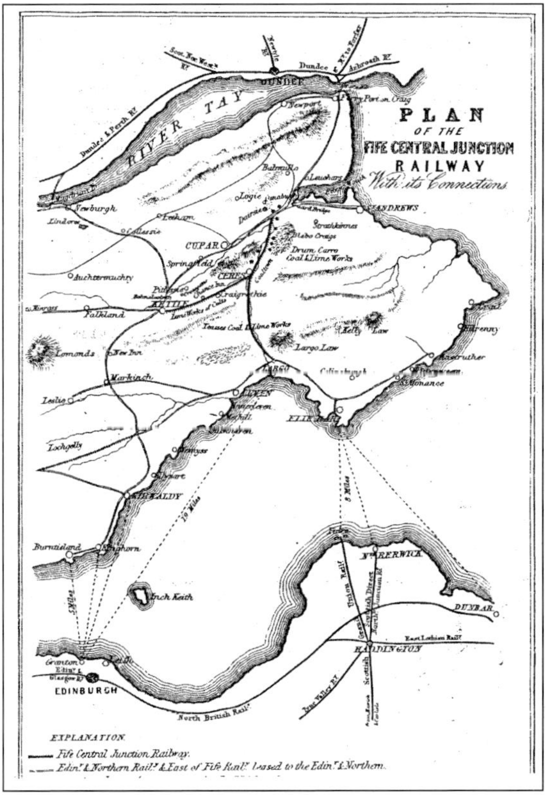

The proposed Fife Central Junction Railway between Elie and Dairsie. Note the connections from the south via Haddington.

Chapter Four

Rails Through the Valley: The Leven Railway 1851-1854

'The cheapest railway bill that has ever been obtained'

John Haig, Chairman, Leven Railway

A railway for Leven

With the demise of the East of Fife scheme there was a temporary lull in enthusiasm for a line to serve the area. However, on 20th September, 1847 the Edinburgh & Northern line was opened as far as Cupar and local stations were provided at Kirkcaldy, Sinclairtown, Dysart and Markinch, with an additional station being opened at Thornton which became known as Thornton Junction not long after the opening of the loop line from Dunfermline, Cardenden and Lochgelly on 4th September, 1848. By now the inhabitants of the Leven area again began to lobby for a branch line to serve them after the failure of the earlier East of Fife scheme and by April 1851 the local newspapers reported that moves were afoot for a local branch line from Thornton Junction to run only as far as Leven. In October 1851 the Leven Railway Company's Prospectus was issued to the public and it was made clear to the prospective shareholders that,

> ... the abandonment of the East of Fife Railway has made it clear that a less adventurous course be pursued to satisfy the more immediate requirements of the district. The promoters therefore propose to limit their efforts to a short branch of six miles from Thornton Station to Leven, with a single line of rails, and to avoid expensive engineering, by adopting as far as possible, the natural gradients of the Orr and Leven Water. They also intend to save entirely on the heavy outlay involved in the purchase of locomotive power and other rolling stock. It is hoped to open the line at an outlay not exceeding £25,000.

The eight promoters of the new company were all well-kent local figures and they were John Haig, Sir Ralph Anstruther, John Wood, George Wilson, Adam Johnstone, James Anderson, Henry Tandy Peter, Alexander Boswell and James Greenhill – the first six of whom later became Directors. Haig, appointed as Chairman, was the owner of the large distillery at Cameron Bridge and lived in Cameron House adjacent to it. The father of 11 children (the youngest of whom, Douglas, became commander-in-chief of the British forces during World War I*) and the brother of Robert Haig, proprietor of the Seggie Distillery at Guardbridge (and a Director of the St Andrews Railway), he was noted as being both a good employer and a successful businessman. Sir Ralph Abercrombie Anstruther, Bt, was a wealthy landowner and lived at Balcaskie House, a couple of miles to the north of St Monance; he became Deputy Chairman of the company and was active in local politics and later became Rector of the University of St Andrews where he 'was all along very popular with the students' as well as Convenor of Fife County ('the highest honour that can be conferred on a country gentleman'). Wood was a banker residing at Colinsburgh, Wilson a businessman who owned the cloth bleaching establishment at Haugh Mill near Windygates, Johnstone was a Writer [solicitor] from Dunfermline, Anderson a partner in the Durie Foundry, Greenhill and Peter were partners in the great local flax and tow spinners at Kirkland Works in Leven and Boswell was the principal of a company of flax spinners, shoe twine manufacturers and herring net manufacturers known as the Hawkslaw Works, also in Leven.

* A Holmes class 'C' (LNER 'J36') 0-6-0 No. 650 was in BR days named in his honour.

Wilkie and Bouch

The Secretary of the Leven Railway was to be Andrew Wilkie, a Writer [solicitor] who had an office in Bank Street, Leven. Wilkie, described by Sir Ralph as 'an exceedingly intelligent and spirited individual', was a fairly extraordinary character, strong in will and determined to do his best for the fledgling company. The son of a tenant farmer and educated at Leven Parish School, he served his legal apprenticeship in Edinburgh and,

> ... during his residence in Modern Athens he had gained considerable experience and become well acquainted with regard to procedure for the promotion of railways. He believed that a railway, consisting of a single line and constructed on economic principles, would not only be of great advantage to the town in which he had taken up his residence, and its neighbourhood, as well as the whole eastern portion of the county; and that it would be remunerative to the shareholders.*

In addition to his legal activities Wilkie was also the local agent of the Western Bank and, following the financial crash of that institution in 1857, was appointed agent for the Royal Bank of Scotland. His style was his own and although the Minute Books for the Leven company have not survived, his letter books have and it is through these that much of the flavour of this small concern has survived. The same account already quoted goes on to make sure that Wilkie's contribution to the success of the project was not to be underestimated:

> There was considerable difficulty experienced in getting up the Leven company, doubts at first being expressed by many parties as to the probability of it paying. Mr Wilkie succeeded in impressing his views on the gentleman who afterwards became the Chairman of the Company ... He also succeeded in thereafter obtaining the co-operation of several of the leading gentlemen connected with the district; but much trouble and exertions were required before the Act for the construction of the line was obtained.

Having learnt a lesson from the collapse of the somewhat overblown and expensive East of Fife scheme, the Leven Railway was now to be built at minimal cost and, following the successful example of the St Andrews Railway upon which construction had just begun, Thomas Bouch was appointed as Engineer, this being his second ever commission. At the time Bouch was highly regarded and was in the vanguard of a movement to create cheap and economic railways† and in the opinion of Sir Ralph 'the company would have gone far before they would have found one better qualified for the duties which he had undertaken'. His star was to set a quarter of a century later with the collapse of the Tay Bridge 'on the last Sabbath day of 1879, which will be remembered for a very long time' but at the time when the Leven Railway engaged him he had not long before been appointed as Engineer to the St Andrews Railway a few miles to the north and was regarded as an able young man of great promise.

The Leven Railway was to be financed by the issue of 2,300 £10 shares, making a total of £23,000 with a provision to raise further capital by way of borrowings on mortgage or bond of £5,000, such sum not to be raised unless and until the whole of the original share capital had been used up. The railway was to consist of three separate but connected lines namely a 'main line' from Thornton Junction to Cameron Bridge and Leven, terminating at a point called Burnmill on the north-western outskirts of the town, a spot apparently chosen because it would be suitable

* From *A Short Account of the Leven and East of Fife Railway Company by One of the Auditors*, an extremely rare publication written after the takeover of the company in 1877 and printed by R. & R. Clark of Edinburgh.

† Bouch, the St Andrews line and the cheap railway movement are dealt with in Chapter Two of *The St Andrews Railway*.

for an eastwards extension of the line towards Anstruther should this later be merited, together with branches to Kirkland mill and Leven Harbour. Private sidings were to be provided at Haughmill, Cameron Bridge distillery and at the Kirkland works. A provisional contract was entered into by the promoters of the new company and the Edinburgh, Perth & Dundee wherein it was agreed that the latter company would work the line under certain conditions referred to later.

At the Gardeners' Hall

At 12 noon on Tuesday 16th December, 1851 in the Gardeners' Hall in Leven, a public meeting was held by the promoters of the Leven Railway at which a number of the Provisional Committee members spoke. Sir Ralph Anstruther, after telling the well attended meeting that this was the first railway in which he had been involved, praised the efforts of those public spirited persons who had 'taken a most active part in surveying, planning and estimating the cost' of the line. He then made reference to the undoubted advantages of railways to the country:

> I may be allowed to call your attention to the fact that those communities which are at a distance from railway communication not only make no progress, but they retrograde and that at a rapid rate. They see the stream of traffic which had formerly flowed past their doors diverted into other channels, and they thus lose the relative position to other places they formerly had. This is universally the case, and hence the anxiety in individuals either to locate themselves in localities where the advantages of railway communication exist, or to bring these to their own doors. Now, as I presume that you have no inclination to quit this sunny side of the hill, and migrate to Markinch, to the higher ground and colder climate, or to add another mile or two to the long town of Kirkcaldy, I think that you will prefer the second part of the alternatives, and be glad if you can bring these advantages to your own doors.

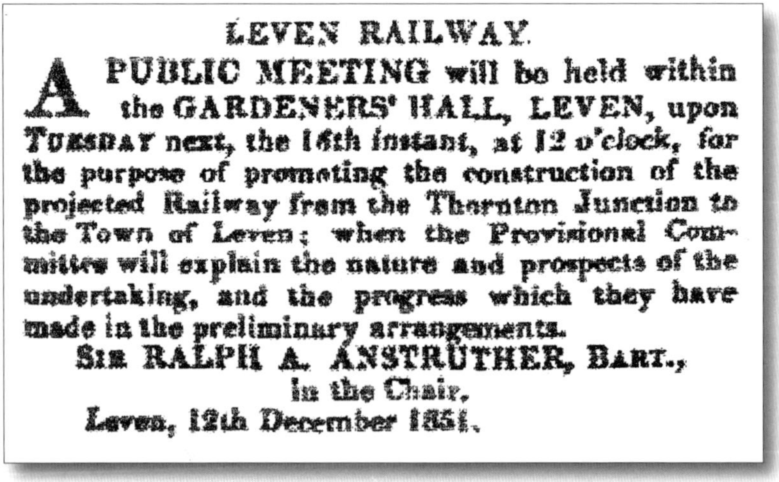

LEVEN RAILWAY.

A PUBLIC MEETING will be held within the GARDENERS' HALL, LEVEN, upon TUESDAY next, the 16th instant, at 12 o'clock, for the purpose of promoting the construction of the projected Railway from the Thornton Junction to the Town of Leven; when the Provisional Committee will explain the nature and prospects of the undertaking, and the progress which they have made in the preliminary arrangements.

SIR RALPH A. ANSTRUTHER, BART., in the Chair.

Leven, 12th December 1851.

The *Fifeshire Journal* intimation of a public meeting.

He then stated that there had been eight offers for constructing the line and that the lowest of these was £13,186, together with a further £1,000 to establish stations at Cameron Bridge and Leven 'which are to be made on the most economical plan'. The successful contractors were Messrs John and Matthew Anderson of Middlesbrough and Sir Ralph emphasised that the meeting had been called only after the promoters had 'chalked out a line of procedure' to ensure that the proposals were only put before the public when all the facts had been ascertained. After dealing with other financial matters he stated that,

> ... the cost of the land would amount to £2,122, to which must be added to tenants' damages and other items, bringing it to £3,123 but in order to make ourselves quite secure, we have stated it at £4,000. This is partly conjectural, because we understand that, in quarters where I should have little expected it, there is likely to be considerable opposition to this line. But things are in a different state than they were several years ago. Then parties in Parliament were against railways, and local juries were also against them; but these railway transactions have become so entirely part and parcel of the country, that no opposition to a railway will be entertained which is not founded upon some right, tangible ground. And as regards the awards of local juries, if there is now any leaning, it is rather towards railways than otherwise; so that if any one is foolish enough to oppose the line, it is not likely that it will be entertained by Parliament; or if the valuation of the land referred to juries, there need be no fear of obtaining otherwise than a just award.

Thomas Bouch was introduced to the meeting by Sir Ralph Anstruther, with the words, 'If you had seen his beautiful plans, and the interest which he has taken in the Railway, I am quite satisfied that you would agree with me in saying that we would have gone far before we found one better qualified for the duties he has undertaken'. Ebullient as ever, Bouch confirmed that the railway could be built at a cheap cost, stating that the trouble with recently constructed railways was that there had been an excessive cost and wastage of capital in their construction. He told those present that many railways in the London area, while carrying great traffic, often paid no dividend while many small railways, even in less populated areas, had much lower costs. He gave the example of the Dundee & Arbroath company which paid a higher dividend than the Edinburgh, Perth & Dundee and the Arbroath to Forfar line gave a better yield than any other railway in Scotland. The Leven Railway, he said, could promise its shareholders 'high returns' because it could fulfil the current need for inexpensive lines.

John Haig told the meeting that, in his opinion, the anticipated railway traffic would be greatly increased if the extension to the Harbour were made, since for a mere additional cost of £2,500, the railway would have run from sea to sea, providing a continuous line of rails from west to east coast from Greenock to Leven, 'the advantages of which were at once apparent'. He then appealed for financial support, stating that the company required to raise £15,000 by 31st December of that year in order to present the Leven Railway Bill before Parliament, and that they were still £2,500 short of this sum. The people of Leven were thus exhorted to take up a small number of shares each and, on account of the benefits which would accrue to them, 'the intelligent and industrious cultivators of the land' and 'the array of able, gallant and hearty fishermen' of the East Neuk were also requested to invest in the line, it being only a matter of time before it would be extended to serve them more directly. The appeal was successful and shortly afterwards the Bill was ready to be presented at Westminster.

An indomitable opponent

The progress of the Bill through Parliament was, unfortunately, beset with difficulties, most of which could be traced back to the indomitable opposition of Mr C. Maitland Christie of Durie. The estate of Durie, which occupied the southern portion of the parish of Scoonie and upon which the entire town of Leven had been feued, had been in the hands of the Christie family for generations and the mansion house of Durie was situated at the north of the town with evidence of the families' small coal pits in the vicinity. The estate owned the harbour at Leven and Christie seems to have been determined to oppose the railway at all costs, possibly because he had decided that it would be deleterious to his interests. In a letter to the *Fifeshire Journal*, published on 12th February, 1852, Christie advised the inhabitants of Leven to object to the Bill on the basis that the two proposed level crossings at the north of the town would present a real danger to the public. He thought that local people had not properly 'contemplated the annoyance, interruption and danger to which the [road] communication betwixt Leven and the interior of the county will be permanently subjected' and that they should 'observe how impossible it will be to get rid of this evil after the railway has been committed'. He followed this letter up by formally opposing the passage of the Leven Railway Bill through the Commons by lodging a petition along with two other local landowners and group who styled themselves as the 'Trustees of the Leven Bridge and Road', all of whom claimed that the railway was not only 'unnecessary' but also 'injurious' to their interests.

Further insult was added to injury when Christie was offered the sum of £1,300 in respect for a portion of land which the railway company wished to acquire and, in rejecting this sum, elected to put the matter before a local jury in terms of his right to do so under the provisions of the Railway Clauses Consolidation (Scotland) Act of 1845. The result was a disaster for him. Contrary to the then popular belief that juries were biased in favour of local landowners, the jurors seem to have favoured the small local company over what they may have seen as the grasping landowner and awarded him some £1,151, £149 less than the railway had offered, and, in so doing, publicly humiliated him. The *Fifeshire Journal* of 24th September, 1853 seems to have taken some delight in the matter when it reported that,

> The jury trial noted in our last edition closed on Saturday night after occupying three days. Some of the evidence was of an extraordinary kind, and will no doubt continue to be animadverted on by all classes for some time yet. It being the first trial of the kind connected with small railroads, it has caused a good deal of sensation, even amongst lawyers. The verdict of the jury has given general satisfaction.

The battle with Christie did not end there. In 1855, long after the railway had opened for traffic, his disenchantment with the Leven Railway was still evident when Wilkie had to write to the company's engine driver that Christie had complained that the he and his brother,

> ... have been poaching on his (Christie's) lands, and on those of Duniface (a farm close by) where he has game, and that one of his servants saw a hare shot by one of you from one of our carriages. I am instructed to intimate that firearms are not allowed to be carried by any of the company's servants on the railway or stations under penalty of dismissal.

The 1852 Act

The Bill eventually made its way through the Commons, two of the petitions having been withdrawn and that of the Trustees being rejected on the basis that they had no locus to act as such. An appeal against the dismissal of one petition (that of Admiral Wemyss, a local landowner) was held up by an unsuccessful appeal to the House of Lords and, on 17th June, 1852, the Leven Railway Act (15 & 16 Vict., cap. xcv) was finally passed. One of the unexpected advantages which the shareholders enjoyed was that, in the words of John Haig at the first ordinary general meeting of the company held in August 1852,

> Notwithstanding the violent opposition ... the expenses which have been incurred have mounted to no more than £1,320, whilst the original estimate for obtaining the act was calculated at £1,270, the excess being only the small sum of £50. Your directors have further to remark that they believe it to be the cheapest railway bill that has ever been obtained. They would further call the attention of the shareholders to the fact that the act has not been encumbered by any of these objectionable clauses which have been almost invariably introduced into Scotch railway bills, such as making the company liable for the debts of the parallel turnpike road, &c, &c.

In section 23 of the Act it was provided that three railways would be built namely:

> A Railway commencing by a Junction with the Line of the *Edinburgh, Perth and Dundee Railway* at or near *Thornton Junction* Station in the Parish of *Markinch* in the County of *Fife* and terminating at or near *Burnmill* in the Parish of *Scoonie* and County aforesaid;
>
> A Branch Railway diverging from and out of the said Railway at a point thereon at or near to where *Burnmill* Lead leaves the River *Leven* in the Parish of *Scoonie* and County of *Fife*, and terminating at or near to *Kirkland* Works in the Parish of *Wemyss* and County aforesaid;
>
> A Branch Railway diverging from or out of the said Railway at or near to *Burnmill* in the Parish of *Scoonie* and County of *Fife*, and terminating at or near the Harbour of *Leven* in the said Parish of *Scoonie* and County aforesaid.

After providing for the commonly dealt-with matters such as the suitability of the junction with the main-line, the period allowed for the works to be carried out, the provision of lodges or stations at level crossings, the maximum rates to be charged for the carriage of passengers and such diverse cargoes as 'Dung, Compost and all sorts of Manure, Lime and Limestone ... Nails, Anvils, Vices and Chains', there were two more unusual provisions. Section 42 gave the company power to enter into 'any Contracts or Agreements with the said *Edinburgh, Perth and Dundee* Railway Company for the Passage over or along the said *Edinburgh, Perth and Dundee* Railway of any Engines, Coaches, Waggons, or other Carriages used by the Company ...' and the following section, 43 was worded as follows:

> That it shall be lawful for the said *Edinburgh, Perth and Dundee* Railway and the Company hereby incorporated to make, enter into, and complete any Contracts and Agreements or Arrangements which may by them be mutually be deemed necessary and advisable for the working and Use of the Railway by this Act authorised, the Management of the Traffic thereon, and generally for and in respect of all such Matters and Things as may be necessary for the proper and efficient working of the said railway when completed, on such Terms and Conditions and in such Manner as may be agreed upon and between the said Companies: Provided always, that all such Contracts and

ANNO DECIMO QUINTO

VICTORIÆ REGINÆ.

****

Cap. XCV.

An Act for making a Railway from the *Edinburgh, Perth, and Dundee* Railway at *Thornton Junction* Station to the Town of *Leven*, with Branches to *Kirkland* Works and to the Harbour of *Leven*. [17th *June* 1852.]

WHEREAS the making of a Railway leading from the *Edinburgh, Perth, and Dundee* Railway, at a Point at or near to *Thornton Junction* Station in the Parish of *Markinch* in the County of *Fife*, to a Point at or near to *Burnmill* in the Parish of *Scoonie* and County aforesaid, with Branch Railways diverging from or out of the said intended Line of Railway to *Kirkland* Works and to the Harbour of *Leven*, would be of great local and public Advantage, by opening an additional, certain, and expeditious Means of Communication between the said Places, and by facilitating Communication with more distant Towns and Places: And whereas the Persons herein-after named are willing, at their own Expense, to carry such Undertaking into execution: And whereas it is expedient that the Company hereby to be incorporated shall be enabled to enter into Agreements as after mentioned with the *Edinburgh, Perth, and Dundee* Railway Company incorporated by "The *Edinburgh, Perth,*

[*Local.*] 15 *R* *and*

The Leven Railway Act, 1852.

Agreements or Arrangements, before they can be put in force, shall be duly laid before the Lords of the Committee of Her Majesty's Privy Council for Trade and Foreign Plantations, and that the same shall have no Force or Effect until the Lords of the said Committee shall have signified their Approbation thereof in such Form and Manner as to them shall seem meet.

The Agreement with the Edinburgh, Perth & Dundee Railway

Long before the public meeting at the Gardeners' Hall the promoters of the Leven Railway had entered into a provisional working agreement with the Edinburgh, Perth & Dundee Railway with whose trains the branch line service was to connect. The main heads of the agreement ran as follows:

First. The Leven Company undertake to find the Capital necessary for the construction of the Branch from the Town of Leven to the Thornton Junction station on the main-line – a distance of about six miles – and to provide a Locomotive for working it. The total capital, in Shares and Loans, is fixed at a Sum not exceeding £28,000.

Second. On the completion of the Branch the Edinburgh, Perth and Dundee Company undertake to work and maintain it, as aforementioned, for a period of twenty-five years, finding the necessary rolling stock, with the exception of the Locomotive, which is to be furnished by the Leven Company.

Third. The earnings of the Leven Railway Company are to be applied in the order, and for the purposes following:- (1st) For the Maintenance of the Railway and Works, and for payment of Taxes and Public Burdens, Salaries and Wages of Officers and Servants, Insurance, and generally all Expenses, excepting those which are incidental to the running of the Trains; (2nd) For payment of Interest and Dividends on Loans (if any) raised by the Leven Company, under the powers of the Act to be obtained – which shall not exceed £5,000 – and on their Share Capital, at a rate not exceeding 4½ per cent per annum; (3rd) For payment by the Edinburgh, Perth and Dundee Company in compensation of the expenses of working the Trains, One Shilling per mile, for each train run by them on the Branch.

Fourth. In the event of there being any surplus revenue, after paying the above expenses, and defraying all necessary and extraordinary charges, that surplus be equally divided between the two companies.

On 31st August, 1852 Andrew Wilkie wrote to the Edinburgh, Perth & Dundee company Secretary to inform him that,

It will be recollected that last year the subject of Working the proposed branch was fully considered by both parties, and that a contingent contract was then concluded between the Promoters and the Directors of the Edinburgh, Perth and Dundee Railway Company. Upon the faith of that Agreement, the Promoters made application to Parliament, and at very considerable expense (increased by an active opposition), obtained an Act, not only authorising them to lay down the proposed Railway, but also conferring powers on the Shareholders of your Company to undertake the Working of the Line. The Promoters also entered into provisional arrangements for the execution of the works so authorised, on very advantageous terms; and by carrying the principles of a strict economy into every department of expenditure, they were enabled to fix the entire cost of the proposed Railway within the limits of £3,500 per mile.

The Directors of the Leven Railway are now desirous to avail themselves of those favourable arrangements entered into by the original Promoters, and to proceed immediately with the works, more especially as, from the recent rise in the price of iron, and in the rate of wages, the undertaking if suspended, cannot be resumed on the same advantageous terms. But, before taking any step in that direction, they deem it necessary to receive the sanction of the Shareholders of the Edinburgh, Perth and Dundee Company to the proposed working agreement.

In drawing your attention to that subject, it will be unnecessary to do more than allude very briefly to some of the most obvious advantages which would accrue to the parent company through the proposed arrangement. At present, the Edinburgh, Perth and Dundee Company, are all but excluded from participation in the Traffic of the important district which extends from Dysart to Anstruther. The proposed branch will be the first step towards developing that new field of Traffic, and it has been so laid out as to bear upon the most productive section of the field. It will command not only a very large Passenger Traffic, but also the carriage of an amount of Goods which no section of the Main Line of corresponding length can boast of; and it will not only be productive of itself but will ensure, at no distant period, by its extension to the eastward, the introduction to the Main Line of a large and profitable Traffic from that district of the County; and with a view to this, preliminary arrangements are now making for the necessary surveys. The Branch to St Andrews has multiplied the Traffic arising from that City to a degree which the most sanguine of its Promoters never anticipated, and is already yielding a return sufficient to recover all expenses, and yield to the Subscribers their anticipated Dividend. But the Leven branch presents conditions still more favourable. Its Cost will be one-third less per mile than that of the St Andrews. Its trains will start from the Junction of the main line with the Dunfermline branch, where the trains from Edinburgh meet those from the North, and hence the Leven Railway will be worked at nearly one half the expense of the St Andrews. Though its Passenger Traffic in summer will not equal that of the St Andrews branch, it will be more uniform throughout the year, and its large Goods Traffic will be such as the St Andrews Line can never command; and, lastly, it presents a prospective Traffic beyond its own immediate resources, while the St Andrews branch is not likely to be extended beyond its present terminus. If the parent company then have cause to congratulate themselves upon the productiveness of the St Andrews branch, they will have much stronger reasons for co-operating in carrying out the present project, and the Directors of the Leven Company confidently claim of your Shareholders the ratification of the Agreement which has hitherto formed the basis of all of these arrangements. It is plain to all external observers that, insulated by the Estuaries of Forth and Tay, the Edinburgh, Perth and Dundee Railway must stand or fall by its Local Traffic and that its only escape from its present embarrassment is in the development of those resources which are independent, and not exposed to abstraction by competing lines; and while one of the most populous and fertile districts of the County is still shut out from Railway communication, it cannot be said that a Railway through Fife has had a fair trial.

The problem appears to have arisen out of the fact that the Edinburgh, Perth & Dundee company was in serious financial difficulty at the time and had appointed a committee of creditors to examine the proposed agreement between the two companies. This committee had expressed serious reservations about the profitability of the arrangement insofar as the larger of the two companies was concerned. In September 1852, however, the Directors of the Edinburgh, Perth & Dundee reported to their shareholders that, despite certain misgivings, they considered it their duty to comply with the request from Wilkie. At the following half-yearly meeting of the Edinburgh, Perth & Dundee, their Chairman stated that,

> Of all the railway lines in Scotland, there was none more dependent than their own on the increase and encouragement of its local traffic. [Cheers] The line went over a very populous district, and if they were vulnerable in a good many points; it was all the more necessary for the increase and efficiency of their own line, and they should encourage branches being formed wherever they could be made useful, and at little expense. I believe that the Leven Railway, as at present proposed, combined many advantages and I have no doubt that although its present terminus would be the town of Leven, that it might be carried still further eastward.

The shareholders duly voted to ratify the Agreement and the way was now clear for the Leven Railway company to move on to the next stage.

A rapid advancement

In August 1852 the company's shareholders were informed that since the passing of the Act they 'have addressed themselves to the subject of land settlements; and from the reception that they have hitherto met with from the proprietors on the line, they are sanguine that they will be enabled to acquire the land necessary on reasonable terms' and that they 'hope to make such arrangements for raising the further capital required, as will enable them to proceed immediately with the construction of the works upon the main-line. This they do, confident that the success of the undertaking is no longer problematic, for the recent experience of the working of cheaply-constructed railways, especially in the case of the St Andrews Railway, has satisfactorily demonstrated that when conducted with due economy, railways may become the subject of investment for capital, equally safe and profitable with any other public works'.

Construction of the line was, therefore, due to start as soon as possible and was originally destined to begin at Thornton where the Leven company's contractor was to carry out the building of the junction between that company's line and the main line of the Edinburgh, Perth & Dundee company. As Anderson began work a letter was dispatched from James Robertson, the Manager of the latter company, to Wilkie in which he was instructed to stop work immediately under pain and penalty. After a sharp exchange of correspondence between Wilkie and Robertson it became clear that it was, in fact, the Leven company who were in the wrong for their Engineer, Bouch, had indeed failed to produce the plans for the junction and it had been an express condition of allowing the contractors to proceed that the plans would not only be produced but also approved by the Edinburgh, Perth & Dundee prior to entering on to their lands. The matter did not end there, however, as Bouch still failed to produce the plans, despite having been instructed to do so in no uncertain terms by the Board on 24th May, 1853 – by October of that year the required agreement had still not been obtained and Bouch was censured for his omission in the company minutes.

Works, however, were being carried on after a fashion and on 16th June the *Fifeshire Journal* commented that, 'the Leven Railway progresses. The number of workmen already employed is somewhere about 150'. On 1st September it was said in the same paper that, 'the formation ... is rapidly advancing and from the fact that only slight cuttings and embankments will be needed, the line will consequently be more speedily and easily completed'. There was, however, trouble in store when the company was in receipt of complaints from various adjoining landowners and more than once Wilkie was forced to tell the contractors not to enter upon particular properties until such time as he gave them the go-ahead. Some of this was due to the fact that local farmers did not wish to see their ripening crops destroyed even though the company had already paid for the land upon which they stood. One landowner demanded that adequate fencing be provided while a neighbouring farmer objected to fences being erected because this would interfere with the positioning of his haystacks. One particular injunction from Wilkie to the contractor read: 'I may mention that the line goes through a splendid field of Oats on Mr Irvine's land worth a considerable amount of money as fodder for horses, therefore, before allowing your workpeople to destroy them, get them cut for your horses'.

The problem with the junction at Thornton was not the first, or indeed the last, run-in with Bouch and there were further letters from Wilkie in which the Engineer was castigated for many things including inaccurate measurements, inordinate delays and a failure to answer correspondence or attend meetings with the company's Directors or officials. Notwithstanding this by 24th November it was being said that, 'the contractors, Messrs Anderson, are getting on with the line very quickly. They are gradually getting possession of the ground as they proceed and it is expected that by May next year the line will be open to the public'. By then, however, another problem had arisen.

Leven No. 1 and its train

It had been part of the original agreement between the Leven and Edinburgh, Perth & Dundee companies that the former would provide the motive power (in the form of a single locomotive) with which the latter would operate the service over the line. But by October 1853 the larger company was in severe financial difficulties and, in view of the growing traffic on its line, was in need of a new heavy luggage (i.e. goods) engine but had no resources with which to buy one. Accordingly they proposed to a deputation from the Leven Railway, composed of the Chairman and Engineer, that the smaller company should advance to them the monies which they had put aside for the purchase of the branch engine in exchange for the Edinburgh, Perth & Dundee handing over one of its own existing locomotives which, the deputation were assured, would be adequate for all their needs. The Leven deputation turned down this 'kind offer' and the upshot was that the Edinburgh, Perth & Dundee representatives, in their fury, condemned the Leven Board to consider not only using their own locomotive but also their own rolling stock and indeed to operate their own trains without any help from the larger company.

Despite the outright hostility displayed by the Edinburgh, Perth & Dundee to any person bold enough to help the Leven company – 'any assistance or accommodation offered to [them] will be held an offence' – Bouch ordered a locomotive from Hawthorn & Company of The Leith Engine Works in Great Junction Street, the locomotive to be delivered by the time that the line was scheduled to open. The locomotive, which was to carry a plate enscribed 'LEVEN No. 1', was apparently a standard design Hawthorn 0-4-0 tender engine costing a total of £1,800, to be paid for in two equal instalments of £900 due in the August and October of 1854. By being able to place this order, the Edinburgh, Perth & Dundee Board realised that they had been outfoxed and, reluctantly, decided that they would have to adhere to their previous agreement after all.

Nothing stands in the way

On 4th March, 1854 the *Fifeshire Journal* reported that some 10 or 12 picks belonging to Anderson's had gone missing from the Leven Railway in the course of its formation near to Cameron Bridge. A week later it was said that an accident had occurred when eight boys were pushing a contractor's wagon by way of amusement when one of them stumbled and fell so that the wheels passed over his left arm, the severe nature of the injury making it probable that, 'amputation of the limb will be found necessary'.

On 20th April the paper announced that, 'The formation of the Leven Railway advances speedily. The rails are now laid down over a considerable length of the road and ere long, the labours of the navvie will enable the snorting "iron horse" to pass from Thornton to Leven, and thus afford us accommodation hitherto unknown in this populous and busy district.' The following month, however, there were two serious accidents within the space of a few days. On 13th May a runaway wagon close to Cameron Bridge struck 'a deaf and dumb mute' named Ogilvie causing him to sustain head injuries and a crushed foot but he escaped with his life 'to the wonderment of all who beheld the accident' although his foot was later amputated. On Wednesday 17th May part of an embankment near Leven collapsed and buried a workman by falling earth. He suffered severe bruising and had one hand seriously injured and later on died as a result.

On a more happy note in the edition of 15th June the paper reported that the workmen employed on the line had presented their time-keeper, Thomas Gray, with 'a splendid silver watch in testimony of their esteem towards him', and then informed its readers that the inhabitants of East Fife would be gratified to learn that the works had almost been completed and in particular that the civil engineering work and the trackwork were ready and that the stations would be roofed and ready for business within a few days:

> Under these circumstances, we understand that it was agreed, at a meeting of the directors held on Friday last, to give notice to the Board of Trade for a formal opening of the line on Monday the 3rd July. Of course, before opening for traffic, the works must undergo government inspection, but this will be merely a matter of course, as it is allowed on all hands that few branches of the same length were ever constructed in a more substantial and efficient manner and the sleepers [are] even heavier than those laid down on the main line of railway. The Directors have already inspected the works, and have expressed themselves satisfied with the manner in which Mr Anderson has performed his contract, and nothing, so far as can be seen at present, stands in the way of a regular commencement of traffic on the first Monday of July. As for plant this, with the exception of the engine, will be supplied by the Main Line, and the engine we understand is all but ready …

One at a time

This press release, which presumably emanated from the Leven Railway itself, was somewhat over-optimistic for it was clear that although the majority of the works had been completed there was still much to be done both in the finishing off and ballasting of the trackwork and in the bridge at Haugh Mills where what had already been constructed had subsided badly and some fairly extensive (and expensive!) remedial works were still required. In addition the level crossing gates at Cameron Bridge required attention, signals were missing and station platforms still required completion. It can thus hardly have come as a shock to the Directors when, three days after the original proposed opening date, they received a communication from Captain Douglas Galton* of the Railway Department of the Board Of Trade in London who enclosed the Inspection Report of Captain Tyler and stated that he (Galton) directed the Leven Railway company to postpone the opening of their line 'for a period of one calendar month from this date' (i.e. until 6th July). The enclosed report read:

> This portion of railway is about six miles in length, from the junction with the Edinburgh, Perth and Dundee Railway at Thornton to the town of Leven; it is laid with a single line of rails, and the permanent way consists of double T rails, weighing 65 lbs. to the yard, in cast iron chairs, affixed by oak treenails to larch sleepers, which are placed four feet apart on the straight portion and three feet apart on the curves. I observe that additional ballast is still required on parts of the line, and that the treenails have not yet been inserted, in some places, on both sides of the chairs. I understand that the traffic is to be worked by a small engine, and at slow speed, but even under these circumstances, I would beg to direct particular attention to the state of the treenails on the curves, the sharpest of which has a radius of 12 chains, as I think it quite possible, that in the course of traffic, the treenails may be found to be cut through between the sleepers and the bottom of the chairs. Should this be the case, I would recommend the use of spikes instead of treenails on the curves. There are three viaducts to carry this railway over the river, each consisting of three openings of 50 feet span on the skew; these are all constructed in a similar manner, with trussed timber girders on masonry abutments and piers, and they appear, as well as one other viaduct, with three openings of 33 feet span each upon the skew, and three other timber bridges of smaller spans, to be sufficiently substantial. A flying arch thrown over the railway near the Haugh Mills has sunk considerably at the spandrels, and some abutments are now being built, from which an arch of smaller span is, I am informed, to be turned. At the Thornton Junction the platform requires to be finished, and the distant signal on the Leven Railway to be fixed. At the Cameron Bridge station, the platforms are not complete, and a signal is required, as well as a distant signal in each direction; and at the Leven station, a signal and distant signal are required. Some additional fencing is wanted in different parts of the line. The gates of a public road level crossing which occurs near the Cameron Bridge Station are constructed so as to fasten across the railway, and I have recommended that the means for fastening them across the road should be added.
>
> For the above reasons, I am of the opinion that the opening of the portion of the Leven Railway extending between Thornton Junction and the town of Leven, would, by reason of the incompleteness of the works, be attended with danger to the public using the same. I am informed that under the 43d clause of the Leven Railway Act of 1852, a contract has been entered into between the Edinburgh, Perth and Dundee Railway Company and the Leven Railway Company, by which the former are to lease and work the Leven Railway, upon obtaining, as required by the Act, the approbation of their Lordships, and upon the completion of the works, and the construction of all conveniences necessary for the traffic, as well as obtaining a report from the officer appointed to inspect the line, of its being completely finished, and ready to open for traffic. As, however, this subject must be brought before their Lordships by the Companies interested, I do not think it necessary to do more at present than thus allude to it.

On the same date (6th July) the *Fifeshire Journal* announced that the line would be open for all traffic on the 14th inst but that, as a result of Captain Tyler's inspection 'the opening of the Leven Railway ... will be postponed until further notice'. This

* The Board of Trade had a statutory duty to inspect new railway lines over which passenger services were to be run and Captain Galton, like the majority of the inspectors appointed by the Board, was an officer in the Royal Engineers.

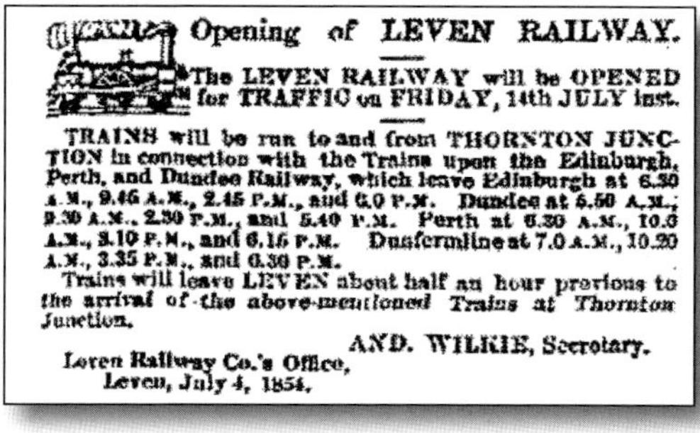

Opening of LEVEN RAILWAY.

The LEVEN RAILWAY will be OPENED for TRAFFIC on FRIDAY, 14th JULY inst.

TRAINS will be run to and from THORNTON JUNCTION in connection with the Trains upon the Edinburgh, Perth, and Dundee Railway, which leave Edinburgh at 6.30 A.M., 9.46 A.M., 2.45 P.M., and 6.0 P.M. Dundee at 6.50 A.M., 9.30 A.M., 2.30 P.M., and 5.40 P.M. Perth at 6.30 A.M., 10.0 A.M., 3.10 P.M., and 6.16 P.M. Dunfermline at 7.0 A.M., 10.20 A.M., 3.35 P.M., and 6.30 P.M.

Trains will leave LEVEN about half an hour previous to the arrival of the above-mentioned Trains at Thornton Junction.

AND. WILKIE, Secretary.

Leven Railway Co.'s Office,
Leven, July 4, 1854.

From the *Fifeshire Journal*.

was something of an understatement for much had still to be done before the company could request that he should inspect the line once again. On Wednesday 2nd August he did so and this time the line passed muster, notwithstanding the fact that in places the line as planned bore little resemblance to the line as actually built, particularly in relation to the sharpness of the curves, the depth of the ballast and the steepness of the gradients – not so much a cheaply built railway as a shoddily built one! Tyler told the Directors that they should expect to receive their certificate showing that the line was fit to be opened for public traffic on Monday 7th August. On 5th August he reported to the Secretary of the Railway Department, Whitehall, that had re-inspected the line and having found that the necessary completion works had been carried out and was therefore, 'of the opinion that this railway may be opened without danger to the public using the same'. He went on to state that he understood 'that the Leven Railway is to be worked, at all events, in the first instance, by the Edinburgh, Perth & Dundee Railway Company, whether the agreement between the two companies referred to in my report of the 4th ultimo, be ratified or not'.

Jumping the gun

It would appear that, notwithstanding the fact that the Board of Trade certificate had not been received, the Leven company effectively 'jumped the gun' and their line was formally opened on Saturday 5th August when, according to the *Fifeshire Journal* of Thursday 10th August:

> We are glad to announce that this important branch line was formally opened on Saturday last, and is open for public traffic today, having now been completed to the entire satisfaction of the Government Inspector, the Directors and the Shareholders of the Company; so that the inhabitants of the thriving town of Leven, and the surrounding district, will no longer be cut off from all the advantages which are the invariable result of the increased facilities of communication afforded by a railway ...
>
> The formal opening of the line on Saturday was not by any means an exciting affair. There was no attempt at display, not even by a decoration of the locomotive, and the entire absence of music and banners almost led one to suppose that the provisions of the new Bribery Act regarding processions were applicable to railway Directors on opening day as well as to candidates for Parliamentary Honours on election occasions! However,

no fault seemed to be found with this specimen of the Board's economy, for shortly before one o'clock, the hour of starting, a great number of ladies and gentlemen, resident in the district, were gathered together, apparently in excellent spirits, in the handsome and commodious station erected at the terminus on the lands of Burnmill. The station is situated at some distance from the town, but this point was chosen, we believe, as the most convenient for carrying out the ultimate designs of the Directors in regard to the extension of the railway. All seemed pleased at the neat appearance of the station, but those who arrived close upon the hour were allowed little time for observation, if they were at all desirous of securing a seat in any one of the seven carriages which were in readiness to convey the party to Thornton Junction. Two of the carriages were quite new, and the locomotive, which is the property of the Leven Railway company, was a new and powerful engine amply sufficient for all demands that will be made upon it, even though excursion trains visit Leven as frequently, and as in as great numbers, as they do now at St Andrews.

Exactly at one o'clock, as if the Directors were desirous to exhibit the Leven line as a model of punctuality, the train left the terminus as quietly and unostentatiously as if the inhabitants of Leven had been accustomed all their lives to see it leave every day at the same hour, or had demanded to show their interest in the newly opened railway in a more substantial and satisfactory manner than by cheers or waving of handkerchiefs. Heedless alike of the enthusiasm or apathy of spectators, the locomotive, entitled 'Leven Railway, No. 1', snorted along, passing the 'precipitous braes' on the lands of Burnmill, so jocularly alluded to by the Lord Advocate at the famous jury trial, and soon leaving behind the lands of Durie, the college lands of St Andrews, and Durie Vale, in a few minutes passed a handsome house now erected by Mr Sang of Kirkcaldy, and arrived at Cameron Bridge station, which is in the immediate vicinity of Cameron House, the residence of Mr Haig, the active and enterprising Chairman of the Company. A house, close to the railway at this point, has been converted into the station-house and will, it is said, suit the purpose admirably. Adjoining the station is the Cameron Bridge Distillery, the property of Mr Haig, to which a siding runs off, and the goods traffic from this part of the line will materially contribute to the success of the undertaking. The inhabitants of Buckhaven on the one side, and of Windygates, and even Kennoway on the other, will find this station of advantage to them, so that a considerable passenger traffic may also be anticipated. At Cameron Bridge, the line near this point crosses the Leven at two places by strong substantial wooden bridges. Shortly after passing Cameron Bridge, the line skirts the estate of Captain Wemyss, along the banks of the Orr, which is crossed at one point by another wooden bridge, and after a short but pleasant ride past the lands of D. Bethune, Esq and O. Balfour, Esq, the main line is reached and immediately afterwards the train arrives safe at Thornton Junction, where additional accommodation has been provided for the passengers. The trip occupied about twenty minutes, including the stoppage at Cameron Bridge, and the smoothness of the ride amply testified to the careful manner in which the line had been finished. The general opinion seemed to be that the line had been constructed with a due regard to economy, care had been taken that the works should be of such a character as to render the maintenance of way a comparatively easy and inexpensive process for many years to come. The train waited for the arrival of the twelve o'clock train from Edinburgh, which brought Mr Haig, Chairman of the Leven company, who had been in London on important business connected with railway matters, along with Mr Lees, secretary, and Mr Robertson, Manager of the Edinburgh, Perth and Dundee company and Mr Bouch, engineer to the Leven Railway. Shortly afterwards the train proceeded on its return trip, and arrived at Leven at three o'clock, where the numerous passengers quietly separated, the ceremony of the opening of the railway ending as unostentatiously as it had begun. The weather was highly favourable and all the passengers appeared pleased and delighted with the first trip on the Leven line.

Not only was there pleasure to be had on that first trip but in the evening 60 gentlemen were invited to a gala dinner at Crawfords Hotel, Leven where what was described as a 'splendid dinner' was served and, after John Haig and Sir Ralph Anstruther had made speeches were made, toasts were proposed to the health of the new railway whose Directors could, it was said, justifiably be proud of their achievements. The same issue of the *Journal* contained another announcement:

EDINBURGH, PERTH & DUNDEE RAILWAY
OPENING OF THE LEVEN RAILWAY

The Leven Railway will be opened for public traffic on Thursday 10 August 1854. Trains, in connection with the Trains on the Main Line, will leave Leven at 7-20 a.m., 10-45 a.m., 3-55 p.m. and 7 p.m. and Thornton Junction, on arrival of the Train from Edinburgh, Dunfermline, Dundee and Perth, about 8-15 a.m., 11-25 a.m., 4-25 p.m. and 7 p.m.

James Robertson, Manager,
Edinburgh, August 7, 1854

and a further report some pages later commented on the initial service provided on the newly opened line:

All the little odds and ends necessary for its safe and efficient working have been completed, this line was formally opened on Saturday last. At present, the trains will run in connection with those on the main line, completing the distance in twenty minutes or thereby and opening up a direct communication for the inhabitants to Edinburgh, to Dundee, to Perth and to Glasgow via Dunfermline. There may be occasionally a few minutes delay at the junction and to render this as little irksome as possible, it is hoped that the Directors of the Edinburgh and Northern [*sic*] will make some efforts to provide better accommodation than they have hitherto done at the important station at Thornton. If it is not their province to do so, we trust the Leven Directors will look to the comfort of their own siding, for we can assure them the want of proper accommodation at Leuchars has been seriously felt by the sister branch of St Andrews. It is one thing to stand shivering for a whole hour in the blasts of December and January with the thermometer some twenty degrees below freezing.

As to the Leven Branch itself, we believe everything possible has been done to render it at once safe and commodious. Starting from the main line at Thornton (where we hope to see some permanent erections by and bye) it proceeds by an easy incline without any very sudden curves along the valleys of the Orr and Leven, by Cameron Bridge and Kirkland to its present terminus, near the town and port of Leven. We say 'its present terminus' for there cannot be a shadow of a doubt that in a year or two the line will be extended to the port of Anstruther.

As a single-line branch of some five or six miles in length, cheaply constructed, passing through a district studded with mills and bleachfields, accommodating the larger works of Cameron Distillery, Kirkland spinning-mills and Leven Foundry and offering new facilities for travelling to the inhabitants of Leven, Largo, Buckhaven, Kennoway and neighbourhood, there is every prospect of the branch, as it stands, being a highly prosperous and remunerative concern. …

Initially only the 'main' line from Leven to Thornton Junction was opened and, as the contemporary reports indicated, the stations were somewhat rudimentary, that at Cameron Bridge using an existing building for the station master's house while the temporary terminus at Burnmill was destined to serve Leven until such time as the promised extension to Largo and Anstruther was built. The Kirkland and Leven Harbour lines were, as yet, unbuilt.

Chapter Five

An Uncertain Beginning: The Leven Railway 1854-1861

'In that once lovely vale ... a crowded train now rattles along leaving a trail of smoke behind.'
Fifeshire Advertiser, 1854

Eve's Fairest Daughters

The Directors were fortunate indeed to have managed to catch the tail end of the holiday season and the line proved to be a considerable boon to at least one section of the community. On 19th August the *Fifeshire Advertiser* reported that in Leven,

> The present season has brought more than an ordinary influx of summer visitors to our town. The Leven Railway has had its effect in bringing those tired of the city or inland country life to our shore for a few weeks, there to taste the health-imparting influence of the sea breeze as it wafts gently on the delicate cheek. Sea bathing is daily indulged in, and the links are beautifully adorned by gay parties of Eve's fairest daughters – the brightest and loveliest flowers in creation.

More prosaically, and notwithstanding the serious problems which the company were having with its locomotive and rolling stock, the new line seems to have been a success and on 7th September, the Leven annual holiday, day-trippers took advantage of the newly opened facilities to travel by train to Edinburgh and Perth, journeys that would not previously have been possible. As the *Advertiser* put it, 'A general holiday is a blessing and the convenience of railways is equally so'. However, the same paper also recorded that, of the countryside the new railway passed through, changes had occurred which had a profound effect on the neighbourhood:

> In that once lovely dale, where the hare and the rabbit sunned themselves undisturbed, a crowded train now rattles along leaving a trail of smoke behind and instead of the call of the wood pigeon, the shrill of the lapwing, or the song of the linnet, can be heard the tramp of the iron steed, the snort of the puffing engine and the sound of the railway whistle.

At the half-yearly ordinary general meeting of the company held in October 1854 John Haig stated to the shareholders that the average number of passengers conveyed weekly in the first two months of operation had been 1,081, compared with the projected figure in the Prospectus of 570. This was, he said, 'beyond our most optimistic expectations' considering that 'goods traffic is not yet in a very workable condition' and that it had been thought necessary to take steps to increase the accommodation for goods wagon shunting at Thornton Junction* and to provide additional facilities for goods at both Cameron Bridge and Leven to remedy this.

Locomotive laments

'Leven Railway No. 1', the locomotive delivered by Hawthorn's in time for the opening, was to put it mildly an unhappy choice. The *Fifeshire Journal* of 5th August

* According to the Edinburgh, Perth & Dundee records this work does not, however, appear to have been carried out until 1857.

1854, perhaps optimistically, stated that 'Mr Nicholson passed here [Kirkcaldy] yesterday with a beautiful new engine bearing the words "LEVEN RAILWAY".' This beautiful new engine might well have been suitable for the Leven line had that line been built according to the original plans submitted deposited for Parliamentary approval but, once again, Bouch had, literally, cut corners and the line as constructed proved to be eminently unsuitable for the hapless engine – surely one of the few times in railway history when it was the line, rather the engine, that was at fault. Within a short space of time the Edinburgh, Perth & Dundee had condemned the 'new and powerful engine', saying that it was unsafe when rounding the curves on the line at the designated speeds necessary to keep trains to the far from punishing schedule of the timetable. A temporary compromise was reached when the operating company agreed to reduce train speeds on an *ad hoc* basis but on the express understanding that the Leven company would immediately order a replacement locomotive from Hawthorn's but, in view of the long waiting period which would be necessary before such an engine could be delivered, that they would forthwith obtain another engine to cover in the interim. On 23rd September, 1854 the Leven Board met and passed a resolution wherein Bouch was ordered to find such an engine. On 3rd October, barely two weeks later, Wilkie wrote to Haig that: 'We have neither seen nor heard from Mr Bouch for a fortnight when he promised to procure us an engine for temporary use on the Leven Railway while a new one is being built to supply the place of the one which he got us and is unsuitable. As the EP&D have intimated that they will not be responsible for the working of the railway longer with the present engine, Mr Bouch's want of attention to our present interests in the matter is beyond our comprehension'.

Beyond comprehension it may have been, but true to form Bouch failed to deliver and the Leven Board were forced to ask Robert Nicholson, the locomotive engineer of the Edinburgh, Perth & Dundee Railway, to find another engine for them, asking him to go south expressly to buy an engine from the Lancashire & Yorkshire Railway. The latter selling some of its surplus locomotives, apparently as a result of its acquisitions of a number of smaller local companies. Nicholson had, in the previous month, been sent on a similar foray by the Edinburgh, Perth & Dundee company but at that time had been unable to find a suitable locomotive to purchase. The Leven Board now gave him authority to use his own judgement and to spend up to £700 on an engine, but on the understanding that he could spend more, 'if the engine justified the price'. He duly purchased a second-hand (and probably rather elderly) Bury 2-2-0 locomotive for £765 from a Chester contractor named Cropper & Bell* and the locomotive was delivered to Burntisland at an inclusive charge, for carriage, of £33 15*s.* 0*d.*, both accounts being settled by the Leven Board on 6th October, 1854. The Bury locomotive appeared at Leven only after certain repairs, which Nicholson deemed to be necessary, were carried out at the Edinburgh, Perth & Dundee Railway works. On 28th October the Leven company sold its Hawthorn locomotive 'Leven Railway No. 1' to the Caledonian Railway for some £1,900 and almost ordered its permanent replacement from Hawthorn's.

* This information was derived from the Leven Railway company's letter book but no contemporary reference to that company can be found and perhaps the reference to Chester should read Manchester, where the Lancashire & Yorkshire Railway's (L&Y) principal works at Miles Platting was situated. The L&Y had certainly been disposing of surplus Bury 2-2-0 locomotives, mostly from its constituent companies, at or about that time - see John Marshall's *Lancashire & Yorkshire Railway*, Vol. 3, (1972).

The Bury 2-2-0, however, proved to be far from satisfactory and not only was it prone to repeated stoppages and breakdowns but even when it did work it had trouble coping with the traffic on the line which seemed to be extremely buoyant – in the period between February and July of 1855 the amount of goods being carried amounted to 14,293 tons with 1,318 sheep and 753 cattle also being conveyed. The Leven company, however, had no option but to soldier on with their dud purchase until such time as Hawthorn's were ready to deliver their new locomotive.

Decree of divorce

A new problem, or rather a previously festering sore, now appeared. The full working agreement which the Leven and Edinburgh, Perth & Dundee companies had entered into prior to the opening of the line had contained two seemingly innocuous clauses, the 11th and 12th, which had been inserted in order to preserve the volume of traffic on the Leven line and to prevent the Edinburgh, Perth & Dundee company from siphoning it off by favouring competing modes of conveyance at the expense of the smaller company. A Joint Committee, composed of the Directors of both companies, had been set up to administer this working agreement and, because of the ill-feeling between the parties to it, the agreement needed not only the ratification of the two Boards but also that of the Board of Trade in London. This ratification was provided on 17th July, 1854 but with certain modifications which deleted the 11th and 12th clauses and shortened the length of the agreement from 25 years to 10 years. The Joint Committee agreed that the matter was unsatisfactory and resolved that a deputation should be sent by the Leven company to London to advise its solicitors there to prepare an appeal to the President of the Board of Trade against the proposed modifications.

Eventually the Board gave its sanction, in January 1855, to clauses 11 and 12 being re-instated but with a new modification to the second of these which, in the view of the Leven Board, was entirely objectionable. The Leven company applied to have the matter ameliorated but the Edinburgh, Perth & Dundee representatives, after another meeting with the Board of Trade, persuaded them to reinstate the original term of 25 years for the subsistence of the agreement. Matters had now reached an impasse and the Leven Directors now felt that they had little choice – they could either accept the agreement subject to the modifications of which they did not approve or abandon it altogether. Matters were, however, taken out of their hands because the Edinburgh, Perth & Dundee Board, before the Leven Directors could consult their shareholders, decided unilaterally that they 'would decline to ratify the agreement in consequence of certain modifications which were required to be made'. Consequently the front page of the *Fifeshire Journal* carried the intimation from Henry Lees, Secretary of the Edinburgh, Perth & Dundee Railway that 'from and after 31st of July current the ... company will cease to work the traffic and passengers, goods and minerals on the Leven Railway, and accordingly that their plant and servants will be withdrawn from the line on the evening of that day'.

The Edinburgh, Perth & Dundee had, apparently had enough and subsequently sought to justify its position by blaming the Leven Board whom, it claimed, had failed to discuss the matter, despite repeated requests to do so. This termination took the Leven Board by surprise, especially since their motive power problems showed little signs of abating. There was little sign that Hawthorn's were in a position to supply the engine ordered by the company so many months before, and in correspondence which passed between Messrs Wilkie and Messrs Hawthorn the company secretary said in relation to their undelivered locomotive: 'Do push it on and drop me a note in due course saying that it will be ready. You know our *friends* the Edinburgh, Perth & Dundee, are to withdraw from working the line on the 31st inst. and we must be in a position to go on'. But there was little the Leven Board could do but to make the best of what meagre resources they already had. The following week another advertisement appeared in the *Journal*, being a direct repost to the previous announcement:

LEVEN RAILWAY

The Edinburgh, Perth and Dundee Railway Company having advertised that, From and After the 31st July current, they will cease to work the traffic passengers, goods and minerals on the Leven Railway and that that their plant and servants will be withdrawn from the line on the evening of that day.

Notice is hereby given that the Leven Railway Company have, in consequence, made arrangements for the working of the line and that trains will continue to run as at present.

By Order, And. Wilkie, Secretary, 12 July 1855

This was a bold step since the branch train mileage worked by the Edinburgh, Perth & Dundee for the last half-year it operated the Leven Railway amounted to 8,196, or approximately 20 per cent less than the mileage worked on the St Andrews Railway, and carried an average of 947 passengers per week, but not only did the Leven company have a defective locomotive, they also had no stock of its own with which to run a service. However, assistance was at hand, and in the words of the author of *A Short Account of the Leven and East of Fife Railway*,

On the abandonment of the working of their line by the Edinburgh, Perth and Dundee Company, the Directors of the Leven Company were placed in a position of great embarrassment. The authorised capital of the Company had been already exceeded by the expenditure. A large additional sum was required for the purchase of engine, carriages and wagons, without which the line could not have been kept open [except] for the purchase of the pecuniary assistance generously offered by General Lindsay of Balcarres, who had taken a deep interest in the undertaking, ordered the purchase of the requisite plant, which was procured and placed on the railway so expeditiously that no interruption in the working occurred.

The Directors subsequently reported to the shareholders that until the surplus revenue was 'otherwise accounted for', they proposed to apply a large proportion of this towards repaying General Lindsay 'for the price of the plant and the keeping of it up'; this seems to have been largely successful for by 1859 £5,864 was appropriated to a Sinking Fund for this purpose.

Escaping steam

On 1st August, 1855 the Leven company began to run its own services, nominally keeping to the existing timetable. Three second-hand passenger coaches were secured from the Scottish Central Railway and a number of goods wagons bought for a total of £364 3*s*. 3*d*. Within a couple of weeks the wagons ordered from Adams arrived, the initial order of 14 arriving from the Midland Works, Birmingham in such a defective state that Wilkie wrote that, although supposedly six-ton wagons, when a one-ton load was placed upon them 'the springs were so depressed that the buffers went under those of the neighbouring wagon'. It appeared that the wagons required a number of new springs to be fitted and when the remaining part of the order was delivered, all of them were found to be defective. Worse was to follow. The wagons required further attention and Adams sent up his own workmen from Birmingham to try to rectify the problems. Even after repair there were still allegations that the wagons were not fit for the purpose for which they were purchased and on one occasion a new axle broke on its very first journey. 'We cannot longer allow the wagons to encumber our stations', said Wilkie and the Board resolved to charge Adams a penalty sum for each day that the wagons lay idle and issued threats to air the matter before the Court of Session if no satisfactory resolution could be reached.

If the wagons fiasco was bad enough, the locomotive problem was a further blow. On 31st August Wilkie wrote to Hawthorn's that,

> Something has gone wrong with our old engine again and we have great difficulty in getting it patched up so as to run all this week, and it is doubtful if we will be able to manage that. I will trust, therefore, to the new engine being here to relieve the old one on Monday morning ... The engine driver has shown me some paints. I like No. 1 and No. 2 the best and would rather prefer 2, but I suppose the engine will be newly painted by this time.*

The new locomotive was not, however, ready and the old one had to soldier on until the following month. Then at the beginning of October 1855 the new locomotive was delivered.

The cost of the engine was £2,000† and was an 0-4-0 tender locomotive with 4 ft 6 in. coupled wheels, 14 in. x 18 in. cylinders and a boiler of the 'longback' type with the dome mounted on a cylindrical base over the firebox.# However, its initial state seemed to be a cause of concern because on 10th October Wilkie was again writing to Hawthorn's in the following terms concerning the new locomotive:

> The steam is escaping from one of the cylinders and also from the boiler near the bottom of the funnel, and there are also some things about the engine that will require to be put right. Be good enough, therefore, to send people to put the engine in order.

Hawthorn's employees arrived on that day although Wilkie expressed some reservations as to how long the remedial works would take. By this time, however, it was becoming clear that all was not well with the line itself and that the failure for this lay, fairly and squarely, with Thomas Bouch himself.

---

* The authors surmise that the locomotive was probably painted in a shade of green.

† This figure may include subsequent repairs or modifications because the Leven Railway accounts show that payment for the locomotive was made to Hawthorn's in four instalments - £700 on 31st July, 1855, £300 on 7th November, £500 on 21st November and a final £500 on 2nd January, 1856.

Possibly this locomotive was similar to, and possibly identical with, 'Leven No. 1' which had been sold to the Caledonian Railway in October 1854. Neither the new Hawthorn nor the Bury or indeed any subsequent engine acquired by the East of Fife or the Leven & East of Fife ever carried any numbers or were referred to by any number.

Bouch bows out

Beset by problems, the Leven Directors decided to take a bold step and to advertise that they intended to walk the whole course of the line themselves, setting out from Thornton Junction at an advertised time and being prepared to receive complaints and comments from delegations and individual landowners en route. This they did and although there were many and varied complaints about the general lack of completion of works all down the line the most frequent and vexed complaints from the public appeared to be directed to the fact that the fencing required by statute had not, in fact, been completed and in some places barely started. This caused the Board to seek out a second opinion from 'an engineer of eminence' and what he found caused them to be further annoyed with Bouch.

Some of the problems were of the nature of fairly minor irritations such as the level crossing gates at Cameron Bridge being of such a nature that, when closed against the railway, they jammed and trains were accordingly delayed for a considerable time. The engine shed at Leven was incomplete, despite Bouch having been ordered a year before to finish it off, and was too small for the locomotive used and, in wet weather, was prone to flooding. The patent signals of Bouch's own design, which he had persuaded the Board to have fitted, did not work and the Board refused to pay for them. If this were not enough, Bouch refused to answer Wilkie's letters and appeared to be deliberately giving the Directors the slip when they attempted to contact him in person.

Eventually the Board had had enough. Anderson, the contractor, had still not been paid in full because Bouch had failed to produce the final report on the line and Wilkie was told by the Board to write to Bouch in the following terms:

> The unsuitability of the [original] engine raised doubts in the minds of the directors that all was not right, but to them you made no disclosure of the defective condition of the works. Again and again they required you to make a private report on those points in regard to which there seemed cause for dissatisfaction, but this request you did not accede to until 21st May last after the line had been open upwards of nine months when you made a communication to me to the effect that the contractor might be paid under deduction of £25. But in this letter for the first time you made known the secret that the curves had not been executed according to the contract and that the special instruction given for their improvement had not received your attention. The details of the curves that you then furnished were totally different from those you had previously returned to the Board of Trade and equally different from those in the contract plans. The directors have had a minute inspection made by an engineer of eminence and have ascertained that in the execution of the works the variation from the plans have been of the most disgraceful character, that the statutory powers of the company have been violated, the Board of Trade misled and the Leven company are exposed to the danger of having the line shut up until the railway is rendered comfortable to the authorised plans and consistent with public security. The directors, I can assure you, have taken up this matter with great pain and reluctance, but as has been seen, while implicitly trusting you, they have been grievously disappointed in the deficiencies accidentally discovered in the works of the railway and they feel that they have the very strongest claims on you for relief for the consequences.

The Leven Railway was not the only company to be having such troubles in getting Thomas Bouch to attend to its affairs – the Crieff Junction Railway was having little better luck with him and the St Andrews company Directors were said to be reaching the end of their tether with him.

The turn of the tide

Gradually the Leven Railway began to turn itself around. At the half-yearly General Meeting held on 28th April, 1856 John Haig informed the shareholders that,

> Your Directors have the satisfaction to report the complete success of the independent working of the line. The anticipated difficulties by which it was sought to alarm the Shareholders have been entirely overcome; and although your Directors can claim no merit for a change which was forced upon them, they cannot help congratulating you upon the happy results which promise to accrue from it. At the close of the half-year to 31 July 1855, when the line was worked by the Edinburgh, Perth & Dundee, after all charges there remained a surplus of £757 applicable to interest and dividends. But of this sum, £111 fell to the Edinburgh, Perth & Dundee as their share of profits, leaving a free balance of only £646. During the last half-year, under independent management, the surplus, after paying all charges, is £1,204.

The fortunes of the company were clearly on the mend and not only was the sole locomotive now a positive asset, but the surplus funds were being applied to remedy the situation in regard to the disreputable rolling stock and the defective permanent way which was a legacy of the Bouch era. The final figure reached for the capital expenditure on rolling stock, inclusive of the 'additional engine' amounted to £5,766 2*s.* 10*d.* but the exact amount expended on making the goods wagons run satisfactorily is unknown. The passenger accommodation had been improved to the extent that the *Fifeshire Advertiser* in January 1857 carried a letter from 'A lover of comfort, Pathhead' stating that 'I have never found such attention paid to the comfort of passengers as those on the Leven Railway' and added that he was particularly impressed by the use of hot water warmers 'to warm the feet of the inmates' in each carriage.

By now construction of the line of the second East of Fife company from Leven to Kilconquhar was underway* and a new joint through station at Leven was under construction. As the East of Fife line opened in stages, the through traffic from Thornton as well as the local traffic began to bring increased revenue to the Leven company and, as from 1st October, 1857, the two companies entered into a working agreement with each other whereby they shared the operating expenses and revenue proportionally and services would be operated under the auspices of a Joint Committee. When the agreement was put before the Leven shareholders at their half-yearly meeting for their approval, their Chairman stated that 'a considerable saving will be effected to both companies and increased facilities for the transmission of traffic will be secured to the public'. The shareholders of both companies, needless to say, approved of the agreement with an apparent amount of enthusiasm and it was becoming increasingly clear that what all wanted was an eventual amalgamation of both companies into a single entity.

The Kirkland Branch

Apart from the Kilconquhar line, other expansion was also taking place, namely of the Kirkland branch. The second of the three lines authorized by the Leven Railway Act, this short line was 18 chains in length, leaving the Leven main line at or near the Burn Mill Dam, some two-thirds of a mile to the west of the terminus at Leven at a trailing junction and running southwards to a wooden bridge over the river and, after crossing the same, running south-eastwards to end adjacent to the

* The Kilconquhar line is dealt with in Chapter Six.

Kirkland Works which, at that time, employed some 500 persons engaged in flax, hemp and jute processing by water, steam and hand power and produced large quantities of calico and sailcloth as well as linen and other goods. The line was single throughout and devoid of any sidings and appears to have been worked by steam power that propelled wagons up to the bridge itself and thereafter by horses into the actual works area. The exact date of the Kirkland branch opening is not clear but at the half-yearly meeting of the Leven railway held on 22nd April, 1858 the shareholders were informed that, 'The branch between your railway and the Kirkland Works has been for some time completed and in use' and since there was no previous mention of the line one can only assume that it was completed and opened at some time after October 1857.

The most profitable of its kind

By this time the financial affairs of the company had become clear and in January 1859 it was declared that a total of £1,165 18*s.* 0*d.* had been incurred on 'Parliamentary Expenses' (Mr Christie having, no doubt, helped to swell this sum), £784 on engineering, £6,826 6*s.* 2*d.* on the acquisition of land and on compensation payments and a further £860 10*s.* 11*d.* on Land Settlements, £15,152 4*s.* 9*d.* on construction of the line, £3,390 5*s.* 1*d.* on stations and sidings and £1,282 5*s.* 8*d.* on miscellaneous expenses making a total, inclusive of the permanent locomotive but excluding rolling stock and the temporary locomotive, of £31,011 10*s.* 7*d.* This was financed by the paid-up share capital of £22,948, debentures issued of £5,000 and debts due of £8,892 13*s.* 5*d.* According to the Board of Trade returns, in the year ending 31st December, 1859 the Leven Railway had a total of two locomotives, three carriages and 54 wagons.

For the six months ending 31st December, 1859 the receipts of the company were as follows:

	No. of Passengers	Receipts £	s.	d.
(1) Passenger traffic				
First class	4,436	243	17	9
Second class	4,773	217	17	9
Third class	17,846	525	11	8
Fourth class	11,638	219	2	4
	38,653	1,197	9	6
(2) Mails, Carriages, Horses and Dogs		44	15	8
(3) Goods, Minerals, Livestock and Parcels		1,613	4	1
(4) Transfer Fees			5	0
(5) Interest		2	16	7
(6) Rent		11	1	3
(7) Sum Received from Joint Committee being the sum received from the company's share of balance arising from agreement with EoFR		352	0	1
		3,221	12	2

In both 1860 and 1861 the Chairman of the Leven company, in declaring dividends of 8 per cent, stated that he believed the undertaking to be 'the most profitable of its kind in Britain'. Matters were, however, moving rapidly towards the formal merger of the Leven and East of Fife companies.

Early days

A handful of early newspaper reports spread some light on the early days of the line. The *Observer* commented in 1861 that,

> Nothing is prospering so well as the goods traffic on the [Leven] railway. Train after train and day after day the long lines of luggage waggons that come with the passenger trains, independent of special ones, are truly astonishing ... Almost every train is from half-an-hour to an hour behind time. This could surely be remedied by the company employing more servants, an arrangement which the community has a right to expect, and more especially when the shareholders are pocketing above eight per cent.

Poor timekeeping was the subject of a letter to the *Scotsman* of 29th September in the previous year:

> SIR – of all the railways with which I am acquainted, there is none, perhaps, so grossly mismanaged as the Leven line running in connection with the Edinburgh, Perth and Dundee. For several of the trains daily a stoppage of nearly an hour (sometimes more) must be submitted to at Thornton Junction, where the accommodation for passengers is of the most wretched description, being nothing more than an open shed, unprovided with the most simple accommodation, exposed to every blast that blows. The second morning train, which leaves Leven at about half-past ten (as also the corresponding train from Edinburgh) takes nearly three and a half hours, which the steamers used to accomplish in two hours. I do not blame the management and that it was of the Leven line for this, as their trains must be run to suit the trains on the main line; but surely some plan might be devised to obviate this tedious detention, or if this is impossible, the station at Thornton ought to be immediately improved. I have heard it stated that the comfort of the local passengers is sacrificed from the desire to benefit the through traffic of the main line, which is far from being productive. There are many who would make Leven their summer residence, so delightfully situated for bathing and golfing, were the locality made more accessible. Yours, etc. 'Viator'

On 7th June, 1860 the *Fifeshire Journal* reported that,

> On Monday afternoon, as the mail train was proceeding from Thornton station to Cameron Bridge, when near that part of the Vale of Orr at Tillybreck, some of the carriages went off the line, which produced considerable alarm among the passengers. They left the carriages and after a detention of about half an hour all was got right and the train proceeded as usual. Little, if any, damage was done.

The company continued to be run in a somewhat amateurish way at this time (which was hardly surprising as none of its early Directors could in any way be described as professional railwaymen) and many years later the *Leven Advertiser & Wemyss Gazette*, in its issue of 14th December, 1910, reported that Henry Hunter, a railway employee of some 53 years' standing had recently retired and, under the heading of 'Early days of the Leven Railway' recounted that the company possessed only two locomotives in number, one being dubbed 'Old Iris', a very primitive machine, being kept in reserve:

> One day an accident happened to the regular engine. Word was sent to headquarters to turn out 'Old Iris' and that it was kindled up at once. The general manager, who was a local magnate, superintended operations, while the engineer fussed about plugging

pipes to keep the water in, and jumping up every few minutes to see if the engine would start. At last it just moved and no more. The general manager was on the footplate ready to go to the scene of the accident. He placed his hands on the boiler, no weatherboard being in the way, and shouted to young Hunter, who was eagerly looking on, 'Shove, man! Shove'. That was my first lesson in push.

Although Mr Hunter did not identify 'Old Iris', she was almost certainly was the 0-4-2 locomotive from Lancashire which appeared to have been kept on the company's books until the mid-1860s.

TO BE SOLD BY PUBLIC ROUP,

On Wednesday the 23d January 1861, at Two P.M., within the Salerooms of Messrs Cay & Black, 65 George Street, Edinburgh,

THE REMAINDER OF THE LEASE, FOR 99 YEARS from Martinmas 1856, of—THE EXTENSIVE

FLAX AND JUTE SPINNING MILLS, called HAUGH MILLS, at CAMERON BRIDGE STATION on the Leven Line of Railway, Fifeshire; together with the WHOLE STEAM ENGINES and MACHINERY, Fixed and Movable.

The Works contain between 4000 and 5000 Spindles for Flax and Tow, for wet and dry spinning. They also contain the requisite Machinery for carding, roving, spreading, and drawing, all on the most approved principles. A great part of the Machinery is quite new, and the whole is in the best working order.

There are Two High-pressure and Condensing Steam-engines, the one 60 and the other 40 horse-power. There is also a Water-wheel of about 25 horse-power. The supply of water from Loch Leven is most regular and abundant all the year round.

There are also upwards of 16 Acres of Excellent Arable LAND attached to the Property, the whole or part of which could easily be turned into a Bleachfield, with plenty of room for extending operations either for Power-loom Weaving, Net Manufacturing, or otherwise.

There is also an Excellent HOUSE, with STABLES, GARDEN, &c., TWO SEPARATE HOUSES for the Manager and Clerk, and a considerable number of WORKMEN'S HOUSES which yield good rents.

The Works are situated on the River Leven, and a Siding runs into them from the Leven Railway, so they are most conveniently situated as regards carriage. Coals from the immediate neighbourhood are delivered at a cheap rate, and the carriage for goods to and from Dundee and the South is very moderate. The Works and Houses are all lighted with gas made on the premises.

The Workers are plentiful, and of a steady class.

The Rent payable to the Landlord is £300 a year.

These Works are well known for their producing the best quality of yarns.

The whole will be exposed at the Low Upset Price of £11,500.

For further information apply to Mr WOOD, Accountant, 7 North St Andrew Street, Edinburgh; Messrs MELVILLE & LINDESAY, W.S., 110 George Street, Edinburgh; or DAVID NICOL, jun., Esq., Leven.

A newspaper announcement of the public roup (auction sale) of the Haugh Mills at Cameron Bridge - note the reference to the railway siding.

Chapter Six

Onwards and Eastwards: The East of Fife Railway 1854-1860

'Ere the railway gradually extended its course along the coast, the East Neuk was remote from the rest of the world and went its way unheeding and unheeded.'
Bygone Fife, James Wilkie (1931)

Eastward Bound

The Leven Railway was always intended only to be the first stage in the railway development of East Fife along the lines of the 1845 scheme and the *Fifeshire Journal*, in an article dealing with the opening of the Leven Railway in its issue of 10th August, 1854, made this quite clear as it went on to comment that,

> At present the whole of the East of Fife is shut out from direct railway communication, the nearest stations being St Andrews on the north and now Leven on the west. It is true that vans and omnibuses run to these stations, and that a steamer plies daily between Anstruther and Leith; but these are tardy conveyances in these days of forty miles an hour, and must of necessity be shortly superseded. With the conjoint populations of Crail, Anstruther, Pittenweem, St Monance, Elie, Colinsburgh and Largo – with a heavy agricultural produce, as witness the shipments of potatoes, live-stock and grain, which were made from the East Neuk last winter – with the largest white and herring fisheries on the Forth – and with the mineral fields of Elie, Pittenweem, Kellie &c., as yet scarcely opened up, there cannot possibly be a doubt that a single line of rails from Leven to Anstruther would be as remunerative to its constructors as it is needed by the district. Let it further be observed, that we are not here speaking of rural and inland villages, but of veritable seaports, all of which have harbours capable of extension and improvement, and in this respect calculated to develop the whole internal wealth of the county, as well as to add materially to the income of the different railways, whether branch or main line. On thus noticing the opening of the Leven Railway, and wishing it every success, we do so regarding it only as the first instalment of an East of Fife line – an undertaking on which we know that an influential section of the eastern proprietors have already set their minds, and only wait for an easier state of the labour and money markets to carry their intentions into effect.

These 'eastern proprietors' included Sir Ralph Anstruther and John Haig, who were already Directors of the Leven Railway, as well as General Lindsay of Balcarres (an estate to the north of Colinsburgh) and William Baird, a wealthy Lanarkshire Ironmaster, who had contributed £2,000 to the Leven company and who was the proprietor of the Elie estates which he had recently acquired. On 24th August, 1854 a Prospectus was issued for 'The East of Fife Railway' and, after noting that the Leven line had been completed and opened for traffic,

> The promoters deem the present a fitting occasion to solicit public attention to a scheme for prosecuting an extension to Anstruther, upon the same moderate and safe principles which have been applied with so much success in the construction of the Leven line. It would be difficult to find conditions more favourable to the application of the economical system of Railway construction, than the projected extension will command. The district to be accommodated is densely inhabited, and its trade and population are located in a chain of Towns and Villages, along which the line of railway will be carried.

A preliminary survey, carefully prepared, by a professional Engineer, shews the face of the County to be traversed is nearly level. The cuttings, embankments, and engineering operations which in other circumstances so greatly enhance the cost of a railway, will thus be of the least expensive character, and the Line, when made, will be capable of being worked and maintained at an unusually low rate. Such are the advantages of the situation that, notwithstanding the rise in the price of labour and materials, the formation of the Railway, including preliminary expenses and land (much of which is Links ground of little value) is estimated not to cost beyond £5,000 a mile...The resources of the District warrant the promoters in anticipating a highly remunerative return upon the estimated expenditure. The Railway is so projected as to secure the traffic of the Towns of Largo, Kilconquhar, Colinsburgh, Earlsferry, Elie, St Monans, Pittenweem, Anstruther and Cellardyke, all within the compass of twelve miles. Several of these towns are shipping ports, and have a large fishing trade. The Country around is a rich agricultural district in a high state of cultivation, and embraces an extensive field of coal and other minerals. The proposed Railway will form a continuation of the great East and West line, which extends from Leven by Dunfermline to Stirling and Glasgow; and will establish direct intercourse with all parts of the County. In it the Fisheries will possess a direct means of transit to Edinburgh, and the great manufacturing Towns in the west and south. It will enable the Agriculturalist to send their produce to the best markets. The connection it will open up with the Iron Works in the neighbourhood of Dunfermline, will tend to develop the mineral resources of the locality. And, when the facilities of railway communication are secured, the excellent Sea-bathing stations, and the many beautiful situations for Summer Residences, which abound upon the line, cannot fail to attract numerous visitors, and to give an impetus to building operations, hitherto only retarded by the isolated position of the coast.

On 7th September, 1854 the *Fifeshire Journal* reported that a public meeting of persons interested in building a line from Leven to Anstruther, chaired by Sir Ralph had been held in Colinsburgh and that it had been well attended. Once again the services of Thomas Bouch as Engineer had been secured and his detailed estimates for the construction of the line were given as follows:

	£	*s.*	*d.*
Cutting and embankment	4,009	10	0
Upper works: Rails, Chairs, sleepers, keys, pins, fencing	21,570	15	0
Ballasting and Boxing	2,770	1	0
Drains and Culverts	800	0	0
Three turnpike Bridges @ £350	1,050	0	0
Viaduct at Largo	2,500	0	0
Occupation Bridges 4 @ £250	1,000	0	0
Retaining Walls	500	0	0
Level crossings (including 4 Turnpike, 10 Public Roads)	1,150	0	0
Stations (5) and 8 Level Crossing Houses	3,660	0	0
Contingencies @ 10% of £39,010 6*s.* 0*d.*	3,901	0	7
Total for works	42,911	6	7
Land for 70 acres @ £150	10,500	0	0
Law, Parliamentary and Engineering Expenses	5,000	0	0
Total	*£58,411*	*6*	*7*

The proposed line was to run eastwards from a new station at Burnmill, where an end-on junction with the Leven Railway was to be situated, and then pass over the Scoonie links from where it would generally follow the coastline to Leven, passing through the undeveloped lands of Lundin Links and to the south of Lundin Mill – these links were of particular interest to the promoters as they were of poor agricultural value and thus could be bought at a reasonable price. Entering the village of Lower Largo, a viaduct across the mouth of the Keil Burn was required and this was to be the only major engineering work upon the line. From here the line followed the shoreline of Largo Bay until turning east across the links and heading directly for Kilconquhar via Muircambus, where it was to cross the Elie to Largo turnpike road and pass just to the north of Kilconquhar village immediately south of the hamlet of Barnyards. The line then passed eastwards via Balbuthie to St Monance where it would then run to the north of Pittenweem and terminate at Anstruther Wester. There were to be five stations, situated at Lower Largo, Kilconquhar, St Monance, Pittenweem and Anstruther, all of them well established as settlements but Elie, which was to be passed to the north, was not to be directly served by the new railway. The capital was to be raised by pubic subscription and the line was to be worked in conjunction with the Leven Railway, with Andrew Wilkie to act as Secretary to the Provisional Management Committee which was set up as a result of the interest generated at the public meeting.

Kilconquhar or Anstruther?

It was, however, realised from early on that the proposed East of Fife Railway was in danger of falling in to the same trap as the earlier proposal bearing the same name – that of being unable to raise locally such a potentially large sum of money in one go. On 30th September, 1854 Sir Ralph wrote to Andrew Wilkie to express his concerns about this, saying that the Provisional Committee would have to seriously consider either building their line in two stages (with Kilconquhar as the temporary terminus) or postponing an application to Parliament for an Act until such time as they could raise sufficient funds.

Although Largo was a small but flourishing fishing port with a growing attraction for the more adventurous holidaymaker and Kilconquhar, an ancient but insignificant village a couple of miles inland, neither were, in themselves, a sufficient financial justification for a railway from Leven. Thus the promoters of the line found themselves at something of a disadvantage in that although they wished to go ahead with the East of Fife scheme, they were not in a position to carry that out, at least in full. At the beginning of October the Provisional Committee met and, reluctantly, took the decision to seek authorization for a line as far as Kilconquhar only with the remaining eastern section of the line to Anstruther to follow as soon as possible thereafter. By the date of their meeting it was clear that they had managed to raised only £15,000, with William Baird as the single largest contributor putting forward £6,000 of his own; other subscribers included Lindsay and Sir Ralph with £1,000 each, Haig and five others with £500 each and a large number of other individuals, mainly local, down to a number of Cellardyke fishermen who were prepared to subscribe £10 each. A week or so later the total of contributions had risen to £18,540 and by the beginning of November to some £23,000 (including a further £2,000 from Baird) or rather less than one-half of the total which would be require to carry the line to Anstruther. However, the decision was not a popular one and it was clear that some of the members of the

Provisional Committee, including the Provosts of Anstruther and Crail, felt that the whole scheme should be postponed until such time as enough money could be raised to proceed with the whole line to Anstruther. At a subscribers' meeting held on 2nd November there was discussion about whether the line was to be carried to the south or north of Kilconquhar Loch and then the vital vote as to whether or not the line should be terminated at Kilconquhar or the whole scheme be deferred for a period of one year. The vote in favour of progressing initially to Kilconquhar was carried with only two subscribers, Philip Oliphant and Michael Connolly, both bankers from Anstruther, voting against the proposal.

The Minister's Glebe or Broomlee Tile Works?

There still remained the question of exactly where the terminus at Kilconquhar was to be situated. The original proposal was to have a terminus 'at a point in or near the Minister's Glebe, near to the town [*sic*] of Kilconquhar'. This terminus would have meant that the line when eventually extended to Anstruther would have passed to the north of Kilconquhar Loch and would therefore have by-passed Elie altogether and the inhabitants of that burgh, together with their most influential resident, William Baird, expressed some disquiet since it was clear that if Elie were to be left off the railway then it would suffer the fate of other places in a similar position and accordingly 'wither on the vine'. It was therefore at an early stage that Baird argued that the Kilconquhar terminus should be moved to a site near to or at his Broomlee Tile Works, half a mile or so to the west of the village, from where an extension could either pass to the south of the Loch and rejoin the originally proposed formation or to deviate a mile or so southwards to serve Elie.

Events were, however, moving swiftly and when the East of Fife Railway Bill was published in December 1854 it appeared that a *fait accompli* had occurred for the terminus was stated to be as in the original proposal, i.e. to accommodate a line passing to the north of Kilconquhar. It was now that Baird began to carry out his own investigations and he managed to ascertain from Robert Keddie, the Parliamentary engineer, that the comparative costs of a deviation from the original line of route where it was to cross the Balchristie Burn west of Muircambus and close to the now abandoned farm of Mount Pleasant to a terminus at Broomlee Tile Works would be £3,372 16*s*. 3*d*. if the line was to pass to the north of Muircambus Mill and £3,677 0*s*. 10*d*. if it passed to the south of the mill as opposed to £5,728 18*s*. 8*d*. for the original route from Mount Pleasant to the terminus between Kilconquhar and Barnyards. Part of these savings resulted from the deviations passing over less valuable agricultural land than the original course would have done and the deletion of the turnpike bridge. Baird then wrote to Wilkie to point out that not only could a saving of some £2,000 or so be made but that the resited terminus would enable the extension to Anstruther to serve Elie as well and thus generate additional traffic.

The Provisional Committee considered the matter further and on 10th April, 1855 John Moffat, an engineer from Ardrossan who had been commissioned by Baird to prepare a report, sent the following communication to Robert Lamond, the Parliamentary agent dealing with the East of Fife application:

> When at Elie yesterday, I was requested by Mr Baird to examine the line of the proposed East of Fife Railway, from the point where it enters his Estate, to the Terminus at Kilconquhar, in order to compare it with another route, which he thinks would be cheaper

> to the Company, and more convenient to the Public. I accordingly examined the ground very carefully, along with Mr Baird and Mr Keddie, the gentleman who made the Parliamentary Survey, and who then took some measurements, in order to find the relative cost of the two routes. Having carefully considered the whole subject, I am decidedly of the opinion that the southern route proposed by Mr Baird is the best and cheapest line, and that, if practicable, steps should be taken to abandon the other and to adopt it ... Merely as a matter of economy it would be better to abandon the Bill at the present stage and bring it forward again next year, than to execute the line as laid down ... The bulk of the passenger traffic will undoubtedly always be got from the coast towns. And there can be no doubt that wherever the terminus may be, the passengers from Pittenweem, Anstruther and the other coast towns, will always pass along the coast road, and through the town of Elie in going to the station. This traffic, besides being the largest, is the one which ought to be most carefully cultivated, on account of the danger of its being diverted from the line by the new and swift steamers that are to be started between Anstruther, Elie and Leith. These passengers would all have to go half a mile further to the Parliamentary station than to the one at the Tile Works. And this additional distance would be sufficient to divert the traffic from the Railway to the Steamers, especially in summer. The next largest item of traffic would be the fish from the coast towns. From Anstruther, Pittenweem and St Monance there would not be any great difference in favour of either station. But for Elie the Tile Work Station would have the same advantages for Goods as for Passengers. The Harbour at Elie has already been improved by Mr Baird. And he proposes to execute further improvements this summer. It is the only point on the coast possessing any natural advantages for Harbour purposes. And I have no doubt that when the contemplated improvements are completed it will command the bulk of Exports and Imports to and from the whole district. It is therefore of the highest importance, not only to the pecuniary interests of the shareholders, but to the general interests of the shareholders, but to the general interest of the public; that the Railway should be constructed in the manner most convenient for the traffic to and from Elie Harbour. And unless there be some reasons not pointed out to me, for following the proposed route between Barnyards and Kilconquhar, it seems to me that it would be very bad policy for the Railway Company to adopt it.

Moffat, described by John Haig as 'an engineer of high character and great experience', went on to point out that although the original terminus might be more convenient for the inland parishes such as Carnbee and Abercrombie,

> … it is not expected that there will be any public conveyance from the Terminus to these parishes. The traffic will therefore consist only of passengers on foot, or in their own carriages and of farm produce. And I do not think that one passenger, or one ton of goods, will be lost by the station being altered to the Tile Works.

The provisional Directors of the company were divided as to whether or not they would wish to adopt Baird's proposal but they could hardly ignore both the views of such an influential shareholder and the advice given to them by Moffat. A further difficulty was the timing of the proposal, because the East of Fife Railway Bill was due to be heard by the Parliamentary Railway Committee in five days' time on 19th April. Wilkie arranged that the correspondence would be forwarded to other Directors and was duly approved. A somewhat curious clause was inserted into the Bill, providing that 'it shall be lawful and in the power of the Company, with the sanction of a general meeting of the shareholders, to terminate such deviated line at a point at or near Broomlee's Tile Works aforesaid, and on the south west side of the turnpike road from Elie to Balchristie'.

There was no further opposition to the Bill and even the Edinburgh, Perth & Dundee Railway saw the potential advantage of yet another feeder line which would cost them nothing, advising their shareholders that the East of Fife 'will prove in every respect advantageous' and that the Bill 'will merit every countenance and support'. On 23rd July, 1855 the East of Fife Railway Act (18 & 19 Vict., cap. clvi) was passed, providing for a railway from a junction with the Leven Railway 'to be made at the sight and satisfaction of the Engineer for the time being of the Leven Railway' to the original terminus in or near the Minister's Glebe at Kilconquhar, with the appropriate provision for a terminus deviation. The authorized ordinary share capital of the company was £32,000, made up of £10 shares, with borrowing powers for a further £10,606 and the first Directors were Sir Ralph Anstruther, James Lindsay, William Baird, John Haig, John Wood and William Ross of Greenside with Andrew Wilkie as the company Secretary. The statutory position was tidied up when the company applied once again for Parliamentary powers in connection with their line, this time to gain sanction for the terminus of their line to be moved from the original site adjoining Kilconquhar village to the new site lying to the north of Muircambus Mill. On 5th June, 1856 the East of Fife Railway (Deviation) Act, (19 & 20 Vict., cap. c.xxiv), was passed unopposed.

From Leven to Lundin Mill

The final route of the new line, which extended to a total of 6¾ miles, started with an end-on junction with the Leven Railway at the original Burnmill terminus of that company. Leaving the newly extended joint station the line ran in a north north-easterly direction to where a horse-drawn tramway was crossed on the level. This tramway connected a clay pit lying 200 yards south of Shotburn Mill and ran a total of about ¼ mile to the Leven Brick, Tile and Ochre Works of John White & Son. Both the works and the tramway pre-dated the railway by some time, having been opened in about 1830 and being responsible for the majority of the bricks from which Leven was built. A siding was provided to serve the Works and this was definitely in operation by 1859. From here the line continued to run in the same direction towards the shores of Largo Bay where it then crossed the almost-deserted Scoonie Links, a wide area of sandy soil covered in turf which was almost useless as agricultural land. Almost 1½ miles from Leven the flax mill at Silverburn was reached. This was rail served, a long siding joining the East of Fife line at the Scoonie parish boundary. The line now crossed Lundin Links and within half a mile the site of Lundin Links station was reached. When the railway was opened there was no community which this station could serve.

The estate of Lundin was a lonely one with few signs of habitation and its principal feature, lying to the north of the Leven to Largo high road, was three tall Bronze Age monoliths known as the Standing Stones of Lundin. A solitary house known as Sunnybraes lay on the road but otherwise the area was a quiet and unfrequented one and entirely undeveloped. Development was, however, in the offing and as part of the negotiations entered into by the East of Fife provisional committee with local landowners, an agreement was reached with the Standard Life Assurance Company of Edinburgh which was to have a far reaching and permanent effect that can still be seen today. Standard Life had acquired the Estate of Lundin in 1852 for the purpose of feuing (dividing the land up into building plots for the purpose of developing a superior residential estate) and, as Clause 36 of the East of Fife Railway Bill was to enact,

LUNDIN LINKS, with LARGO BAY and LAW.

Lundin Links as yet unbuilt on - note the fishing vessel and the train in the background.
From Fairnie's Handbook to the Fife Coast, 1860

Lundin Links in about 1900 - the wedge-shaped building on the platform is the original Standard Life station with its NBR replacement to the right. *P. Westwater Collection*

And whereas the Standard Life Assurance Company, the owners of the Estate of Lundin in the parish of Largo, have laid out a portion of the said Estate on the proposed line of the Railway to be let in lots or feued for Building ... the [Railway] Company shall erect and maintain a temporary goods and passenger station at or near to Sunnybraes, or at any other point on the said Estate which may be agreed upon by and between the Company and the owners of the said Estate for the time, and at the said station ordinary traffic shall stop for the purpose of traffic.

Provision was made for the situation where, if after five years from opening, the traffic generated was not sufficiently remunerative for the railway company, then the obligation to keep the station open was no longer binding on them. Lundin Links station was opened along with the rest of the line in August 1857 with a temporary building but in September 1858 an agreement was reached between the East of Fife company and Standard Life that the station was to be completed as a permanent structure. Standard Life contributed £450 out of a total cost of £800 for the station and its approach road and would also undertake to construct four villas by the station. At the following EoFR half-yearly meeting the shareholders were told that this agreement 'cannot fail; to promote the development of traffic at that station'.* Development at Lundin Links was, however, slow and it was many years before the station was surrounded by 'a village of villas and commodious houses, with a contented, well-to-do air about it'. Fairnie's 1860 *Hand Book of the Fife Coast* stated, perhaps optimistically that,

Lundin Links lies in the recess of Largo Bay, which is said to rival the beautiful bay of Naples in point of scenery; and no where on the coast are there such eligible sites for marine villas. The stretch of view seaward is magnificent, embracing a panorama of the opposite coast from the Bass to the shores of Edinburgh by Inchkeith. The landscape of the surrounding district is equally beautiful and interesting from its historical associations and antiquities. As a sea-bathing station and resort for valetudinarians, the locality cannot be excelled. The sites are contiguous to the beautiful links of Lundin and Leven, which bid fir soon to surpass the far-famed links of St Andrews as a golf centre. The East of Fife Railway affords abundant means of communication, there being a station on the ground. The feuing has already commenced, two handsome villas having been constructed and more are in progress.

Beyond Lundin Links lay Lundin Mill, originally a scatter of houses originally centred on the British Linen Company's flax mill but by the time the railway had arrived there was already development in the area and a number of houses had already appeared on the Emsdorf road.

Largo and onwards

The only substantial engineering work on the new line was now reached, the viaduct over the Keil burn, a handsome structure of four spans, one of which crossed the burn itself and the other three the den,† two of the spans being over 60 feet high. Farnie picturesquely described the scene saying that the line,

* A separate local contractor was used for the permanent station which was built to a distinctive double-gabled design quite unlike the standard EoFR pattern used at other stations on the line.

† 'A somewhat remarkable surface feature of Fife, especially in its eastern portion, is its numerous dens or deans. These have been cut out of solid rock by the age-long action of what may now appear quite inconsiderable streamlets, in which the declivity of the channel has compensated for volume of water ...' (*Cambridge County Geographies – Fife.*)

> ... suddenly comes upon quite a precipitous ravine, crossed by a tall and imposing viaduct, through the arches of which the Kiel burn flows cannily. Down in this ravine, at the mouth of the burn, lies green-mossed and linen thatched Largo built on both sides of the Kiel, which is crossed below the railway viaduct by a foot suspension bridge. The hamlet on the western side is called Drummochie and was anciently a fisher-village ... in contradistinction the other side goes by the name of Temple of Strathairlie, but more commonly the two are joined together as Nether or Lower Largo.

Lower Largo or Seatown of Largo was known as such to differentiate it from Kirkton of Largo or Upper Largo (also known as Nether Largo), situated half a mile to the north on the high road. Chambers, in his *Pictures of Scotland* published in 1827, described Lower Largo as as 'an extensive fishing village' with a pier from which coal was exported. The village had a small tourist trade helped, in no small measure, by the fact that it had a twice-daily steamship connection with Leith. Its fishing trade was not insubstantial, there being in 1855 eighty men and boys employed on the 36 herring boats based in the harbour. Fairnie commented that,

> There is little trade now of any kind in the Largos. Immediately below the railway bridge, on the banks of the Keil, are a water mill for cleaning flax and a steam and water-mill for manufacturing it. But it is now some time since they were in operation, and from the present proprietorship it is not probable their walls will ever tremble with the dull throbbing of machinery. At Lundin Mills, a small village near Nether Largo, are flour mills which confer the distinguishing appellation on the village, and which do considerable business. The villagers at Upper Largo are principally engaged in hand-loom weaving and agricultural occupations, and the same is the case with Lower Largo, with the addition of sea fishing ...

Lower Largo, however, had another claim to fame, and as *Slater's Directory* of 1860 put it, 'The village would have remained amongst the most obscure of coast villages but for the circumstances of its having been the birthplace of Alexander Selkirk, rendered famous by the pen of Defoe as Robinson Crusoe'. Running then eastwards along the shores of Largo Bay the line then continued in the same direction while the coastline swung away to the south until crossing the Cocklemill Burn the terminus was reached next to the Largo to Elie road, a good half mile or so from the nearest house in Kilconquhar village – given the fact that the station served very little in the immediate vicinity, it was given the somewhat optimistic initial name of Kilconquhar and Elie.

Towards completion

Construction began promptly, the contractor being Matthew Anderson of Granton near Edinburgh and the engineer being Thomas Bouch's assistant Mr Martin, Bouch's services having been dispensed with because of his debacle with the Leven Railway Directors. On 10th July, 1856 the *Journal* commented that the formation of the line was proceeding rapidly, that about 130 navvies were currently being employed in its construction and 'that in about four months the trains will be running to Largo'. There were, however, unfortunately a series of accidents which marred the otherwise smooth progress of the line. In October 1856 a labourer, George McKinlay, a native of Ross-shire 'aged about 45' was struck by a load of sleepers when a chain, being used to lift the sleepers on to some scaffolding at Largo, gave way. Death was reported as having been instantaneous. The following month it was reported that close to Sunnybraes (adjoining the links) one of the contractor's horses had been so injured when it fell and was run over by a truck that it had to be destroyed.

In an interesting entry in the company's letter book, dated 23rd September, 1856, Wilkie wrote to Messrs Hawthorn & Co., Engine Builders, Leith that, 'I have been instructed by the Directors to take in offers for a locomotive engine with tender for the East of Fife Railway Co., identical to the one which you supplied to the Leven Railway and which is presently working on that railway. I will be glad to receive an offer from you'. In due course such a locomotive was delivered by Hawthorn's. Wagons were also required and on 6th December Wilkie wrote to Joseph Wright & Sons, wagon builders of the Saltley Works in Birmingham, sending them £500 on account for 10 wagons which they had supplied with the statement that, 'I am aware that the money has been far too long due and we thank you for your forbearance'.

The formation was sufficiently advanced that Wilkie could write to William Baird on 5th January, 1857 in the following terms:

> We had an engine over the railway as far as the Largo viaduct on Saturday and the Directors are to have a meeting tomorrow to go over that portion of the line and decide if it shall be opened for goods traffic which some of them are anxious for. We have had a rather severe storm yesterday of wind and snow from the East and today it is not much better.

The inspection duly took place, with the Directors, Wilkie 'and a few others interested in the success of the undertaking' travelling from Leven to Drummochy, the *Fifeshire Journal* commenting that they 'passed along the line in a gaily decorated train which created considerable sensation among the good folks of Largo' and were met at Largo by the town band. On 7th January Wilkie wrote again to Baird to tell him that, 'The Directors had a fine trip on the East of Fife from Leven to Largo yesterday. The train went beautifully. It is proposed to open that portion of the line for goods traffic in about a fortnight. The storm still continues, but this morning the wind has changed to the South-West and there is approaching a change of weather'. The Directors now resolved to open this part of the line for goods only, and they gave the temporary terminus at the western end of the uncompleted Largo viaduct the name of Lundin Mill, somewhat misleading as it was a quarter-mile downstream from the settlement of that name and actually situated in the hamlet of Drummochy. The opening took place on 1st February, 1857 and the traffic seems to have justified this partial opening for in the following month the *Fifeshire Journal* reported that,

> The iron horse of commerce may now be seen sweeping on is iron path across the once quiet links twice a day as far as Lundin Mill, with its loads of merchandise and animals. Direct communication having now been opened up between Largo and all large manufacturing towns, it is not unlikely that we may soon hear of some enterprising tenant for the Drummochy Spinning Mill, lately occupied by Messrs Swan of Kirkcaldy. We are glad to observe that Mr Grainger the contractor is pushing on with the rest of the works with his usual energy. The viaduct at Largo is the most formidable part of the undertaking and the finest piece of architecture in the vicinity now nears completion, for two miles beyond the permanent rails are laid and if operations go on as present the line soon must be completed.

By the end of April the viaduct, the contract for which was awarded to John Wood, engineer, was all but finished and the remaining engineering works were

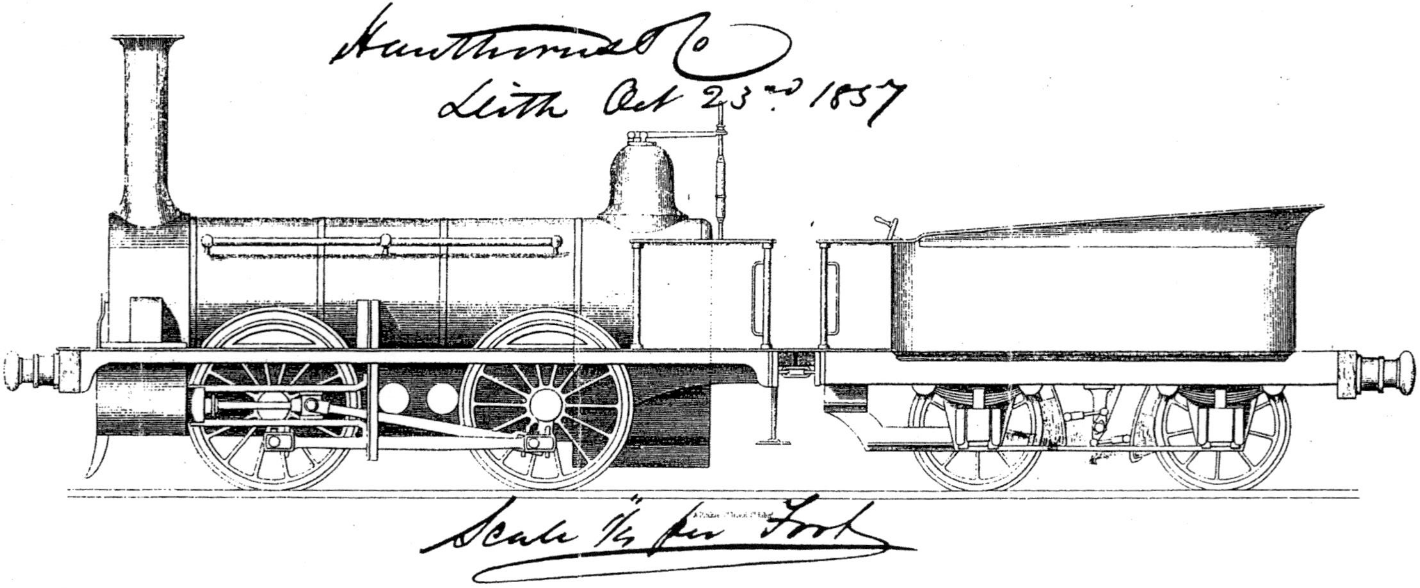

The plan of a Hawthorn 0-4-0 sent to Andrew Wilkie in 1857. The three LEoFR Hawthorn locomotives were identical and the wording on the plan tends to suggest that this was the third engine ordered in 1857 and delivered in 1863. *Authors' Collection*

completed within a short time, leaving work to be carried out on the stations, the track and fencing. Then, on 27th July, 1857, Captain Tyler of the Royal Engineers submitted a report to the Board of Trade stating that he had inspected the line and found that,

> The permanent way is a slight one, being composed of a rail weighing 65 lbs to the linear yard, placed upon sleepers averaging three feet apart, and being secured at the joints by a cast-iron chair and wooden key only. The traffic is not expected to be heavy, and the speed will be moderate; but it would be better if one of the various improvements which have been made of late years in securing the joints of the rails had been adopted. The ballast is composed of sand and gravel. There are no public level crossings on the line. A culvert near Largo has sunk two or three inches for a portion of its length. It appears that this happened from an inequality in the foundations when it was first built, and that it has not since altered. I do not therefore apprehend any danger from it, but it should be carefully watched. The permanent way wants packing, and putting in order on some parts of the line, and some of the fencing has yet to be completed. At a ¼ of a mile from Leven there is a tram-way level crossing,* which must be either removed or properly protected by signals, and supplied with a signal man's box. A siding at a temporary loading bank, and a ballast siding, are to be removed. Some 6-inch planking employed to carry the rails between the cast-iron girders of two of the bridges should be replaced by 8″ planking. I have not yet received the necessary certificate in regard to the working of the line, which is single. For the reasons given above, I am of the opinion that the opening of the line would, by reason of the incompleteness of the works, be attended with danger to the public using the same.

Two days later Captain Galton, on behalf of the Railway Department of the Board of Trade, sent a copy of the report to the Secretary of the East Fife company and, in a covering letter informed him that the opening of the line to passengers was to be delayed by one month to enable the outstanding matters to be remedied. The company acted quickly and within days the Secretary and Engineer sent a letter to Captain Tyler certifying that the requirements detailed in his report had been completed together with a certificate signed by the Deputy Chairman and Secretary to the effect that the line would be operated on the 'one engine in steam' principle. Captain Tyler reported to the Board of Trade on 4th August, 1857 that, accordingly, the line forthwith 'may be opened without danger to the public using the same' and three days later a letter was sent to the East of Fife company informing them that there would be no further objection to the line being opened to the public 'provided that not more than one engine in steam (except where two are required for one train) be allowed upon the line at one and the same time'.

Open for business

Before this sanction had been given, an unofficial opening had already taken place. On Friday 31st July the *East Fife Record* reported that,

> The directors and shareholders, accompanied with a number of friends, made several trips along this line, which is now completed from Leven to Kilconquhar. The day was remarkably fine, and at every station and at several places along the line, the people had collected in considerable numbers from the adjoining villages to greet the passing train with cheers. The line appears to be in most excellent order, reflecting great credit upon

* The Leven Brickworks Tramway referred to in Chapter Two.

all who have had anything to do with its construction. ... This railway promises to be of immense advantage to the district through which it passes, affording a quick access to various markets for the agricultural produce, and the produce of the extensive fisheries along the coast. To excursionists the East of Fife line should present many attractions. It passes through beautiful country, and for a considerable distance quite near to the coast of the Firth of Forth, ending for the present at Kilconquhar – a most delightful place to spend a holiday. That the East of Fife Railway will be incomplete till it reaches Anstruther is very evident; and it is to be hoped that a vigorous and united effort will at once be made to accomplish this most desirable and important object. It is a trite observation to say that railways have introduced a new order of things in the trade and commerce, and even in the social relations, of our country.

A celebratory dinner was held at the Kilconquhar brickworks and was attended by those who had travelled on the first train. The public opening took place 12 days later on 11th May, 1857. The opening services consisted of four trains in each direction and the initial service was as following:

Up trains		*1*	*2*	*3*	*4*
		am	*am*	*pm*	*pm*
Kilconquhar & Elie	*dep.*	6.45	10.15	4.20	6.40
Largo		6.57	10.27	4.32	6.52
Lundin Links		7.00	10.30	4.35	6.55
Leven		7.15	10.45	4.50	7.05
Cameron Bridge		7.23	10.55	4.59	7.13
Thornton Junction	*arr.*	7.43	11.13	5.20	7.33

Down trains		*1*	*2*	*3*	*4*
		am	*am*	*pm*	*pm*
Thornton Junction	*dep.*	8.13	11.38	5.45	7.58
Cameron Bridge		8.32	11.55	6.00	8.15
Leven		8.40	12.03 *pm*	6.08	8.23
Lundin Links		8.47	12.10	6.15	8.30
Largo		8.50	12.13	6.18	8.33
Kilconquhar & Elie	*arr.*	9.10	12.28	6.30	8.53

Passengers change carriages at Thornton Junction.
Notes: Train 1 – 1st, 2nd & 4th class and mail; Trains 2 and 4 – 1st, 2nd, & 3rd class; Train 3 – 1st, 2nd, 3rd class and mail.

Connections were provided at Thornton for Edinburgh departing at 7.45, 11.20 am, 5.22 and 7.35 pm, arriving there at 9.30, 1.00, 7.00 and 9.10 and for Dundee and Perth at 8.10, 11.35 am, 5.40 and 7.54 pm and arriving at Perth at 9.30, 12.45, 6.57 and 9.04 and at Dundee at 10.05, 11.25, 7.37 and 9.40. Down train connections were similar, with the last connection of the day from Edinburgh leaving at 6.25 pm. A coach ('for which the Railway Company are not responsible') was run by Andrew Marshall of Anstruther and was advertised to leave Anstruther at 5.35 am and 3.00 pm with two return services. Return fares to Kirkcaldy from Largo and Lundin Links were 2*s.* 6*d.* first and 1*s.* 11*d.* second (no third or fourth class returns were issued) and to Edinburgh, Leith or Granton returns were 6*s.* 6*d.* first class, 5*s.* 3*d.* second, 3*s.* 8*d.* third and 3*s.* 4*d.* fourth; single tickets were issued at two-thirds of the return fare.

The effect of the first train to be run was still remembered 75 years later when it was said that,

> The first train came to Largo in 1856 [*sic*]. Prior to that the railway stopped at Leven and there are still people who can remember walking across the links to Leven to catch the train there. Mr Lindsay in the Kirkton tells me he was in the little school in Emsdorf Road then, and his master let him out to see the first train pass. They all stayed out longer than he said they might, and were all smacked with the tawse, except Mr Lindsay who was so wee that he was forgiven. [The passage ended with the wry comment that] the trains are still not very numerous nor very rapid.*

Running the line

During the first month of operation, it would appear that passenger receipts on the newly-opened line had far exceeded the Directors' anticipations and it was announced that in the first five days that 575 tickets had been sold, while the figure for the week ending 22nd August was 940 and 895 'exclusive of return tickets from Edinburgh' for the following week. It was said that these figures, in the face of competition by sea, promised well for the passenger traffic 'and a fair amount of goods traffic has likewise been obtained, which will go on increasing as the season advances'.

At the East of Fife Railway half-yearly meeting in October 1857 John Haig told the shareholders,

> That the passenger traffic should have amounted to 1,000 per week, was not only satisfactory, but surprising. If you consider that but a few years ago the district could not support a two-horse coach – that not very long ago there was not a conveyance all round the coast from St Andrews to Kirkcaldy, save one old post-chaise at Anstruther, they would agree with him that a wonderful change had taken place in the locomotive habits of the people, and that there is some truth in the statements that railways make traffic. He accounted for the smallness of the goods traffic by the fact that the line had been opened when the two chief sources of traffic – fish and agriculture – were unproductive; the herring fishing have been just concluded – and an unfortunate season it had been – while no white fish had come into the market, and in agriculture the harvest was not cut, and the potatoes in the ground. But even with all these drawbacks, if the traffic be compared with the first few weeks of the Leven line, opened at the same period of the year, there will be found no very great difference, although the Leven was not so dependent as the east of Fife was on agriculture and fish traffic. There was another encouraging feature in the traffic. In the three weeks of August the goods traffic had been 324 tons; value £33 1*s*. 7*d*. In September the traffic had been 473 tons, value £62 6*s*., and October promises to have a still greater increase, so he thought he had good reason to congratulate them on the infant steps of their line. As to the working agreement with the Leven line, our great difficulty was of a novel character, viz. that we were so much agreed.

The meeting concluded with thanks being given to various of the officials and Directors of the company and a clear indication that the object of both the East of Fife and Leven companies was 'to become one at as an early period as possible'. Acknowledgement was given to the fact that there were those who were still unhappy at the delay in prosecuting the line as far as Anstruther but, on the basis that 'half a loaf was better than none', those people would have to be patient.

At the following half-yearly meeting, held in April 1858, it was said that the total

* *The Largo Village Book*, Largo Women's Rural Institute, 1932.

ISSUE

IN THE CAUSE IN WHICH

WILLIAM TULLOCH, residing in Earlsferry in the County of Fife, and one of the Magistrates of that Burgh; and ROBERT PATTIE, Farm Servant, residing in Earlsferry—are *Pursuers;*

AND

WILLIAM BAIRD of Elie, and JOHN WOOD, Bank Agent in Colinsburgh; and the East of Fife Railway Company—are *Defenders.*

IT being admitted that the Defender William Baird of Elie, is proprietor of the lands of Dumbarnie, and the defender John Wood, is tenant thereof, and that the defenders, the East of Fife Railway Company, have constructed a railway from the town of Leven to Kilconquhar.

WHETHER for forty years and upwards, or for time immemorial prior to the 10th day of April 1858, being the date of raising this action, there has been a public road or right of way, for carts, horses, and foot passengers, or any and which of them, leading from the burgh of Earlsferry, by the farms of Grange, Grangehill, and Kincraig, through the links of Saint Ford, then crossing the burn or stream, called the Cockle Mill Burn, by a timber bridge through Muircambus Mill Links, thence through the lands of Balchristie, and thence through the links of Dumbarnie across the site now occupied by the line of said railway to the turnpike road between Pittenweem and Largo, at or near Dumbarnie farm-steading.

Authenticated as finally settled by Interlocutor of date 11th June, and signed 15th June 1859.

(Signed) DUN. M'NEILL, *I.P.D.*

The formal question posed to the jury in the Dumbarnie case.

expenses of operating the line amounted to £448 19*s*. each for the Leven and East of Fife companies and the operating surplus for each company amounted to £861 4*s*. It was stated that the number of passengers in the last six months had been 17,930, being divided up between classes at 1,955 first, 2,073 second, 8,694 third and 5,208 fourth. Capital expenditure to date was given as £36,606.

Operated on the same basis as, and in conjunction with, the Leven Railway the East of Fife company had its own locomotive, the Hawthorn 0-4-0 ordered by Wilkie. Goods rolling stock consisted of 20 wagons but it appears that these were not enough because in April 1858 it was reported to the shareholders that, 'the supply of wagon plant at the disposal of the joint committee has not been so ample as your directors could have wished, but a further supply of both goods and cattle trucks has now been secured, sufficient, in the opinion of the [joint] committee, to meet every requirement of the traffic'.

Although the number of passengers showed a slight increase in the following six months, revenue from goods traffic showed little increase which was attributed by the company to the fact that there had been a universal stagnation in business and that there was a general falling off of trade on the 'established lines of railway'. The *Fifeshire Journal* of 8th October, 1859 mentioned that with regard to what was described as coach accommodation,

> ... there is at present no lack of conveyances between the Kilconquhar railway station to the eastwards as far as Crail. Mr. T. Smith, who has for a number of years run his omnibus between Anstruther and St Andrews, has now discontinued that road, and commenced to run twice daily between Crail, Anstruther and the Kilconquhar station. Mr Marshall's coach, conveying the mails twice daily, also occupies the same road – so that we now have a coach both to meet the arrival and departure of the four daily trains. It is much doubted whether there is sufficient traffic on the road to pay all these coaches – we rather think not, especially during the winter season; but the rivalry has commenced, and the time will tell whether the proprietors will be able to afford the public what, in the absence of a railway, is without doubt a great accommodation.

The Dumbarnie case

What was described at the time as 'an extraordinary litigation' and a local *cause celebre* came before the Court of Session in 1858 when the action known as Tulloch against Baird came before the court. The substance of the action was that certain residents of Earlsferry, namely William Tulloch, a magistrate, Robert Pattie, a farm servant, Andrew Rolland, a collier and Mary Harris, described as 'spinster, residing at Grange Hill' wished to obtain a declarator to the effect that a right of way for pedestrians and wheeled traffic existed over the East of Fife line where it crossed the Dumbarnie Links between Largo and Kilconquhar. In addition they sought damages and an order that a gated and manned level crossing should be provided where the alleged right of way crossed the railway. The defenders in the action were William Baird, 'proprietor of the lands of Dumbarnie', John Wood, bank-agent of Colinsburgh and tenant of those lands, and the East of Fife Railway Company. It is difficult to see how the expense of this action bore any proportionate relationship to the value of the benefit claimed, particularly when the defenders readily conceded that there was a pedestrian right of way but not a vehicular one, and this may have been the reason why certain of the pursuers promptly disassociated themselves from the proceedings by writing to the company's solicitors leaving only William Tulloch and Robert Pattie to attempt to establish that 'for forty years* and upwards ... there has been a public road or right of way for carts, horses and foot passengers'. After sundry procedure† the case eventually came before a civil jury in the Court of Session in Edinburgh and, at the beginning of January 1860, the trial took place with 19 witnesses being led by the pursuers Tulloch and Pattie, and 23 for the defenders who were represented by the Lord Advocate, James Moncrieff. After 1 hour and 20 minutes of deliberations the 12 jurors unanimously returned a verdict for the defenders, i.e. that there was no vehicular right of way and thus no necessity for a level crossing, and the defenders were awarded their legal expenses. A subsequent attempt by the pursuers to have the verdict set aside on the basis that it was contrary to the evidence led at the trial was unsuccessful.

The impact of the railway

In December 1859 the *Fife Journal* commented that with regard to Lower Largo there had been great improvements since the coming of the railway including the construction of a new paved road through the village which was paid for out of the £200 compensation provided by the East of Fife company for taking part of the village bleaching ground to build the line. Another benefit that Largo enjoyed was a revival of the fishing trade in Largo, 'a fair complement of fishing boats being indicative of the great influx of capital because of the means of taking fish to the principal markets'. However, the real impact of the line locally may have been considerably less since both Largo and Elie were still well served by the steamer services across the Forth and there was little time advantage between the steamers and the combined service of three trains and a ferry necessary to travel by the newer rival. Indeed proposed improvements to local harbours including Elie were being discussed during 1859 and the Elie scheme was proceeded with for, it was said, the benefit of both the local fishing industry and the Forth steamer services.

* The statutory prescriptive period at that time.

† See *Tulloch & Others v Baird & Others* – reported in the Session Cases (the official Scottish law reports) at (1859) 21 D 807 [title to sue and parties to the action] and (1859) 21 D 957 [form of issues to be put before jury].

Chapter Seven

Stringing the Pearls: The Leven & East of Fife Railway 1859-1866

'The ride between Anstruther and Leven is a delightful one, the traveller having both land and sea scenery at his command as he speeds along ...'

The East of Fife Record

Strength in unity

In November 1859 the Parliamentary notice of the long-awaited intended extension of the East of Fife Railway to Anstruther was published and the local newspapers, after extolling the virtues of the scheme so far as the communities to be served by it, commented that,

> As to the financial aspect of the question, if the Leven and East of Fife Railways, during the last half-year, yielded such a handsome return to its shareholders, it is not difficult, with the additional traffic that will ensue by its extension to Anstruther, to see that the scheme will be a paying one. The construction of the extended line will also be favourable to the shareholders, for not only is the price of iron at present low, but some of the proprietors through whose lands the line will pass are to give every facility for forwarding the undertaking. There will be no engineering difficulties to overcome, and it is calculated that, should the bill pass next session, the line will be opened for traffic in 1861. The expense of working the extended line will also be comparatively small, for the same plant of carriages, engines &c., will suffice for the working of both lines and the saving will consequently be greater.

For the half-year ending 31st July, 1860 the receipts and expenditure of both companies was as follows:

RECEIPTS	*Leven Railway*			*East of Fife Railway*		
	£	*s.*	*d.*	£	*s.*	*d.*
Passenger Traffic	1,034	1	10	613	14	5
Goods, minerals, live stock, parcel traffic, &c and sum received from the Joint Committee being the company's share of balance under working agt	2,049	4	3	1,134	2	6
	3,083	6	1	1,747	16	11
EXPENDITURE						
Traffic dept.	604	14	1	350	2	5
Loco dept.	450	10	3	430	12	0
Maintenance	261	4	5	126	5	9
General charges & Pass. Duty	333	4	7	203	17	11
	1,649	12	4	1,120	18	1
BALANCE	1,433	13	9	626	18	0

Both companies' receipts had fallen as a result of the poor weather which had plagued the area but notwithstanding this the Leven company declared a dividend of 8 per cent, and the East of Fife 2 per cent. This reflected the difference in the profitability of the two companies, largely caused by the fact that the former company served an industrialized and well populated area whereas the latter served a largely agricultural and undeveloped tract of coastal land.

The amalgamation of the Leven and East of Fife Railways, 'though very desirable, cannot be accomplished without some difficulty in the meantime'. The difficulty appears to have been a financial one related to the valuation of the respective shareholdings of the two companies and the likely traffic on the extension line rather than any great difference of opinion between the two Boards. While these matters were being discussed, the inhabitants of the towns to be served by the proposed new line were becoming restless. Further meetings took place between the Directors of both companies and it became clear that the question was no longer one of whether or not amalgamation or the building of the extension would take place but of when. By the autumn of 1860 the companies were agreed on their course of action and at the half-yearly general meetings of both the Leven and East of Fife, held on the same day, Monday 22nd October, a report detailing a scheme of amalgamation and the extension of the line to Anstruther was put forward and approved by the shareholders. William Haig, Chairman of the Leven Railway, told his shareholders that,

> ... with regard to the proposal for extending the East of Fife line to Anstruther, he might say that they had received a great many letters urging such an extension, and he believed himself that such a scheme was now practicable. Nothing had as yet been done to carry it out, but he believed that Mr Baird of Elie, to whom three-fourths of the land belonged that would be required, had intimated his intention of assisting in the extension, if the two companies could agree upon amalgamating. The whole subject would, of course, require full discussion, but he must say that he hailed the proposed extension as one means of greatly increasing the prosperity of the Leven company, because the additional traffic would, of course, go over their portion of the line.

At the end of October a conjoint meeting of the two sets of Directors was held and they resolved to carry out the amalgamation of the companies and to proceed immediately with the extension upon the condition that part of the sum which they would require to build the line, namely £11,000, would be put forward by local investors. As the *East Fife Record* reported on 3rd November,

> ... of that there can be little doubt, as since Monday nearly the half of that sum has been subscribed, with little or no agitation on the part of those gentlemen who are taking an interest in the matter. The Parliamentary notices, we believe, will appear in a few days; and as no opposition is anticipated by any of the parties through whose property the line will pass, the works will in all likelihood proceed in a very short time.

The joint Directors resolved that Philip Oliphant, Writer, Anstruther be responsible for raising this local capital and he met with some success for within a week over £7,000 had been promised and within three weeks stock to the amount of £13,000 had been taken up. The investors, numbering over a hundred, were spread throughout the East Neuk but, as expected, the greater part of the capital raised came from the Anstruther area. Individual shareholdings amounted to between £10 and £500, the latter amount being contributed to by the local member of Parliament,

£3,000 by the inhabitants of Anstruther, £800 by the fishermen of Cellardyke and £780 by the folk of Pittenweem with a further £1,180 from the same source if and when a station was provided for that town. William Baird of Elie 'has also entered heartily into the project' and was prepared to sell the land required at a very reasonable price. The Directors of the new Leven and East of Fife Railway were similar to the original companies and comprised Haig, Baird, Wood, Johnstone, Anderson and Sir Ralph Anstruther with the addition of John Luke of Muircambus (near Kilconquhar).

Routeing the Railway

On 17th November, 1860 it was reported that the Parliamentary notices for both the amalgamation scheme and the eastwards extension had just been published and that the new line was described as,

> ... commencing by a junction with the East of Fife Railway at a point thereon near to the Kilconquhar station, and terminating in a small field or enclosure at the west end of Anstruther Wester, opposite the first milestone there ... together with a branch or loop railway diverging from the main line of the said intended railway, at a point thereon on the lands of Elie, situated about two and a half furlongs northward of the Independent Chapel at Elie, and terminating by a junction with the said main line on the east links, at a point about four furlongs eastwards of John's Place, Elie.

Stations were proposed at Elie, St Monance and Anstruther but not at Pittenweem which had been effectively by-passed by the line about three-quarters of a mile to the north. However, after effective lobbying by the town council of Pittenweem and some intervention on the part of Edward Ellice, MP*, a station was considered by the Directors but, on the basis that it would be of doubtful financial merit, they rejected the request. The 'loop line' was intended as a coastal alternative to the line passing to the north of Elie and some controversy was raised by this proposal. On 22nd November the *Fifeshire Journal* published a letter in which the writer stated that,

> In your paper lately, a wish was expressed for a railway nearer our doors. It appears now that our wishes will soon be realised, as there is every prospect of a line being formed either on the north side of the town, or immediately in front of our sea bulwarks. It often happens that in public questions opinions differ. Some parties belonging to the better class, who reside near the sea, think the latter plan would prove detrimental to the beach as regards sea-bathing, and thereby prevent visitors taking their abode here in the summer season, and that it would mar the beauty of our pretty little bay. They also think that the line immediately on the north side of the town is better adapted for the formation of a railway than that on the sea side but some of the people who live in North Street express a contrary opinion. They say that nothing could suit better than the sea links.

The 'seaside faction' attracted considerable support, including some from the 'better class' who felt that ample sea-bathing facilities would remain if the line took this route but that a lasting benefit to the town would be given in that the railway would run along a breakwater which would 'completely shelter the harbour in western storms, adding greatly to its safety and prosperity'.

---

* Ellice was the member for the Fife Burghs and his name is commemorated by Ellice Street in Cellardyke.

The Act accomplished

On 7th March, 1861 the Parliamentary Committee on Scottish Railways considered the proposed amalgamation of the Leven and East of Fife companies, and gave their approval to the scheme. However two petitions against the Anstruther extension line were lodged, one from the inhabitants of Pittenweem who had been informed by the Directors that 'a station there is not practicable or for the interest of the line', and one by 'certain parties' in Elie who were against the routeing of the line past the harbour there. A deal was then done with the former, who withdrew their opposition on the basis of an agreement being reached on 2nd April, 1861 between the railway and the town council that a station for passengers and goods would be provided and maintained at Pittenweem and that all ordinary trains between Anstruther and Elie would stop there. In June the Elie harbour loop was deleted from the plans, largely as a result of opposition from the Admiralty. The *Scotsman* reported that,

> The Admiralty Report on the Bill has been presented. It states that the interference with their Lordships' jurisdiction consists in the main-line at 1¼ miles from its commencement being carried in front of the town and shore at Elie for a distance of nearly 2000 feet and projecting into the sea, below the high-water mark to the extent of about 200 feet at the widest place and generally to the extent of about 140 feet; and from 2¼ miles from the commencement to 3¼ miles, the railway skirts the shore of the Firth of Forth, the limits of deviation extending below the high-water mark. Their Lordships consider that such a line would, if sanctioned, interfere most seriously with the interests of navigation by preventing access to and from the shore by the inhabitants of the place and others, as well as to fishing boats and other craft. Their Lordships have had to complain, at various places, of the dangers to boats and small craft caused by the landing shores and beaches being intercepted by walls and breastworks and must, therefore, withold their assent to the proposed line of shore railway which appears hardly to be required, as the other line to the North-East of the town of Elie may be constructed without inconvenience or detriment to the inhabitants and fishermen ...

On 22nd July, 1861 the necessary legislation was passed. The Leven and East of Fife Railway Act (24 & 25 Vict., cap. clviii) amalgamated the two systems by dissolving the existing companies and creating in their place a new entity named the Leven and East of Fife Railway Company, with two distinct classes of shareholders namely those holding Leven stock and those holding East of Fife stock. The Leven stock, issued to existing Leven shareholders at par, comprised of £23,000 of shares together with a further £14,000 of shares authorized by the Act for the purpose of settling the existing liabilities of the Leven company. The East of Fife stock consisted of £32,000 of shares issued at par to that company's existing shareholders and a further £3,000 in authorized share capital to cover the East of Fife company's debts, thereby making a total of £37,000 worth of Leven stock and £35,000 of East of Fife stock. The revenue of the new undertaking, after payment of interest on the new Extension Debentures and the payment of the dividend on the Extension or Preference stock was for the remainder to be divided as to two-thirds to Leven stockholders and one-third to the East of Fife stockholders. Traffic and dividends on the former line had been consistently higher than that of the latter line. Following on this legislation was The Leven and East of Fife Railway (Extension) Act (24 & 25 Vict., cap. clix) which authorized the extension of what was now the East of Fife Section of the new company from the existing terminus at Kilconquhar to a new terminus at Anstruther and, in order to finance this, a new form of preference stock with a fixed dividend of 4½ per cent, 'Leven and East of Fife Extension Stock', to a value of £40,000, was issued together with authorized borrowings of £13,000. The total rolling stock possessed by the combined companies was, according to the Board of Trade annual returns, as follows:

	Locomotives	*Carriages*	*Waggons*
From Leven Railway	2	3	54
From East of Fife Rly	1	2	56
	3	5	110

One 'other vehicle' (unspecified) was also listed.

A commencement has been made

On 8th February, 1862 the *East of Fife Record* reported that surveyors were to be seen at work in the vicinity of Elie and that it appeared that they were surveying a line to pass to the north of the town, rather than by the abandoned seaward route which 'a good many will still regret has not been allowed'. On 24th March, 1862 the contracts for the extension to Anstruther, totalling a line length of 6 miles 624 yards, were being advertised and although the contracts were divided into three separate sections, namely from Kilconquhar station 'to a point near Ardross farmhouse', from there to 'a point near to the western boundary of the parish of Pittenweem' and the last section from there to the proposed Anstruther terminus, it was open to any single contractor to submit tenders for all three sections. All tenders were to be received by Wednesday 16th April, the Directors 'not being bound to accept the lowest offer'. The Engineer appointed by the new company was John Sang, CE of Kirkcaldy.

On 21st June, 1862 the *East of Fife Record* reported that:

> We are glad to say that a commencement has at length been made in the formation of the railway line from Kilconquhar to Anstruther. This is more particularly so at the west end, where workmen have commenced the erection of some of these bridges which cross the public roads in the neighbourhood of Elie, and in diverting portions of the road so as to secure a straight line for the railway. A large portion of the iron rails have also arrived at Elie Harbour in two vessels, and another cargo is, we believe, to be landed at Anstruther. These iron rails will not be laid until the crops are off the ground in autumn, but in the meantime the erection of all the bridges and stations can be proceeded with.

Three months later the same newspaper stated that the formation of the line was making steady progress and that on the section near to Elie and St Monance several of the bridges and part of the cuttings were in a state of completion. In addition work on one of the bridges near Milton Dam, half a mile west of Anstruther, had just been started. Since a large number of men were being currently employed on bridgework it was expected that all of these bridges would be completed within a short time. Once the grain harvest was in from the fields, the remaining work on the cuttings would then be completed without delay.

At the end of May 1863 it was reported that the work on the line in the vicinity of Anstruther was making 'visible progress every day' and that the construction of the

LEVEN & EAST OF FIFE RAILWAY.

TIME-TABLE FOR APRIL 1862.

UP TRAINS—GOING WEST.

Stations	Class 1 2 3 4	Class 1 2 3	Class 1 2 3	Class 1 2 3
Coach leaves	A. M	A. M	P. M.	P. M.
Anstruther - - - - -	5 30	9 0	1 55	5 15
Trains leave				
Kilconquhar - -	6 40	10 5	3 5	6 30
Largo - - - - -	6 52	10 17	3 18	6 42
Lundin Links - -	6 55	10 20	3 21	6 46
Leven - - - - -	7 10	10 33	3 33	6 57
Cameron - - - - -	7 15	10 43	3 43	7 5
Leave Thornton J. for Dundee, &c.	7 40	11 5	4 14	7 35
Do. for Edinburgh	7 45	11 32	4 8	7 30
Dundee - - arrive at	9 30	12 55	6 15	9 30
Perth - - - - -	9 0	12 15	5 30	8 50
Edinburgh - - - -	9 30	1 15	5 50	9 5

DOWN TRAINS—GOING EAST.

Stations	Class 1 2 3 4	Class 1 2 3	Class 1 2 3	Class 1 2 3
From	A. M.	A. M.	P. M.	P. M.
Edinburgh - - - - at	6 0	9 30	2 45	6 0
Dundee - - - -	5 50	9 45	2 20	5 40
Perth - . .	6 30	10 40	3 0	6 15
Trains will not leave				
Thornton Junction - before	7 50	11 35	4 20	7 38
Cameron Bridge - -	8 9	11 52	4 38	7 56
Leven - - - - -	8 17	12 0	4 46	8 4
Lundin Links - -	8 24	12 7	4 53	8 11
Largo - - - - -	8 27	12 10	4 56	8 14
Kilconquhar - - - -	8 47	12 25	5 12	8 30
Coach arrives at				
Anstruther, about -	10 0	2 5	6 20	9 5

Passengers change carriages at Thornton Junction.

By Order, AND. WILKIE, Secretary.

An 1862 timetable published in the *East of Fife Record* and showing the horsebus connections between Kilconquhar and Anstruther.

station house there, described as being 'built of bricks and in a rather tasteful style', was 'well forward in its erection'. Other works at the station, including the platform, and goods shed, were nearly finished and sidings there were being laid out. Over the whole of the new line rails had been laid on the greater part of the formation with the exception of two gaps, one for a distance of about 1½ miles between Pittenweem and St Monance, and the other a half-mile gap between Milton Mill and Anstruther station. By the following month the works were almost complete and the *Record* of 27th June stated that,

> As the line now approaches completion, great interest is manifested by the public regarding it, and at various portions along the line it is daily visited by a large number of people. The permanent rails are now all laid, with the exception of about 200 yards next the Anstruther station, and these too will be laid in a few days. The ballast engine and trucks are traversing the extended line, and the rails daily adjusted and levelled previous to the finishing and dressing up of the works. The different station houses are also in a nearly finished state, the plastering and woodwork now being proceeded with. A good deal of work is yet to be done on the siding embankments for loading or unloading goods at the various stations, but a week or two will find them ready for the work. It is thought at present that the line will be ready, at least for goods, by the beginning of August and consequently in time for the herring fishing.

Two weeks later it was being said that for some time past a locomotive had been in constant use on the new line for the purpose of transporting the top dressing, the siding rails, material for the station houses, etc. and that the inhabitants of the East Neuk 'have already become familiar with the peculiar warning whistle of an approaching train'. St Monance station was in the course of erection 'and bids fair to be both neat and commodious', while the sidings for goods traffic were nearly all laid but that 'the road to the goods station will not be finished for a week or two'. There was, however, considerable local disappointment with the length of time which the construction had taken, particularly given the fact that there was an absence of any substantial engineering works on the line and no bad weather or labour difficulties to account for any delay.

Somewhat rough and uneven

On 8th August, 1863 the *Record* informed its readers that,

> ... no official notification has yet been made as to the day on which the extended line is to be opened, as the Government Inspector has not yet arrived to survey the line. The line is, however, ready for the goods traffic, and in a few days will be so far finished as to commence the passenger trade, which only awaits the sanction of the Government official.

It had been generally anticipated that the new line would have been opened in the third week of August but such was not the case as the government inspector only went over the line on Thursday 13th August. The *Record* two days later reported that,

> A beautiful new and large engine was employed on the occasion,* and the government inspector was accompanied by a number of the directors, the Secretary, Mr Wilkie, Mr Sang the engineer, and others. After going leisurely along the line, stopping here and there at

* The locomotive was a Hawthorn 0-4-0 identical to the Leven Railway and East of Fife Railway two Hawthorn locomotives. No. 3 was apparently built in 1857 but not bought by the LEoFR until the opening of the Anstruther line in 1863.

short distances, and minutely inspecting all the works, the party reached Anstruther at about two o'clock. It is of course not known what the actual report of the inspector was, as the Govt official makes his report direct to the Board of Trade, but we understand he expressed to the officials of the railway his general approval of the whole works, with the exception of some wooden fencings at the different stations, which the Board of Trade now insist on being put up on all railways, in consequence of the great number of accidents that have lately occurred from the rails being unprotected from the incursions of cattle etc.

On that day, August 15th, Colonel Yolland reported to the Board of Trade as follows:

I have inspected the extension to the Leven and East of Fife Railway from Kilconquhar to Anstruther station, a length of 6 miles and 18.43 chains. The line is single throughout, both the over and under bridges have only been constructed for a single line on the 4 feet 8½ inch gauge, but sidings have been provided at all the stations on the line, viz. Elie, St Monans, Pittenweem and Anstruther and there is 6 feet space between the main line and the siding. This is an extension of a small local line, and the permanent way is, I am informed, precisely similar to that laid down on the portion already opened about 13 miles. The width at formation level is 15 feet in cuttings and 16 feet on embankments. A single headed rail weighing 65 lbs per linear in lengths of 18 and 21 feet is fitted in cast iron chairs by wooden keys, the joint chairs weigh 36 lbs each and the intermediate chairs 24 lbs each – the chairs are fitted on transverse sleepers by wrought iron spikes. The points of the rails are not fished. The sleepers consist of creosoted Scotch fir and larch in equal proportions, 9 feet long by 11 ins x 5½ ins for the joint and 9 ins x 11½ ins for the intermediates. The ballast is of broken stone and gravel and stated to be 16 inches deep below the water surface of the sleeper.

There are 8 over and 6 under bridges – two of the over bridges are constructed with stone abutments and cast-iron girders and the whole of the other bridges are built entirely of stone. They are all of small span, and are well constructed and sufficiently strong. An engine turntable has been provided at Anstruther station. There are no unauthorised level crossings on the line.

The report then went on to list defects and omissions found, namely that portions of fencing needed to be completed 'and the entrance to stations require to be closed from the public roads' and he concluded that,

The line has been finished off during very dry weather, and it is somewhat rough and uneven, so that it requires to be lifted and carefully packed – and it would be better that goods traffic should be worked over it somewhat before it is opened for passenger traffic – under any circumstances from the nature of the permanent way laid down, it should not be worked at a higher maximum speed than from 25 to 30 miles an hour. I have now therefore to report that by reason of the incompleteness of the works, the opening of the portion of the Leven and East of Fife Railway between Kilconquar and Anstruther station for traffic cannot be sanctioned without danger to the public using the same.

An undertaking was included from John Haig and Andrew Wilkie, dated 12th August, to the effect that they certified,

... that in working the Leven & East of Fife Railway, the mode of working by a train staff will be adopted. In working the line between Thornton and Leven, a train staff or train ticket square and coloured red will be carried to and fro with each engine. Betwixt Leven and Kilconquhar a train staff or train ticket round and coloured blue will be carried to and fro and betwixt Kilconquhar and Anstruther a train staff or train ticket coloured white will be carried to and fro with each engine.

A week later Andrew Wilkie confirmed to the Board of Trade that the fencing along the whole length of the line had been completed and added that 'I have further to state that as recommended by Colonel Yolland, C.E., the goods traffic has been wrought over the extension line and goods trains have run along it every day since the 14th inst'.

Open for business

On 24th August a Minute Paper recorded from Colonel Yolland that he was of the opinion that there was no longer any objection to the line being opened for traffic 'provided that it is worked at low speed' and notification of this was apparently received by the company on the evening of Friday 28th August. The following day the *East of Fife Record*, which had presumably gone to press prior to this, stated that,

> No notification has yet been given by the railway company as to the time when the newly extended line is to be opened to the passenger trade and the public, who have been so often and long disappointed and somewhat annoyed at the delay in completing the works, must yet wait patiently, and be thankful for railway accommodation if it be given within another month. The delay which has taken place in the construction of the line has been unaccountable. The works were commenced fourteen months ago, and although there was no great engineering difficulties to contend with, no stoppage from bad weather during the whole of that time, no tunnelling or extensive excavating, the greatest railway contractor in Scotland has been unable, for some cause or other, to complete a short line of little more than six miles only at this date.
>
> At first it was given out by this company that we would without fail have the line completed and trains running by the end of March last. Nearly six months have elapsed since then, and the line is not yet in a complete state, except perhaps for goods traffic, and a great deal of work still remains to be done even for that department. If this be the celerity and 'railway speed', the public have in prospect for their accommodation, the old slow coach state of matters would almost be preferable.

The public, however, did not have to wait long for on Saturday 5th September the *Record* was pleased to tell the inhabitants of the East Neuk that the position had now altered for the better:

> After all the delay that has occurred in the construction and completion of the extended line of rails from Kilconquhar to Anstruther, it has at length been opened to the public. The Directors received, on Friday evening last, the sanction of the Board of Trade to open the line, and they lost no time in issuing bills announcing that the railway would be opened for passenger traffic on the 1st September. No public demonstration of any kind took place, owing no doubt to the short time that elapsed between Saturday and Tuesday morning preventing arrangements being made for this purpose, and accordingly, with the exception of a considerable crowd who had assembled at the station to witness the novelty of a railway in operation, everything passed off quietly. The first train in the morning containing about eighty passengers from Anstruther station, and the great majority of these were half dealsmen* on their way home from the fishing. On Tuesday there were only altogether about 150 passengers who left the

* Half-dealsmen were fishermen who did not have a share in providing the gear for a boat and they normally had other seasonal occupations such as farming, crafting or, especially in Fife, coal mining.

station by the whole three trains – a small number considering the fine weather and the favourable opportunity the public had for taking a short trip along the line to view the works.

The ride between Anstruther and Leven is a delightful one, the traveller having both land and sea scenery at his command as he speeds along – some of it barren enough, no doubt, as at Lundin Links, but in other portions passing through highly cultivated tracts of country, the richly wooded hills of Balcarres, Largo Law, and Kellie Law on one side, and on the other, as the train here and there emerges from some deep embankment, a beautiful view is had of the Firth of Forth, with the Pentland hills, Bass Rock, Berwick Law, and the Isle of May in the distance, and the various ships, steamers and boats as they pass up and down the Forth. On the newly extended line there have been four new stations planted for the public convenience – at Elie, St Monance, Pittenweem and Anstruther – the whole distance traversed between these places being about five miles, or six and a half between Anstruther and Kilconquhar, where a new station house has also been erected. At present there will only be three trains each day to and from Anstruther, Pittenweem. And St Monance and the reason given out officially for this is that the train leaving Edinburgh at 4.15pm, and Thornton at 5.58pm would not have time to come further than Elie, and be back at Thornton in time to catch the last trains on the main line.

Kilconquhar to Anstruther

The new line to Anstruther made an end-on junction at Kilconquhar with the existing terminus where a new station building was provided. Leaving Kilconquhar it headed abruptly south-east past the farm of St Ford and running over a short embankment before passing under the Elie to Largo turnpike road (the present A917) before entering a cutting between the northern edge of the town and the policies of Elie House, where William Baird lived. Passing again under the turnpike road, Elie station was situated at the eastern extremity of the town and served both Elie itself and its twin settlement of Earlsferry, which adjoined Elie to the west and was a Royal Burgh although its days of importance as the northern landfall of the pilgrim's route from North Berwick to St Andrews were long over. By the time that the railway reached Elie, local industries were at a low ebb and, according to *Slater's Directory* of 1860: 'the trade of the place is confined to the export of grain and potatoes ... and at Earlsferry village, which joins with Elie, the weaving of ticks and checks for distant houses and the coal works are the chief employment and support of its inhabitants'.

The coal works were listed as being owned by Robert Keddie, coal and ironmaster* and such local coal as was mined came from the miniscule pits adjacent to his Grange Coal and Iron works on the Cadger road, near to which ironstone was quarried. Elie also boasted a smithy and a brewery while just over the border in Earlsferry, there was a small gas works with its own gas holder; none of these establishments were ever rail served. There was no rail connection to Elie harbour, which had been recently enlarged and improved with new stonework at the expense of William Baird, as little fish was landed here, local boats preferring the more established (and less exposed) fishing harbours to the east. The harbour, however, retained its importance for some time and in April 1858 the *Fifeshire Journal* recorded that,

* Keddie had been one of the reluctant pursuers in the Dumbarnie Links litigation who had later parted company with William Tulloch.

> Several pretty large vessels, principally English, are loading and unloading in our harbour at present. We have the *Pettrill* of Fleetwood, discharging seed potatoes, the *Star* of Faversham, a large brigantine and the *Mary and Ann,* schooner of Portsmouth, both loading potatoes. One vessel has left laden with iron stone from Grange coal works and another cargo lies on the pier ready for shipment.

In the following decades, however, traffic at the harbour went in to a slow and inexorable decline until it was little used for commercial purposes. The principal inward traffic from Elie station included coal, lime, and fertilisers and outward traffic consisted of agricultural produce and livestock being dispatched to market. Probably, however, the principal source of revenue from Elie was to be the passenger traffic and, as Farnie's *Handbook of the Fife Coast* put it:

> Very little manual employment of any kind goes on in Elie. The majority of the inhabitants appear to cultivate the genteel business of letting their houses in summer, and occupying them in winter. Elie has always been a favourite spot for sea-bathing quarters, and no doubt will flourish more abundantly in that respect, when its advantages become more known.

The summer trade did, indeed, flourish and the railway encouraged the well-to-do inhabitants of Edinburgh's New Town to switch over their allegiance from the Leith steamers and although the town grew in a discreet and tasteful manner its social character changed little, still earning it the soubriquet of 'New Town on Sea' long after the demise of the railway.

On leaving Elie the railway turned north-east and followed the coast line across the links for a mile or so, passing the ruins of Ardross castle and, a mile or so further on, Newark castle, while the line then passed inland crossing the Inverie burn close to the imposing kirk at St Monance where the station was situated close to the junction of the main road and the road leading from Abercrombie to St Monance harbour. This station served the small fishing port and surrounding landward area including Balcaskie House and the small settlement of Abercrombie. The principal inward traffic here consisted of lime, fertilisers and general goods and outward traffic consisted of fish, livestock, potatoes and grain.

Leaving St Monance station the line now continued in a north-easterly direction but was a good half mile inland. There were few earth works of any note and the principal feature was the bridge at Waterless over which the Colinsburgh road (the present B942) was carried. Entering a short cutting, the line was crossed by the Pittenweem to Carnbee road and the station at Pittenweem was reached. The distance of the railway station from the town, half a mile or so, was due to the existence of the ancient raised beaches which lay to the south and made it impractical to site the station closer to the town. This meant that fish traffic from the busy harbour of Pittenweem tended to be dispatched by rail from either St Monance or Anstruther. The main traffic handled at Pittenweem included coal, fertilisers and general goods and in the outward direction small amount of fish, and some livestock, grain and potatoes. Leaving Pittenweem the line continued eastward for just under one mile to the terminus at Anstruther. This short distance saw few features of note passing through open farmland with the farm of Milton Mill on the northern side of the line and that of Milton Muir on the southern side. At Anstruther the station was situated at the western end of the High Street of Anstruther Wester and on the banks of the Dreel Burn and it would be another 20 years before the burn was to be bridged by the railway.

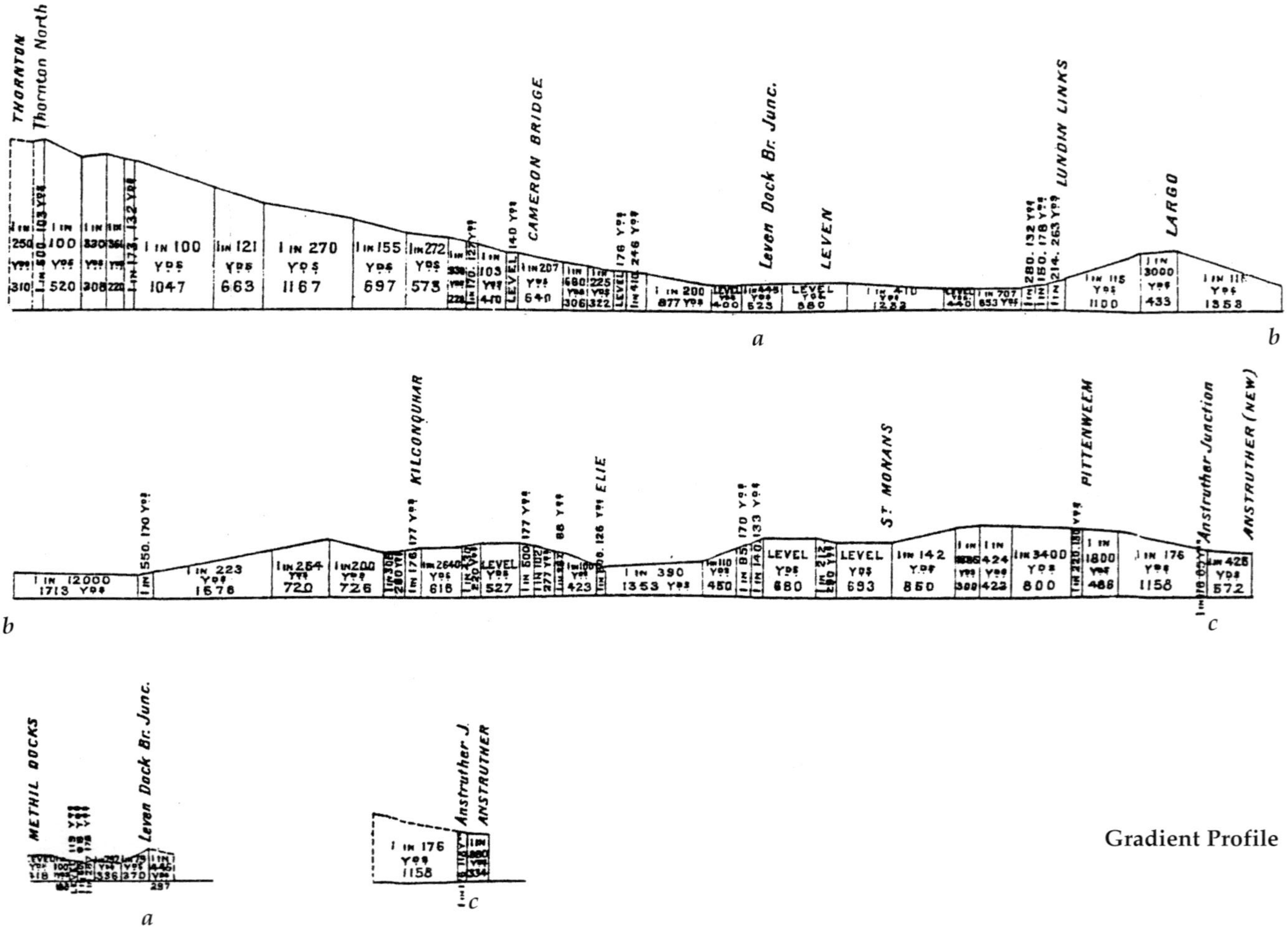

Gradient Profile

The passenger station had but a single platform with a single-storey building containing the usual offices. The standard of workmanship at the terminus, however, seems to have left something to be desired. On 5th September, 1863 the *East of Fife Record* reported that, 'the brick house at the station, intended for sheltering and cleaning the engine, the building of which was nearly complete, gave way in part on Saturday last'. The collapse of the east gable was said to be the caused by heavy rain saturating the foundations and an excess of bricks stored on the scaffolding. Two months later the 40 ft high retaining wall next to the station house collapsed but as the *Record* happily related the cost of the reinstatement of the same would fall on Grainger, the contractor. The arrangements at the terminus for both passengers and goods seem generally to have been somewhat sparse but coal depots were provided there for three different coal agents; the passenger accommodation was soon augmented as evidenced by a report in the same paper on 17th March, 1865:

> A good many improvements for the comfort and convenience of the public are presently being effected at the railway station here, and it promises in a short time to be one of the most commodious and complete stations on the line. A large awning shed or covering is being erected over the platform, which will add greatly to the comfort of passengers in wet weather when trains arrive and depart; and though there are comfortable and neatly-fitted up waiting rooms adjoining, the new erection will be a decided advantage in many ways to the public. A large goods shed, for the storing and keeping dry of goods, is also in course of erection on the south side of the station, which will also be of great advantage to the traders on the railway. The soft and muddy state of the approach to the station house from West Anstruther, however, especially in wet weather, is almost the only drawback, but this arises from the unconsolidated state of the new road. In the course of time that also will be remedied, and we will then have a terminus here which, considering everything, leaves little else to be desired. The number of passengers on the line, as well as the goods traffic, is now rapidly on the increase, and we may soon expect to receive an addition to the number of daily trains.

The Buckie House, Anstruther, *circa* 1900. The original LEoFR terminus was behind the houses to the right of the wagon. The scene will be familiar to modern residents.

Alan Brotchie Collection

Three trains a day

The opening service consisted of three trains per day from Thornton to Anstruther and back and an additional Thornton to Elie return working, with connecting coach services to and from Crail and St Andrews connecting with certain of the trains at Anstruther. First, second and fourth class carriages were conveyed on the first train in each direction, while the other trains conveyed first, second and third classes only. All trains were nominally mixed and all passengers had to change at Thornton Junction. A definite pattern was thereafter established with separate summer and winter timetables, the main difference being in the last train of the day from Anstruther which, from October to May, ran on Saturdays only. A third locomotive had been acquired, another Hawthorn 0-4-0 which appears to have been identical to Nos. 1 and 2, acquired respectively in 1855 and 1857; No. 3 was built in 1857 but not delivered to the company until the time of the opening to Anstruther. A separate goods service was run but these goods workings also conveyed third class local passengers. The Summer timetable for down trains in June 1865 is given here:

		am	*am*	*pm*	*pm*	*pm*
Thornton Junction	*dep.*	8.05	11.35	4.00	6.00	8.27
Cameron Bridge	*dep.*	8.24	11.54	4.20	6.15	8.44
Leven	*dep.*	8.32	12.02 *pm*	4.52	6.23	8.52
Lundin Links	*dep.*	8.39	12.10	5.00	6.29	8.57
Largo	*dep.*	8.42	12.13	5.06	6.34	9.02
Kilconquhar	*dep.*	8.54	12.25	5.20	6.46	9.14
Elie	*dep.*	9.00	12.32	5.26	6.51	9.19
St Monance	*dep.*	9.09	12.40	5.36	–	9.27
Pittenweem	*dep.*	9.17	12.47	5.44	7.03	9.34
Anstruther	*arr.*	9.23	12.52	5.50	7.08	9.39

Notes: 8.24 1st, 2nd, 3rd & 4th class; 11.54, 6.00 and 8.27 1st, 2nd and 3rd class passengers only; 4.00 for goods only.

Traffic, particularly passenger traffic, was heavy and the Directors intimated to the shareholders in April 1864 that they had previously told them that the extension line would be a success 'and that they are now happy to state that the traffic has fully justified that belief'. In the six months ending 31st January, 1865 60,174 passengers were carried with 5,251 being first class ticket holders, 5,770 being second, 33,507 being third and 15,616 being fourth. The locomotives were worked hard and in a not untypical incident on 14th March of that year an incident occurred to the mid-morning up train from Anstruther when, at St Monance, the connecting rods of the engine broke 'but there was no injury done to life or limb'. The damage done to the engine was soon repaired and it was at work again in the afternoon.

Here and there

The timetable does not, however, seem to have been adhered to with any due regard to punctuality and the *East of Fife Record* on 13th November stated that,

> As showing the dilatoriness of our railway, and the unpunctuality in the arrival of our trains, we may mention that this (Friday) morning, the mail gig, which receives the bag

as formerly at Kilconquhar station, reached Anstruther ten minutes before the train – a mail gig running at the rate of some six or eight miles an hour thus beating a railway which ought, even including stoppages, to run at least double that speed. Great complaints are made as to the late arrival of almost every train, and there is evidently good ground for complaint, for almost all of the trains are in general 20 or 30 minutes behind the advertised time. As regards the mail, the railway has yet been of no advantage in this quarter.

One case of delayed running was an unpleasant incident which occurred six weeks earlier and was recounted in the local press under the title of 'Fiendish Attempt to Upset a Railway Train':

A most diabolical action was performed on our railway , by some person or persons as yet unknown, on Monday morning last. As one of the platelayers employed on the line, named David Honeyman, was passing along the railway that morning, he discovered a large stone, weighing at least 80 lb., lying across one of the rails. This was on a curve of the line between Newark and Ardross, and on the top of a deep embankment, and had the discovery not been fortunately made, the consequences could have been frightful. The train was due half an hour after the stone was found. From the great weight of the stone, it could not have been placed there by children, and must have caused some labour and trouble, and was evidently done with the fiendish purpose of upsetting the train, which undoubtedly it would have done, had the obstruction not been discovered. No clue has been found of the perpetrator of this diabolical action, though every attempt is being made by the police. It is supposed to have been done by two men who were seen in the neighbourhood poaching a day or so previously, and who, to avoid apprehension, were found to have left the locality the same morning.

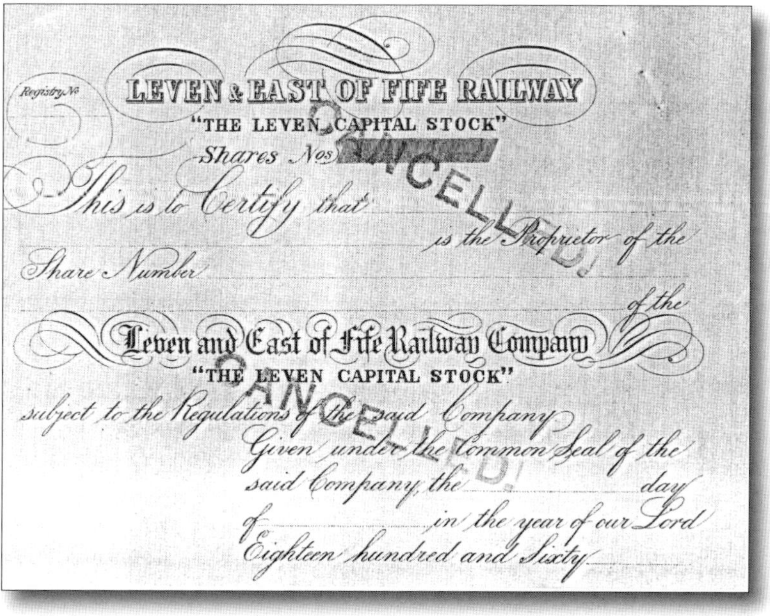
Registry No

LEVEN & EAST OF FIFE RAILWAY

"THE LEVEN CAPITAL STOCK"

Shares Nos [redacted]

This is to Certify that .... is the Proprietor of the Share Number .... of the

Leven and East of Fife Railway Company

"THE LEVEN CAPITAL STOCK"

subject to the Regulations of the said Company.

Given under the Common Seal of the said Company, the .... day of .... in the year of our Lord Eighteen hundred and Sixty........

CANCELLED

CANCELLED

Chapter Eight

Of Harbours and Herring: The Leven & East of Fife Railway 1866-1877

'The districts through which the line passes have very greatly benefitted from the railway.'

A Short History of the LEoFR

An increase of traffic

Additional rolling stock was required if the line was to cope and in April 1865 John Haig, the company Chairman, stated to the shareholders that they were aware

> ... that considerable outlay has taken place in the erection of suitable station buildings at Thornton Junction, the construction of which was authorised at the last meeting. There has also been considerable outlay in making an iron bridge over the Leven at Cameron Bridge, in place of the former wooden one, which had given way to such an extent as to have become unsafe. In order to supply the want occasioned by the increase of traffic on the line, your directors sometime ago ordered 6 cattle waggons, which have now been delivered; and they have also contracted for 25 merchandise waggons which they expect to be on the line before the autumn fish traffic begins.

Six months later the shareholders were told that a further £500 had been set aside for an additional supply of wagons, 'necessary by the increased traffic' and that the Directors now wished to build additional siding accommodation at Cameron Bridge and to make a short siding or branch to an adjoining coal pit 'which they cannot do without Parliamentary authority' – the latter was the first mention of what was to become the Muiredge branch. Other improvements included a 'considerable expenditure' on the extension of the passenger station buildings at Thornton Junction.

In October 1865 the *East of Fife Record* carried an interesting paragraph entitled 'Pittenweem Harbour Traffic' showing just how successful the Leven & East of Fife Railway had become that,

> ... the effect of the railway on the harbour traffic has gone beyond anything ever anticipated, even by those who have a taste for looking at the dull side of things. Potatoes, grain and coals, the principal articles from which the revenue of the harbour is mainly derived, are almost all swallowed up by the inhospitable rail. At one time no less than 30,000 bolls* of potatoes were shipped here in one season: while this year, little over 3,000 bolls would take in the whole quantity sent by sea from this place. The herring fishing, which used to be looked on as a great item in the revenue of the harbour, is every year becoming gradually less. It was rather a lucky thing that a new table of rates was adopted, for the sum that would have been derived had the old table of rates been in use, would not have paid the expense of collection.

However, a counter-balance to this was provided by the same paper which reported in December 1866 that, in connection with a new proposal for a direct steamship to Leith from Anstruther,

* A measure of capacity used in Scotland for potatoes, grain etc. and equivalent to 6 bushels or 48 Imperial gallons.

The railway, it has been observed with truth, is quite sufficient to overtake all the

> present trade of this locality; but its rates are deemed quite high enough ... One great complaint against the railway is the dilatoriness in the prompt forwarding of goods. We have heard repeated complaints regarding this, and cases alleged where packages, that should not have occupied more than two days in transit, were detained about a week ere they reached their destination. This has naturally soured some traders against the railway. That such delays should take place on a railway where trains start two or three times a day, is quite inexcusable ...

This showed that, despite its perceived advantages, there were still problems with the railway and the competing steamship service for goods and passengers was able to soldier on for another decade or so.

Fish

Given the fact that one of the most important cargoes to be carried over the line was, of course, fish landed at the harbours of Largo, Elie, St Monance, Pittenweem and Anstruther, it is perhaps surprising that none of the harbours involved was ever directly served by a railway branch off the Leven and East of Fife line. In the case of Largo the station and harbour were close to each other but separated by a steep incline but in any event the harbour was being used less and less by the fishing trade. Elie harbour was to have been connected to the line by a spur that had been planned but never executed and it again was not a major fishing port. St Monance and Pittenweem were both uphill from their respective harbours but in the case of the former the railway yard was sufficiently close to be used by the fish dealers while in the case of the latter the distance was more formidable. In all cases fish had to be landed off the boats and manually loaded onto horse-drawn wagons or bogies and then taken to the relevant station where it would once again be transhipped to railway wagons. Much of the herring caught was smoked, salted and cured locally so that the importance of speedy transport was not as important but, concomitant and caused by the arrival of the railway, a new and growing market in fresh white fish was being developed. This market, which relied on fast transit to the major towns in Scotland and England, often by dedicated trains and in specially adapted wagons, was one from which the Leven & East of Fife, in common with many other railways serving the East Coast ports, was anxious to make money. There was a certain amount of inward traffic of herrings from other ports which were to be processed in the East Neuk and some outward herring traffic by sea to northern European ports and, initially at least, to North Berwick for the Manchester market before the East of Fife line opened.

When the line was opened the fisheries were going through an extremely prosperous period and in the case of Anstruther this prosperity was greatly increased by the proposal to build a Union Harbour there. This ambitious scheme, partly funded by monies made available from Parliament under a Harbours of Refuge scheme, was a joint effort by interested parties in Anstruther Easter, Anstruther Wester and Cellardyke. It involved the construction of a new East Pier and the upgrading of the existing harbour and construction began in 1866, the engineer being Thomas Stevenson, son of Robert Stevenson who surveyed the original Edinburgh to Dundee Railway nearly half a century before, and father of the poet and novelist Robert Louis Stevenson.*

* Robert Louis Stevenson himself came to Anstruther to glean some engineering experience from the building of the new breakwater and famously described the town as a 'gray, grim, sea-beaten hole' of which he was 'utterly sick'.

The Anstruther Harbour Line

In December 1867 negotiations were underway between the Anstruther Harbour Commissioners, the Fishery Board, the Leven & East of Fife Railway and the coalmasters of the Wemyss Estate 'with the aim of having the west breakwater of the new harbour converted into a traffic pier, effecting a junction between the harbour and the railway and the shipment of coals'. At the end of the following month the company's Engineer was seen in and around the town making a survey of the ground and properties lying between the present west pier and the station and in April 1868 Andrew Wilkie was present at a meeting of the Harbour Commissioners when he stated the case for the building of a line to the harbour. He stated that,

> The access to the harbour could be gained by two routes – the first, by starting from a point at the present goods shed at the station, and crossing the public road to Pittenweem by means of a bridge – thence down the lane by the parish school, through some garden property there, on to the beach and the pier-head. The estimated cost of this line would be £4,065. The other route could be made from starting from near the same point as above, on the north side of the present line, crossing the West Anstruther bleaching-green and the burn, and thence along it to the bridge; then by cutting off a portion of the churchyard (which has never been made use of for interment) and the abutment known as the old Castle of Dreel, a straight line could be acquired down to the beach and harbour. This would be the most expensive route, though in every respect the most desirable one, and the estimated cost of construction, not including the erection of a bridge, would be £5,370. One proposal had been made in regard to the bridge here – and which would be a most decided to the improvement of the town – was to place a bridge across what was once the old ford on an old road leading into the town from the west: that is, running it in a straight line across the burn from Miss Lees' house in West Anstruther to the Post Office ... It would greatly improve the properties there, shorten the road considerably, and enable the railway to get down to the harbour with greater facility. He thought, however, taking into account the great expense of erecting a bridge, that in the meantime, some temporary arrangement could be made whereby the railway trucks could go through the present bridge and there be drawn by means of a horse down the line of rail, which would then be laid on wooden or iron girders, to the harbour. This might save £2,000 of outlay in the meantime, and if it were deemed advisable afterwards, the proper bridge could be erected.

Wilkie then laid before the meeting the Engineer's plans of both routes and emphasised that if a wet dock was constructed at the new harbour at least 1,500 tons of coal could be exported from there each week. At the present time the coal harbours of Fife were at Tayport and Burntisland and if the line were built then this monopoly could be successfully challenged by Anstruther, whose harbour would have a greatly increased trade and revenue in consequence. Six months later the Harbour Commissioners minutes reveal that 'no steps had yet been taken regarding the proposed extension of the railway' and by June this position was repeated when the local press said that, 'No decision has yet been come to as to the proposal for altering the western breakwater into a landing pier, and the conditional proposal by the Railway Company to extend their line of rails down to the harbour; but we are led to believe that the negotiations are now going on with the view of accomplishing the desired improvements, and that everything is progressing satisfactorily'.

Further meetings took place with shippers and importers in the Leven and Wemyss areas and in October 1868 the company's Engineer, Wood, was again surveying possible routes, this time for the purpose of drawing up plans for Parliamentary approval. At the company's half-yearly meeting held on 30th October, 1868 the shareholders were told that the Directors

> ... are informed that the Anstruther Harbour Commissioners expect to be assisted by the government to construct a floating dock at the harbour. Should this be done it will greatly add to the traffic on your railway by affording facilities for the shipment of coals as well as for the import of the various raw materials used in the numerous manufacturies in the district traversed by the railway and which are at present brought by small coasters from Dundee and Leith. Should this dock be made, the siding to connect with the railway will be constructed solely on the security of a small rate for the traffic passing over it and without any guarantee whatsoever from this Company which your Directors would not in any circumstances recommend.

The Harbour Commissioners, however, dragged their heels and the government money was not forthcoming. Although the proposed harbour railway was mentioned again in their minutes, the scheme came to naught and with the building of the Methil docks further up the coast the impetus insofar as coal was concerned was lost. The fish trade, however, continued to boom.

More Fish

As the fish trade became concentrated at the harbours at Pittenweem, St Monance and above all Anstruther, these three ports between them began to handle a very considerable proportion of all of the fish landed in Fife. The trade had its fluctuations but when the 'herring drave' was in full swing (which in the Forth was a winter activity unlike the other herring fishing areas of the east coast) then the roads from the harbours to the railway stations were congested and littered with fish scales and other debris. An early complaint was made by the Provost of Anstruther who, in February 1868, said that,

> ... great complaints had ... been made to him regarding the desecration of the Sabbath by several of the English buyers carting barrels and herring to the railway station on Sunday last. He explained that the fish came in late on Saturday night, and were packed and then to the railway station on Sunday in order to be sent off by the first train on Monday morning. As the train did not leave until half-past six on Monday, there was no occasion to do the work on Sunday, so it could easily have been done on Monday morning. The herrings were principally carted from Crail, and he believed that the gates at the railway station were broken open to allow the carts to get into the station.

On 5th February, 1869 the *East of Fife Record* carried a graphic account of the congestion at Anstruther station caused by fish:

> Owing to the heavy fishing of the last two days, the carrying powers of our railway company have been taxed to an extent beyond any former occasion; and at one time yesterday it seemed almost beyond its capabilities. There were a great many of Wednesday's catch which could not be forwarded that day, and some slightly salted had purposely kept back by buyers for transmission yesterday. From five o'clock yesterday morning, cartload after cartload of these began to pour into the station. Some trucks were attached to the early passenger train, while an early extra train was run with fish alone, so as to ease the regular traffic; and the 10 o'clock passenger train as usual

had what trucks remained sent on by it. These three trains would take on some 40 trucks, laden with 30 barrels each, but there still remained 150 on the 'bank', while the large bulk of that day's catch had not as yet come forward. On the departure of the 10 train, the gates were ordered to be locked, and the confusion thus avoided at the station was transferred to the highway, where the carts formed a double line reaching from the gate down beyond the port, and at one time numbering upwards of forty. The appearance of the road at this time, with the excitement of the buyers and the eagerness of the carters, who were anxiously watching their turn for the opening of the gate when the promised empty trucks should arrive, was a source of merriment which the unusual occurrence had collected together. When they did arrive, and the gates opened, a scene of the wildest confusion ensued – their tacit agreement to stand their turn was completely ignored by all, and their mad attempts to enter the gateway, two at a time, was not only the cause of much delay, but also of great danger. One man, in his attempt at one of those 'double entries', was caught up off his feet betwixt the horse and shaft of his opponent's cart, but without hurting him. The loading bank was now a scene of still greater confusion, being entirely blocked up with carts which could get moved neither way, and it was not until one of them got overturned and the barrels smashed that any idea of the necessity for some order prevailed. As there were about 30 trucks, the pressure slackened gradually, but other loads came dropping in until and after these were also filled. It is a pity that this should take place when a perishable cargo like herrings cannot find a ready despatch. It tells much against all concerned; but we believe every exertion has been made to prevent a recurrence of any similar inconvenience, for which those connected with our line, we are happy to learn, were in no way to blame.

There were, unfortunately, near repetitions of such scenes in subsequent years and although the railway attempted to anticipate sudden large landings it was a difficult problem for them to overcome, being only a small company with a limited number of daily services and a comparatively small number of locomotives and wagons. On 8th March, 1872 the *Record* noted that,

On Tuesday the loading bank at the station became so blocked up that it was necessary to close the gate at the goods entrance for a short time. An additional goods train was despatched on that afternoon, and by this means the whole of Tuesday's catch was despatched in time to catch the train leaving Edinburgh in the evening for the English markets. No less than 40 trucks left with one train on that day. On Wednesday the steamer 'Forth' which came down on her usual passage from Leith in the morning, got a full cargo of herrings, and left for Leith again in the afternoon, so as to get these fish sent off by the evening train from Edinburgh.

The Muiredge Branch

The Leven & East of Fife had only one branch line of any length, namely the Muiredge branch which served collieries lying to the north of the small coastal town of Buckhaven just to the west of Leven. The branch left the main route east of Cameron Bridge station and headed for a mile or so south to terminate at a point slightly to the north of the Kirkcaldy to Leven coast road. The colliery at Muiredge had originally been worked by the Wemyss estates but had later been abandoned. In 1864 the mineral rights were leased by the Wemyss estates to Bowman & Cairns, whose two partners came from Crossgates in West Fife and who proceeded to develop the colliery and transformed it into a very successful operation. The *Fifeshire Advertiser* of 11th June, 1864 reported that, 'The coal pit close to this village

[Buckhaven], and known as the Muiredge pit of the Wemyss collieries, has been let upon lease to parties residing about Crossgates in the Dunfermline district. If they intend working the valuable seams of coal here to advantage, they cannot afford to lose a moment in procuring a communication per rail'. The firm working the pit later became known as Bowman & Company.

The Leven & East of Fife Board realised that to serve the Muiredge pit a connection with its own line would be desirable and in 1865 they instructed its Engineer, John Sang of Kirkcaldy, to draw up plans for the same; the other stated purpose of the branch was to serve a public goods station at its terminus which would form 'a considerable attraction for the general traffic from the prosperous fishing and manufacturing town of Buckhaven'. In November of that year the plans were submitted to Parliament and, with little opposition either internal or external, the Leven & East of Fife Railway Act (29 & 30 Vict., cap. clxvii) was passed on 16th July, 1866. This Act, whose full title was 'An Act for authorising the Leven and East of Fife Railway Company to make and maintain certain branches in the parishes of Markinch and Wemyss in the County of Fife and for other purposes...' described in Section 4 two separate branches to be built namely:

1. A Branch Railway (hereinafter called 'Railway No. 1'), one mile and four furlongs in length, commencing in the Parish of Markinch and County of Fife by a junction with the Leven and East of Fife Railway at the western end of Cameron Bridge station, and terminating in the Parish of Wemyss and county aforesaid in a field owned by Joseph Thomson, on the north side of the Sawmill ford turnpike road, and one hundred and thirty yards or thereabouts eastwards of Percival Toll Bar.
2. A Branch Railway (hereinafter called 'Railway No. 2'), one mile four furlongs and one hundred and ten yards in length, commencing by a junction with the first-mentioned branch at its terminus as described and terminating at the north-west corner of the harbour at Methil.

The Act introduced an important restriction on the type of traffic to be permitted on this second proposed line and stipulated that it 'shall not be used for the conveyance of passengers, but for goods and mineral traffic only'. However, Railway No. 2 was, in fact, never built because the Leven & East of Fife Board decided that there would never be enough potential traffic to justify the expense of its construction and although powers had been obtained to build the line, these powers were allowed to lapse – a major miscalculation that in time was to cost the company and its successors dearly.

The contractors for the Muiredge branch were Messrs J. & W. Grainger of Perth and the project was financed by the issue of 4½ per cent preference shares issued under the 1866 Act; the construction cost was estimated at £6,200. Despite the fact that the only engineering work of any importance was the bridge over the River Leven, there was a considerable delay between the passing of the Act and the start of any work on the construction of the new line caused, no doubt, by the uncertain state of the money market following the crash of the London discount house of Overend, Gurney & Co. in 1866. On 5th October, 1867 it was, however, reported that operations had begun on the construction works with the clearing of land and the shareholders of the Leven & East of Fife were told at the end of October 1868 that the Muiredge branch was 'now ready for opening'. Two months later it was stated that the 'branch line of railway between the coal field in the locale and the Cameron Bridge station has been opened insofar as an engine has passed several times along it'. No passenger service was ever operated over this undulating single-track line which had in its short length from Cameron Bridge to Muiredge 10 separate changes of gradient, the steepest of which was 1 in 54. The terminus consisted of a small goods shed on the north side of the Buckhaven to Methil road and upon opening was named Muiredge Sidings (Goods) although in June 1878 it was re-named Buckhaven and later still (from 5th May, 1887) Buckhaven (Old) to distinguish it from Buckhaven on the newly-opened Wemyss and Buckhaven Railway.

The subsequent history of the Muiredge branch is a complicated one. Bowman's Muiredge Colliery was, within five years, connected to Methil Harbour by a private tramroad and coals were transported over this line in horse-drawn wagons to the harbour from where it was shipped in small boats of between 50 and 200 tons. In 1870, when the output of coals had increased so that horse power was no longer feasible, a locomotive was then used. Later on a number of private lines connected with the Muiredge branch proper and these lines served the collieries of the Pirnie Coal Co. and, later, the Fife Coal Co. Ltd. The Fife Coal Co. started operations in the east of Fife in 1877 when it commenced the sinking of the Leven colliery, which lay to the east of the Muiredge branch. A private connection was laid to the Muiredge line from the new workings and in June of that year it was reported that the colliery connection was 'wearing fast to completion' and that a number of trucks conveying wood and bricks had already been run close to the pits. In the following month it was said that locomotives were now running to the pithead with materials and that the branch from Methilhill to the colliery was nearly completed. The Fife Coal Co.'s lines were private mineral branches which led off to the east and were connected with the Muiredge branch and although initially were operated by North British locomotives they were later worked by the coal company's own locomotives. A connection was later installed between the Muiredge branch and the NBR Buckhaven to Wemyss line opened in 1881.

Further Developments

As traffic begun to increase and heavier trains were run, the Leven & East of Fife Board had to upgrade the line even more, especially in relation to the original Leven line. In April 1868 it was reported that instead of renewing the two wooden bridges across the River Leven 'which had become decayed' the Directors had decided to replace them with 'substantial iron ones'. In April 1870 it was announced to the company's shareholders that, 'the wooden bridge across the Orr, having become decayed, your Directors, instead of reconstructing it in the same material, have replaced it by a substantial iron one, the cost of which, £377 4*s.* 6*d.*, has been paid out of the fund set aside to meet similar contingencies, at the credit of which there still remains a considerable balance'. By May 1872 it was reported to the shareholders that the last of the wooden bridges on the Leven line, dating back to the Bouch era, had now been replaced by a substantial malleable iron structure, while in the following year the shareholders were told that there had been further heavy expenditure caused by the replacement of the original iron rails by more expensive but durable steel rails.

On the locomotive front there were developments when in 1870 the company ordered additional motive power in the form of No. 4, the first of two 0-4-0 locomotives from Black, Hawthorn of Gateshead-on-Tyne at a cost of £2,280.* Then,

* The Bury engine had, by then, been long gone.

in 1872, the original Leven Railway Hawthorn engine No. 1 was sent to the Cowlairs works of the North British to undergo a complete rebuild from which it returned in the guise of a saddle tank with distinct features common to Wheatley locomotives. Two years later No. 5 appeared, another 0-4-0 from Black, Hawthorn, at a cost of £1,602.* This had minor detail differences from No. 4 such as an absence of brass beading on the splashers and the low-pitched running plate of the earlier locomotive, springs suspended close to the track rather than laminated springs seen in full view on No. 4 and the absence of the additional pair of stays securing the cab roof to the front of the side-boxes. In October 1874 the company's shareholders were told that the chief cause of the fall in profits in the preceding half-year had arisen 'from one of the locomotive engines having had to undergo extensive repairs, and the necessity of having to hire another engine to supply its place while repairs were being executed'.

A short line of railway

The harbour at Leven, which had never been rail served despite the provision for such a line in the Leven Railway Act of 1852, had always been regarded as difficult to access, largely due to the shifting sandbanks near to the mouth of the River Leven. With the rapid expansion of the coal mining industry in the Leven area, local interests determined that the harbour should be improved by dredging and the construction of new harbour walls and a wet docks and the Christie family of Durie, who owned the surrounding land, transferred their rights to a new company for this purpose. The new company, the Leven Harbour Dock & Railway Co., promoted a Bill to authorize the construction of the new harbour and an associated railway was promoted. The Leven Harbour Act (39 & 40 Vict., cap. lxxiii) was passed on 24th July, 1876 and apart from the harbour provisions the Act also provided for,

> ... a short line of railway five furlongs and one chain in length to commence by a junction with the Leven & East of Fife Railway at a point thereon two hundred and forty yards or thereabouts measured in a southerly direction ... from the engine house at the Leven station ... to terminate at a point in the harbour at Leven.

The Secretary of the Leven Harbour Dock & Railway Co. was Andrew Wilkie and the contractors for the works were, once again, J. & W. Grainger of Perth. The capital of the company was made up of £25,000 in ordinary shares (£5,000 of which was acquired by the North British Railway as successors to the Leven & East of Fife) and £8,000 in debentures and the total expenditure was estimated at £40,000. The later history of the Leven Dock railway, however, belongs to the North British era.

Management, Staff and Finance

The Leven & East of Fife Railway Co. had a small Board of Directors, initially six in total in addition to the Chairman, John Haig and the initial Board comprised the familiar names of Sir Ralph Abercrombie of Balcaskie, Adam Johnstone of Kingswood, William Baird of Elie, John Wood of Colinsburgh, James Anderson of the Durie Foundry, Leven and John Luke of Brownhills. By 1870 the survivors were Haig, Wood, Anderson and Luke and the others, having died or retired, were not replaced – the

* A lower price than No. 4 which led some modern commentators erroneously to suggest that it may have been built as a tank locomotive.

1861 Act had allowed the total number to vary between a minimum of three and a maximum of seven. By the final year of independent operation Haig, Luke and Johnstone were still Directors, William Baird had rejoined them and a new Board member had joined, Sir Coutts Lindsay, Bart., of Balcarres. The day to day management of the company was left to a small group of trusted officers, namely Andrew Wilkie as Secretary and General Manager, Edward Kellow as superintendent, Alex McLellan as accountant and cashier, John Brown as rolling stock superintendent and John T. Forster who bore the imposing title of 'Superintendent of the Permanent Way'. These officers, with the exception of Alex McLellan who was succeeded by a Perthshire man, George Irons, all served the company virtually throughout its existence but little is known about them or they way in which they operated. Unfortunately, the company's Minute Books have not survived although some letter books and accounting records have but there is nothing to suggest that relations between the Board and their officers was anything other than harmonious and the fact that the latter group served for so long would tend to corroborate this view. Relations with the staff were, however, not always that harmonious and in 1873 the Anstruther station master, J.C. Gray, tendered his resignation because of a breakdown in communication with some of the company's officials. Things had become 'of so unpleasant a nature that he felt he could not with any self-respect or satisfaction continue to hold the appointment' despite the fact that he had 'gained for himself the respect and confidence of all those with whom he had come in contact'.

The mileage worked for the six months ending 31st July, 1876 is recorded as being 44,231 made up of 27,282 passenger and mixed miles and 16,949 goods miles while the relevant figures for the following period ending in July 1877 were 46,379, 28,124 and 18,255 respectively. The revenue earned from the line had shown a steady increase and as the author of the *Short Account of the Leven and East of Fife Railway* recorded:

> During the first two years, 1856-57, when the Leven Section only was in operation, the revenue for the former year was £4,217, and for the latter £4,815. During the following six years, 1858-63, when the line was extended to Kilconquhar, the revenue gradually increased from £7,111 to £9,415, the average for the whole six years being £8,650. After the extension to Anstruther was made, and until the Muiredge Branch the revenue has shown the remarkable increase from £16,605 in 1869 to £22,765 in 1877, being fully 37 per cent, without any further addition to the mileage of the undertaking. The earnings per mile of railway in 1856 were £703, and in the year 1877 they were £1,138.
>
> These results plainly show that the district through which the line passes has been very greatly benefited by the railway. The continued increase in the traffic indicates the continued and increasing prosperity of the district, and there is no doubt that the mining, manufacturing and agriculture interests of the southern and eastern portions of the county have all been promoted by the railway facilities which have been afforded to them, and that means and comfort of the various classes of the community have been enhanced.
>
> The dividends paid to the shareholders have borne corresponding increase with the increase in traffic – those to the Shareholders of the Leven Section having gradually advanced from 4½ to 10½ per cent; and to the Shareholders of the East of Fife Section from 2½ to 5 per cent ...

The final capital structure of the Leven & East of Fife was, at 31st July, 1877, authorized stock of £130,000 (£129,910 of which had been paid-up) divided as follows:

Leven Railway Stock, 1852, issued at par	£23,000
East of Fife stock, 1856, issued at par	£32,000
Leven & East of Fife stock, 1861	
For Leven Railway, issued at par	£14,000
For East of Fife, issued at par	£3,000
Leven & East of Fife Extension Stock –	
Preference stock at 4½% fixed dividend	£40,000
Leven & East of Fife 1866 Act stock –	
Preference stock at 4½% fixed dividend	£18,000
	£130,000

The total amounts of capital received by the company amounted to £174,302 made up of £129,910 worth of paid-up shares and stocks, £37,850 in loans, £6,000 received as compensation from the government in return for the nationalization of the telegraph system in 1870* and a cash balance of £542. The total amount expended amounted to the same total and was comprised of £42,000 by the Leven Railway, £45,600 by the East of Fife Company and £86,702 for the Anstruther Extension and the Muiredge lines.

The Leven Railway Workshops

In common with many small railway companies of the period, the Leven & East of Fife had its own workshops at which minor running repairs and other maintenance work could be carried out on the locomotives and rolling stock of the company without the necessity of using the facilities of the North British or the locomotive manufacturers. The works, which combined its function with that of the engine shed, were a modest affair under the control of John Brown, who is described in the 1871 census return as 'Locomotive Engineer, age 40, residing at 22 Haughbank Terrace, Leven'. Situated close to the Leven passenger station, the works had been inherited from the Leven Railway and employed a staff of about 20 including smiths, mechanics, joiners and labourers – the 1871 Census for the Parish of Scoonie includes entries for Andrew Finlay (Railway Blacksmith), James Robertson (Railway Engine Fitter), George Kilgour (Railway Engine Driver, age 34, residence: 218 Bleachfield, Leven) and John White (Railway Guard, 17 Haughbank Terrace, Leven). By 1877 the works were responsible for maintaining five steam locomotives (the two original locomotives inherited from the Leven and East of Fife companies respectively and another three which had been acquired after the amalgamation), 186 open goods wagons, four covered goods wagons, 20 cattle trucks and two coal trucks. The coaching stock consisted of one first class carriage, two composites, one second class, five third class, two horse boxes, two brake vans and two brake carriages making a total of 237 vehicles – an impressive figure for a small and relatively insignificant company. Upon the Leven & East of Fife being absorbed by the North British Railway the works were closed down and its functions absorbed by the North British at Thornton and elsewhere.

* This was the 'public', i.e. non-internal system which had been installed by the company; the internal railway telegraph system remained under the company's control.

Accidents and Incidents

The Leven & East of Fife line seems to have attracted a fair amount of accidents and these may well have been due to the rather relaxed operating standards which the company had set itself. An early example was the collision which occurred within a few months of the opening of the extension line when a goods train, proceeding westwards 'ran violently into some empty goods trucks which were standing on the line at St Monance station, owing to the signals not being correctly given on the approach of the engine. Fortunately, no person was on the waggons at the time. The force of the goods engine completely smashed one of the trucks, and damaged the others, but no other damage was done to either life or property'.

Other incidents involved the destruction of a whole herd of cows by a train at Ardross near St Monance. On 3rd August, 1871 the *Fifeshire Journal* reported that,

> An accident, which might have been attended with serious consequences, but which, fortunately, was productive of no loss of life, occurred on the Leven and East of Fife Railway on Saturday afternoon. Just when the train which leaves Leven for Thornton station at fifty-seven minutes past one o'clock was passing a little to the west of Cameron Bridge, the engine, tender and a number of trucks containing goods ran off the rails down the embankment on the south side of the line. The engine driver, Charles Bell, under the critical circumstances, did all in his power to prevent the consequences from being fearful by letting off the steam, and the carriages containing the passengers, which were at the end of the train, were thus kept upon the rails. Barring the alarm and great excitement caused by the mishap, nobody was injured but the driver, who was hurt by some barrels toppling over above him from a truck With all possible sped another engine was secured, and the passengers conveyed onward. It has been stated that the points, at the place where the accident took place had inadvertently been left open.

The sequel to this was that John Walton, railway porter at Cameron Bridge, was sentenced to 30 days' imprisonment at Cupar Sheriff Court for 'culpable neglect of duty in connection with the recent accident at the Haugh Mill siding'.

Another incident involved the derailment of the early morning train on entering Leven station in March 1874 due to 'some irregularity of the points' although passengers were transferred to another train 'which proceeded with only a few minutes delay' – something that would be unlikely to happen today! An explanation of this incident appeared under the title of 'Meddling with the Railway Points' in a later edition of the *Dunfermline Journal* when readers were informed that,

> David Chapman and Thomas Hunter, two boys belonging to Broomieknowe, were charged at the Cupar Sheriff Court on Wednesday with having on 1st March placed and left on the Leven & East of Fife Railway, near to the station of Leven, a railway wooden key, and in such a manner as to open the connecting points at said station, whereby an engine was forced off the line ... The boy Chapman failed to appear. Hunter pled guilty and was sent to prison to receive six stripes.*

Persons trespassing on the line were another recurring hazard and six months after the derailment at Leven it was reported that,

> On Thursday afternoon, about four o'clock, an accident of a serious nature befell a miner named John Laing, belonging Cowdenbeath, about half a mile to the East of Thornton Junction on the Leven & East of Fife Railway. Laing, it appears, had some business at

* 'Stripes' were lashes of the birch common when corporal punishment was still approved

Wemyss during the day and returning home, he was walking on the line about the place mentioned. The line is single and Laing was met with a passenger train. Although the driver did all in his power to alarm the man, he could not attract his attention and the consequence was that he sustained serious injury by being struck by the engine.

An accident that perhaps sums up the prevailing attitude to safety in the independent era was provided by an accident which occurred at Anstruther on 2nd June, 1875.

Last Thursday evening, while the railway officials were shunting a number of carriages not required for the last train to Thornton, one of them was forced over the embankment at the entrance to the road leading to the station. Fortunately no one was near enough to be injured, but two of the carriages were considerably damaged. A considerable number of people collected at the spot about ten o'clock, and the successful pulling up of the carriage on to the rails again was saluted by cheers.

One of the few recorded accidents on the Kirkland branch arose on 1st October, 1877 and provides an interesting insight as to how that short branch was worked. A report in the *St Andrews Citizen* stated that,

A serious accident occurred at about 11 o'clock on Monday forenoon to the bridge over the Leven, which is in connection with the branch line to the Leven and East of Fife Railway to Messrs H and T Peter's works at Kirkland, about a mile from Leven. It appears that while a heavily-laden wagon of jute was being driven along the bridge by a horse, assisted by a number of men, the bridge suddenly gave way in the centre ... precipitating wagon, horse and men into the stream. The bridge, which is of wood resting on heavy beams clamped with iron rails, was damaged during the late floods.

One man, a Mr J. Ramsay, was killed in this incident.

The end of the Leven & East of Fife

By the 1870s the North British was well on the way to becoming Scotland's largest railway company in terms of route mileage, staff employed and capital resources and, having absorbed a myriad of large and small companies, was poised to complete its grand trunk route to the North via Bouch's ill-fated Tay Bridge. This near monopoly of East Coast travel in Scotland did not bode well for the continuing independent existence of small connecting lines such as the Leven & East of Fife which, although not struggling to make ends meet, could see the writing on the wall for a number of different, but equally compelling reasons. The company, well managed and still reasonably prosperous, was in a vulnerable position and its Board were well aware that things were moving swiftly in favour of absorption by its larger neighbour.

The reasons were obvious. At that time the general economy of the United Kingdom was slipping into what would become a prolonged trade slump and Scotland was no exception. Past prosperity of the railway and the level of dividends declared in prior years could not be assumed to continue if traffic revenues declined and a tie up with a larger organization, with all the advantages of economies of scale and easier access to capital markets, was highly desirable. The Leven & East of Fife was a single-track terminus branch line some 20 miles in length, having an end-on junction with the North British over which the majority of its traffic passed. Local journeys wholly on the company's line, whether for passenger or goods, were small in number and thus the question of through traffic rates via the North British were crucial to the prosperity of the company, even though in May 1875 an agreement had been reached with the North British to run through carriages between Anstruther and Burntisland by certain named trains. The company had found it difficult to raise the substantial amounts of capital needed to extend the line to Anstruther and much of the infrastructure including the locomotives and rolling stock were in need of replacement or refurbishment. A larger organization, with larger cash flows from substantial traffic, would find the raising of fresh capital much easier. From the North British point of view, absorption was desirable because it was seen by them as the way forward and in Fife the Edinburgh, Perth & Dundee, the Fife & Kinross, the Stirling & Dunfermline and the Leslie railways had all already fallen under their control. The building of a new coal shipping dock at Leven and the development of the coalfield in the nearby Wemyss coalfield was certain to increase railway revenue locally and the North British also wished to acquire railway access to the new dock, given that they were already handling traffic originating from other parts of Fife such as Kelty, Lochgelly and Cowdenbeath. All in all, a deal would certainly be favourable to both the larger and to the smaller company and after a great deal of discussion and agreement between the two Boards, an agreement was reached and duly ratified by the shareholders of both companies.

The author of *A Short Account*, ignoring some of the evidence to the contrary, neatly summed up the matter by stating that,

> Although the Company, after the first year, became independent of the Edinburgh, Perth and Dundee Company, and thereafter worked their own line ... they nevertheless continued to be in close connection, as regards the regulation of trains and otherwise, with that Company, till it became amalgamated with the North British Railway Company; and since that time the relations of the Leven and East of Fife Company with the North British Company have always been of the most friendly character. The proposal for an amalgamation with the North British Railway Company had been mooted before; but last year the Directors of the North British proposed to take over the line on terms which, on due consideration by the Directors of the Leven and East of Fife Company, were deemed to be fair and reasonable.

On 28th June, 1877 the North British Railway (Amalgamation) Act (40 & 41 Vict. cap. lxi) received the Royal Assent and both the St Andrews Railway and the Leven & East of Fife passed into history. The latter, referred to in the Act as 'the Fife Company', capital of £129,910 had divided into ordinary stock of £72,000 and 4½ per cent preference stock (i.e. stock with a guaranteed annual dividend) with mortgaged borrowings of £37,950 plus the £5,000 invested in the shares of the Leven Harbour Co. The Act made the following provisions for the Leven & East of Fife shareholders:

> The preference stock of the Fife Company amounting to the sum of sixty-two thousand, nine hundred and ten pounds shall, on the date of the amalgamation become North British Lien Stock of the same amount and entitled to a fixed preferential dividend at the rate of four pounds ten shillings per centum per annum [i.e. 4½ per cent], and the North British Lien Stock is in this Act called the 'Fife No. 1 Lien Stock'.
>
> And the Leven Ordinary Stock of the Fife Company amounting to the sum of thirty-seven thousand pounds shall, on and from the date of the amalgamation, become North British Lien Stock of the same amount and entitled to a fixed preferential dividend at the rate of ten pounds ten shillings per centum per annum [i.e. 10½ per cent] and that North British Lien Stock is in the Act called 'Fife No. 2 Lien Stock'.

And the East of Fife Ordinary Stock of the Fife Company amounting to the sum of thirty-five thousand pounds shall on and from the date of the amalgamation become North British Lien Stock of the same amount entitled to a fixed preferential dividend at the rate of five pounds per centum per annum [i.e. 5 per cent] and the North British Lien Stock is in the Act called the 'Fife No. 3 Lien Stock'.

To recap, therefore, the 'Fife No.1 Stock' consisted of £62,910 of 4½ per cent North British Lien Stock issued in exchange for the same value of 4½ per cent Leven & East of Fife preference shares comprising of £40,000 of shares issued under the 1861 Act, £17,910 issued under the 1866 Act and £5,000 of shares issued to pay for the company's investment in the Leven Harbour Company. The 'Fife No. 2 Stock' consisted of £37,700 of 10½ per cent North British Lien Stock issued in exchange for the same value of £23,000 of Leven Railway stock issued in 1852 and £14,000 of Leven & East of Fife Stock issued for Leven Railway debt in 1861. The 'Fife No. 3 Stock' consisted of £35,000 of 5 per cent North British Lien Stock issued in exchange for the same value of £32,000 worth of East of Fife 1855 stock and £3,000 of Leven & East of Fife Stock issued for the East of Fife debt in 1861.

The date of the amalgamation was fixed as Wednesday 1st August, 1877 and, from that date, the assets, contracts, obligations and debts of both the Leven & East of Fife Railway and the St Andrews Railway vested in the North British Railway with control passing from Fife to the company's headquarters across the Forth in Edinburgh. The local newspapers duly reported the amalgamation in a generally favourable way and recorded for posterity the final actions of the Leven & East of Fife Railway Company. The last half-yearly meeting was held in the Caledonian Hotel, Leven on Wednesday 31st October, 1877 with John Haig presiding as Chairman, a position he had held for more than quarter of a century since the inauguration of the railway back in 1852. Speeches were made but the general tone of the meeting was somewhat subdued, hardly surprising in view of the fact that many present realised that the management of a major business undertaking had now been lost to the town for ever. Thanks were given to the officers and servants of the company, the sum of £500 was unanimously voted to Andrew Wilkie 'in acknowledgement of the valuable services which he had rendered to the Company'* and a final dividend of 10½ per cent for Leven stock and 5 per cent for East of Fife stock was declared and that was that – the end of the line had been reached. The company's workshops at Leven had already gone – on 13th September they had been closed down and 'the various workmen, smiths, mechanics, joiners and labourers' employed there were dismissed but offered work elsewhere with the North British after 'a final social parting meeting' at the Caledonian Hotel. Various other dinners and socials had taken place for retiring officials. On 6th October, 1877 it was reported that 'Mr E. Kellow, passenger and traffic superintendent of the Leven and East of Fife Branch of the North British Railway was waited on the other day at his residence, 26 Sutton Place, Edinburgh, by a deputation of the officials in connection with the late Leven and East of Fife Railway, and presented with a silver salver and purse of sovereigns as a mark of respect'. He was then aged 58 and presumably retired from railway service.

The final act occurred on Friday 9th November, 1877 when 'about forty gentlemen met in the Caledonian Hotel to do honour to Mr G. Irons, on the occasion of the winding-up of the Leven and East of Fife Railway for which Mr Irons has acted as accountant for the last eighteen years'. Mr Irons had tied up all the loose ends and the Leven & East of Fife Railway Company was no more.

* Unfortunately he did not live long to enjoy the money and died in the following year; his gravestone can be found in Leven cemetery.

No. 483, the Black Hawthorn 0-4-0 supplied to the LEoFR in 1874 in its original form at an unknown location about 1878. *NBRSG, Hennigan Collection*

No. 483, by now 483A, at Leven in 1884 with a group of railwaymen including driver John Patterson and permanent way inspector J. Foster. *NBRSG, Hennigan Collection*

Chapter Nine

Slow and Even Slower: The Leven & East of Fife Line 1877-1899

'I do not think any of these trains on that branch line are worthy of the name of an express as we understand it now-a-days.'

Thomas Robertson, General Manager, GNR(I)

Under New Management

With the transfer of the Thornton to Anstruther line to become the Leven & East of Fife Section of the North British Railway, the way forward seemed to be one of consolidation and prosperity, notwithstanding the agricultural and trade depression of the period. The only major capital investment that the independent company had been undertaking, the Leven Harbour branch, was continued by the North British but there was a general reluctance to spend money on the updating and replacement of the stations or structures on the line, despite many of these still dating from the era of the 'cheap railway' a quarter of a century before. The next quarter century would, at the end of it, see the beginning of major improvements to the structures and operation of the line, especially after the opening of the Forth Bridge brought an influx of through traffic and added to the already increasing goods and passenger traffic that the line would attract.

The five surviving Leven & East of Fife locomotives had a mixed fate and none survived World War I. No. 1, the replacement locomotive delivered in October 1855 by Hawthorn's and rebuilt as an 0-4-0ST at Cowlairs in 1872, became North British No. 481 and then transferred to the duplicate list in 1883 as 481A. It underwent two further changes in numbering to become 836 in 1895 and 1036 in 1901 before being withdrawn in 1907 for scrapping. No. 2, built for the East of Fife Railway in 1857, became North British No. 484 and was subsequently rebuilt as a Holmes saddle-tank similar to No. 481, both having dumb buffers, the water intake being placed ahead of the centrally placed dome and both had a square sandbox on the running plate between the wheels giving gravity sanding to the rear wheels only. There were, however, certain differences between the two locomotives as No. 481 had the cylinder pipes hidden beneath flat plates and an inverted egg-cup type of dome while No. 484 had curved smokebox saddles and lock-ups on an ordinary dome. No. 484 became in due course 484A and then 839 and 1039 in the subsequent renumbering schemes before being scrapped in 1911. No. 3, the locomotive delivered for the Anstruther extension had a very limited lifespan as a North British engine despite it nominally being the youngest of the three sisters. Becoming NBR No. 485 it was never rebuilt and, it being decided that it was badly worn out and only fit for scrapping, was withdrawn in December 1877, some five months after its acquisition. The two Black, Hawthorn engines, Nos. 4 and 5 became 482 and 483 in the North British stock list and both were rebuilt as 0-4-0 saddle tanks in the early 1880s. No. 482 acquired a low-pitched running plate and laminated springs in full view above plain splashers and an additional pair of stays securing the cab roof to the front of the side boxes whereas 483 had brass beading on its splashers and its springs suspended close to the track and out of sight behind the wheels. No. 482 became, in 1883, 482A, 837 in 1895 and 1037 in 1901 and its sister was renumbered 483A, 838 and lastly 1038. Both barely outlasted their earlier stable mates with No. 483 the last to go in 1912 and thus the locomotives of the Leven & East Fife became extinct 35 years after the company itself had ceased to exist.

No. 1037, the rebuilt engine supplied by Black, Hawthorn in 1870 to the LEoFR; this photograph shows the engine in its rebuilt state and shortly before it was scrapped.
NBRSG, Hennigan Collection

No. 1038, formerly 483, seen here in rebuilt form working as the Rose Lane pilot in about 1905 with driver Will Wright. *NBRSG, Hennigan Collection*

The Leven Harbour Branch

On 18th November, 1879 the first vessel sailed into the new Leven Harbour, the *Dahlia*, carrying coals from Newcastle. Nine days later an agreement was concluded between the Leven Harbour Co. and the North British Railway which provided that the branch railway from the Leven & East of Fife line to the harbour be built and equipped to the satisfaction of James Carswell, the Engineer of the North British, with all additional sidings being supplied by and at the cost of the harbour company. It was further provided that the harbour line should be treated as a siding of the North British and that the gross receipts over the line should be divided in the ratio of the mileage of traffic generated (the branch being treated as being eight-tenths of a mile long.) Any local traffic on the branch was to be worked by the harbour company and the gross receipts of any such traffic were to be retained by the harbour company. With regard to through traffic over the branch, the North British was to work the same and entitled to retain one half of the gross receipts relating to that traffic and the harbour company entitled to the other half. The agreement specifically excluded the working or maintenance of sidings for the Fife Coal Co. and the agreement was to subsist for a period of three years after the opening of the harbour branch.

On 18th February, 1880 James Carswell reported to John Walker, General Manager of the North British, in the following terms which gives a good contemporary description of it before the rebuilding at the beginning of the 20th century. Walker states that John Bell Jnr, engineer, inspected the branch on February 12th and 13th and reported:

> This branch, which is 1,144 yards in length joins the Siding lately put in by the Harbour Commissioners parallel with our main line. This siding is 337 yards in length measured from the point of the switches and the harbour branch joins the siding at a point 233 yards from the point of the switches on our line, leaving a distance of 104 yards to enable a train to enter on to the branch.
>
> *Under bridges:* There are two underbridges, one over the Burnmill lade and the other over the lade near to Messrs Balfour & Co's foundry. The bridge over the Burnmill lade is 32′9″ span and consists of malleable iron beams resting on timber frame abutments. The construction of this bridge is too light for our own heavy engines. The distance between the flanges is 9′6″ which does not admit of the Board of Trade regulations width between the rail and the girder.
>
> *Over bridge near terminus of branch:* The bridge over the mill lade near Messrs Balfour & Coy's foundry is 12 ft span … and is in good order. The bridge carrying the turnpike road to Kirkcaldy: the abutments and wing walls are of square snecked block rubble masonry. The arch is of ashlar. The span between the abutments is 13 feet which does not admit of the Board of Trade Regulation width from the rail to the abutments. This bridge is in good order.
>
> *Level crossings:* There are two crossings, one a 9 feet field crossing and the other a 15′7″ crossing over the Saw Mill Road. This crossing is furnished with 15′7″ gates and locks. Lamps are required for the gates and also a gate-keeper to attend to them.
>
> *Rails:* The rails are of steel, flat bottomed in 19 & 20 feet lengths and weigh from 63 to 68 lbs per yard. The fastening in connection with the switches and crossings are of a very temporary description and are quite unfit for our heavy engines working over them.
>
> *State of the line:* The line in several places is out of both line and level. In order to put the branch in good order it will be necessary to give it a two inch lift and adjust the rails to line and level.

> *Siding to Messrs Balfour & Co's foundry:* The siding is on a sharp curve and falling gradient and quite unfit for our engines to work over.
> *Miscellaneous:* There are no signals in connection with this branch. I enclose a sketch shewing the length of the branch and the radius of the curves.

Carswell concluded that, 'Owing to the light construction of the branch, I cannot recommend our engines to work over it'. However, the report was amended on 2nd March when, among other things, it was agreed that North British engines would be permitted to work over the line but only on the basis that the harbour company would indemnify them for any loss caused by a derailment or other accident caused by the state of the line.

The Leven Harbour Co. was not, however, a profitable undertaking due to both its chronic lack of funding and the continuing silting of the badly-situated dock at the mouth of the River Leven which necessitated continuous dredging just to keep it open. Although the branch saw local traffic of coal from the pits in the Leven area (including the newly opened Rosie Pit), which travelled there on a very roundabout route via the Muiredge branch and goods and materials to and from Balfour's Durie Foundry, the railway to the dock never fully achieved its potential.

Anstruther & St Andrews

On Saturday 1st September, 1883 the Anstruther & St Andrews Railway opened the first part of its line from an end-on junction with the Leven & East of Fife line at Anstruther. Trains began running from Pittenweem to Boarhills, the starting point of the service being necessitated because the new passenger station at Anstruther on the far side of the Dreel Burn was not yet fit for traffic and the terminus being an interim one until the line to St Andrews was complete, the latter task not being fulfilled until 1st June, 1887.* On 27th December, 1883 the new passenger station at Anstruther Easter was opened for business and with its opening the old station at Anstruther Wester was closed to passenger traffic and adapted for general goods purposes and, particularly, for the burgeoning fish traffic. The *Fife News* of 31st October, 1885, reported that:

> A most important improvement is in course at Anstruther railway station in connection with utilising the old station for fish traffic. With the double rails on either side of the spacious esplanade, there will be accommodation for 40 wagons in connection with the fast trains that will run during the season. English buyers were formerly particularly exposed to annoyance and loss by limited facilities at the station, where it was not unusual on the first day of a heavy fishing to lock the gates in face of the traffic. Herrings were carted from pier to station at 3*d*. per barrel which led to bickering and delay but now the railway has arranged to convey them in lorries at a charge of 1s 0d a ton, to be included in the through rate.

These facilities were indeed necessary for on Tuesday 26th January of that year the greatest number ever of winter herring were landed at Anstruther and the North British required to dispatch 280 wagons of herring that day. A year later 190 wagons were dispatched in a single day in February, with 176 on the next day and a higher number on the day after that. The same newspaper then commented that, 'we may observe that the change from the old to the new platform has proved a notable convenience, as it leaves the first free for just such a pressure as occurred this week'.

---

* The full history of this line is recounted in our companion volume *The Anstruther & St Andrews Railway* (Oakwood Press, 2009) – the date of the opening from Boarhills to St Andrews was erroneously printed there as 1st *July* 1887 rather than 1st June.

The effect of exporting such large quantities of fresh fish to home markets by rail was a virtual change in the eating habits of the British public. The falling price of fish led to a vastly increased consumption of fried fish by the working classes and the rise of the fish-and-chip shop. Special fast trains ran from Anstruther during the season, connecting with London- and Manchester-bound services and there was some lobbying of Parliament by the assessor for the Burgh of Anstruther Wester, in favour of the Bill introduced by Sir Edward Birkbeck, MP for the Eastern Division of Norfolk. This was designed to secure a uniform scale of rates and charges for the carriage of common types of fish by the railway companies in the United Kingdom and in consequence the railways managed to carry a great deal of fish until after World War II.

The Leven Connection Railway and the Rise of Methil

At the same time as Leven Dock was opened, the coal production of the small coalfield situated to the south-west of the town and in the hands of Bowmans, the Fife Coal Company and, most significantly of all, the Wemyss Estates was flourishing. Some of this travelled by rail to Leven Dock but coal from the west of the area travelled a considerable distance over the North British to Burntisland. There were, however, already plans for a more ambitious scheme which would result in the building of a new dock at Methil, close to Leven, which would eventually result in virtually all of the coal produced in Fife being exported through this port and the total eclipse of Leven Harbour. The driving force behind this was Randolph Wemyss* and other Fife coalmasters (including his tenants the Fife Coal Company and Bowmans) and their aim was to redirect the coal traffic to Methil which, until it was developed by them, was little more than a small and peaceful fishing village. In the 1870s a railway was proposed to run from Thornton Junction to Buckhaven, to be constructed independently but operated by the North British. On 21st April, 1879 an agreement was entered in to between the Wemyss Estates, who had financed the line, and the North British in relation to the working of the line and subsequently the coalmasters of the Leven area pits agreed to ship their coal via Randolph Wemyss' proposed new Methil dock.

The North British did not view the provision of a new dock that would be independent of them with favour, especially when the Wemyss Estates had pre-empted any opposition from the stricken Leven Harbour Co. by, on 15th August, 1883, purchasing the Leven Dock and its associated branch line for £12,000 – a considerable loss to the harbour company's shareholders. Wemyss then entered into an agreement with the North British and Wemyss and Buckhaven companies, dated 21st May, 1883, whereby he was to extend his Buckhaven line to Methil, working it as part of the Wemyss and Buckhaven Railway and to provide suitable storage sidings at Methil. In order to preserve traffic on the Muiredge branch and other North British lines various rates for coal carriage were agreed as was the construction of a line known as the Leven Connection Railway, which provided for the construction of a short line from the Leven Dock branch to Methil Dock.

The Leven Connection Railway, two miles in length and extending from Leven to Buckhaven, left the Leven Harbour branch south of the Leven bridge and crossed the River Leven on a three-span girder bridge before following the coastline past

* The full history of the Wemyss Coal Co. and Methil Docks is covered admirably in *The Wemyss Private Railway* by Alan Brotchie (Oakwood Press, 1998).

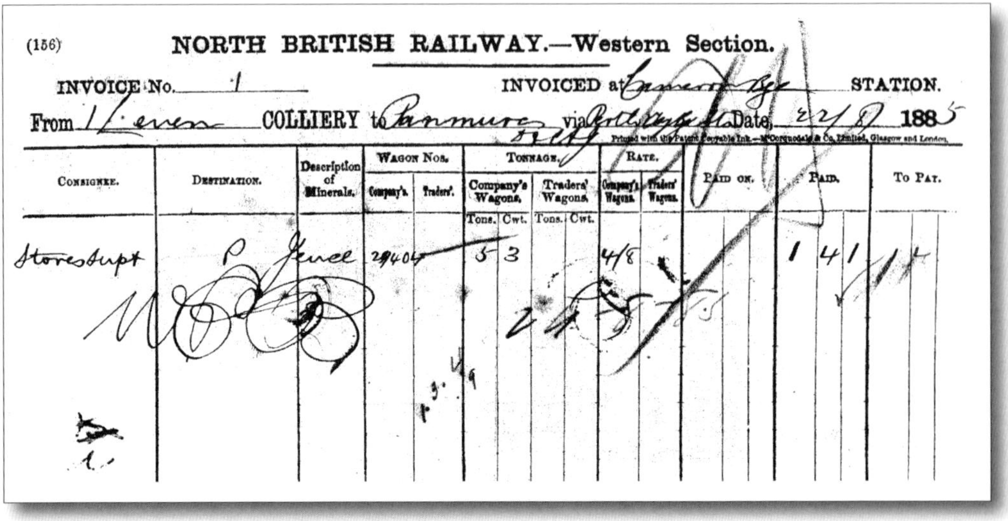

(156) **NORTH BRITISH RAILWAY.—Western Section.**

INVOICE No. 1 INVOICED at Cameron Bge STATION.

From Leven COLLIERY to Panmure via ... Date 22/8/ 1885

Printed with the Patent Copyable Ink.—M'Corquodale & Co. Limited, Glasgow and London.

Consignee.	Destination.	Description of Minerals.	Wagon Nos. Company's.	Wagon Nos. Traders'.	Tonnage Company's Wagons Tons.	Tonnage Company's Wagons Cwt.	Tonnage Traders' Wagons Tons.	Tonnage Traders' Wagons Cwt.	Rate Company's Wagons.	Rate Traders' Wagons.	Paid on.	Paid.	To Pay.
Stores Supt	P	Fence	29404		5	3			4/8			1 4 1	1 1

An invoice issued at Cameron Bridge station for conveyance of coal from Leven Colliery.

The original Leven Railway Hawthorn locomotive of 1855 in its rebuilt guise as NBR No. 1036 and acting as St Leonards pilot in about 1905 with driver J. McArthur.

NBRSG, Hennigan Collection

Innerleven, where a steeply graded line ran down from the Leven No. 1 and 2 pits. The Fife Coal Co., who were to make use of the line to export their coal via Leven Dock until the new Methil Dock was opened, paid for the Leven girder bridge. The Leven Connection Railway was opened on 17th September, 1884, six months after the construction of the new Methil Docks had commenced. On 5th May, 1887 the passenger line from Buckhaven to Methil was opened, together with Methil Dock and the railway lines leading to it. The effect on the Leven Harbour branch, owned by Wemyss but operated by the North British, was immediate and traffic levels fell to such an extent that the North British had to apply to Randolph Wemyss asking him to work the traffic to and from Balfour's Durie Foundry, since it would be no longer economically practicable to keep an engine solely to work this traffic. Events, however, continued to unfold and on 1st February, 1889 Wemyss sold the Buckhaven & Wemyss, Leven Harbour and Leven Extension Railways and certain connecting lines joining the Muiredge branch, together with the Methil Dock, to the North British for the sum of £225,000 . In due course as the coal output of the Fife pits, and the demand for them, increased additional dock facilities were provided at Methil but the connection with the Leven Harbour branch saw comparatively little use until the construction of Kirkland Yard in the first decade of the 20th century.

Durie Colliery and Silverburn Sidings

To the north of the line and immediately to the east of the original waggonway-served pits at Sauchenbush and Sillerhole and unconnected with the Scoonie and Durie of the 1850s workings, new shafts were sunk in the winter of 1887 by the Fife Coal Company in connection with their development of the Nos. 1 and 2 pits of their new Durie Colliery. It was said that 'when it is in full operation it is hoped that the pit will give a much needed impetus to the town and trade of Leven' but unfortunately the workings were prone to persistent flooding throughout the short life of this colliery. Situated close to Scoonie Cotton and near to Blacketyside, the colliery was served by a short branch line off the Leven and East of Fife line between Brickworks and Silverburn sidings work on which began on 18th February, 1888. The siding was opened for temporary use by 31st March of that year and permanently by 19th April. Durie Colliery produced up to 400 tons per day and at is height employed some 185 underground and 42 surface workers. Unfortunately, even the 'very elaborate' pumping arrangements did not prove adequate to the task of removing the 1,150 gallons of water per minute needed to keep the pits workable and on 19th January, 1903 the colliery was abandoned. The Durie Colliery siding remained in place for a short period thereafter, being listed in the NBR sidings register as being closed and by 1914 was disconnected apart from a short stretch alongside the main line and still connected to it. This remnant, re-named the Durie siding was still in use in 1956. In the case of Silverburn the siding laid originally in 1857 was lifted in about 1870 but was subsequently re-laid and opened again on 12th June, 1888. Although the siding remained in use all flax production had ceased. A stub of the original siding remained in use until at least 1957 and the authors assume that this was because it was used as a ballast siding.

Cyanide and telegraph poles

In late Victorian times a number of industrial premises were connected by privately-owned or tenanted sidings to the Leven and East of Fife section. Travelling westwards the first private siding reached was Haughmill siding opened in 1854 and built to serve the mill of the same name. Latterly tenanted by G. & W. Beveridge, flax mill owners and linen manufactures and by the Haugh Bleaching Co., the siding appears to have closed down and in 1897 was renamed the Drumcaldie Distillery siding to serve the new works of the Fife Distillery Co. This distillery had a short existence only before closing down in 1903, when its premises (and siding) were acquired by Distillers Co. Ltd (DCL) and incorporated into their adjacent Cameron Bridge distillery which had been owned by the Haig family and whose family name is perpetuated in one of their blended whiskies. Approaching Leven was the east-facing Kirkland branch which, by 1880, had been lifted and its bridge over the River Leven demolished. Kirkland works had laid derelict for a number of years until they were acquired in 1896 by the Scottish Cyanide Co. Ltd who were manufacturers of cyanide which was used in large quantities to extract the gold from gold-bearing rock. The Kirkland branch was apparently re-laid on its existing formation. Much of their product was used in South Africa and the Boer War and its aftermath so lessened the demand for cyanide that the works closed in 1905 and the Kirkland site was again to remain derelict for another few years. To the west of the Kirkland branch, lay and joined to the main line by an eastward-facing siding, the creosote works of Alexander Bruce & Co. who were manufacturers of telegraph and telephone poles and railway sleepers. Indeed such was their specialization that they were known as the only telegraph pole depot in Scotland. Forced out of their existing premises by the building of the No. 2 dock there, they leased a four-acre site at Leven in 1899 and had two sidings put in. On the Leven Dock branch itself were two private sidings, the first of which was the Durie Foundry siding opened in 1880 and serving this long-established works. The foundry also contained a network of standard gauge lines upon which wagons could be detached and then horse-drawn around the foundry. The second was Donaldson & Sons Wemyss Saw Mill sidings opened in 1890 when Donaldsons transferred part of their business from Tayport. Acquiring the sawmills from John Balfour & Sons in December 1889, they managed to negotiate a favourable rate for the carriage of imported timber from the newly-opened Methil Dock to their Leven site via the Leven Connection line. An NBR working timetable of 1902 states that, 'The Leven Dock branch pilot works Donaldson & Sons Siding, Bruce & Co's Creosote Siding and Cyanide Siding when required'.

Summer Visitors and Day-trippers

As Queen Victoria's long reign continued, the small burghs along the East Fife coast became increasingly popular as seaside resorts, both for day-trippers and excursionists and for longer-term stays by the middle classes of Glasgow and Edinburgh, the latter giving the town of Elie the soubriquet of 'Newtown-on-sea'. On 11th May, 1888 the *Fifeshire Journal* reported that there was some competition for this traffic and that, 'The better class of houses in Elie and Earlsferry are well let, and every day parties in search of summer quarters are to be seen. The outlook at present is favourable, and the increased facilities afforded by the landing stage in course of erection should lead to a greater patronage by the Galloway steamers. The first trip for the season was made on Monday, when about 50 passengers were landed'.

The *Ordnance Gazetteer for Scotland* commented in relation to that town that it had once been a place of some importance, and that although it retained a few antique mansions in a street near the beach, it mainly consisted of modern well-built houses and 'for long been place of considerable resort for summer sea-bathing, and is even claimed by some as one of the best health resorts, particularly in winter, of any place in Scotland', while another contemporary source said that the town was 'after a sleep of centuries awakening to renewed life and activity'.

However, Elie was not the only watering place to flourish - Lundin Links, Largo, St Monance and Pittenweem, and to a greater extent Anstruther, were all beginning to develop as summer seaside resorts at this time. But, although the opening of the Anstruther & St Andrews Railway to Crail and Boarhills brought a slight increase to the traffic over the Leven & East of Fife line, it was not until the opening of the Boarhills to St Andrews section and the commencement of through services over the whole line that Crail began to take off as a resort. Largo retained its tourist trade despite the unsuccessful attempts to revive its regular paddle-steamers from Granton and Leith and 'upwards of twenty boarding establishments' there were advertised to cater for this trade, Perhaps a little surprisingly, Kilconquhar enjoyed a considerable trade as an inland holiday centre and a place for picnics and rambling in the countryside. St Monance enjoyed popularity as a Victorian centre for artists, both amateur and professionals, while Pittenweem catered for those who appreciated its antique aspects and varied coastline. Both Leven and Anstruther tendered to cater for daytrips and family holidays and even busy Cellardyke had its share of visitors. There were few hotels for tourists, Lundin Links being the exception with its large turn-of-the century hotel but Largo and Elie also having some 'superior' establishments. Many of the visitors sought summer lodgings with families or in their homes as the inhabitants went, in the best Scottish traditions, to live in annexes or sheds at the bottom of the garden.

The holiday traffic was, however, by no means a one-way one and although there may have been little in the way of outward traffic of holidaymakers going to other resorts for a week or month's holiday, there was a healthy traffic in both day trippers to local attractions such as the East of Fife Agricultural Society's annual summer show at Colinsburgh served by Kilconquhar station, and to the annual Lammas Fair at St Andrews. The Anstruther and Cellardyke Merchants' Association for many years organized quite elaborate excursions to destinations in Fife, Angus and Perthshire and there were other organized excursions by church and Sunday school groups, local societies and clubs and by the railway themselves who were always quick to encourage such trade.

On 25th May, 1888 the *Journal* reported that,

> Yesterday was observed as the Queen's Birthday Holiday in Anstruther and the East of Fife, with the exception of Cellardyke. The same delightful weather which has been experienced since last Saturday was continued yesterday, and outdoor recreation was continued yesterday. The railway company offered special terms to Glasgow in order to enable visitors to see the exhibition, but unfortunately only a few availed themselves of the advantage. From Crail and Anstruther only 19 passengers were booked by the first train, 12 from Crail and 7 from Anstruther. At different places along the coast to Leven the passengers were more numerous and at Leven especially a good number left with the train. The other trains were not patronised more than usual. To mark the event of the Queen's birthday, flags were hung on the town houses of Easter & Wester Anstruther.

ANNUAL SHOW
OF THE
EAST OF FIFE AGRICULTURAL SOCIETY
AT
COLINSBURGH (KILCONQUHAR STATION),
THURSDAY 19th APRIL 1888.

GRAND SHOW of CATTLE, DRAUGHT HORSES, HUNTERS, ROADSTERS, PONIES, SHEEP, PIGS, POULTRY, EGGS, BUTTER, BREAD, AGRICULTURAL PRODUCE, FOX HOUNDS, COLLIE DOGS, and IMPLEMENTS.

HORSE JUMPING (13 Entries) at Twelve o'clock—Water, Turf Dyke, and Hurdle Jumps.
LADIES' PONY DRIVING COMPETITION (9 Entries) at One o'clock.
PONY JUMPING (13 Entries) at Three o'clock.

AN INSTRUMENTAL BAND WILL PERFORM DURING THE DAY.

LUNCHEON and REFRESHMENTS at Moderate Rates may be had on the Grounds.

ADMISSION TO THE SHOW YARD—
From 10 o'clock till 2, One Shilling ; after 2, Sixpence ; Reserved Seats, One Shilling Extra.

Return Tickets for a Single Journey Fare will be issued from all Stations of the Leven and East of Fife and Anstruther and St Andrews Branches to Kilconquhar, and Return Tickets at Reduced Fares will also be issued from Leuchars, Cupar, Ladybank, Newburgh, Markinch, Dunfermline, Kinross, Kirkcaldy, and Burntisland. A Special Train will be run from Kilconquhar to Thornton, in connection with the Last Trains on the Main Line, leaving Kilconquhar Station at 7·54 ; the Special Stock Train leaves at 8·50. Particulars as to Fares will be got from the Companys' Handbills and from the Station Agents. Members are requested to Pay their Subscriptions at the Secretary's Office in the Show Yard.

NOTICE TO EXHIBITORS.
The Show Yard will be Open at 8·30 A.M., and will be Closed for the Admission of Stock at 9·45. Nothing can be removed (except for Mr Bowman's Sale) till after 4.

LEITH, ELIE, METHIL, AND NORTH BERWICK.

THE SPLENDID SALOON STEAMER,

TANTALLON CASTLE,
WILL SAIL AS UNDER, WEATHER &c. PERMITTING.

JUNE 1888.

MONDAYS (Down) from LEITH, 10 A.M. ; ELIE, 12.45.

MONDAYS (Up) from NORTH BERWICK, 4 P.M ; ELIE, 5 P.M.

TUESDAYS (Down) from LEITH, 10 A.M. ; NORTH BERWICK, 12 Noon ; ELIE, 1 P M., (for BELL ROCK, or other Trip).

TUESDAYS (Up) from ELIE, 5 P.M. ; NORTH BERWICK, 6 P.M.

WEDNESDAYS (Down) from LEITH, 10 A.M. ; ELIE, 12.45 P.M., (For MAY ISLAND).

WEDNESDAYS (Up) MAY, 4 P.M. ; ELIE, 5 P.M. ;

THURSDAYS (Down) from LEITH, 10 A.M. ; NORTH BERWICK, 12 Noon, (for MAY ISLAND and ELIE.)

THURSDAYS (Up) from ELIE, 3 P.M. ; MAY, 4 P.M. ; NORTH BERWICK, 5 P.M.

FRIDAYS (Down) from LEITH, 10 A.M. ; ELIE, 12 Noon, NORTH BERWICK, 1 P.M., (for a Cruise.)

FRIDAYS (Up) NORTH BERWICK, 4 P.M. ; ELIE, 5 P.M.

SATURDAYS (Down) from LEITH, 10 A.M. and 3.30 P.M.

Fares from Elie—Single to North Berwick or Leith, Saloon, 1s 6d ; Steerage 1s. Return Fares—May Island or Bell—Saloon, 2s ; Steerage, 1s 6d.

Note—The Steamer will not call at Methil regularly as previously advertised.

These advertisements appeared in the local press in 1888: the agricultural show at Colinsburgh includes Kilconquhar railway connections while Galloway's steamer notice gives Elie excursions to and from Leith.

Eight years later, on 1st May, 1896, the same paper under the heading of 'Anstruther Local Intelligence' stated that,

> In addition to the increased railway facilities to be given during the summer season, Fife is to benefit from a series of cheap fares which the railway company have arranged for the Wednesday half-holiday. The cheap Saturday bookings – mostly single fares for double journeys – are to be applied to Wednesdays after twelve o'clock beginning with Wednesday 6th May, and the tickets will be available for travelling by any ordinary train after that hour. It may also be noted that the North British Railway Company continue the privilege inaugurated last summer, and not sufficiently known, of a pleasure sail by the ferry steamer, Burntisland to Granton, and back, both ways for sixpence.

Improvements expected

As railway passengers themselves became more sophisticated, or at least more critical, comments about the poor facilities provided at some local stations began to be regularly expressed. In June 1888 it was noted that at Anstruther,

> This week workmen are engaged in taking the water from the town's main into the waiting and station premises. The want of water has been greatly felt, and the offices will have some pretence to cleanliness after this. It might be as well were the Co to paint the waiting rooms. The walls especially are anything but tidy or clean, and some improvement is urgently required.

Wheatley 0-6-0 No. 155 seen at Anstruther in January 1887 with driver John Pirnie and other staff. *NBRSG, Hennigan Collection*

On 9th August, 1889 the *Journal* reported that,

> It has long been hinted that something was to be done to Elie station, but apparently no steps have been taken as yet to make this fashionable resort a station worthy of the traffic that is carried on there during the summer months. Then there is Largo. It has one of the ugliest, and what is worse, one of the most dangerous stations on the system. The platform is extremely narrow all over, and at the present time when there are so many visitors arriving and departing from it something should be done to remedy the dangerous crushes which often occur. We are glad to hear that a strong desire has been expressed to have this station altered. The company have not the same excuse to plead as they offer in regard to other stations – the want of room. At Largo there is plenty of ground on the opposite side to make a handsome and comfortable station. The accommodation for the officials and the public is very meagre at present and when there is room to erect as fine a station as at Leven the head officials of the railway should determine that before next season at any rate a large and commodious station should be erected at Largo.

Some curious incidents

On 15th December, 1879 the afternoon goods train to Anstruther came to grief at Pittenweem and some of its wagons were derailed and overturned thus blocking the line. When it was clear that the afternoon train from Thornton could go no further the 'passengers, mails, fish &c.' were dispatched to Pittenweem and it was found that the only damaged sustained to the train was 'the breaking of one rail and the loss of a few pounds of flour'. In February 1882, Thomas King, one of the porters at Anstruther station had 'an accident of a somewhat alarming nature' when, 'in attending to some shunting operations and by some means or other he fell in front of the engine'. His foot was crushed and he was promptly conveyed to the Edinburgh Royal Infirmary where an operation was successfully carried out. This type of accident appears to have been fairly common-place for two months later Robert Wright, a cooper employed at the Cameron Bridge distillery, was seriously injured when a locomotive passed over one of his feet. A third serious accident in that year involved the death of a boy who was hit by a train on a level crossing at Largo, and this was followed by another level crossing accident reported in the *Journal* of 2nd November, 1883:

> Much alarm was occasioned in this locality on the evening of Friday last when it became known that a train on the Leven & East of Fife Railway had run into a cart passing along the level crossing at Haugh Mill, and a little to the west of Cameron Bridge Station. It appears that Thomas Walker, carter to the bleaching company at Haugh Bleachfield, had been crossing the line at the level at about six o'clock, when a goods train dashed forwards and struck the cart, whereupon the horse, which at the moment had just crossed the rails, making a bolt and breaking the harness, escaped uninjured. The driver also providentially escaped, but the cart was dashed to pieces (the axle was broken and twisted as if it had been a bit of wire), and the yarn therein scattered about. Some of it was carried far forward on the line. The shock caused a large noise, and was heard a far way off. With all speed the line was got cleared. The level crossing where this collision occurred is made use of by the numerous workers both at the Haugh Bleachfield and at Haugh Spinning Mill, and also by the inhabitants at Haugh Mill and by the general public, and it is surely necessary that a man be stationed to open and shut the gates for the safety of people going in that direction. A light should also be put up during these dark nights. The sooner this matter is properly seen to the better for the Railway Company and the public.

Eventually a permanent crossing keeper was employed at Haugh Mill Crossing, but this did not occur until the doubling of the line there in 1910.

On 30th May, 1887 a goods train became derailed 1½ miles east of Largo when, according to the *Fifeshire Journal,*

> The train, consisting of a bogie engine, seven wagons (two with cattle) and a brake van, ran for a distance of about 50 yards after leaving the metals, when the engine half-buried itself in the side of the cutting. The wagon next the engine telescoped into the engine as far as the boiler, and it is marvel how the driver and fireman escaped without serious injury. The latter was hurt about the legs. The wagon was smashed to matchwood, while the others were much damaged. A cattle wagon was thrown on its side, but the cattle were got out safely. The road was torn up and broken, but total damage to plant has not yet been ascertained. Passenger traffic was stopped.

On 2nd February, 1888, under the heading of 'Narrow Escape', it was reported that,

> On Friday, shortly after the goods train left Cameron Bridge, the driver observed something wrong, and drew up the engine to see what it was. On examination this proved to be one of the axles of the tender broken off close to the journal. Wishing to clear the road, he drove slowly down to Leven, the wheel keeping on the metals so long as the train went forward. It took about half-an-hour to do the 2 miles between the places. On leaving Leven the driver attempted to back the train into the loop, but here the difficulties commenced, for as soon as the motion was reversed, the wheels dropped off and the tender went down on the metals, resting on the brakes, which had all the time been keeping the wheels in position. An attempt was made to proceed forward again, but in vain. The fish train from the east had by this time come up, and with the assistance of it they managed to get the disabled engine on the line again, and dragged along to the brickwork siding, the fire flying from the rails all the road. The breakdown having been reported to headquarters, a squad with new axle and wheels was sent on from Ladybank, and after five hours work was all put right. There had only been a small bit in the centre of the axle solid. There was no one hurt, and no damage done to the permanent way.

On 28th May of the same year another broken axle caused an accident, this time with more severe results:

> On Tuesday morning, while a cattle train from Anstruther was about a mile from Largo station, one of the axles of the brake van broke while the train was going at a considerable speed. The guard and his assistant leaped from the train, sustaining severe injuries, both being cut about the head. The train was into the station before the driver knew that anything was wrong, as the engine being a heavy one, the dragging of the brake van was not felt. The sleepers for some distance were damaged, and a number of chairs broken. The first passenger train going west was detained three-quarters of an hour in consequence.

A few years later a more alarming accident at Cameron Bridge occurred:

> Last Friday morning the station here was the scene of a startling and rather serious accident, but one, very fortunately, which was unattended by any personal injuries. As is well known, there is a gradual, but very perceptible fall in the gradient between Thornton and Cameron Bridge, and a train running in this direction consequently soon

gathers way. The train which occasioned the smash was the 5.45am fish truck special, loaded up with goods from Thornton to Anstruther, and it seems that soon after leaving the Junction one of the wagon couplings had stopped, and the train, thus separated, had so to run to Cameron Bridge. In the darkness of the early morning, the driver of the train could distinguish nothing clearly, but still had the impression that something had gone wrong. He had not long to wait, however, for in the slowing down to pick up the tablet here 'the breakaway' had, as it is called on the railway, crashed with tremendous force into the front portion and in an instant all was chaos and confusion. The engine fortunately had kept to the metals but the succeeding seven or eight wagons were reduced to splinters and thrown the one over the others. Heavy wagon wheels and axles, brake blocks, broken railway chairs and goods consisting of groceries, boxes of biscuits, bales of cloth, butter, dishes, boots etc. were lying about in a confused and heterogeneous mass.

Pittenweem scorned

In May 1888 the town council of Pittenweem learned that the North British were planning to run a summer express train, the 6.25 pm Thornton Junction to Anstruther which had a direct connection off the 5.00 pm Edinburgh to Aberdeen express, and which was to be booked to call only at Leven and Elie. The town, in the person of its Provost Gilchrist, objected most strongly and caused the clerk to write to John Walker, the General Manager of the North British. He stated that the omission of a stop at Pittenweem was in direct contravention of the agreement entered in to with the promoters of the Leven & East of Fife Railway in 1856 when they withdrew their opposition to the promoters' bill in exchange for a promise that all ordinary trains would call at the station. Walker requested a copy of the agreement and on 1st June replied to the council that the company doubted if the agreement really did oblige them to stop express trains at Pittenweem but, rather than dispute the matter, the train in question would stop at that station from Monday next. The *East of Fife Record* reported that the Provost welcomed the decision with the comment, 'That is very satisfactory' and the July timetable was amended accordingly. This was not, however, the last time that the town of Pittenweem was to be in dispute with the North British.

Forth bridged

The late Victorian agricultural and trade depression in East Fife was both long-lasting and comprehensive and although the coastal burghs attempted to alleviate its effects by developing tourism the prospects of attracting industry to the area were remote. However, undoubtedly the biggest drawback so far as the local railway system was concerned was the need to transfer passengers and their belongings from the train to the railway-owned ferries at Burntisland and again to tranship them at Granton for the short journey to Edinburgh. It was thus a relief when the Forth was finally bridged and the line from Saughton to the south end of the now-famous cantilever bridge and the connecting line from the north end of the bridge to join the existing line at Burntisland were finally opened on 5th March, 1890. The revolution that this was to have on Fife's railway network was keenly anticipated and a few days previously the *Record* reported that, 'An Edinburgh correspondent' had said that,

> We are now within a couple of weeks of the opening of the Burntisland and Inverkeithing Railway to passengers and I am assured on the best authority that it will create a complete revoloution in the way of speedy transit to the East of Fife. At present the journey from Anstruther via the ferry is rarely done in under 3½ hours while the new service, particularly the morning and evening trains, will do the journey from the East Neuk in 1½ hours. This is a consummation devoutly hoped for by those whose lot requires them to travel by that route daily or even weekly.

In the event there were relatively few daily or even weekly commuters from further east than Leven and the journey was not reduced to a figure like the 1½ hours hoped for. At the end of the century seven trains per day were using the line from Thornton to Anstruther and journey times from Edinburgh varied between 1 hour 50 minutes and 2 hours 30 minutes depending on how long passengers had to wait at Thornton – a veritable revolution indeed. In order to make this revolution complete, however, much needed minor improvements had to be made to the Leven and East of Fife line. In order that signalling could be improved a number of passing loops with second platforms would be provided at intermediate stations. Although Leven station had been rebuilt with a new two-storey structure opened on 12th December, 1885 the other stations on the line apart from Anstruther were largely untouched even though the increase in traffic was now making them inconvenient and unworkable. At Leven a new platform, signal box and bridge were erected while at Largo a new station building, platform, passing loop and signal box were opened on 6th July, 1894. At Pittenweem alterations were carried out in March 1898 so that luggage and fish traffic could now be taken over the road bridge to the single platform there rather than by crossing the running lines. At Elie a new loop, up platform with a passenger building and loading bank and signal box was completed on 11th November, 1898 when, after a frantic day, a squad of men from Ladybank replaced the entire signalling and pointwork. At St Monance a new loop, platform with shelter, footbridge and signal box came into use on 21st September, 1900 along with a new loading bay for goods provided at a cost of £2,725. That the improvements were needed was beyond doubt – the *Record* of 5th August, 1898 commented that,

> The train service was completely disorganised the end of the last and the beginning of this week. The morning trains were fairly up to time , but in the afternoons and evenings they ran 2 to 3 hours late. The last train arrived in Anstruther 10 minutes before 12 and in Crail early on Sunday morning. A large number of special trains were run daily, but did little to expedite the exceptionally heavy traffic. Some of these specials were from 3 to 4 hours late in reaching their destination, and there was a good deal of grumbling amongst the summer visitors especially at the long delay.

Other more unpredictable events could also delay trains and in the same issue it was recounted that two shunting engines had been derailed at Elie station on the Saturday evening and that the line was blocked. The train from Thornton was delayed by an hour and a half before a breakdown squad from Thornton had been summoned.

A better ruling spirit

At the end of 1890 a series of strikes by railway servants crippled the Scottish railway companies and the North British was amongst those hit hardest. The causes were multiple and trade depressions causing economies and the keeping down of

Elevation of Waiting-rooms etc to Railway

Leven with the main brick station building   NBR original plans, 1887

Back Elevation of Agent's House & Waiting Sheds

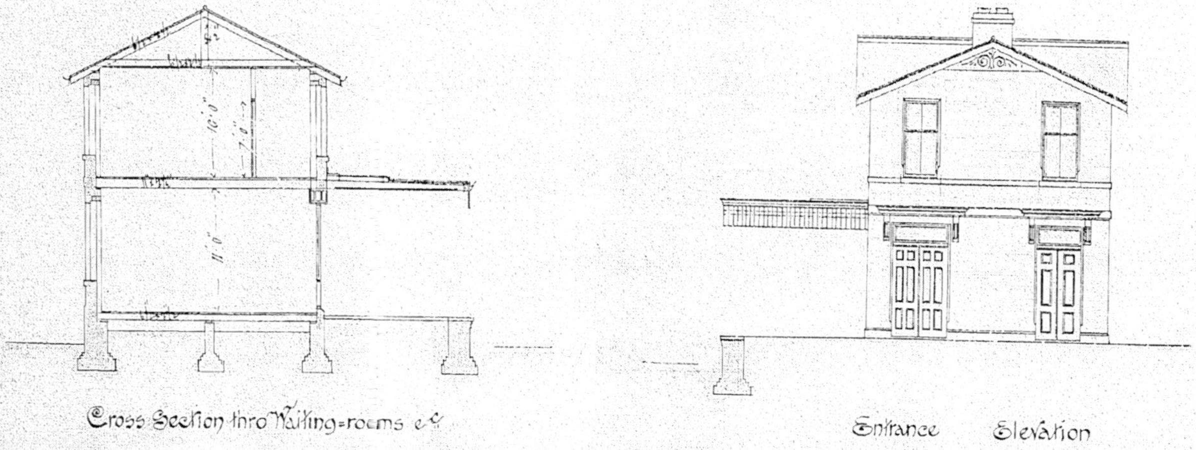

Leven with the main brick station building NBR original plans, 1887

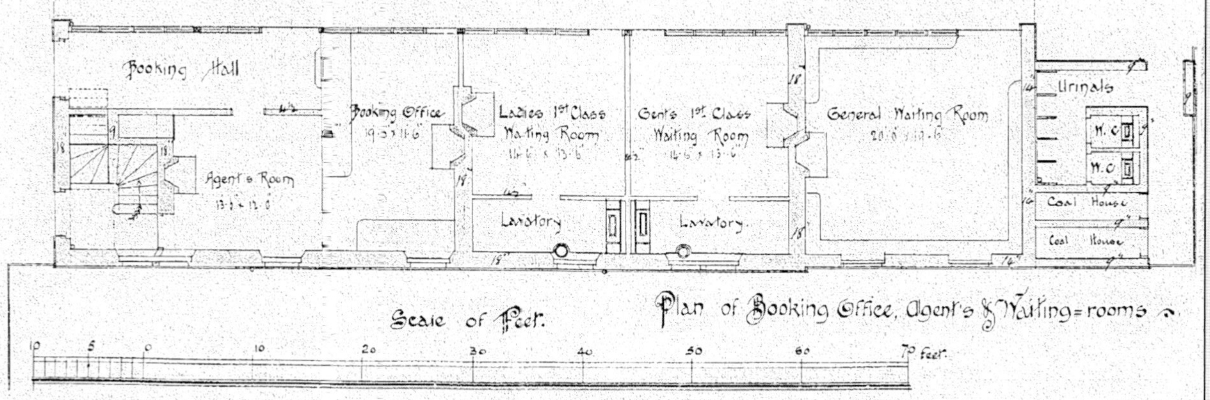

wage increases, grievances over hours worked and the lack of promotion and the growing power of the trade unions led to the North British curtailing services throughout its system. Many members of the public were sympathetic and felt that the railwaymen's concerns were justified but resentment was expressed by traders, particularly where perishable goods were concerned. The strike began two weeks before Christmas and much disruption was caused to travellers and merchants in the East Neuk. By the last week of December a handful of trains were again running and one passenger train had 22 wagons of fish attached to it on its run from Anstruther and St Monans to Glasgow. Gradually traffic picked up again and one evening train from Thornton to Anstruther and Crail conveyed the newspapers and mail, 'the first to have done so in nearly a fortnight'. At Cameron Bridge the *Fife News* of 24th January, 1891 reported that, 'much irregularity prevails in connection with service on the railway here as regards deliveries and despatches of goods, but the passenger traffic is pretty regular. The public works here have had regular supplies of coal to keep up steam, etc. from collieries close at hand'. Other strikes were to follow in subsequent years but the effects were often felt in the long term and it was over a year later before the *Fifeshire Journal* reported that there was once again a growth of the spirit of *esprit de corps* among railwaymen in Fife and it was said that that was definitely a change for the better.

Ordinary Trains, Extraordinary Results

One unintended result of the introduction of the new services introduced with the opening of the Forth Bridge was, however, the extraordinary series of actions in which the North British now found itself embroiled. The cause was that the two nominally 'fast' or 'express' trains which now ran from Edinburgh to Anstruther but omitted to call at Lundin Links station were a direct contravention of the agreements entered into between the Standard Life company and the East of Fife Railway in 1855 and 1858 and reflected in section 36 of the East of Fife Railway Act 1855. The agreement had, it was claimed, placed an obligation on the North British as successors to the East of Fife to run trains that stopped at Lundin Links, the section in question stating that, 'at the said station ordinary trains shall stop for the purpose of traffic'. Standard Life, unable to fully develop the estate as they had intended because of water and drainage problems, sold it in 1872 to Allan Gilmour, a Glasgow ship-owner and on his death in 1884 the Lundin estate passed to his son John Gilmour of Montrave. By now the problems of sewage and a clean water supply had been overcome and the feuing of the estate was progressing satisfactorily. When John Gilmour learnt that the two best trains of the day were omitting the Lundin Links stop he wrote in protest to the North British, pointing out that they were legally obliged to make these trains call there. The failure to do so was harming the development of the village and that, 'visitors and golfers complain that the most convenient trains from and to Edinburgh and Glasgow do not stop at Lundin Links station' and that instead Largo and Leven were preferred by summer visitors 'who require to travel frequently to all their places of business'.

The North British was unconvinced and John Gilmour then raised an action in the Court of Session for declarator that the company were required by the agreement to stop all ordinary trains at Lundin Links. The case was heard on the procedure roll before Lord Stormonth Darling in January 1893 when the company presented a preliminary legal argument to the effect that Gilmour had no title to sue because the original agreement had not been made by him and that in any event it only related to the temporary station. The court rejected these arguments and allowed Gilmour a proof, i.e. a hearing at which he could lead witnesses to prove his contentions. The North British reclaimed, i.e. appealed and on 24th February the First Division of the Inner House of the Court of Session upheld its argument in relation to the temporary station and, reversing Lord Stormonth Darling on this point, dismissed the action.* Undeterred, Gilmour appealed to the House of Lords who in June reversed the judgement of the Inner House and held that the obligation imposed on the railway company to stop all ordinary trains at Lundin Links remained after the station became permanent.† Accordingly Lord Stormonth Darling began to hear evidence in the case in December 1893 where Gilmour sought to show that the trains in question were ordinary trains in the usual sense of the word and that even if not ordinary they did not merit the description of fast or express trains as argued by the North British.

John Gilmour's counsel opened the case with his first witness, Andrew Dougall, the General Manager of the Highland Railway who, at the age of 62, deponed that he was the oldest General Manager in the United Kingdom. Having studied the timetables of the North British and 'speaking as a railwayman', he said that he considered that the disputed trains were, in fact, ordinary trains, even though this was not generally a term used in railway timetables and that the main distinction to be drawn was between an 'ordinary' train and a 'special or excursion' train. Similar evidence was given by James Hurman, the former traffic manager of the Taff Vale Railway and that speed was irrelevant. They were followed by Thomas Robertson, General Manager of the Great Northern Railway of Ireland, who said that 'fast' was not a helpful definition and that, 'I do not think any of the trains on that branch line are worthy of the name of express as we understand it now-a-days' and he attempted to show that the 'fast' trains were, in fact, slower than the ordinary trains if allowance was made for station stops.

A number of local witnesses were then called. George Bruce, a partner in the Leven solicitors firm representing Gilmour, said that he was a regular traveller on the line and that he could detect few differences between the express trains and the others on the line. He stated that he had that very morning travelled by the 7.45 from Anstruther and observed that 'We had to wait outside Cameron Bridge to get water for the engine, although we were not timed to stop at Cameron Bridge. That takes place five times in the week. It does not happen on the Monday, as there seems to be a sufficient supply on that day; water seems to be abundant over the Sunday'. After Bruce, James Gillespie, a St Andrews architect, William Scott Bonthron, an Anstruther fish salesman and ship manager and auctioneer, and William Davidson, the keeper of livery stables at Lundin Mill and Largo, all gave similar evidence to the effect that the ordinary and 'fast' trains were virtually similar in all respects.

The North British relied on John Conacher, its General Manager, who said that the omission of the Lundin Links station stop by certain trains was nothing new and he relied upon the fact that technically the ordinary local trains and the express trains were different, that the relative speed of the two express trains was on average some 32 per cent faster than the ordinary trains and that the express trains kept the same engines throughout from Anstruther to Edinburgh and that they had been put on for the special purpose of accommodating the Anstruther and sea-side traffic. The final witnesses were Henry Lambert, General Manager of the Great Western Railway and Henry Tennant, former General Manager of the North Eastern Railway, both of whom were of the view that an 'ordinary train' was a term understood by

* Both Lord Stormonth Darling's judgement and that of the Inner House are reported in Session Cases at (1893) 20 R 409.

† Reported in Session Cases at (1893) 20 R (HL) 53.

Hurst 0-6-0 No. 190 at Anstruther *circa* 1890 with fireman George Pitbladdo.
NBRSG, Hennigan Collection

NBR No. 375, a sister engine to 190, at Anstruther with driver Jock Brown and fireman Tam Milner.
NBRSG, Hennigan Collection

A Leven train stands in the northern bay at Thornton with a Drummond 4-4-0T, No. 110 *Kinross*, in charge while alongside stands a Holmes 'N' class 4-4-0 (later LNER class 'D25') on the 1.50 pm Edinburgh to Aberdeen express. *NBRSG, Hennigan Collection*

railwaymen (in contrast to the views expressed by Dougall and Robertson) and that the trains in question were obviously not ordinary but 'fast' trains.

Lord Stormonth Darling delivered his judgement in December 1893 and, in granting Gilmour his declarator, said that.

> ... but that this definition might not be appropriate to a main-line upon which true express trains were run but the character of these trains enables me to decide the case in favour of the pursuer, without attempting any precise definition of the word 'ordinary' as used in the Act. I defer to the notion that a railway company can convert a train from an ordinary to an extra-ordinary train by simply putting on discs or running it past a few stations and then calling it 'fast'. If the East of Fife had become a great through route between (let us say) Dundee and Edinburgh with real express trains running over it, the change of circumstances might have been so great as to make it unreasonable to hold that the parties had such trains in contemplation when they framed the clause in question. But the trains in question had no such character. They were essentially local trains, serving not termini but a district, just as the trains on that line have done all along; and if they are local trains of best class, that only makes it the more natural that the landowner should desire to have the benefit of them. He must be held to have stipulated for something which the voluntary action of the company was not likely to give him. When, therefore, he stipulated that all ordinary trains should stop, I think that the agreement as that all trains should stop which did not clearly belong to some other category; and I am of the opinion that the trains in question do not belong to any other category.

The North British, unsatisfied, reclaimed once again and on 17th May, 1894 the First Division issued their judgment but this time upholding the decision of Lord Stormonth Darling, Lord McLaren observing that 'on this little line ... every train which appears on the company's time-tables, and is one that is run daily for the conveyance of passengers, is to be called an ordinary train'.* The company immediately complied with the judgement issuing a notice stating that, 'The public are respectfully informed that, commencing on Friday 18th May, and until further notice, the express trains between Edinburgh and Anstruther will call at Lundin Links ...'

* Both Lord Stormonth Darling and the First Division's judgements are reported at (1894) 20 R 765.

The main up platform at Thornton Junction *circa* 1890 with Drummond 4-4-0T No. 103.
NBRSG, Hennigan Collection

NBR No. 187 at Haughbank Villas, Leven in about 1895. *NBRSG, Hennigan Collection*

Chapter Ten

New Century on the North British: The Leven & East of Fife Section 1900-1922

'Everyone on the East of Fife, whether visitor or resident, has seen and chuckled over a postcard entitled 'The Local Express' in which the short-comings of a certain railway comes in for severe caricature.'

East of Fife Record

A new century

By the turn of the century what was generally seen, at least in retrospect, as a golden age of peace and prosperity had begun. The coastal towns enjoyed ever increasing popularity as resorts for excursionists and holidaymakers alike and, with no serious rivals, goods traffic reflected a trade boom that was felt throughout the area while coal exports at Methil were reaching their peak and the local fisheries were doing extremely well. But things were not always what they seemed and by the middle of the first decade of the new century the North British was financially struggling and social unrest and industrial action were looming on the horizon. Nevertheless, in the second decade the East Fife railways reached the zenith of their popularity and usage and a spate of station improvements, better trains (including the now-fabled 'Fifeshire Coast Express') and rising traffic figures, peaking in the year immediately preceding the Great War all contributed to a feeling that the Thornton to Leuchars line, together with its burgeoning industrial branches and sidings, was probably the linchpin of the local economy and that the railway was unassailable and omnipotent. But change came with a war that destroyed the British economy and at the same time opened up a powerful rival that would eventually not only seriously challenge the railway but eventually defeat it completely. But this was all in the future and in the meantime East Fife had other concerns.

Some East Fife Improvements

In 1900 improvements were made to the station access at Anstruther and a new footbridge and an improved access between the passenger and goods station were provided. At the eastern end of the line, it was becoming increasingly obvious that the single line between Thornton and Anstruther was coming under severe pressure not only from the heavy summer weekend and bank holiday traffic, which resulted in a large number of special and relief trains occupying every available siding and platform, but also by a steady growth of goods traffic in the Leven area which caused severe congestion on the original Leven Railway section. As far back as 1898 the question of doubling the whole of the line at least as far as Anstruther, and with a separate double-track section between St Andrews and Leuchars to cope with the traffic on that section – St Andrews being said at times to be the busiest station on the North British between Dundee and Edinburgh – had been raised. The North British took its time to consider the matter but in the interim several pressing improvements of a more minor nature were carried out. Anstruther Town Council requested the North British to properly light up the station road in their town, the *East Fife Record* commenting that,

Leven harbour in the late Victorian period - contrast this view with the following picture.
P. Westwater Collection

The Bawbee bridge over the River Leven with the Wemyss tramway in the foreground, and the Leven Dock branch, Leven Dock sidings and Methil East signal box in view.
P. Westwater Collection

More light is greatly needed on this dark road. The company have a lamp in the centre of the road but this is seldom or very rarely lighted simply to save a few pence in the year. The company have done well in erecting several large lamps on the loading banks this year to assist porters in their work at nights and especially in the winter herring season.

The company agreed to the council's demand but within days similar complaints were being made about St Monance station when it was said that the gas lights there were turned out, rather than down, when no train was in the station and in consequence it was difficult to walk safely to the station in the dark. In August 1905 the North British announced that it intended to improve services over the coastal line by rebuilding the station at Kilconquhar as a passing place with an island platform, although this work was somewhat delayed. It eventually was only carried out when a loop was installed at a windswept location close to the Dumbarnie links where a lonely signal box named Kilconquhar West was opened on 28th July, 1907.* This left Pittenweem and Lundin Links as the sole stations without passing loops and second platforms, a fact that, in the case of Pittenweem, was much resented locally although the North British investigated the possibilities of such facilities and draw up detailed plans for the same. Eventually the plans were rejected, having been supplanted by the crossing loop at Kilconquhar West, and a further plea for improved passenger facilities including a full-length canopy beneath which travellers could shelter from the rain were also eventually rejected, the company stating that the traffic at the station appeared to be in decline and did not warrant such attention – yet another slight to the burgh.

Other improvements included the 1906 provision of a station master's house at St Monance,† the extension of the Elie down platform in 1908, station improvements at Lundin Links and Largo and the construction of a number of private sidings in the Leven area to serve industrial concerns there. In October 1907 the *East Fife Record*, commenting upon the last of the coast line stations to receive the telephone, stated that,

For some time past, Mr Mitchell Hughes, fishcurer, has been carrying on a correspondence with Mr Deuchars of the North British Railway with the view of having the telephone extended to the railway station at Pittenweem for the benefit of traders and others who have the telephone in their premises. At the end of last week, Mr Hughes received an intimation from Mr Jackson, the General Manager of the Company, stating that he had given instructions for the telegraph superintendent to arrange for Pittenweem station being connected with the telephone exchange. Much satisfaction has been expressed in Pittenweem at this concession.

At Strathairly, a mile to the east of Largo, a siding was built at a cost of £383 by the noted firm of civil engineers, Robert McAlpine & Sons, for their own use. First mentioned in the North British Works Committee minutes of 14th May, 1908, the siding's purpose was to enable McAlpine's to remove sand from behind the foreshore for use in the production of concrete for the new harbour works at Methil.

* The schedule and specification of works for Kilconquhar West signal cabin still exists and a copy can be found at BR/NBR/3/42. The successful contractor was Alex. Fraser of the St Clair Stone Dressing Works, Millie Street, Kirkcaldy, whose offer was accepted on 7th June, 1907 with the exhortation that, 'the signal cabin is required to be erected with the utmost speed'. The crossing loop itself cost the NBR £1,753 3*s*. 11*d*.

† The cost was £346 4*s*. 8*d*. and was completed in the summer of 1907. Other station agent's houses included Elie in 1901 and Largo in 1903.

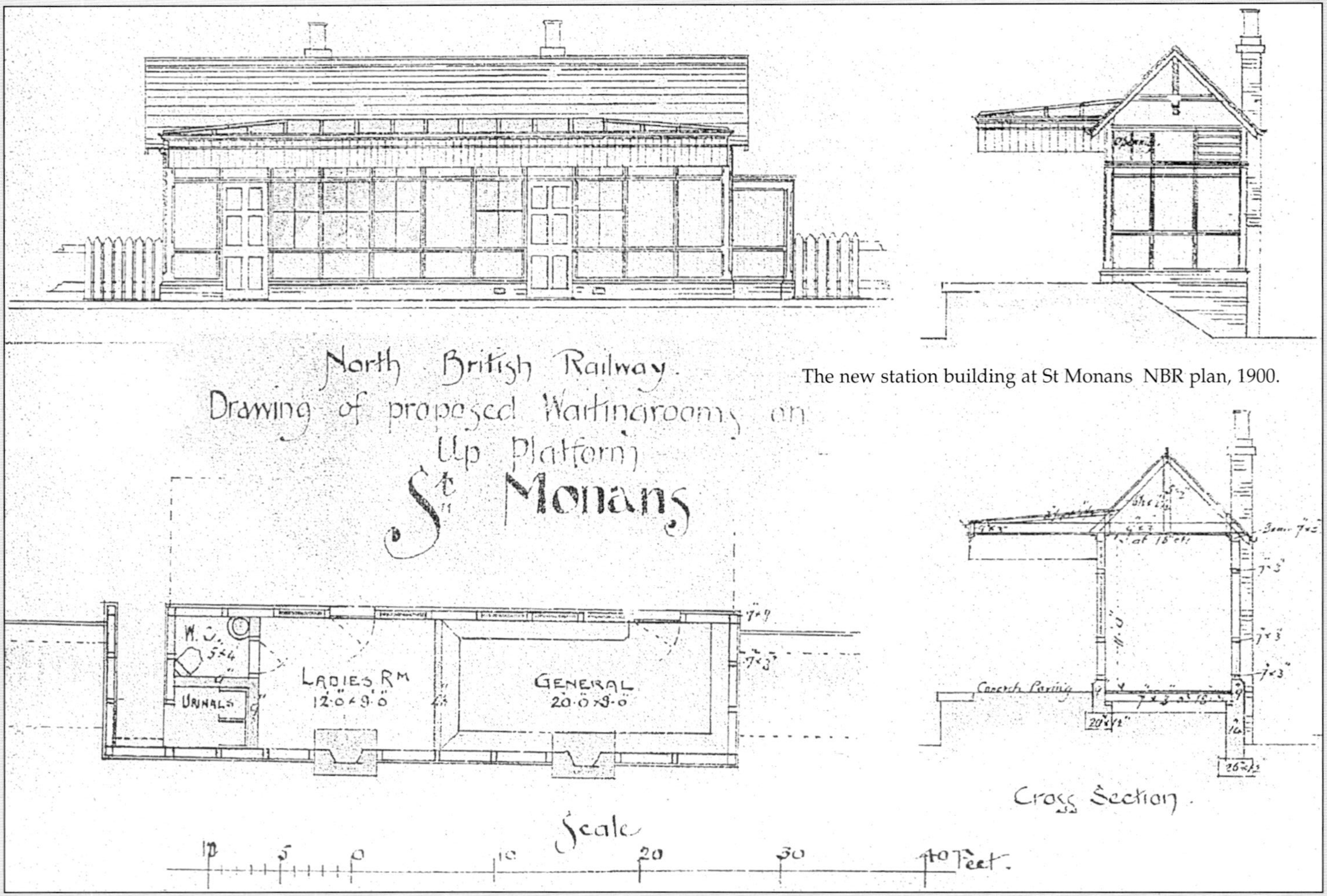

The new station building at St Monans NBR plan, 1900.

Between 1910 and 1912 an amount of sand in excess of 30,000 tons was conveyed by rail between these points,* the siding remained in use for a considerable time thereafter and was used again in 1920 in connection with house-building activities.

Passengers protest

In the early years of the century the local newspapers contained a series of complaints about the East Fife passenger service or, rather, the way in which it was being run. A daily traveller claimed that he regularly had to wait half-an-hour or more at Thornton for connections and not only did the local services come under fire for the poor quality of the rolling stock used but the connecting main-line services appeared to be little better. A prescient letter from 'NBR victim' in connection with the shortcomings of the existing train service, published in the *Record* of 1st September, 1905, reads that, 'I believe that a motor car service all along the Fife coast, say from Kirkcaldy to St Andrews, by way of Sinclairtown, Dysart, Thornton, Leven etc., would be a great success and convenience. We commercials would patronise the same largely as we could be along the coast transacting business instead of wasting time at Thornton and also waiting at every station for the belated trains'.

The most compelling objection, and the only one to be successful, came from the governors of the Waid Academy, a successful local school whose premises abutted the new station.† David Cook, a local solicitor who was also clerk to the governors, wrote to the North British Board:

> A meeting of the governors of the Waid Academy was held yesterday as to consider making a representation to your company against the withdrawal of the train leaving Anstruther at 4 pm. It was then resolved to represent to you that the withdrawal of this train seriously affects the working of the Academy and to ask you to continue this train, if it is at all possible for you to do so. The facts of the matter are as follows. The total number of pupils in attendance at the Waid Academy is 150 and of these 43 are in the habit of using this 4 pm train – the particulars are given in a note appended hereto. The working day is already very short and if another 40 minutes is to be taken off it will destroy the efficiency of the school to a great extent. The 4 pm train has existed for such a number of years that it has been looked upon as a permanency and arrangements have been made for the development of the Waid Academy on the anticipation that this train would not be interfered with. In particular it may be mentioned that the governors are at present engaged in a scheme for the enlargement, to a considerable extent, of the school buildings and this development may be to a great extent be rendered futile if the attendance is diminished through lack of reasonable transport facilities. Another matter which hampers the teaching staff at the Waid Academy is the fact that whereas pupils arrive in the morning from the west at 8.52 they do not arrive from the east until 9.16, the latter train is frequently very late. It is practically 9.30 before the work of the school can be fully started in the morning. If the school is to be closed at 3.15 to suit the altered arrangements of the trains, this means that the working hours of the Academy can only extend to 5¾ hours and an interval for lunch is absolutely necessary. The governors cannot, of course, expect that you provide a service of trains solely for the benefit of the pupils at this academy ... but they trust that you will give this representation due weight ...

* In 1910 the tonnage of sand extracted from here and sent to Methil amounted to almost 20,000; the sand was dark in colour and, not being sea-sand, was suitable for building purposes.
† The school was founded in 1886 as a result of an endowment from the estate of Andrew Waid, a Royal Naval officer; the school still flourishes today as a comprehensive but its more far-flung pupils now have to travel to and from it by bus.

St Monance at the turn of the last century with local humans and a dog and a varied collection of NBR coaches on an up train. *Authors' Collection*

St Monance station staff *circa* 1905. *Authors' Collection*

A schedule showed that 22 pupils attended from the east (14 from Crail, seven from Kingsbarns and one from Boarhills) while from the west the number was nine from Pittenweem, four from St Monance, 12 from Elie, seven from Kilconquhar and 10 from Largo.* The Fife County Education committee backed up this representation and as W.F. Jackson, General Manager of the North British, stated, the Directors 'in view of the evident great inconvenience caused to the public generally by the withdrawal of the [4 pm] train they have decided that, as from 1st proximo, it will be restored'. Once again, the Waid pupils were able to enjoy their lessons without fear of interruption and continued to use the 4 pm train and its successors until the eventual withdrawal of passenger services.

An Electric Rival

Although the private motor car was still in its infancy and the few local attempts to set up motor bus services largely ill-founded, one rival that did affect passenger traffic from Leven was the inauguration of the Wemyss and District Tramways Company service from Leven to the Kirkcaldy Corporation Tramways system at Gallatown on 25th August, 1906. Running mainly across his own lands on a route through Methil, Denbeath, Muiredge, East Wemyss and Coaltown of Weymss, the 7½ -mile tramway had been promoted and built to a gauge of 3 ft 6 in. by Randolph Wemyss, proprietor of the Wemyss Coal Co. Electricity to power the trams was originally generated at the coal company's Denbeath generating station which had been built to serve the Wellesley colliery complex. On 27th September, 1906 the service was extended from Gallatown over the Corporation tracks to a terminus at Whytescauseway in the centre of the town and reasonably close to the railway station at Kirkcaldy. The effect on local passenger traffic was, it was felt, bound to be significant, particularly over the parallel North British branch line from Methil to Wemyss Castle (East Wemyss) and Thornton Junction but also to the passenger traffic between Leven and Kirkcaldy via Thornton. In both these cases a roundabout journey often involving a change at the rather bleak junction station was replaced by a direct and cheaper modern alternative, although potential first class passengers would have been loath to mix with the miners who made up a substantial part of the tramway's clientele – in the event passenger bookings at Leven station appear to have been largely unaffected but traffic on the Methil branch line was hard-hit.

On 7th September, 1906 the *East Fife Record* reported that the Leven cars were so popular at the weekend that many passengers were climbing in through the windows in their eagerness to obtain seats. Three weeks later the same newspaper reported that,

> The parcel department of the [tramways] Company has been a great success. One day this week nearly 100 parcels were delivered in [Leven] town. It is understood that the Company contemplate extending the parcel system to Anstruther, daily deliveries being made by parcel van from the Leven terminus. Meantime the carriers take practically a couple of days to make deliveries in Anstruther and other coast towns from Kirkcaldy, so that they will not be able to compete with the car auxiliary, either as regards dispatch or rates. Shopkeepers no less and carriers and the railway Company have been severely hit since the introduction of the cars over this considerable stretch of the business portion of East Fife.

* However, as Donald Cattanach pointed out in 'Pupil Power', *North British Railway Study Group Journal 90,* it is unclear as to how the St Monance and Kilconquhar pupils returned home on the 4.00 pm train as in 1908 it omitted to call at these stations and it was not until 1910 that this train became an all-stations service.

What was perhaps even more of note were the fact that in 1908 'new motor-car danger signal posts' had been erected at the crossroads at Tollcross, Pittenweem to obviate the chance of an accident there, and that about the same time the road between the bridge and paperworks at Guardbridge had been tarmacadamed. This was to be followed by a stretch of the main road between Lundin Links and Silverburn, the latter being said to be the heaviest trafficked road in the district. And, even though it was only on a small scale, the first motor-buses appeared in the district.

Highdays and Holidays

As the holiday traffic increased steadily there were calls to install yet further passing places or to double the line as far as Anstruther and, separately, to augment local trains by introducing steam railcars to provide additional services. The *East of Fife Record* of 25th May, 1906 stated that,

> The North British Railway Company are at present building some steam cars which are to be tried experimentally on the East of Fife Railway. The great development of the East of Fife holiday resorts has caused the demand for an improved railway service during the summer months, and as the line between Leven St Andrews and Leuchars Junction is a single line it is thought that a car service is likely to meet the demands referred to.

The North British immediately denied this rumour. The following summer the same paper commented that the annual invasion of tourists to Anstruther was underway:

> Every year Anstruther and district seems to becoming more popular with visitors from Glasgow and elsewhere and during the past weekend an unusually large number arrived at Anstruther station. On Friday and especially on Saturday the special and ordinary trains were filled and from Friday to Monday night no less than 1178 tickets had been collected from pasengers on their arrival. Of that no, close on 800 were from Glasgow and the west of Scotland, while the others were from other places in Fife and Stirlingshire. To the 1178 should be added the large numbers of children that had travelled free, and for whom no tickets were required.

Two weeks later the same paper reported that,

> During past fortnight traffic on the railway has been exceptionally heavy. In addition to the large number of ordinary trains, several specials have been run from Glasgow and Edinburgh, with the result that nearly 40 trains passed the station in one day last week. The traffic has been very heavy for a single line and the necessity of arrangements being made by the Company to continue the doubling of the line from Leven to Anstruther at least.

In 1908 there were further complaints about the lack of facilities at the station for holidaymakers and the paper warned ominously that, 'they were waiting for improvements'. The same heavy summer traffic, and the carping about the facilities, was replicated at numerous locations down the line as the East Fife holiday trade reached its zenith.

New lines, new bridges

The increasing coal traffic to Methil, and the continual lobbying of Randolph Wemyss on behalf of the Wemyss estates, led to the North British proposing to build a new and much larger dock at Methil, together with two necessary railway improvements in order that the Leven Dock branch could become the principal artery for traffic from the West Fife coalfields to Methil Docks in place of the steeply graded Buckhaven and Methil branch. These improvements were authorized by the North British Railway Act passed on 2nd August, 1907 (7 Edw.7, cap. Ciii) which provided for the construction of a new railway line some 6 furlongs 8.40 chains in length running parallel to the existing Leven Harbour branch and leaving the Leven and East of Fife line 'at a point on that railway 480 yards or thereabouts measuring in a south-westerly direction from the bridge carrying the public road over the said railway at the Leven goods station and terminating in the parish of Wemyss near to the proposed wet dock'. Section 6 of the Act provided for the acquisition by the company of land to build suitable storage sidings on either side of the existing line at Kirkland and section 37 provided for the widening of the existing line 6 miles and 3.60 chains in length between Thornton Junction and 'a point 220 yards north east of the booking office at Leven station'. Other provisions included the construction of a number of new and replacement bridges between Methil and the junction with the line at Kirkland, the construction of two new sidings at the Durie Foundry and the construction of a new siding to serve the Leven Mills at an annual payment by John Balfour of some £50 per annum. Public roads and the Wemyss and District electric tramway were all to be protected and kept in serviceable condition and some new and diverted public and private roads were to be constructed.

The total cost of the scheme was £500,000 and the contractors for the improved railway facilities were Symington & Sons of Glasgow, while the construction of the new Methil No. 3 Dock was to be undertaken by Sir William McAlpine & Sons. The doubling of the line from Thornton to Leven necessitated the reconstruction of every bridge en route together with the complete rebuilding of Cameron Bridge station and the provision of a second passenger platform at Leven. A new double-track connection was to be installed between Cameron Bridge and the Leven Dock branch and a large marshalling yard covering 15 acres at Kirkland containing some 12 miles of sidings was to be constructed. A new Leven River crossing, upstream from the original single-track bridge built for the Leven Connection Line, was also to be built. New signalling was to be installed and level crossings at Cameron Bridge, Glenlyon Road and Sawmill Road were to be replaced by bridges. Although the scheme was to be undertaken primarily for the rapidly expanding coal traffic the potential for relieving passenger train congestion at holiday periods was also recognized and welcomed as a useful collateral benefit.

Work commenced within a short period of time from the contract having been awarded, the contractor rapidly having a large number of men on the job. According to the *East of Fife Observer*, 'the works were tackled in a thoroughly workmanlike manner' and the only major difficulties encountered were the diversion of the Burnmill lade, the construction of some 15 new bridges for the railway and the fact that mining subsidence was causing problems with the existing stations at Leven and Thornton. At both places the line had to be continually made up since it had sunk some 10 feet or so into the ground and the stability of both buildings was compromised.

A historic collection of private owner wagons at Leven Dock including Fife Coal Co. and Largoward Colliery examples; 1902. *Alan Brotchie Collection*

The reconstruction of the Leven Dock branch at Iron bridge also known as Sawmill bridge in 1909. *Alan Brotchie Collection*

Right along the line

On 1st July, 1908 the *Record* stated that,

> In connection with the doubling of the line, considerable improvements were to be made at Leven station. A platform is to be constructed on the north side, a suite of waiting rooms is to be erected, and a footbridge constructed although a subway would be preferable to a bridge, but the Company are not likely to face the expenditure which a subway would entail. Win last few days the ground for northern platform has been marked off with encroachments on to a grazing field and nursery. Rapid progress is being made.

On 8th September the *Leven Advertiser & Wemyss Gazette* reported that,

> Right along the line from Thornton to Leven there is no mistaking the determination and engineering skill which Messrs Symington & Son are throwing into their contract to double the railway and all that involves. At Leven the skeleton of the new platform is run along its full length and at leisure the staff will get the ground made up for the office etc. The new half bridge, the continuation of the girder bridge at Glen Lyon Road 18 months ago, is ready for the girders and the road is virtually ready for the permanent way between Leven and Cameron Bridge. A concrete wall, 18 feet high, is being formed at the side of the Leven at Cameron Bridge so as to give room for another line of rails.

On 17th March, 1910 the *East Fife Record* reported that,

> Every day, Sundays included, squads of men are engaged pushing forward the doubling operations on the Leven to Thornton line. At Leven work is almost completed, except the levelling of the new platform. At Cameron Bridge, which, owing to the contracted area and the amount requiring to be done, has formed the key to the situation, very little remains to be done. The new offices and platform are finished, and the road deviation almost ready for opening. The deviation will carry the traffic over the lines, and abolish the much talked of level crossing. Many new bridges have been constructed, and old ones widened. The line is linked up to Thornton, but the work at Tullybreck is still in course. It is hoped that the contractor will be all clear of the job in April.

The works at Cameron Bridge also involved the construction of a new girder bridge to carry the diverted Kirkcaldy to Windygates road over the railway and River Leven, the construction of a new island platform at the station, the widening of the bottleneck at the north end of the station by demolishing part of the existing distillery building and the building of a new signal box. The construction of the new bridge allowed the level crossing at the station to be abolished which in the words of the *Record* were often a source of considerable detention while shunting operations were being carried out and 'farmers, proprietors of posting establishments and owners of motor cars who are ever in a hurry are rejoicing that the detention days are over'. A footbridge was provided at the station to keep the right of way open. The demolition of part of the distillery was apparently done 'without disturbing the innumerable casks of "Cameron Bridge" which for many long years have been lying in bond'. Most of the work was carried out on Sundays so as not to disturb the regular traffic over the line. On 4th May of that year it was said that the new buildings on the down platform at Leven were practically finished. The following week it was reported that the final stretch of the new road built as a

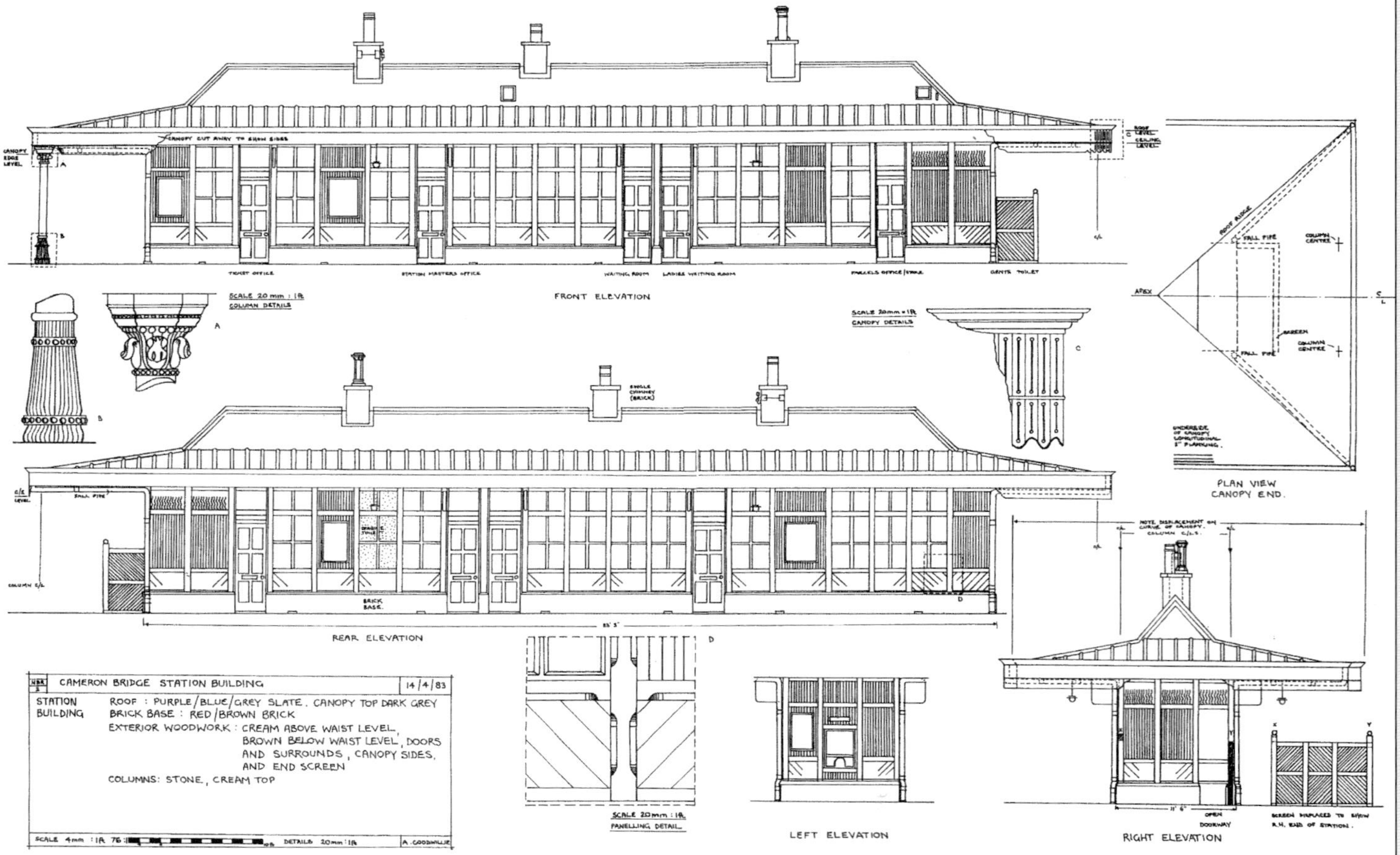

The new (1910) station building at Cameron Bridge.

Drawing by Alan Goodwillie

bypass to the level crossing had been opened to traffic and that, 'it was a great improvement on the old dip and long haul up to Greenfield, but the former road is not to be completely discontinued'.

The new Leven River bridge at Dubbieside was a substantial structure carrying four tracks, two between the central girders and one on either side and the eight main girders were of the steel plate web girder type resting on a central pier and two masonry end abutments spanning 107 ft; the width of the bridge was 60 ft and the steelwork alone weighed 200 tons. The bridge carrying the public road and tramway consisted of 11 main girders resting on two end abutments and two cross girders supported by columns resting on concrete piers. Two principal girders ran along each side of the bridge, the span between the abutments was 62 ft and the width of the roadway was 36 ft. The bridge over the mill lade at the sawmill had a clear span of 10 ft, the abutments were of concrete and the girders were rolled steel joists and the deck was made of creosoted planking. The Sawmill bridge, carrying the new public road over the river and new line was of the bowspring type where it spanned the river (span 120 ft) and plate girder type where it spanned the railway (50 ft); the width of the road was 18 ft. The bridge carrying the new Kirkland walk over the railway was of plate girder construction spanning 79 ft between the abutments on a skew and the width of the roadway was 12 ft. The river itself was now restrained by retaining walls parallel to the new line.

The new works were completed by the summer of 1910 and tested by the running of a heavy ballast train over the line on Sunday 18th June, the official opening taking place on the following day, although the official Board of Trade inspection, carried out by Major Pringle, did not take place until Sunday 23rd July; he appears to have been entirely satisfied in all respects. In a report in the *Leven Advertiser and Wemyss Gazette* it was said that of the Kirkland Yard there were 12 miles of sidings capable of storing 30,000 tons of coal and that most of the collieries on the North British system fed into its hoists. In the years before World War I private owner wagons from almost every Fife coalowner could be seen in the yard.

Muiredge severed

In connection with the development of the Wemyss Coal Company's pits and the growth in trade from the Bowman & Co. pits in the Leven and Methil areas a new single track private mineral railway was built and opened in December 1900.* Prior to the opening of the Wemyss Private Railway the good-only Muiredge branch had enjoyed a good service with four trains per day running as follows:

		am	*pm*	*pm*	*pm*
Thornton Jn	*d.*	9.05	12.00	2.35	–
Haugh Mill Sdg		9.20	–	–	–
Cameron Bridge	*a.*	9.25	12.15	2.50	–
	d.	10.00	12.25	3.10	4.30
Pirnie Colliery		10.15	12.40	3.25	4.45
Buckhaven Old	*a.*	10.20	12.45	3.30	4.50

		am	*pm*	*pm*	*pm*
Buckhaven Old	*d.*	10.25	12.50	3.35	4.55
Pirnie Colliery		10.40	1.05	3.50	5.10
Cameron Bridge	*a.*	10.50	1.15	4.00	5.20
	d.	11.05	1.50	–	6.20
Haugh Mill Sdg		–	–	–	–
Thornton Jn	*a.*	11.20	2.05	–	6.35

The Pirnie and Leven pits were served by the Fife Coal Company eastwards line from the Muiredge branch and Bowmans Isabella pit from a westwards branch but the building of the Wemyss line severed the Muiredge branch at The Plunks, about a mile south of Cameron Bridge, so that it was now operated as two separate lines

* The full history of this line is covered in Alan Brotchie's *The Wemyss Private Railway* (Oakwood Press, 1998).

NBR Holmes 'M' class 4-4-0 No. 734 at Leven *circa* 1910; this locomotive survived until May 1939 having been transferred by the LNER to the former Great North of Scotland Railway lines in 1926. *NBRSG, Hennigan Collection*

'Eve's fairest daughters' at Elie, in the summer of 1910. *Authors' Collection*

namely the northern section from Cameron Bridge to Plunks with a junction with the Wemyss line and a southern section from Plunks to Buckhaven; there was no direct connection between the two junctions at Plunks with the northern and southern sections and direct running between Cameron Bridge and Buckhaven was no longer possible. Although a connection had been made between Buckhaven and the Wemyss and Buckhaven branch of the NBR in 1881, traffic on the two remnants of the Muiredge branch was diminished owing to the Wemyss line siphoning off the traffic from the mines. Buckhaven (Old) goods depot was closed and subsequently the Wemyss Coal Co. had the sole use of the northern part of the Muiredge branch from 1917 onwards as there was now no other traffic on that part of the line.

Anstruther Harbour: A Second Attempt

The winter herring trade showed few signs of abatement and indeed in February 1902 it was reported that, with four successive days of good catches, the railway goods yard at Anstruther was almost totally overwhelmed and that at one time there were a total of 60 carts that had made their way up from the harbour and were waiting to unload their contents in to railway vans. This congestion, to say nothing of the added delays, expense and inconvenience, led to calls for the revival of the suggestion of half-a-century earlier, that of the construction of a branch line to give direct access to the harbour. In 1911 such a plan was advanced but with one essential difference to the previous scheme which had envisaged a level crossing or reduced clearance bridge over the main road between the station and harbour and the running over a partially culverted Dreel Burn. The proposal was now for a longer branch line leading off the main line at Milton Muir between Pittenweem and Anstruther, tunnelling under the high road between these two towns and emerging to cross the golf course, reaching the coast in the vicinity of the present club house. The line was then to pass behind Shore Road and, passing the old Wester Anstruther pier, would then pass in front of the picturesque houses of Castle Street and in front of the line at this point there was to be an extensive land reclamation scheme to accommodate several sidings upon which fish wagons would be stored. The branch would then cross the Dreel Burn on a bridge before reaching the Union Harbour at Anstruther; an extension parallel to Shore Street and leading to the lifeboat station was also proposed. The line was never built for purely financial reasons since it would have been an expensive solution to a recurring but temporary problem; environmental and aesthetic considerations do not seem to have featured to the same extent which, given the contemporary examples of Leven and Methil was, perhaps, not surprising.

The 'Fifeshire Coast Express'

In the summer of 1910 the only named train to operate over the East Fife line was inaugurated when the 'Fifeshire Coast Express' began to run as a Fridays-only 4.20 pm Glasgow Queen Street to Crail service which ran fast to Leven, 66½ miles from Queen Street via the Winchburgh and Dalmeny line and then called at all stations to Crail excepting Kilconquhar and St Monance. The return working left early on the Monday morning. In the following year the service became a daily one and continued to run every season until the outbreak of the war. The Fifeshire Coast

Kilconquhar with passengers, a bicycle and some interesting enamel advertisements, *circa* 1910.
NBRSG, Hennigan Collection

No. 769 at Leven with the 'Fife Coast Express' in 1912; this Holmes 'N' class 4-4-0 survived until the last month of the LNER's existence, December 1947. Driver David Scott, fireman Jimmy Allan, fireman Jimmy Lawson (a friend of the photographer), signalman Clark and guard Bob Harper can all be seen.
NBRSG, Hennigan Collection

Express was joined by a southern counterpart, the 'Lothian Coast Express' which ran from Glasgow and Edinburgh to Gullane, North Berwick and Dunbar. The 'Fifeshire' was, in 1911, joined by a special golfer's train which left Edinburgh on Saturday afternoons, calling only at Leven, Anstruther and Crail, arriving at 3.30 pm and departing again from Crail at 7.45 pm, arriving back in Edinburgh just after 10 o'clock. Providing that the weather was good and the service ran on time, golfers could enjoy a good game and take advantage of the longer northern evenings before returning to the capital for late evening. Other through trains ran between Crail and Glasgow and Edinburgh. The North British, spurred on by the increased traffic and the two railway-owned luxury hotels to be built (one by the Glasgow & South Western Railway at Turnberry and the other by the Caledonian Railway at Gleneagles) even contemplated a Fife golfing hotel between Largo and Kilconquhar but presumably the windswept Dumbarnie links were not so appealing to the Board and the plans were shelved.

Industrial Unrest

The early years of the 20th century saw great industrial unrest and this affected East Fife with its coal mines and associated works. A threatened railway strike in August 1911 was, according to the *East of Fife Record*,

> … the sole topic of conversation in the East of Fife during the weekend. There was a run on the evening newspapers on Saturday night to hear the latest details ... and great relief was felt when it was bruited abroad that the strike in the meantime had been averted. While sympathy was expressed for the men in the several grades of the service for the long hours and miserable pay, strong condemnation was passed on the riots and disorder in the different parts of England which had, unfortunately led to bloodshed. The wages now and such questions are at the bottom of the widespread unrest, and something will have to be done to improve the conditions in these respects.

In 1912 there was a prolonged coal strike which affected East Fife badly. The strike, which was for a minimum wage for miners, was resisted by the Scottish coal owners who said that it would result in an annual loss to them of between £4 million and £5 million, resulted in the temporary closure of all local pits including Largoward. Services over the coast line were affected with the withdrawal of six trains and 'prospective passengers will do well to consult the railway officials, as if the strike is not settled promptly, further curtailment of the service may be expected'. Easter holiday arrangements were adversely affected and the *Record* of 4th April commented that,

> Coming after the dreary winter months, Easter is the most welcome of the year, but on most lines the holiday period has either been abandoned, or much reconstructed and a very large number of people have been unable to get away to their favourite resorts. There are, of course, alternatives and compensations, and those who have been compelled to spend their holidays at home – walking, cycling, gardening, or on other outdoor recreations – will probably benefit as much in health, and at less expense, than if they have gone away. Still, the coal strike has deprived very many people of their Easter holidays of their choice, and the hotels, boarding houses, tradesmen and those who let apartments, will suffer accordingly.

A 1920 view of the beach looking west at Lundin Links with the footbridge over the line visible on the right. *P. Westwater Collection*

Illustration of St Monans from the NBR tourist guide of 1914; the East Neuk harbours are still popular with artists a hundred years later.

NORTH BRITISH RAILWAY.

FAVOURITE RESORTS

IN

FIFESHIRE.

Increased and improved MORNING TRAIN SERVICE from, and AFTERNOON TRAIN SERVICE to, the Favourite Resorts in Fifeshire.

		a.m.	a.m.	a.m.	a.m.	a.m.		a.m.	a.m.	a.m.	a.m.	
St Andrews	leave	...	6 10	6 10	7 10	...	...	8 10	9 0	...	9 55	...
Crail	„	5 49	5 49	......	......	7 30	......	......	......	9 7	......	......
Anstruther	„	6 1	6 1	...	...	7 40	...	...	...	9 16	...	...
Elie	„	6 19	6 55	6 55	......	7 50	......	......	......	9 30	......	......
Largo	„	6 33	7 6	7 6	...	8 1	...	...	...	9 43	...	...
Lundin Links	„	6 36	6 36	......	......	8 4	......	......	......	9 46	......	......
Leven	„	6 44	7 12	7 12	...	8 10	...	...	...	9 52	...	...
Burntisland	„	7 36	7 57	8 15	......	......	......	......	......	10 43	......	......
Aberdour	„	7 42	8 4	8 23	...	...	...	...	..	10 50	...	...
Edinburgh (Waverley) ...	arrive	8 34	...	9 10	9 24	9 24	...	9 58	11 29	11 29	12 p 2	...
Glasgow (Queen St. High Level)	„	......	9 30	......	......	10 43	......	10 43	......	12p50	12 50	......

		p.m.	p.m.	p.m.	p.m.	p.m.	p.m.	p.m.	p.m.	p.m.	Wed. only.	Sat. only.
Glasgow (Queen St. High Level)	leave	...	...	4 7	4 7	4 7	5 35	5 35	...	8 15		
Edinburgh (Waverley) ...	„	3 55	4 25	......	4 50	4 55	6 40	......	7 12	......	9p15	10p30
Aberdour	arrive	4 28	...	...	...	5 40	...	...	7 55	...	...	11 31
Burntisland	„	4 36	......	......	5 30	5 48	......	6·52	8 5	9 32	9 48	11 41
Leven	„	...	...	...	6 1	...	...	9 9	9 9	...	...	...
Lundin Links	„	......	......	......	6 6	......	......	9 14	9 14	......	......	......
Largo	„	...	...	...	6 9	...	...	9 17	9 17	...	...	...
Elie	„	......	......	......	6 20	......	......	9 34	9 34	......	......	......
Anstruther	„	...	...	...	6 35	...	...	9 50	9 50	...	...	...
Crail	„	......	......	......	6 49	......	......	10 † 3	10 † 3	......	......	......
St Andrews	„	...	6 16	6 30	...	...	8 20	...	10 0	...	...	...

† Saturdays only.

Fortnightly and Monthly Season Tickets at Moderate Rates, and Cheap Week-end Tickets issued from Edinburgh (Waverley) and Glasgow (Queen Street) to—

Anstruther, Aberdour, Burntisland, Crail, Elie, Largo, Leven, St Andrews, &c.

Eventually the coal strike was settled, but further industrial unrest was expected. Other day-to-day minor occurrences unconnected with the strike included break-ins at stations, often marked by the low value of articles stolen compared with the damage done by the burglars. On one Saturday night in 1909 Largo station was robbed of the total sum of fourpence while Lundin Links' losses amounted to two tins of tobacco stolen from a parcel.

The Lights Go Out

On 3rd August, 1914 Great Britain, ostensibly in defence of the neutrality of the Belgian nation, declared war on Germany and the resulting four-year long war had a profound effect on the railways of the country. The first and immediate effect was the taking under government control of the national railway system including that of the North British and the vesting of this control in the committee of railway managers known as the Railway Executive Committee. The second, and more insidious effect, was the gradual draining away of manpower, money and other resources and it was this effect which was most widely felt in the East Fife area. Although railwaymen were exempt from conscription, being in a 'reserved' occupation, many joined the forces as soon as they could and accordingly the resulting manpower shortage was overcome by the employment of notionally retired railwaymen and by the widespread use of women in positions which they had not normally previously occupied. Locally it was noted that the holiday trade had fallen off and comments were made in the press that there was a marked absence of holidaymakers all along the coast and that, especially in Elie, it was the absence of young men that was particularly striking. As the war progressed, however, tourist traffic made a partial recovery and any losses were off-set by a modest amount of additional military traffic seen at Elie, where a military convalescent home (auxiliary hospital) was established in the latter days of the war and at Largo, where the former Cardy net factory was used as a billet for the Highland Cyclist Batallion. Rationing and other restrictions gradually came into effect. Since much of the East Fife coastal line lay within sight of the Forth estuary, the amount of light allowed to be displayed from railway carriages after dark was regulated by the compulsory use of drawn blinds due to the risk of enemy airships and vessels, including submarines, obtaining a fix on bearings – a very real threat given that Leith was subjected to Zeppelin bombardment during the war.

Goods traffic was also affected by the war especially as some of the local manufacturing industries were involved in emergency production work such as work on shell cases and parts for artillery pieces which generated additional traffic at Guardbridge and, in the Leven area, where Balfour's Durie Foundry, the National Steel Foundry and the Boase Spinning Mills were all kept busy. Food production was increased to offset the blockade of British shipping by the German High Fleet but the level of fishing locally was severely restricted due to the apprehended risks from mines and U-boats. In a direct consequence of this, the herring export traffic all but disappeared; one unintended but no doubt beneficial effect of the closure of the North Sea fishing grounds was that they were given a chance to naturally restock after having suffered from over-fishing in the immediate pre-war years. Similarly, seasale coal exports from Methil Docks dwindled from record levels to almost nothing because the traditional markets in Germany and the Baltic were either lost to the Central Powers or, if those markets were in neutral countries, because they were well aware of the risks of the German U-boat campaign to their shipping.

Total War

Some of the flavour of the war locally can be gained from the pages of the *East Fife Record* which comments on the downturn in visitors at Anstruther and Cellardyke and other resorts, particularly during the Glasgow and Edinburgh holiday weekends. The *Record* of 14th January, 1915 reported that on the previous Monday afternoon, an armoured train passed over the East of Fife line, travelling from Thornton to Leuchars, the train consisting of several wagons with a locomotive in the centre.* Then from April 1915 onwards another armoured train, based in Edinburgh, appeared on the coast line and continued its patrols up and down the lines between Rosyth and Thurso, including the East Fife coastal line, for the remainder of the war.† Other reports note that the extensive repairs, including replacement of some of the girders, was undertaken at the two Elie bridges in 1915, that in July 1916, as the result of a severe rainstorm, 39 to 40 yards of the embankment between Ardross and Newark Farm, just west of Elie, collapsed leaving the rails unsupported. The Balcomie Golf Club was in severe financial difficulties in the same year and the temporary closure of the Links Hotel due to the fact the German proprietor had been interned, that local postal services were partially curtailed and that George Morris, the North British carter at Pittenweem for half a century, was relinquishing his post 'owing to his other work and his son having answered his country's call, which left him short-handed' were also noted. In 1916 serious flood damage to the coastal line occurred after torrential rainfall in July, leaving part of the track between Elie and St Monance hanging in mid-air. Large numbers of people from as far away as Anstruther walked to the scene at Ardross to survey the damage for themselves; services were resumed within several days with the help of a large workforce from Ladybank and Leven. One new source of traffic locally was sphagnum moss for use in the manufacture of wound dressings and bags of this, collected and cleaned by volunteers, were regularly dispatched by rail from Anstruther to the offices of the Sphagnum Moss Committee in Edinburgh. Two months previously the paper reported that the southern embankment at Anstruther station had been dug up and planted with potatoes and cabbages by local railwaymen and it commented that this was 'a good way to practice the national dictum to economise and make the best of things'.

Another way to practice this national dictum was a curtailment in passenger train services over the coastal line, put into effect with the publication of the March 1916 timetable. This principally affected early morning and evening services with the cancellation of the first train of the day from Dundee to Thornton and the last eastbound train of the day plus the mid-afternoon train to Dundee, used by the Waid Academy pupils to travel to Crail and beyond. After some lobbying by the inhabitants of Crail the servce was restored in June and it was said that the avoidance of '... the pleasure [*sic*] of a four-mile tramp' was 'greatly appreciated by some of the Waid Academy pupils, especially when the weather is in one of its uncongenial moods, as it is so often in these parts'.

Worse was to come. In an effort to sustain wartime production and discourage unnecessary passenger traffic the Whitsuntide holiday of 1916 was cancelled by the government so that it would not detract from the great offensive on the Western

* It is not clear what the make-up of this train would have been as the only East Coast armed train in service at that time appears to have been the recently-converted 'War Office Armoured Train No. 1' stationed at North Walsham, Norfolk.

† Armoured Train No. 2, converted at the Crewe Works of the London & North Western Railway and subsequently named 'Alice' was drawn by a Great Northern 'N1' class 0-6-2T No. 1590. For full details of this train see Balfour, *The Armoured Train*, 1981, pp. 43-45.

Front and this was followed by a cancellation of the August bank holiday. The *Record* commented that, 'the time for holidays will come later' but that 'Crail is full of expectation that, notwithstanding the embargo as to holidays, August will prove to be a record month for visitors'. It was later recorded that all of the coast towns appeared to have enjoyed a late surge in numbers of visitors arriving by train despite the absence of any official holiday. But the autumn holiday was disappointing 'in striking contrast to what it used to be on such occasions previous to the war'.

On 1st January, 1917 the most stringent measures yet were put into effect by the Railway Executive Committee. Passenger fares throughout Britain were raised by a uniform 50 per cent in order to combat galloping inflation with striking downturns in the number of tickets issued at local stations during that year especially as tourist and other discounted fares had already been abolished in 1915. In order to prepare for a massive push on the Western Front and to release men, coal and locomotives for France, other measures were also put into effect and these included the closure for the duration, under the auspices of the Board of Trade, of some 400 stations throughout the country, including some 51 on the North British system. Five Fife closures were announced in the national press on 22nd December, 1916 and these included, on the coastal line, Mount Melville, Boarhills and, somewhat surprisingly, Pittenweem; the other Fife stations were Halbeath and Sinclairtown. Although Mount Melville and Boarhills might have been regarded as quiet wayside halts, Pittenweem was quite different for in 1916 it had handled a respectable 17,000 passengers, 8,500 tons of goods and 2,100 head of livestock. The North British Directors had exercised their judgement and the inhabitants of Pittenweem felt that they had done so in error. At a town council meeting held the same night as the closure announcement was made it was recorded that,

> Pittenweem Parish has a population of 1,912 (within the Burgh – 1,888) and the station serves a large country district including Carnbee and Arncroach. There is a large business done at the station. The Gas Company alone imports about 1,000 tons of coal per annum and despatch coke used in munitions factories. Last month it was calculated that 350-400 tons were received at the station and from 80-100 forwarded, even in these days of restricted trade. There is at all times a large business in potato and other farm produce and even a very considerable necessary passenger traffic even allowing for the embargo on all unnecessary travelling. There are also barrel manufactories which despatch large quantities of barrels and receive equivalent quantities of rough wood. Pittenweem has always a very large export of fish and at present the port is the only fishing centre on the coast. No station between St Andrews and Thornton except Elie and Leven has so large an amount of trade and yet in the section of line between Kingsbarns and Thornton – about 28 miles – Pittenweem is the only station which is ordered to be closed, whilst the unimportant stations of Kilconquhar and Lundin Links, though Elie and Largo are respectively adjacent, are being left open. The trade at Pittenweem will have to be handled at Anstruther which will tend to congest that station and hamper traffic seriously. More horses and men will be required for transit of goods by road to and from Anstruther and, as labour is scarce and the military claiming every available man, so difficult to see where additional labour will be found, and in any case a much greater expense will be incurred than if Pittenweem station was retained. A serious handicap will also be placed on farmers with their depleted staffs in getting produce despatched. Closing will be a serious blow to the Burgh and will, it is feared, ruin the town in all its trade interests.

What now followed was a concerted campaign to persuade the North British to recognize its 'mistake' and to have the station re-opened. Early on Herbert Asquith, the Liberal Member of Parliament for East Fife since 1886 and Prime Minister until his resignation in 1916, promised his help and, asking for all the relevant details to be sent to him, said that he would contact the Railway Department of the Board of Trade. Others promised their help too and the local member for the St Andrews Burghs, Colonel Anstruther-Grey and senior politicians such as Bonar Law and even David Lloyd George himself were enlisted to argue the case. All this was in vain and even though it was said at a public meeting at the end of February 1917 that a railway official who had visited the town was astonished to see so many houses and to find out how much trade was carried on there he was also credited with the remark, 'We have closed the station; we will keep it closed'.

And keep it closed they did with the only concession being that, with effect from 21st March, 1917 the station would be reopened on alternate days of the week as a goods siding for full wagon loads at 'station to station' rates, inwards and outwards, on the condition that the consignors and consignees undertake the loading and unloading, covering and uncovering of the traffic. Passengers for Pittenweem were expected to walk the mile or so from the town to Anstruther or St Monance stations unless they could rely on the kindness of others to give them a lift on farm carts or the still rarely seen motor cars of the wealthy.* The town council would not accept defeat and they even went as far as seeking the opinion of counsel as to whether the North British could be challenged in relation to an agreement made by the Burgh with the Leven and East of Fife Railways as far back as April 1861 in relation to a promise by those companies to stop all ordinary trains at Pittenweem (in an echo of the earlier litigation relating to Lundin Links station). Counsel wisely informed them that the agreement might well be binding but that the closure of the station had been authorized under the emergency legislation passed by the government and that accordingly the actings of the North British in that regard would not be susceptible to judicial review. The Burgh, undaunted, kept up its pressure on the railway company but, alas, to no avail.

For the railway the war was not, however, all doom and gloom as additional crops were grown in the area as the German U-boat blockade intensified; a good example was the flax grown at Ardross, Balcormo and Ovenstone and transported by rail from Pittenweem to the flax mill at Silverburn. There were a number of temporary military installations constructed along the route of the coastal line and these generated a certain amount of additional traffic. The first of these was an army camp and coastal gun battery at Kincraig Point, which lay between Largo and Elie. The nearest station was Kilconquhar and stores and ammunition for the battery were taken by horse and cart or motor lorry up to the camp as well as troops arriving at the station and bound for the camp. In addition there was a military shooting and rifle range near to Kilconquhar West signal box although whether this generated much additional traffic is not known. The major works in the district were, however, situated further north in the Crail and Leuchars districts where, in the last year of the war, two airfields were constructed to house that new phenomena, the flying machine.

At Crail the airfield was constructed on open land between Crail and Fife Ness and the contractor used was the large civil engineering firm of John Laing & Sons, who employed some 300 labourers and craftsmen on the construction works. A special workmen's train was run for the conveyance of Laing's staff during the construction period, leaving Thornton Junction at 5.15 am and calling at all stations

* A local garage proprietor was fined 10s. at Cupar Sheriff Court in November 1917 for permitting a motor car to used as an unlicensed taxi at the instigation of travellers unable to use the station and wishing to travel to Anstruther or St Monans. The closure of the station was doubly galling given that the *Coast Burghs Observer* of 16th July, 1917 reported of Anstruther that, 'with the advent of the Glasgow Fair holidays, there has been a record influx of visitors to the town'.

with the exception of the closed Pittenweem to Crail, where it arrived at 6.20. The return journey left Crail at 6.30 pm, again calling to set down at all stations excepting Pittenweem and arriving back at Thornton at 7.33 pm. This additional service seems to have been well-used while it lasted and in particular Anstruther was a favoured town for the workers to reside in, giving a lively air to the town which, given the paucity of visitors, was greatly appreciated.*

Peace and boom

In the immediate aftermath of war the railways of East Fife attempted to return to normal. As from 1st February, 1919 the stations at Pittenweem, Mount Melville and Boarhills were re-opened and although the additional wartime traffic disappeared passengers returned in great numbers. In the first two or three years of peace the coastal line stations all enjoyed record numbers of passengers as holidaymakers returned with a vengeance. In March 1919 the North British announced that for the summer season (1st June to 30th September) the 'Fifeshire Coast Express', suspended for the war, would be reinstated and would consist of two separate trains, namely a 7.15 am Crail to Glasgow service, calling at Anstruther, Pittenweem, Elie, Largo, Lundin Links and Leven only and arriving at Queen Street at 9.40 am and another train bound for Edinburgh which left Crail 10 minutes later and called at the same stations with an arrival at Waverley at 9.14 am. The return workings left Glasgow at 4.05 pm arriving at Crail at 6.27 and from Edinburgh at 4.50 pm arriving at 6.38 pm with the same intermediate stops as the outward journeys. These trains operated on Mondays to Fridays only but there was an additional Saturday working from Edinburgh to Crail which left at 1.06 pm in the path of the previous golfers' train. The advertisement for the service contained an 'Important Note', namely that 'A Breakfast Car will be provided on Train to Glasgow in the morning, and a Tea Car on the Train from Glasgow in the evening. (This train runs daily except Saturdays)'. As to this facility, the *East Fife Observer* proudly commented that, 'A dining car is attached to each train, which is an innovation on the East of Fife line'. The purpose of the Expresses was clear – the Scottish habit of taking a house for a month in the summer was still current and it was important for businessmen, lawyers and other heads of the family to be able to visit their places of work in Glasgow and Edinburgh when they needed to, hence the desire for fast and comfortable services such as these. During the day the Glasgow portion was held at Cadder Yard and the Edinburgh portion at Craigentinny sidings. For the 1920 season the Glasgow expresses were extended back to St Andrews which they left at 6.50 am and returned from Glasgow at 4.10 pm, arriving at St Andrews at 6.55; they ran 'fast' between Crail and St Andrews stations; the restaurant cars were, however, withdrawn as from 13th August, 1920.

Other passenger improvements were in the air. The timetable was restored to its pre-war state although the East Fife services had hardly been the jewel in the crown of the North British – one curious reinstatement was the 7.30 pm Edinburgh to Anstruther service which, apparently, was well-known locally under the title of the 'Boozers' Train'. Minor works were carried out to the station buildings at Elie and new bookstalls were erected at Anstruther and Elie, the old bookstall at the latter station being converted into a summer house at a nearby tea-garden. On the goods front traffic rapidly returned to pre-war levels and in the short-lived economic boom that followed on from the war local goods yards and sidings were all busy with, once-again, record amounts of merchandise, coal, minerals and livestock being carried between about 1919 and 1922.

* For fuller details of the Crail airfield and its effect upon the railway in both World War I & II, see *The Anstruther & St Andrews Railway* and in respect of Leuchars see *The St Andrews Railway.*

Winds of Change

All, however, was not well. During the war the government had paid the railway companies a rental equivalent to the net revenue earned by the companies in the year 1913 although rampant inflation throughout this period had effectively halved the value of money. Wages had been greatly increased and the government had promised the railway unions an eight-hour day as soon as the war was over. As a result of the breakdown in negotiations between the government, company Directors and the railway unions, a national railway strike commenced at midnight on 26th/27th September 1919. The *Leven Advertiser* of 2nd October reported that,

> Local railwaymen in particular, and the public in general, were amazed on Friday afternoon, when they got to know a railway strike would start at midnight. At first, indeed, the whole affair was looked upon as a species of practical joke, and the many holidaymakers who arrived in the district during the afternoon and evening were quite certain that everything would be as usual before many hours had passed. Disillusion came on Saturday: the holidaymakers found themselves cut off from home and railway workers discovered themselves on strike and wondering, like Little Peterkin, what all the trouble was about. Saturday passed very quietly, but several little incidents all ending against the strikers, took place on Monday. It became known that the Coast Express, which had arrived on Friday evening, would run to the city [Edinburgh] on Monday morning and anticipating of travelling on it, over 200 prospective passengers assembled at Leven station. Starting from Anstruther, the train reached Lundin Links all right, but there a picket endeavoured to stop further progress. The engine was uncoupled and with jocular unconcern the driver got down from his cab. While he was exchanging pleasantries with the picket and so keeping their attention, the fireman quietly coupled up and before the strikers could grasp that they had been sold, he had started the engine and the driver had swung himself aboard and the train was proceeding on its journey. Another strong picket at Leven and they were all ready for a determined effort to stop the train when the driver, obeying signals, put on speed. Leven passengers got off opposite the Kirkland [National Steel] foundry. A last attempt to prevent the train continuing on its journey was made at Thornton. At that place the strikers were ignominiously routed, futile stone throwing expressing their chagrin.
>
> Pickets also tried to prevent raw materials being taken from the goods yard to the paper mill and the rope works, but at both cases the coal and the material were eventually secured while the Strike Committee were pleased to give Messrs H. Balfour & Co permission to lift a cable and carry it from the goods yard to Durie foundry. Arrangements were made last week by the management of the Kirkland Works for a large supply of coal. Before this could be given effect to, however, the strike came on, the result being that on Monday the firm had with great regret to dispense with the service of the moulders. But for the fortunate fact that water power is available, practically the whole works would have had to shut down. Methil Docks are at a standstill, the trimmers being thrown idle, but the pits have not so far been severely affected. Several trains were run on Thursday and yesterday and there are hopes that in the course of a day or two a service almost up to the usual will be maintained with the help of the many men who have offered their assistance.

Locally the response of staff was almost unanimous with few trains being run and no local deliveries being made. St Andrews, Leven and Anstruther were designated as food-distribution centres and were served by road although rationing was re-introduced on a temporary basis. Newspapers and mails were carried by road and pickets were in evidence at several local stations. Coal was immediately restricted to one hundredweight per customer but this restriction was soon rescinded. From 2nd October men began returning to work and services were improved and the strike ended on 5th October with the government effectively conceding defeat. One legacy was that in future the government would cooperate with the railway unions but the real result was an immediate increase in the wage bill of the North British, an estimate of the increase in wages for the 10 years from 1913 being in the order of 148 per cent. This was partly off-set by an increase of passenger fares of 75 per cent between 1913 and 1919 and of goods rates by almost 100 per cent, by notable falls in both short-haul goods traffic and, more significantly, in a significant slump in first class passenger traffic. Another effect of the strike was to have a permanent effect for there was little local sympathy for the striking railwaymen who were attempting to preserve their wages in an era of inflation and change. Instead local people and visitors turned to the increasingly readily-available alternative road services which, boosted by an influx of cheaply available lorries and chassis suitable for buses and a number of men trained by the Army in driving skills, had provided a stop-gap during the strike and were to prove a permanent addition to the local scene. As the *East of Fife Observer* of 14th October, 1920 put it:

> This is the age of the motor, and as a rival to the railway train bids fair to be a success. Increased railway fares and the increased rates on goods carried by rail have given the motor easy introduction. The motor service commenced between Anstruther and Leven is a sign of the times and there is little doubt that the enterprising firm will reap the benefit. Cheaper rates may not be the immediate outcome of this venture, but that it will eventually result in less expensive means of transit is likely and for this reason alone it deserves the patronage of all.

A welcome post-war development, triggered off by the realisation that the returning servicemen were entitled to a better standard of housing than they had formerly been subjected to, came in May 1920 when the town council of Leven requested a temporary siding to be laid next to the line just to the east of the station in connection with the building of council houses there. The council were willing to pay a charge for its use 'in addition to the ordinary Leven station rates'. The Leven Council siding, lengthened to accommodate five wagons, was authorized in October 1920 at a cost of £276.

Another national coal strike in April 1921 had a severe effect on local railway services. Coal for household use was rationed and certain local gasworks temporarily closed. However, ostensibly as a result of both the war and the strikes, the government were now inclined to continue with their supervision of the railways by setting up a Ministry of Transport and by putting into effect a scheme of concentrating the haphazard and competing 121 or so pre-war railway companies into four major groupings formed on a geographical basis, by voluntary means or otherwise. When the Railways Act 1921 was eventually passed it was clear that an east coast grouping was to include both the North British and Great North of Scotland companies and William Whitelaw, the ebullient Chairman of the North British, was to become Chairman of the new London & North Eastern Railway.

Chapter Eleven

Holidays with Pay: The London & North Eastern Railway 1923-1947

*'Never before has such a one-day rush had to be coped with ...
Holidays with pay has had a marked effect.'*

The Leven Mail

All Change!

The North British Railway was absorbed into the new London & North Eastern Railway (LNER) on New Year's Day 1923 and it did not take long for the change in ownership to be physically manifest on local stations and trains. One early change concerned a station name - because of a duplication of Thorntons on the new systems,* Thornton in Fife became, officially, Thornton Junction with effect from 1st July, 1923. A couple of months earlier *The East of Fife Observer* observed that at a social event held for local railwaymen in Anstruther reported under the heading of 'Railwaymen Make Merry – Successful Whist Drive and Dance', spirits were high and it was said that these occasions would help to perpetuate friendship amongst all London & North Eastern employees in the area. It was, however, noted by one speaker that local railwaymen would have to be able to meet the challenge of the ever-present and growing competition from motor traffic.

In October 1920 John Dewer, trading as the Caledonian Motor Engineering Co. Ltd of Mitchell Street, Leven commenced running a four-times daily (three on Sundays) service using two Belsize motor buses between Leven and Anstruther via Lundin Links, Upper Largo, Colinsburgh, Kilconquhar, Elie, St Monance, Pittenweem and Anstruther. These journeys were slow and well over an hour was allowed between Leven and Anstruther, due to a combination of the poor road surfaces and primitive nature of those early buses. Even though Dewer's buses were particularly prone to accidents and breakdowns, the *East of Fife Observer* was able to comment in 1921 that the service had been 'exceptionally well-patronised during the summer months'. Tom Gardner, whose Gardner's Motor Services operated out of the Harbourhead Garage at Anstruther, commenced a regular service from Anstruther to Crail and St Andrews via the coast in 1923 while the Wemyss Tramways Company commenced a Kirkcaldy to Anstruther bus service in 1924. What the motor buses were able to do, and the railway was not, was to reach the centres of the towns and villages, important in the case of St Monans and Pittenweem where the station was uphill and some distance away, and in the case of Colinsburgh, Upper Largo and Kilconquhar which, in effect, were not served by the railway.

The strike to end all strikes

In January 1924 local drivers and firemen joined in the national strike of footplatemen called to resist a cut in wage rates and this had some effect on East Fife trains, particularly on goods services; the National Union of Railwaymen did not, however, join in the action although an interesting news item reported in the *East Fife Observer* of 24th January was that pupils at the Waid Academy who lived in

* Other LNER stations of similar name were Thornton (Great Northern), Thornton Abbey (Great Central) and Thornton Dale (North Eastern).

No. 9149 approaches Saughton Junction, Edinburgh with a special train from the East Neuk on 15th May, 1926. The General Strike only ended on the railways on the previous day.
J.J. Cunningham KC

'D28' class 4-4-0 No. 10387 leaves Largo with a Dundee to Edinburgh working on 9th June, 1926.
J.J. Cunningham KC

Kingsbarns and Crail 'were forced to patronise the motors, believing that the train which they usually depended upon to convey them to Anstruther was "off". As a matter of fact, on Monday and Tuesday at least, a train did run from Crail'. Two years later, however, railway services throughout Britain ground to a halt when railwaymen of all grades and in both major unions decided to join in a General Strike called to show solidarity with the miners. Since East Fife included a coal mining area that had been known for a certain degree of militancy, the response was a solid one.* The strike began on Tuesday 4th May, 1926, when the majority of local LNER employees failed to turn up to work, and all trains were cancelled. However, some men had begun to drift back to work by the end of the week and on the Friday, 7th May, it was resolved to run a passenger train from Edinburgh to Anstruther and back by way of Leven. The train reached Anstruther with little comment, although its progress was noted by a large number of bystanders and the return journey commenced from Anstruther at 12.55. By the time Leven was reached there were many passengers on board, this having been the first train to run over the line for several days. At 1.35 William Rattray, station master at Leven, gave the orders to the crossing keeper at Burnmill to close the gates there against the road but on trying to set the signals for the train it was found that one was not working, apparently having been tampered with. The train set out but on reaching Burnmill crossing found its passage blocked by a crowd of between three and five hundred persons standing within the gates. An attempt was made to send a union picket to speak to the driver, Robert Paxman and his fireman, David Keir, but Rattray refused their request, despite being a union member himself. A separate deputation then called the guard, John Will, a blackleg and scab and threatened to decant Rattray, who was now present in the guard's van, 'into the water'.

The crowd were now turning restless and starting shouting abuse and throwing stones at the train, so that the county police were summoned to assist the sergeant and two constables already present. Inspector Clark of the Methil sub-division arrived on the scene by car about half an hour later, together with six other officers, and requested the crowd, which by now had been swollen to over a thousand, to disperse immediately. When they did not do so, the Inspector ordered a baton charge and, according to a passenger, the strikers scattered 'like rabbits'. By 2.15 the train was able to set out again but only for a short distance for on reaching East Fife Central Junction it was found that the points leading on to the Lochty line had been tampered with and the train was diverted off the main line, coming to an abrupt halt on the branch line. Hundreds of strikers from the Leven area, including many of those who had gathered at Burnmill, now arrived on the scene and began to insult the passengers with shouts and threats of physical violence and 'an ugly situation then developed'. A band of young men then jumped the fence, lifted some heavy stones and began to throw them at the elderly driver, who was standing beside the engine; one of the stones struck him in the face. The passengers, both male and female, then began to shout 'Shame!' and 'Un-British!', and many ran to the driver's assistance. Stones were then flung at the train and the passengers had to take refuge on the floor of the carriages until the police arrived and restored order, making three arrests of the alleged ringleaders. The points were found to be so mutilated that it was a good two hours before they could be repaired and the train eventually backed down off the Lochty line and proceeded on its way, some three hours late. The strike held for a few days more, but within a week virtually normal services were

* The LNER had already decided that during the strike an engineer's sleeping van would be stationed at Anstruther for the use of 'loyal staff and volunteers' and that there would be a feeding point for them at that station, the food being procured from local restaurants and cooked on the railway premises.

THORNTON JUNCTION to LEUCHARS JUNCTION, via ANSTRUTHER.

20th Sept. 1926

WEEK-DAYS.

DOWN TRAINS. Stations and Sidings.		Distance from Thornton		1 Railway Workmen.	2 Railway Workmen.	3 Railway Workmen.	4 Railway Workmen.	5 Light Engine	6 Em'ty Carriages	7 Goods	8 Railway Workmen.	9 Goods	10 Pass.	11 Pass.	12 Pass.	13 Em'ty Carriages.	14 Pass.	15 Goods Leuchars 2nd Pilot.	16 Pass.	17 Pass.	18 Goods
Departs from		...	...	...	...	...	...	...	...	...		*Burntisland* a.m. 5 0	...	...	...	...	...	*Leuchars Junc.* a.m 10 5	...	...	...
		Miles	*Chains*	MO a.m.	MX a.m.	a.m.	a.m.	MX a.m.	MO a.m.	a.m.	a.m.	a.m.	a.m.	a.m.	a.m.	a.m.	a.m.		a.m.	a.m.	a.m.
—Thornton Junction...	dep.	...	...	12 15	1 30	3 5	4 35	5 45	5 45	5 50	6 10	6 40	...	...	7 48	...	8 43	a.m.	...	...	...
Drumcaldie Distillery Siding	,,	3	45	...	...	...	...	...	...	...	...	...	...	...	...	...	...	...	...	...	...
—Cameron Bridge ...	arr.	3	61	...	...	...	...	...	...	...	...	...	...	...	7 55	...	8 50	...	...	...	...
Cameron Bridge...	dep.	3	61	...	...	...	...	...	...	...	...	...	...	...	...	...	...	...	...	...	...
Pirnie Colliery ...	,,	4	50	...	...	...	...	...	...	...	...	...	...	...	...	...	...	...	...	...	...
Cameron Pit Sidings ...	arr.	4	57	...	...	...	...	...	...	...	...	...	...	...	...	...	...	...	...	...	...
—Cameron Bridge ...	dep.	3	61	...	...	...	...	...	...	...	...	7 5	...	...	7 56	...	8 51	...	...	...	...
—East Fife Central Junction...	,,	4	51	...	...	...	...	...	...	6 5	...	...	...	...	...	...	...	...	...	...	...
Kirkland Yard ...	,,	5	23	12 30	1 45	3 20	4 50	...	...	...	...	...	...	...	...	...	...	...	...	...	...
—Leven ...	arr.	5	77	...	...	...	...	5 57	5 57	...	6 27	7 15	...	...	8 1	...	...	...	...	...	...
—Leven ...	dep.	...	...	...	...	...	...			6 20	...	...	...	...	8 3	...	8 57	...	...	...	...
Leven Brick Work Siding ...	,,	6	18	...	...	...	...	Works 6-20 a.m. Passenger train, Leven to Edinburgh.		...	...	...	...	...	...	...	...	...	...	...	...
Silverburn Siding ...	,,	7	16	...	...	...	...			...	...	...	...	...	...	...	...	...	...	...	...
Lundin Links ...	,,	7	60	...	...	...	...			6‡35	...	...	...	...	8 8	...	9 2	...	...	...	...
—Largo ...	,,	8	50	...	...	...	...			6 55	...	...	...	...	8 13	...	9 6	...	...	...	...
—Kilconquhar West ...	,,	11	59	...	...	...	...			...	...	...	...	...	...	...	...	...	...	...	...
Kilconquhar ...	,,	12	39	...	...	...	...			7 15	...	...	...	...	8 21	...	9 14	...	...	...	...
—Elie ...	arr.	13	71	...	...	...	...			7 20	...	...	...	...	8 25	...	9 18	...	...	...	...
—Elie ...	dep.	...	...	...	...	...	...		Works 6-20 a.m. Passenger train, Leven to Edinburgh.	7 44	...	...	...	...	8 28	...	9 21	...	...	...	...
—St Monan's ...	,,	15	78	...	...	...	...			8 46	...	...	...	...	8 34	...	9 35	...	...	...	...
Pittenweem ...	,,	17	42	...	...	...	...			9 0	...	...	...	...	8 39	...	9 40	...	...	...	...
—Anstruther Signal-box	,,	18	33	...	...	...	...			9 5	...	...	...	...	...	...	...	...	...	...	11 25
Anstruther (New Station)	arr.	18	52	...	...	...	...			...	...	...	...	...	8 43	...	9 44	...	...	...	...
Anstruther (New Station)	dep.	...	...	...	...	...	...	...		...	...	...	...	...	8 45	...	9 46	...	...	...	...
—Crail ...	,,	22	74	...	...	...	...	...		...	...	...	...	...	8 54	...	9 54	...	...	...	12 5
—Kingsbarns ...	arr.	25	61	...	...	...	...	...		...	...	...	...	...	9 0	...	...	...	...	...	...
—Kingsbarns ...	dep.	...	...	...	...	...	...			...	...	...	...	...	9 7	...	...	...	...	...	12 25
Boarhills ...	arr.	27	27	...	...	...	...		...	...	...	...	...	...	...	...	...	...	...	...	...
Boarhills ...	dep.	...	...	...	...	...	...	5a	...	...	...	...	...	...	9 12	...	...	...	...	...	12 45
Stravithie ...	,,	29	44	...	...	...	...		...	...	...	...	...	...	9 19	...	...	...	...	...	1 15
Mount Melville ...	,,	32	1	...	...	...	...	Pass.	...	...	...	...	...	...	9 26	...	...	...	...	...	1 35
—St Andrews (New Station)	arr	33	76	...	...	...	...	a.m.	...	...	...	...	...	...	9 30	...	...	...	...	...	...
—St Andrews (New Station)	dep	...	...	...	...	...	...	7 13	...	...	...	...	8 0	8 40	9 33	9 40	...	...	10 42	11 40	1 45
—St Andrews (Links Station)	,,	34	24	...	...	...	...	...	...	...	...	...	...	...	...	...	...	...	...	...	1 47
—Guard Bridge ...	,,	37	67	...	...	...	...	7 22	...	...	...	...	8 9	8 49	9 42	...	...	10 30	10 51	...	...
—Seggie Siding ...	,,	38	8	...	...	...	...	...	...	...	...	...	...	...	...	...	...	...	...	...	...
—Leuchars Junction .	arr.	39	1	...	...	...	...	7 25	...	...	...	...	8 12	8 52	9 45	9 50	...	10 39	10 54	11 50	...
Arrives at		...	...	*Methil (East)* 12 32	*Methil (East)* 1 47	*Methil (East)* 3 22	*Methil (East)* 4 52	...	...	*Thornton Jct.* 1 38	...	*Aberdour* 11 36	...	*Dundee* 9 11	*Dundee* 10 7	...	...	*St. Andrews* 11 30	...	...	*Anstr'ther* 4 45

All the Railway Workmen's trains working between Thornton Junction and Methil, and vice versa will call at Cameron Bridge if required. After 10·0 p.m. Saturdays, trains terminate Kirkland Yard.

‡ No. 7.—Calls at Lundin Links for Live Stock and Road Van traffic only.

No. 9.—Engine, Guard, and Van return to Thornton to work 9-12 a.m. Goods train, Thornton to Aberdour.

No. 11.—To be worked by Leuchars No. 2 Pilot.

No. 18.—Engine and Guard turn out at 9-45 a.m.

Fish Specials and Extra Goods Trains will be run when the Traffic requires it.

From the LNER Working Timetable, 20th September, 1926. *Authors' Collection*

WEEK-DAYS.

DOWN TRAINS. Stations and Sidings.		19 Min.	20 Pass.	21 Pass.	22 Goods Leuchars 2nd Pilot.	23 Pass.	24 Goods	25 Goods Leuchars 2nd Pilot.	26	27 Pass.	28 Pass.	29 Stores Thurs See p. 135 for dates.	30 Em'ty Carriages	31 Goods	32	33 Pass.	34 Pass.	35 Goods	36 Goods	37 Pass.	38 Pass.
Departs from		...	*Edinburgh* a.m. 9 5	...	*Leuchars Junc.* a.m. 11 15	...	...	*Leuchars Junc.* 11 15	...	...	...	*Stirling* 8a49	...	*Leuchars Junc.* p.m. 2 20	...	...	*Edinburgh* p.m. 1 14	...	...	...	...
—Thornton Junction	dep.	TO THO SO a.m. 9 5	a.m. 10 21	p.m. ...	SO p.m.	p.m. 12 4	p.m. 12 20	SX p.m.	...	SO p.m. ...	p.m. ...	p.m. 12 42	p.m. ...	p.m. ...	...	SX p.m. 2 25	SO p.m. 2 31	p.m. 2 40	p.m. 3 30	p.m. ...	p.m. 5 35
Drumcaldie Distillery Siding	„	...	...	...	...	...	...	...	...	...	...	...	...	...	...	...	...	...	...	...	...
—Cameron Bridge	arr.	9 25	...	...	...	...	...	...	...	...	...	12 49	...	...	...	...	...	...	3 43	...	...
Cameron Bridge	dep.	...	...	...	...	...	...	...	...	...	...	...	...	...	...	...	...	...	...	...	...
Pirnie Colliery	„	...	...	...	...	...	...	...	...	...	...	...	...	...	...	...	...	...	...	...	...
Cameron Pit Sidings ...	arr.	...	...	...	...	...	...	...	...	...	...	...	...	...	...	...	...	...	...	...	...
—Cameron Bridge	dep.	10 45	10 29	...	...	12 12	...	...	...	...	...	12 52	...	...	...	2 35	2 39	3‡15	...	...	5 43
—East Fife Central Junction ..	„	...	...	...	...	...	12 33	...	...	...	...	...	...	...	...	...	...	3 18	...	...	...
Kirkland Yard	„	...	...	...	...	...	...	...	...	...	...	...	...	...	...	...	...	...	...	...	...
—Leven	arr.	10 52	10 34	...	...	12 17	...	...	...	...	...	12 59	...	...	...	...	...	...	...	...	5 48
	dep.	...	10 35	...	...	12 21	1 0	...	...	...	...	1 2	...	...	...	2 42	2 45	3 38	Suspended on Saturdays.	...	...
Leven Brick Work Siding ...	„	...	...	...	...	...	...	...	...	...	...	...	...	...	...	...	...	...	...	...	...
Silverburn Siding	„	...	...	...	...	...	...	...	...	...	...	...	...	...	...	...	...	...	...	...	...
Lundin Links	„	...	10 40	...	...	12 26	1 15	...	...	...	...	1 7	...	...	...	2 47	2 50	3 48	...	...	...
—Largo	„	...	10 44	...	...	12 30	1 50	...	...	...	...	1 11	...	...	...	2 57	2 57	4 35	...	...	...
—Kilconquhar West	„	...	...	...	...	...	...	...	...	...	...	...	...	...	...	...	...	...	...	...	...
Kilconquhar	„	...	10 52	...	...	12 38	2 10	...	...	...	...	1 22	...	...	...	3 5	3 5	4 55	...	...	...
—Elie	arr.	...	10 56	...	...	12 42	2 15	...	...	...	...	1 26	...	...	...	3 9	3 9	5 0	...	...	...
	dep.	...	10 58	...	...	12 44	2 30	...	...	...	...	1 32	...	...	...	3 12	3 12	5 13	...	...	...
—St Monans	„	...	11 3	...	...	12 49	3 0	...	...	...	...	1 39	...	...	...	3 18	3 18	5 43	...	...	...
Pittenweem	„	...	11 8	...	...	12 54	3 12	...	...	...	...	1 46	...	...	...	3 23	3 23	5 55	...	...	...
—Anstruther Signal-box ...	„	...	...	...	...	...	3 20	...	...	...	...	...	...	...	...	...	...	6 3	...	...	...
Anstruther (New Station)	arr.	...	11 12	...	...	12 58		...	...	...	...	1 49	...	...	...	3 27	3 27	*Thornton Jt.* 10 30	...	...	...
	dep.	...	11 14	...	...	1 0		...	...	...	...	1 52	...	...	...	4 3	3 29		...	...	...
—Crail	„	...	11 23	...	...	1 10		...	...	...	...	2 2	...	...	...	4 13	3 37		...	...	...
—Kingsbarns	arr.	...	...	...	...	...	Suspended.	...	...	...	...	2 9	...	...	...	...	...		...	...	...
	dep.	...	11 30	...	...	...		...	...	...	...	2 11	...	...	...	...	...	...	...	...	...
Boarhills	arr.	...	...	...	...	...		...	...	...	...	...	...	...	...	...	...	35a	...	...	...
	dep.	...	11 35	...	...	...		...	...	...	...	2 18	...	...	...	...	...		...	...	...
Stravithie	„	...	11 42	...	...	...	...	...	...	...	...	2 31	...	...	...	...	...	Pass.	...	...	...
Mount Melville	„	...	11 48	...	...	...	...	...	...	...	...	2 38	...	...	...	...	...		...	...	...
—St Andrews (New Station)	arr.	...	11 52	...	...	...	...	...	...	...	...	2 42	...	...	...	...	...	p.m.	...	...	...
	dep.	...	11 59	12 28	...	...	...	...	...	2 7	2 35	2 45	3 30	...	...	...	...	4 13	...	5 35	...
—St Andrews (Links Station)	„	...	...	...	1 0	...	...	1 40	...	...	...	...	...	3†40	...	...	...	...	...	...	...
—Guard Bridge	„	...	...	12 37	1†28	...	...	1†55	...	2 16	2 44	2 56	...	4 0	...	...	...	4 22	...	5 44	...
Seggie Siding	„	...	...	...	...	...	...	...	...	...	...	...	...	...	...	...	...	...	...	...	...
Leuchars Junction	arr.	...	12 9	12 40	1 35	...	...	2 2	...	2 19	2 47	3 0	3 40	4 10	...	...	...	4 25	...	5 47	...
Arrives at		*Lochty* 1 25	*Dundee* 12 28	...	*Guardbridge* 2 45	*Glasgow* 5 30	*Thornton Jct.* 8 15	*Guardbridge* 2 45	...	*Dundee* 2 45	...	*Dundee* 4 0	...	*Tayport* 4 57	...	...	...	*Dundee* 4 57	*Thornton Jct.* 6 50	...	*Thornton Junc.* 6 19

No. **19**.—Shunts Sidings at Cameron Bridge.

† Nos. **22** and **25**.—Call for Road Van Goods.

† No. **31**.—Only starts from St Andrews when required to lift Live Stock for beyond Leuchars Junction.

‡ No. **35**.—Calls at Cameron Bridge to lift traffic.

THORNTON JUNCTION to LEUCHARS JUNCTION, via ANSTRUTHER—*continued.*

20th Sept. 1926

DOWN TRAINS. Stations and Sidings.		WEEK-DAYS. 39	40	41	42	43	44	45	46	47	48	49	50	51	52	53	54	55	SUNDAYS. 1	2	4	5
		Pass.	Goods		Pass.		Pass.	Pass.			Goods	Pass.	Pass.		Pass.	Pass.	Railway Workmen	Railway Workmen	Railway Workmen	Railway Workmen	Railway Workmen	Railway Workmen
Departs from		...	*Leuchars* p.m. 5 25	...	...	...	*Edinburgh* p.m. 5 0	*Edinburgh* p.m. 5 55	...	...	*Cameron B'dge* 6p35	...	...	...	...	...	...	...	...	...	...	...
		p.m.	SX p.m.		p.m.		p.m.	p.m.			p.m.	THO p.m.	TH X p.m.		p.m.	SO p.m.	p.m.	p.m.	a.m.	a.m.	a.m.	a.m.
Thornton Junction ...	dep.	...	...	...	...	...	6 9	7 42	...	...	8 0	...	...	...	9 20	...	10 20	11 15	1 30	3 5	4 35	5 45
Drumcaldie Distillery Siding	,,	...	...	...	...	...	...	...	...	...	...	...	...	...	...	...	...	...	...	...	...	...
Cameron Bridge ...	arr.	...	...	...	...	...	...	...	...	...	...	...	...	...	...	...	...	...	...	...	...	...
Cameron Bridge	dep.	...	...	...	...	...	...	...	...	...	...	...	...	...	...	...	...	...	...	...	...	...
Pirnie Colliery ...	,,	...	...	...	...	...	...	...	...	...	...	...	...	...	...	...	...	...	...	...	...	...
Cameron Pit Sidings	arr.	...	...	...	...	...	...	...	...	...	...	...	...	...	...	...	...	...	...	...	...	...
Cameron Bridge ...	dep.	...	...	...	...	...	6 17	7 50	...	...	8 25	...	...	...	9 30	...	...	...	...	...	...	...
East Fife Central Junction ...	,,	...	...	...	...	...	...	...	...	...	8 35	...	...	...	...	...	...	...	...	...	...	...
Kirkland Yard ...	,,	...	...	...	...	...	...	...	...	...		...	...	...	...	...	10 35	11 25	1 45	3 20	4 50	6 0
Leven ...	arr.	...	...	...	...	...	6 22	...	...	...		...	...	...	9 35	...			...	...	...	...
	dep.	...	...	...	...	...	6 24	7 56	...	...		...	...	...	...	...			...	...	...	...
Leven Brick Work Siding ...	,,	...	...	...	...	...	...	...	...	...		...	...	...	...	...			...	...	...	...
Silverburn Siding ...	,,	...	...	...	...	...	...	...	...	...		...	...	...	...	...			...	...	...	...
Lundin Links ...	,,	...	...	...	...	...	6 29	8 1	...	...		...	...	...	...	...			...	...	...	...
Largo ...	,,	...	...	...	...	...	6 34	8 6	...	...		...	...	...	...	...			...	...	...	...
Kilconquhar West ...	,,	...	Leuchars No. 1 Pilot.	...	...	...	6 46	...	...	...	Suspended on Saturdays.	...	...	...	...	...	Worked by Leven Dock Pilot.	Worked by Engine of 9-55 p.m. Passenger train, Edinburgh to Thornton Junction.	...	...	...	...
Kilconquhar ...	,,	...		...	...	...	6 49	8 14	...	...		...	...	...	...	...			...	...	...	...
Elie ...	arr.	...		...	...	...	6 53	8 18	...	...		...	...	...	...	...			...	...	...	...
	dep.	...		...	...	...	6 56	8 21	...	...		...	...	...	...	...			...	...	...	...
St Monans ...	,,	...		...	...	...	7 1	8 27	...	...	...	...	...	...	...	...			...	...	...	...
Pittenweem ...	,,	...		...	...	...	7 6	8 32	...	...	...	...	...	...	...	...			...	...	...	...
Anstruther Signal-box	,,	...		...	...	...	...	...	...	...	...	...	...	...	...	...			...	...	...	...
Anstruther (New Station)	arr.	...		...	...	...	7 10	8 36	...	...	...	...	...	...	...	...			...	...	...	...
	dep.	...		...	...	...	7 12	...	...	...	...	...	...	...	...	...			...	...	...	...
Crail ...	,,	...		...	...	...	7 21	...	...	...	...	...	...	...	...	...			...	...	...	...
Kingsbarns ...	arr.	...		...	...	...	...	...	...	...	...	...	...	...	...	...			...	...	...	...
	dep.	...		...	...	...	7 28	...	...	...	...	...	...	...	...	...	...		...	...	...	...
Boarhills ...	arr.	...		...	...	...	...	...	...	...	...	...	...	...	...	...	...		...	...	...	...
	dep.	...		...	...	...	7 33	...	...	...	...	...	...	...	...	...	...		...	...	...	...
Stravithie ...	,,	...		...	...	...	7 40	...	...	...	...	...	...	...	...	...	...		...	...	...	...
Mount Melville ...	,,	...		...	...	...	7 46	...	...	...	...	...	...	...	...	...	...		...	...	...	...
St Andrews (New Station)	arr.	...		...	...	...	7 50	...	...	...	...	...	...	...	...	...	...		...	...	...	...
	dep.	6 23		...	7 30	...	7 52	...	...	...	...	8 55	9 30	...	...	10 13	...	...	...	...	...	...
Do. (Links Station)	,,	...	7 15	...	...	...	...	...	...	...	...	...	...	...	...	...	...	...	...	...	...	...
Guard Bridge ...	,,	...	7 50	...	7 39	...	8 1	...	...	...	...	9 4	9 39	...	...	10 22	...	...	...	...	...	...
Seggie Siding ...	,,	...	...	...	...	...	...	...	...	...	...	...	...	...	...	...	...	...	...	...	...	...
Leuchars Junction ...	arr.	6 33	7 58	...	7 42	...	8 4	...	...	...	...	9 7	9 42	...	...	10 25	...	...	...	...	...	...
Arrives at		...	...	...	...	...	*Dundee* 8 21	...	...	...	*Thornton Jt.* 11 0	*Dundee* 9 23	...	...	...	...	*Methil (East)* p.m. 10 37	*Methil (East)* 11 27	*Methil (East)* 1 47	*Methil (East)* 3 22	*Methil (East)* 4 52	...

No. 48.—Takes South traffic Cameron Bridge to Kirkland Yard.

LEUCHARS JUNCTION to THORNTON JUNCTION, via ANSTRUTHER.

20th Sept. 1926

WEEK-DAYS.

UP TRAINS. Stations and Sidings.		Distance from Leuchars Junction.		1	2	3	4	5	6	7	8	9	10	11	12	13	14	15	16	17	18
				Railway Workmen	Railway Workmen	Railway Workmen	Railway Workmen	Pass.	Goods Leuchars No. 2 Pilot.	Cattle	Pass.		Pass.	Pass.	Pass.	Min.	Pass.	Em'ty Carriages	Goods	Goods Leuchars 2nd Pilot.	Pass.
Departs from...				*Methil (East)* a.m. 12 40	*Methil (East)* a.m. 1 55	*Methil (East)* a.m. 3 53	*Methil (East)* a.m. 5 20							*Dundee* a.m. 7 52		*Thornton Jt.* a.m. 9 5			*Thornton Jt.* a.m. 5 50		
		Miles	Chains	MO a.m.	MX a.m.	a.m.	a.m.	a.m.	a.m.	MO a.m.	a.m.		a.m.	a.m.	a.m.	TO THO SO a.m.	a.m.	WSO a.m.	a.m.	a.m.	a.m.
—Leuchars Junction...	dep.	...	...						5 30				7 40	8 25	9 6		10 2			10 5	11 12
Seggie Siding ...	,,	...	73																		
—Guard Bridge	,,	1	14						5 40				7 44	8 29			10 6			10 11	11 16
—St Andrews (Links Station)	,,	4	57						5 54												
—St Andrews (New Station)	arr.	5	5										7 52	8 37	9 16		10 14				11 24
	dep.	...	...											8 39							
Mount Melville	,,	7	0											8 45							
Stravithie	,,	9	37							6 15				8 54							
Boarhills	arr.	11	54																		
	dep.	...	...							6 25				8 58							
—Kingsbarns	arr.	13	17											9 2							
	dep.	...	...							6 35				9 5							
—Crail	,,	16	7							7 16	6 57			9 13							
Anstruther (New Station)	arr.	20	29								7 5			9 21							
	dep.	...	...								7 6			9 24							
—Anstruther Signal-box	,,	20	48							7 35									10 10		
Pittenweem	,,	21	39								7 10			9 28					10 22		
—St Monans	,,	23	8							8 6	7 15			9 34					10 40		
—Elie	arr.	25	10							8 14	7 20			9 39					10 47		
	dep.	...	...							8 32	7 23			9 41					11 35		
Kilconquhar	,,	26	42							8 43	7 28			9 46					11 48		
—Kilconquhar (West)	,,	27	22																		
—Largo	,,	30	31							9 16	7 36			9 54					12 32		
Lundin Links	,,	31	21							9 25	7 40			9 58					12 50		
Leven Brick Work Siding	,,	32	63																		
—Leven	arr.	33	4								7 44			10 2							
	dep.	...	...					6 20		9 40	7 45			10 4		11 20		11 45	1 10		
—East Fife Central Junction	,,	34	30													11 40			1 25		
Kirkland Yard	,,	...	...	12 42	1 57	3 55	5 22														
—Cameron Bridge	,,	35	20					6 25						10 9							
Cameron Pit Sidings	dep.	...	...																		
Pirnie Colliery	,,	...	...																		
Cameron Bridge...	arr.	...	...																		
—Cameron Bridge	dep.	35	20					6 26		9 50	7 51			10 10							
—Thornton Junction...	arr.	39	1	12 57	2 12	4 10	5 37	6 34		10 5	7 59			10 18				11 57	1 55 2 10		
Arrives at								*Edinburgh* 7 49			*Edinburgh* 9 2			*Glasgow* 12 48		*Lochty* 1 25		*Kirkcaldy* 12 7		*Leuchars Junc.* 10 39	

All South traffic, except for Carlisle Route, must be left off at Kirkland Yard. Trains for Thornton must have West traffic next Engine and North traffic on Van. Wagons to be marshalled before leaving Kirkland.

No. 6.—Shunts sidings at St Andrews Links until 8-15 a.m. Works 8-40 a.m. Passenger train, St Andrews to Dundee, thereafter as presently booked.

No **7**.—Engine and Van leave Thornton at 4-50 a.m. for Stravithie. On return trip calls where required to lift Live Stock traffic. Stations to wire Control, Burntisland, by 11-0 a.m., Sats., number of wagons of Live Stock to lift. Stations between Stravithie and Crail to advise Agent, Anstruther, on Saturday forenoon, number of wagons to lift.

No **11**.—Luggage and Parcel traffic for St Andrews off the 6-25 a.m. train from Edinburgh to be kept back at Leuchars Junction for 9-6 a.m. train from Leuchars.

LEUCHARS JUNCTION to THORNTON JUNCTION, via ANSTRUTHER.

20th Sept. 1926

WEEK-DAYS.

UP TRAINS. Stations and Sidings.		19	20	21	22	23	24	25	26	27	28	29	30	31	32	33	34	35	36	37	38
		Goods	Pass.		Pass.		Pass.	Pass.	Goods	Pass.	Pass.	Goods	Pass.	Min.	Min.	Pass.	Pass.	Pass.	Goods	Goods	
Departs from...		Guard bridge a.m. 10 30	...	...	...	...	...	...	Ans-tr'ther a.m. 11 25	Dun-dee p.m. 1 0	Thorn ton Junc. p.m. 12 4	St An-drews p.m. 1 0 SO 1 40 SX	Dun-dee p.m. 2 25	Lochty p.m. 1 45	Lochty p.m. 1 45	Dun-dee p.m. 2 15	...	Thorn ton Jt. p.m. 5 35	Thorn ton Jt p.m. 3 30	Thorn ton Jt. p.m. 12 20	...
		a.m.	a.m.		p.m.		p.m.	p.m.	p.m.	SO p.m.	p.m.	p.m.	p.m.	TO THO p.m.	SO p.m.	p.m.	p.m.	p.m.	p.m.	p.m.	
—Leuchars Junction ...	dep.	11 15	...	...	12 10	...	...	1 11	...	1 44	...	2 20	2 48	...	...	3 4	3 14	...	...		...
Seggie Siding ...	,,	11 21	...	...	...	...	...	...	...	...	...	‡	...	...	...	...	...	...	...		...
—Guard Bridge	,,	...	...	...	...	...	...	1 15	...	1 48	...	2†45	2 52	...	...	3 8	...	...	...		...
—St Andrews (Links Station)	,,	11 30	...	...	...	...	...	...	2 10	...	...	2†55	...	...	...	...	...	...	...		...
—St Andrews (New Station)	arr.	Leuchars 2nd Pilot.	...	...	12 20	...	...	1 23	...	1 56	...	Leuchars 2nd Pilot.	3 0	...	...	3 16	3 24	...	...		...
	dep.		...	...	...	...	...	...	...	...	...		...	...	...	3 18	...	...	...		...
Mount Melville	,,		...	...	...	...	...	...	2 30	...	...		...	...	...	3 24	...	...	...	Suspended.	...
Stravithie	,,		...	...	...	...	...	...	2 50	...	...		...	...	...	3 33	...	...	...		...
Boarhills	arr.		...	...	...	...	...	...	...	...	...		...	...	...	...	...	...	...		...
	dep.	...	...	...	...	...	...	...	3 10	...	...	...	...	...	...	3 37	...	...	...		...
—Kingsbarns ...	arr.	...	...	...	...	...	...	...	...	...	...	...	...	...	...	...	...	...	...		...
	dep.	...	...	...	...	...	...	...	3 46	...	...	...	...	...	...	3 41	...	...	...		...
—Crail ...	,,	...	...	...	...	...	12 44	...	4 35	...	2 16	...	...	...	...	3 50	...	...	...		...
Anstruther (New Station)	arr.	...	...	...	...	...	12 52	...	...	...	2 24	...	...	...	...	3 58	...	...	...		...
	dep.	...	11 40	...	...	...	12 58	...	...	...	2 26	...	...	...	...	4 1	...	...	...		...
—Anstruther Signal-box	,,	...	...	...	...	...	...	...	4 45	...	...	...	...	...	...	...	...	...	...	4 15	...
Pittenweem ...	,,	...	11 45	...	...	...	1 3	...	...	...	2 30	...	...	...	...	4 6	...	...	...	4 30	...
—St Monans ...	,,	...	11 51	...	...	...	1 9	...	...	...	2 35	...	...	...	...	4 12	...	...	...	5 5	...
—Elie ...	arr.	...	11 56	...	...	...	...	...	...	...	2 40	...	...	...	...	4 17	...	...	...	...	...
	dep.	...	11 59	...	...	...	1 16	...	...	...	2 43	...	...	...	...	4 19	...	...	...	5 25	...
Kilconquhar ...	,,	...	12 4	...	...	...	1 21	...	...	...	2 48	...	...	...	...	4 24	...	...	...	5 40	...
—Kilconquhar (West) ...	,,	...	12 7	...	...	...	...	...	...	...	...	...	...	...	...	...	...	...	...	...	...
—Largo ..		...	12 12	...	...	...	1 29	...	...	...	2 56	...	...	...	...	4 33	...	...	...	6 35	...
Lundin Links	,,	...	12 16	...	...	...	1 33	...	...	...	3 0	...	...	...	...	4 37	...	...	...	6 45	...
Leven Brick Work Siding ...	,,	...	...	...	...	...	...	...	...	...	...	...	...	...	...	...	...	...	Suspended on Saturdays.	...	...
—Leven ...	arr.	...	12 20	...	...	...	1 37	...	...	...	3 4	...	...	...	...	4 41	...	...		...	...
	dep.	...	12 22	...	...	...	1 39	...	...	...	3 6	...	...	...	...	4 43	...	6 5		7 10	...
—East Fife Central Junction ...	,,	...	...	...	...	...	...	...	...	...	...	...	...	3 45	3 45	...	...	...		7 40	...
Kirkland Yard ...	arr.	...	...	...	...	...	...	...	...	...	...	...	...	...	...	...	...	...		...	...
—Cameron Bridge ...	,,	...	12 27	...	...	...	...	...	...	...	3 11	...	...	3 50	3 50	4 48	...	...		...	...
Cameron Pit Sidings	dep.	...	...	...	...	...	...	...	...	...	...	...	...	...	...	...	...	...		...	...
Pirnie Colliery ...	,,	...	...	...	...	...	...	...	...	...	...	...	...	...	...	...	...	...		...	...
Cameron Bridge...	arr.	...	...	...	...	...	...	...	...	...	...	...	...	...	...	...	...	...		...	...
—Cameron Bridge ...	dep.	Leuch-ars Junc-	12 28	...	...	...	1 45	...	...	...	3 12	...	...	4 0	5 40	4 49	...	6 11	6 35	8 0	...
—Thornton Junction ..	arr		12 37	...	...	...	1 53	...	...	...	3 20	...	...	4 20	6 0	4 57		6 19	6 50	8 15	...
Arrives at ...		1 35 SO 2 2 SX	Edin-burgh 2 1	...	...	...	...	...	...	...	Glas-gow 5 30	...	...	...	...	Edin-burgh 6 9	Leuchars (Empty) 3 40	...	East Fife Ct. Jt. 8 35	...	...

No. 29.—† Runs forward to St Andrews only when required to lift Live Stock. ‡ Shunts Seggie Siding.

Nos. 31 and 32.—Leave at Kirkland Yard all wagons for South of the Forth and for Methil Branch (Live Stock excluded).

No. 32.—Reliefmen to be sent from Thornton Junction to Cameron Bridge by the 2-40 p.m. Goods train, Thornton Junction to Anstruther.

No. 33.—All Stations sending Fish traffic by this train for South of Edinburgh must wire Station-master and Parcels Agent, Edinburgh, full particulars, giving number of packages and destination of each consignment.

LEUCHARS JUNCTION to THORNTON JUNCTION, via ANSTRUTHER.

20th Sept. 1926

UP TRAINS.		WEEK-DAYS.																SUNDAYS.			
Stations and Sidings.		39	40	41	42	43	44	45	46	47	48	49	50	51	52	53	54	1	2	3	4
		Pass.	Pass.		Goods	Pass.		Pass.	Pass.	Railway Workmen	Goods	Pass.	Pass.	Em'ty Carriages	Goods	Railway Workmen	Pass.	Railway Workmen	Railway Workmen	Railway Workmen	Railway Workmen
Departs from...		...	*Dundee* p.m. 4 57	...	...	...	...	...	...	*Methil (East)* p.m. 9 20	*Thornton Jt.* p.m. 2 40	*Dundee* p.m. 9 35	...	...	*Thornton Jt.* p.m. 8 0	*Methil (East)* p.m. 11 35	...	*Methil (East)* a.m. 1 55	*Methil (East)* a.m. 3 53	*Methil (East)* a.m. 5 20	
					SX							TH O	TH X	SO			SO				
		p.m.	p.m.		p.m.	p.m.		p.m.	p.m.	p.m.	p.m.	p.m.	p.m.	p.m.	p.m.	p.m.	p.m.	a.m.	a.m.	a.m.	a.m.
—Leuchars Junction	dep.	4 34	5 19	...	5 25	6 7	...	6 46	8 6	...	...	9 55	9 55	...	...	...	10 37	...	...	...	...
Seggie Siding	,,	...	...	...	...	...	...	...	...	...	...	...	...	...	...	...	...	...	...	...	...
—Guard Bridge	,,	4 38	5 24	...	5 50	...	...	6 50	8 10	...	...	9 59	9 59	...	...	...	10 43	...	...	...	...
—St Andrews (Links Station)	,,	...	...	...	6 0	...	...	...	...	...	...	...	...	...	...	...	...	...	...	...	...
—St Andrews	arr.	4 46	5 32	...		6 17	...	6 58	8 18	...	...	10 7	10 7	...	...	...	10 51	...	...	...	...
	dep.	...	5 34	...		...	...	...	...	...	...	...	...	...	...	...	...	...	...	...	...
Mount Melville	,,	...	5 40	...		...	...	...	...	...	...	...	...	...	...	...	...	...	...	...	...
Stravithie	,,	...	5 49	...		...	...	...	...	...	...	...	...	...	...		...	...	...	...	...
—Boarhills	arr.	...	...	...		...	...	...	...	...	...	...	...	...	...		...	...	...	...	...
	dep.	...	5 53	...		...	...	...	...	...	...	...	...	...	...		...	...	...	...	...
—Kingsbarns	arr.	...	5 56	...		...	...	...	...	...	...	...	...	...	...		...	...	...	...	...
	dep.	...	5 57	...	Leuchars No. 1 Pilot	...	...	...	...	...	...	...	...	...	...		...	...	...	...	...
—Crail	,,	...	6 5	...		...	...	...	...	...	...	...	...	...	...		...	...	...	...	...
Anstruther (New Station)	arr.	...	6 13	...		...	...	...	...	...	...	...	...	...	...		...	...	...	...	...
	dep.	...	6 16	...		...	...	...	...	...	...	...	...	...	...		...	...	...	...	...
—Anstruther Signal-box ..	,,	...	...	...		...	...	...	...	...	7 15	...	...	...	...		...	...	...	...	...
Pittenweem	,,	...	6 21	...		...	...	...	...	...	7 30	...	...	...	...		...	...	...	...	...
—St Monan's	,,	...	6 27	...		...	...	...	...	...	7 55	...	...	...	...	Worked by Engine of 9-55 p.m. Passenger train Edinburgh to Thornton Junction.	...	...	...	...	...
—Elie	arr.	...	6 32	...		...	...	...	...	...	8 1	...	...	...			...	...	...	...	...
	dep.	...	6 35	...	...	...	...	...	...	...	8 23	...	...	...	Suspended on Saturdays.		...	...	...	...	...
Kilconquhar	,,	...	6 40	...	...	...	...	...	...	...	8 33	...	...	...			...	...	...	...	...
—Kilconquhar (West)	,,	...	6 46	...	...	...	...	...	...	...	...	...	...	...			...	...	...	...	...
—Largo	,,	...	6 53	...	...	...	...	...	...	...	8 58	...	...	...			...	...	...	...	...
Lundin Links	,,	...	6 57	...	...	...	...	...	...	...	9 9	...	...	...			...	...	...	...	...
Leven Brick Work Siding ...	,,	...	...	...	...	...	...	...	...	...	...	...	...	...			...	...	...	...	...
—Leven	arr.	...	...	...	...	...	...	...	...	...	9 14	...	...	...			...	...	...	...	...
	dep.	...	7 3	...	...	...	...	...	...	...	9 23	...	...	9 42			...	...	...	...	...
—East Fife Central Junction ...	,,	...	...	...	...	...	...	...	...	...	9 53	...	...	...	10 15		...	...	...	...	...
Kirkland Yard	,,	...	...	...	...	...	...	...	...	9 22	...	...	...	...	...	11 37	...	1 57	3 55	5 22	6 8
—Cameron Bridge	,,	...	7 8	...	...	...	...	...	...	...	...	...	...	...	...	...	...	...	...	...	...
Cameron Pit Sidings ...	,,	...	...	...	...	...	...	...	...	...	...	...	...	...	...	...	...	...	...	...	...
Pirnie Colliery	,,	...	...	...	...	...	...	...	...	...	...	...	...	...	...	...	...	...	...	...	...
Cameron Bridge... ...	arr.	...	...	...	...	...	...	...	...	...	...	...	...	...	...	...	...	...	...	...	...
—Cameron Bridge	dep.	...	7 9	...	...	...	...	...	...	...	10 10	...	...	...	10 40	...	...	...	...	...	...
—Thornton Junction	arr.	...	7 17	...	...	...	...	...	...	9 37	10 30	...	...	9 54	11 0	11 50	...	2 12	4 10	5 37	6 18
Arrives at		...	...	...	*Leuchars* 7 58	...	...	...	...	...	...	...	...	...	...	...	...	...	...	...	...

No. **40.**—Must not work extra Vehicles. Conveys Fish and Yeast traffic in van, total quantity not to exceed 30 cwts.

No. **42.** — Works Seggie Siding.

No. **47.** — Worked by Leven Dock Pilot.

No. **52.**—Takes traffic for South of Berwick to Thornton for 9-40 p.m. **SX** (9-35 p.m. **SO**), Dundee and Tweedmouth train. Traffic to be left off in East of Fife Dead End Siding for a "Catch-on."

resumed although the rancour remained. In a sequel at Cupar Sheriff Court at the end of the month, 12 of the Burnmill picketers were each fined £3 for obstructing the crossing, despite their solicitor's pleas that a conviction would lead, being railwaymen, to their instant dismissal by the company. The long-term consequence of the strike was that, once again, the public turned to other forms of transport and, as the traffic figures reflect, the business of the railways in East Fife continued to decline.

Economies abound

On 12th September, 1926, following upon certain economies which had been put in place between Anstruther and Crail, the arrangements at Anstruther were rationalized by the closure of the Anstruther Station signal box (thus saving on both its maintenance and staffing costs) and the re-naming of the existing signal box at Anstruther Junction as 'Anstruther'. Track alterations were put into effect with the shifting of the crossing loop to the west of the passenger station and the lifting of the eastern end of the former loop by the placing of buffer stops at the eastern end of the down platform. So while the up platform remained bi-directional the down platform could only be used as a starting or terminating point for trains from the west. This new arrangement appears to have worked quite satisfactorily and was followed, in 1932 by further signalling alterations being made, this time at Kilconquhar West. Here, as part of a drive to cope with changing traffic patterns on the coast line, provision was made for the switching out of the signal box with the result that the box and loop there were only used at peak periods in the summer season. Whether these economies were enough was debatable as the great trade depression following the stock market collapse in 1929 and the consequent world recession affected the LNER both nationally and locally and a decline in both goods and passenger traffic, exacerbated by competition from the unregulated motor lorry and bus, made substantial inroads into the company's revenues. The acquisition of local bus services by the railway companies should have stemmed the passenger decline but even at that stage there was little real co-operation between the two forms of transport apart from agreements as to inter-availability of tickets. The net result was that the bus continued to abstract revenue from local stations, particularly in view of the fact that many local stations were situated at the edge of the towns that they purported to serve while the bus ran through these settlements. If this was not enough, the private car was also making inroads into passenger traffic that had formerly been the sole preserve of the train and the first class compartments on local trains became completely empty for much of the day. One local rival did, however, disappear – the Wemyss Tramway which was acquired by the Scottish Motor Traction Co. from its previous owners, Balfour Beatty, and closed down completely at the end of January 1932. Another casualty of this era was the Muiredge branch. The part of the section from Cameron Bridge and the Plunks had been used by the Wemyss Coal Co. (WCC) since 1923 but in 1936 the LNER intimated it was were intending to close the whole of this section of line. Instead it sold this part of the branch to the WCC who wished to lift the track and use it elsewhere and on 10th November, 1936 the dismantling of the line commenced. In March 1938 the southern part of the branch was purchased by the WCC at a cost of £1,500 and the Muiredge branch of the NBR became history.

The herring desert

The once-vibrant fish traffic by rail from the East Neuk ports to the southern markets collapsed between the wars, partly due to intensive competition from motor lorries and because the herring themselves eventually deserted the Forth. The 1924 Railway Strike caused poor results to the fishing trade because many of the larger fishing boats stayed in port and one perhaps unforseen consequence of the 1926 Strike was that many of the local steam drifters began to get their coal directly from Methil dock rather than take it on at Anstruther, to where it had been delivered by rail. The service of fish trains to London continued, there being one dedicated train in the season and a second train which ran if required but the traffic was vulnerable to road competition and as local lorries, which had the great advantage of being more flexible in their operation and able to serve the harbours directly, began to take more of the trade from the railway, the existing service was in danger of becoming uneconomic to maintain. The 7th March, 1936 was a record day for winter herring landings at Anstruther but, being a Saturday, the railway was unable to cope with the landings and it was recorded that lorries replacing the trains ran direct to a German export ship at Methil. By 1939 a fair proportion of the fish traffic was travelling by road and when war broke out the fish catches landed at Anstruther and the East Neuk ports ceased almost entirely. Immediately when the war ended the hand of fate caused the herring to leave the Forth and the fishing trade collapsed. A partial revival followed with white fish landings mainly at Pittenweem but by this time little fish of any sort travelled by rail and the glory days of the Anstruther fish trains were over.

Austerity and Hope

Although few long term plans or improvements were being made in an age of austerity forced upon the railways by economic necessity, the government did promulgate a capital credits scheme whereby major labour-intensive schemes whose aim was the alleviation of unemployment would be underwritten by grants. Among those which the LNER considered applying for was that to build a new and more direct line between Leven and Kirkcaldy, which would by-pass Thornton Junction and use, in parts, a much improved trackbed of the Weymss and Buckhaven line. It is not clear how far these proposals went before the scheme was abandoned, but one can hardly blame the company for not having the courage to undertake such a major work against the economic background of the early 1930s. Indeed towards the end of that decade the LNER gave some consideration to abandoning completely the section of the Fife coast line between Crail and St Andrews on account of its poor revenue potential but it is doubtful if the government would have sanctioned this, given the threat of war with Germany. On a more positive note when, in February 1937, severe storm damage occurred between Temple and Viewforth, lying just to the east of Largo station, and a quarter-mile of the trackbed was almost completely washed away causing the cessation of all traffic between Largo and Kilconquhar and the diversion or bus replacement of services, the LNER acted promptly. Accordingly hundreds of tons of redd (the rock and debris waste from coal mining) was brought in by rail from pits in West Fife and the Wemyss and tipped into the breach until the embankment was restored. The works were finally completed in time for the holiday season and the summer trains ran. At Largo, where difficulties were encountered in carting holidaymakers' luggage from the station to their summer quarters in the village below, the LNER proposed to construct a pedestrian walkway on the north side of the viaduct with steps leading down to Burnbank Terrace but nothing came of this proposal.

KY149, *The Restless Wave*, sets out from Pittenweem harbour in 1925; steam drifters like this vanished from the Fife fisheries after World War II and the sole remaining British example is now in a Yarmouth museum. *Authors' Collection*

A postcard view of the beach at Lundin Links with the railway to the right. *Alan Brotchie Collection*

Busy summers; quiet winters

The coastal stations continued to be busy with holiday traffic and outwardly there was little change from the pre-war position. The local newspapers reflected the great numbers of people who still travelled to the seaside resorts by rail and the traditional pattern of taking houses for the summer continued even if some of the well-heeled holidaymakers now came by car. Local journeys were increasingly made by bus and especially those made by local people in winter but the buses could not cope with heavy luggage, prams and bicycles and longer-distance journeys in any season and the railway managed to hang on to much of this lucrative traffic. The special and excursion trains continued to run and were as popular as ever, even if they were now competing with local charabanc proprietors who were able to undercut rates and provide a wider range of options for East Fife residents. Cheap tickets were issued, including afternoon and evening excursion fares and special deals for Wednesday half-day closing trips and Saturday journeys were heavily promoted locally. St Andrews not only managed to retain its pre-war passenger figures but actually increased them as the town was seen as a positive draw to both day trippers and holidaymakers and a series of art deco posters promoting the virtues of the town was issued by the LNER.

As the trade depression lifted, the traffic increased and, towards the end of the 1930s, a new source of holidaymakers appeared with the introduction for the first time of statutory paid holidays for many employees. On 20th July, 1938 (nine days before the Act came into force but when, for many, its effect was already being felt) the *Leven Mail* reported that, in connection with the Glasgow Fair holidays, Leven had been invaded by 20 special trains from that city and other towns in the West on the previous Friday and 30 on Saturday and that it was estimated that between 10,000 and 12,000 people had used the services. On 19th July, 1939 the paper reported that on the previous Friday and Saturday some 25,000 passengers disembarked at Leven station:

> The first of the visitors, in appreciable numbers, made their appearance on Thursday. By Friday they began to come thick and fast. Leven station staff dealt with crowds off 14 special trains from Glasgow and the West of Scotland in addition to the normal service trains. About 5,000 holidaymakers came by train. But that number paled into insignificance when Saturday came round. From early morning till late night special after special streamed noisily into the station and disgorge a seemingly never-ending stream of holidaymakers. About 20,000 tickets were collected by the station staff on Saturday. Never before has such a one-day rush had to be coped with – there were 24 special trains! Holidays with pay has had a marked effect.

Within a few weeks Britain was again at war and all excursion trains and special fares had been suspended.

Leven's Level Crossings

One perennial problem during the LNER period was that of the two town centre level crossings in Leven, namely the Laundry (or Aithernie Road) and Waggon Road crossings. A census in November 1935 showed that a daily average of 3,200 people used the former crossing and that, 'the crush of passengers at meal hours made the crossing exceedingly busy' while at the Waggon Road crossing in the same week some 25,816 pedestrians, 708 motor vehicles, 387 vans and 4,427 cyclists passed over. This situation had arisen because of the northwards spread of the town since the railway had been built

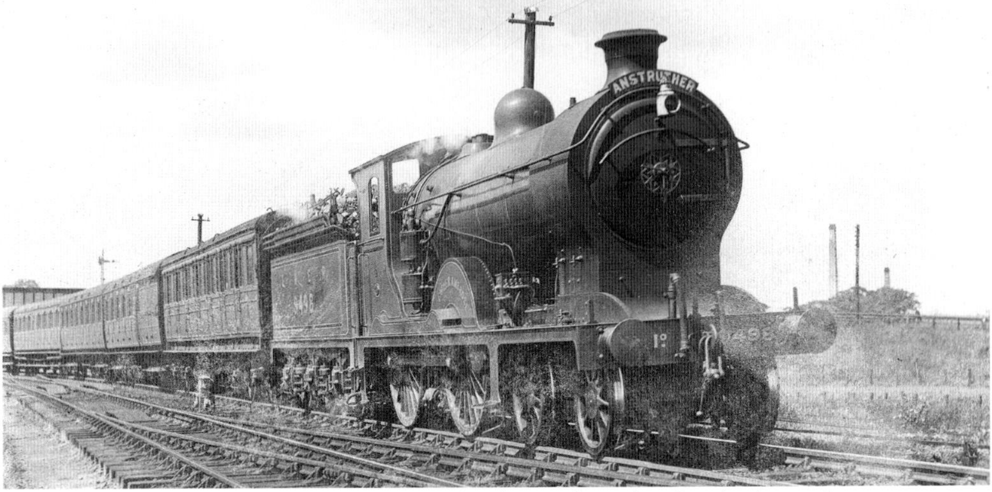

The immaculate No. 9498 *Father Ambrose* in lined green livery heading for Anstruther.
W.D. Yuill Collection

Anstruther on a summer Sunday in 1929 with three special trains from Glasgow with 'D30' class 4-4-0 No. 9497 *Peter Poundtext* ('Anstruther'), 'D34' 4-4-0s No. 9153 ('Glasgow') and No. 9406 ('Crail'). The Eastfield crew of the latter comprised driver Davie Wilson and fireman Peter Nimmo.
NBRSG, Hennigan Collection

No. 9410 *Meg Dods* leaves Elie with a Glasgow service in the 1930s. *J.J. Cunningham KC*

St Monance garden and station staff in the 1930s. *NBRSG, Hennigan Collection*

Above: No. 9291 *Glen Douglas* at Anstruther shed on 17th June, 1936 with driver Jock Barbour and fireman Jock Millar.
NBRSG, Hennigan Collection

Right: 'D34' No. 9406 with driver Jimmy Dobson and fireman Alex Hendry.
NBRSG, Hennigan Collection

and what had originally been provided only as accommodation crossings were now unable to cope. The problem continued to grow and a collision between some passenger coaches being shunted and a lorry at the Waggon Road crossing in 1942 only helped to fuel the anxieties of the council. In February 1947 the council had further discussions with the LNER, arising out of further concerns with shunting operations leading to prolonged delays at the Laundry crossing and 15-minute waits at the Waggon Road crossing. Various suggestions were made to alleviate the problems such as having the Laundry crossing gates operated from Leven station and having the Waggon Road crossing-keeper close the gates against the railway when no trains were due. One councillor mentioned that pedestrians late for work sometimes 'jumped' the gates and found themselves fined and he also had concerns that the Burnmill level crossing to the west would also be seriously congested when it became the main route to the hub of the new town at Mountfleurie. The company replied that the Laundry and Waggon Road crossings were still classified as private crossings and in any event they were closed to vehicles on Sundays. Although estimates had been prepared for a signal box and signals at Waggon Road in 1937, the council had rejected these on the grounds of cost. The company was willing to look at the matter again should circumstances merit it. The matter was not revisited until 1956 when the British Transport Commission proposed the closure of the Laundry and Waggon Road crossings but this never took place and the three crossings remained as a traffic hazard until the eventual closure of the line.

Hitler's War

The outbreak of war on 3rd September, 1939 coincided with the end of the summer tourist season and there was an immediate reduction in passenger services with several trains withdrawn for a number of days before a normal service was resumed a week or so later. As in World War I, the government took overall control of the railways and on 19th September the following appeared in the *Leven Advertiser* amidst paragraphs headed 'Methil Victim of Black-Out Tragedy' and 'Call to Holders of Allotments':

> In a statement issued on Friday, the Railway Executive Committee regretting the inconvenience caused by the reduction of train services state, 'The railways have a very heavy and military traffic to deal with which is of an urgent and exceptional character. It is essential for the welfare of the country that freight and military traffic should be punctually and efficiently handled. Subject to this the railway companies are doing and will do everything they can to give the public the best passenger service that is within their power. Each company is watching the situation from day to day, and will put on such extra trains as working conditions permit ...'

Within a short time East Fife passenger services were largely run as normal, notwithstanding the imposition of the blackout and any reduction in holiday traffic was more than offset by additional traffic of military and naval personnel. In 1940, when there was a very real feeling that Britain was in danger of being invaded, Polish army engineers were billeted throughout the area for the purpose of constructing the defences along that part of the coast between Burntisland and Montrose. In East Fife the Poles were stationed, amongst other places, at Tayport, St Andrews and Largo and needed a large amount of stores and cement for the construction of the concrete anti-tank blocks which can still be seen in a state of decay at various points on the coastline; in addition to the engineers, Polish paratroopers carried out their training in the Largo area. Other new flows of traffic included stores and fuel for the convoys which were awaiting naval escort at Methil and these included ships bound for the Soviet ports of Archangel and Murmansk. In general the docks at Methil saw a dramatic reduction in coal exports with the consequence that rail traffic over the Leven Dock branch lessened considerably.

In the eastern part of the county there were a number of airfields in operation, all of which generated additional rail traffic. The former Royal Naval Air Services aerodrome at Crail was reinstated and modernized and became operational on 1st October, 1940. In anticipation of the additional wartime traffic that would be generated by it, the viaduct at Largo was re-inforced in the winter of 1939/1940 to enable heavier rolling stock and locomotives to reach Crail. Other additional traffic was caused by the fact that the factories and foundries of the Leven area were involved in much war-related production and the drive to grow food for the war effort also led to an increase in agricultural traffic handled at the goods yard in the area; however, the shortage of grain also caused the Cameron Bridge distillery to cease production between 1941 and 1947.

An unusual local railway cargo was mentioned in the *LNER Magazine* of October 1945:

> During the course of the war a considerable number of invasion barges were constructed by Messrs. Henry Balfour and Company, Durie Foundry, Leven, whose works have no direct access to the sea, thus necessitating the barges being conveyed by rail to Methil Dock where they were unloaded by crane direct from the railway vehicle intro the water. The journey by rail, although only some two miles in distance, was extremely hazardous owing to the barges being far outside the normal railway loading gauge, the measurements being 42 feet 9 inches long, 14 feet by 9 feet high. The dimensions required both lines to be kept clear, the gauge on one side being the greatest problem as two overline bridges had to be negotiated, one of them carrying the Leven road allowing a fractional clearance of one-half inch.

One proposal that would have greatly affected the line but was never carried out was a plan to build a large relief port on the coast between Pittenweem and Anstruther. Intended to be an auxiliary port and a replacement for Leith Docks, in the event of the latter having suffered serious damage through bombing, the new port would have capable of taking vessels of up to 10,000 tons displacement and would have been served by its own short branch off the Pittenweem to Anstruther section. The Anstruther golf course and the beach at Billowness would have been the main casualties and both burghs would have been altered irretrievably.

In the event the East Neuk villages and burghs suffered less than many places and bombing was confined to a single raid on Cellardyke and Leven but the tourist trade and fishing ceased for the duration. Thankfully, casualties among local servicemen were less than in World War I.

Pittenweem Dissatisfied – Again!

In the summer of 1945 many of the wartime travel restrictions were lifted and holidaymakers began to come back to the East Fife resorts. But the railways were tired and the lack of maintenance of locomotives, carriages and the infrastructure had led to a general shabbiness and lack of purpose on the part of the railway company. Complaints were made about the poor timekeeping of local services, particularly those east of Leven. In March 1946 the Pittenweem Town Council received a letter from the divisional manager of the LNER in reply to a very specific complaint made by them:

> In recent years, because of the war and other essential commitments, the Company regret that they had not been in a position to carry out their normal programme of repairs, renovations

and painting at stations. With things now returning to normal, they have prepared a list of those stations which were to receive attention this summer, and Pittenweem has been included amongst them. It is hoped that after painting and other renovation work has been carried out, the station will be found to be in a satisfactory state.

Doubts were, however, expressed by several of the town councillors with Provost Lawson stating unequivocally that 'Pittenweem was the worst station along the whole line in East Fife' with Councillor Robertson commenting that the entrance to the station was 'terrible'. If these criticisms of the modest little wayside station that dated back to 1863 and bore witness to the parsimony of the cash-strapped Leven & East of Fife Railway seem harsh, Councillor Millet went further and said that 'painting alone will do little good' and that what they really wanted was a new station altogether and that the Council should press for this – a motion which was readily agreed to by all present. The LNER ignored this request but they had other much more pressing things to worry about at that particular time, such as a chronic shortage of money and the looming spectre of nationalization of the railways, against which latter prospect they were engaged in a spirited but ultimately futile fight.

Swansong

But life on the East Fife lines continued in its same steady pattern as three random items which appeared in 1946 in the *East of Fife Observer* testified to. At the end of January a correspondent commented that,

> The time taken for journeys to Edinburgh and Glasgow is still far too long. The afternoon train from East Fife to Glasgow is one of he slowest of all … Leaving East Fife at around three o'clock, it goes to Thornton and then proceeds to wind its way round West Fife to Dunfermline, then turn back by Rosyth Halt to Inverkeithing, across the Forth Bridge, and so to Glasgow, reaching there after six o'clock. Sometimes it gets in near seven – and that for a journey which could be comfortably accomplished in a little over two hours. Surely if East Fife people wish to go to Glasgow it shouldn't be necessary for them to do a Cook's Tour of West Fife!

On 25th April the paper reported that two LNER lorry men based at Anstruther, Messrs A. Gardner and A. Bogie, were presented with gold medals to mark their having completed 10 consecutive years of motor driving free from accident. On 26th December a more sensational report stated that, 'During the absence on holiday of the attendant, Miss Isa Cormack, the bookstall at Anstruther station has been broken into by thieves. A quantity of cigarettes in packets is missing, but until the return of the attendant from her holiday in Leicester, the full extent of the robbery cannot be ascertained'. It can only be added that this as certainly neither the first nor the last time that the bookstall at the station had been raided, its secluded location making it an ideal target while trains were not running.

The winter of 1947 was a harsh one with trains on the coast line held up by snowdrifts, freezing points and coal and staff shortages. But the LNER soldiered on and, at the end of that year, managed to pass on to the new nationalized set-up a local railway system that was essentially in good order but one whose basic infrastructure was, indeed, little changed from the days when the North British had operated it a quarter of a century before.

'D11/2' class 4-4-0 No. 2680 *Lucy Ashton* enters Lundin Links on 11th April, 1947. *J. Boyd*

No. 2403 *Sir Walter Scott* at Largo on 18th August, 1947. *NBRSG, Hennigan Collection*

Chapter Twelve

Weeping in Sympathy: British Railways 1948-1969

'As the train made its last run in to Leven station,
the clouds opened and the rain came down, as if weeping in sympathy.'

The Fife Mail

No change

In the immediate post-war period there were more pressing problems than those of the railways and in retrospect it is easy to see that a certain complacency had set in; so much so that the Fife County Council, in the report of their Planning Advisory Committee, issued in 1946, could say that, 'It does not appear that many changes or improvements will be necessary on the railway system in the near future. Electrification, though desirable on the grounds of amenity, is hardly likely to become urgent so long as coal remains plentiful'. The mines, nationalized in 1947, were still struggling to cope with the demand for coal, a demand heightened by extreme winters and a struggle to supply both the home and export markets despite the privations of war, and the newly formed National Coal Board had great plans for the expansion of the industry in Fife. The following year the British Transport Commission was formed, its railway arm being, somewhat unadventurously, titled British Railways (BR) and within weeks of New Year's Day 1948 the new name began to appear on the tanks of East Fife locomotives stabled at Thornton shed, and on publicity. Gradually rolling stock began to appear in a uniform maroon livery, relieved by a cream band for express passenger stock, and a new motif, that of an emaciated lion balancing upon a wheel, replaced the plain lettering on the locomotives. These, however, were the only real changes, at least initially, that the local traveller would have seen and services and facilities were to all intents and purposes unaltered. The holiday trade had returned in force and in the early years, with travelling restrictions to abroad still not lifted and austerity still in vogue, was even enhanced over that of pre-war levels. In addition local traffic, both passenger and goods, still appeared to be flourishing even if, behind that facade, problems were mounting.

The Fife Coast Express revived

One of the features of the coastal line that had been in abeyance during the war years was the summertime 'Fife Coast Express' which was revived with a 7.15 am departure from St Andrews calling at Crail, Anstruther, Elie, Leven, Kirkcaldy and Burtntisland and arriving at Glasgow Queen Street at 9.50. The return journey left Queen Street at 4.07 pm and called at the same stations in reverse order arriving back at St Andrews at 6.53 pm. The stock for the train was unusual to say the least for it was provided by a five-coach set of Gresley streamlined stock that had been built for the pre-war 'Silver Jubilee' express of the LNER. Refreshment facilities were once again provided but these were short-lived, being withdrawn again in 1952. There was no corresponding winter service, the purpose of the 'Express' being the same as the original 'Fifeshire Coast Express' of the North British but times were changing and the Express ran for the last time in the 1959 summer season, its traffic having been largely lost to the private car and bus and to changing customs in work patterns and holidays for the middle classes. When the Express finally

No. 2442 *Simon Glover* at Largo, 7th April, 1948. *NBRSG, Hennigan Collection*

'K2' class 2-6-0 No. 61755 approaches Kilconquhar on 26th July, 1952 with Largo Law in the background. *W.J.V. Anderson*

'B1' class 4-6-0 No. 61403 with the eastbound 'Fife Coast Express' approaching Elie in June 1952.
W.J.V. Anderson

'B1' class 4-6-0 No. 61172 with the eastbound 'Fife Coast Express' at Ardross between St Monans and Elie June 1952; note the LNER 'Silver Jubilee' streamlined coaches. The location will be familiar to all those who have walked the coastal path. *W.J.V. Anderson*

Gresley 'K2' class 2-6-0 No. 61755 with a mixture of coaches leaves Kilconquhar for St Andrews on 26th June, 1952. *W.J.V. Anderson*

'J37' 0-6-0 No. 64588 with a westbound 'Coast goods' on Largo viaduct in 1956. *W.J.V. Anderson*

departed, its passengers had already deserted and the replacement train, which ran in July and August calling at all stations between Thornton and Inverkeithing, was a pale imitation, with a winter down service which operated only as far as Leven.

Declining Fortunes

The ending of restrictions on the use of private cars and the rise of the motor lorry and motor bus began to undermine the railway again and in the *Third Statistical Account of Scotland*, the Fife volume, published in 1952, it is noticeable that, in the case of virtually every parish mentioned, not only was passenger traffic under serious competition from the bus, but that the bus appeared already to have gained an upper hand. Thus in the case of Leven, 'Though the railway station is on the East Fife branch line, the town is rather better served than the communities to the east, for it has the advantage of a number of extra trains to Edinburgh and Glasgow, which reach here and go no further. Bus transport however, has reached incomparably greater proportions'. Leven was noted as being the terminus for a quite remarkable number of long-distance services as well as local ones, 'and it has been suggested that no other town in Scotland of comparable size figures so frequently on the destination board of buses'. Another contributor claimed that 'with a frequent bus service in both directions, there are few more assiduous travellers in Scotland than the people of St Monance' and attributed the coming of the bus with the gradual disappearance of the individuality of the town and its inhabitants. In Kilconquhar the 'cheap and convenient bus service' was blamed for the decline of the local shopkeeper, while in Largo the 'excellence' of local bus services is mentioned with the concluding comment that, 'Both Lower Largo and Lundin Links also have railway stations' added as something of an afterthought. Possibly even more telling is that in a number of the other East Fife parishes which still had stations serving them no mention is made of the railway or its services.

Goods traffic was also in decline and here there were a number of factors at work. Much of the shorter distance traffic was peculiarly vulnerable to the increase in the ownership of vans and light lorries by local farmers and businessmen. Once such people were free of the vagaries of the railway timetable and need for transhipment with the consequent evils of delay and damage to goods and, unfortunately, theft by railway employees and others, they tended to stick with their own transport. The nationalized British Road Services began to compete with BR for longer-distance traffic and deregulation then increased that competition. One form of revenue that was increasingly lost by the railway locally was what remained of the fish traffic which now had a guaranteed 'next-day' lorry delivery to many parts of Britain from the East Fife ports; another loss was the transport of livestock. With economic factors counting against freight by rail, the national railway strike of 1955 only helped to lose yet further traffic and what was eventually left east of Leven was the wagonload transit of household coal and potatoes and the varied, but largely unprofitable, quantities of sundries and miscellaneous parcels bound for local businesses and residents. In an effort to compete, BR developed an extensive road delivery network, locally epitomised by the Scammell tractors and trailers based at Leven and Anstruther which took the goods to places where the railway, even in its heyday, had never dreamed of serving.

A series of fatal accidents occurred in the early years of nationalization and, although unconnected, displayed an alarming tendency for locals and trains to come into violent contact with unfortunate results. In July 1949 a young Guardbridge man was taking a Sunday evening stroll with his girlfriend along the line near to Largo when he was struck

Glen Orchy crosses Largo viaduct with the 2.38 pm Thornton to Crail service on 2nd April, 1957. *W.A.C. Smith*

No. 62467 *Glenfinnan* close by the shore at Largo in August 1957. *W.J.V. Anderson*

by the locomotive of a Crail to Glasgow special working and killed although his companion managed to jump to safety. It was said that neither of them heard the train until the last possible moment, its sound being drowned out by high winds and heavy seas but this did not, apparently deter others from trespassing on the very same stretch of line. A year later a man playing golf at Lundin Links was killed by a train when he strayed on to the line, apparently to play a shot during a game. It was said that the accident had occurred because he was so intent on his golf that he was oblivious to the approach of the engine, a situation exacerbated, or so it was claimed, by his apparent hardness of hearing.

Delightful and inexpensive

A feature of the East Neuk for many years was the presence of railway camping coaches at various locations along the coast. These coaches, which were converted out of old passenger carriages, were intended to provide simple and relatively cheap self-catering accommodation for families or groups of friends holidaying together. The annual BR leaflet entitled 'Camping Coaches for delightful, inexpensive holidays' contained useful information for would-be campers including 'Make a friend of the Station Master who will be glad to help you in any way he can to make your holiday a success. He knows the locality and can advise on outings, fishing, golf and in many other ways' while campers were also advised that 'all coaches are fully equipped with crockery, cutlery, cooking utensils, towels, table and bed linen. Lighting, cooking and heating is ... by paraffin fuel, the cost of which is not included in the rental. Supplies are obtainable from the Station Master at a moderate charge'. The Fife coaches were all six-berthers and were available between March and October at an inclusive weekly rent of between £7 and £12 10*s*. A minimum of four full-fare (children counting as half-fare) tickets from the campers' home station had to be purchased and 'as the demand for camping coaches greatly exceeds the accommodation available during the holiday months, it is inevitable that a number of applicants must be disappointed. In allocating the available accommodation the management give preference to parties travelling the longest rail distance'.

Camping coaches, which were originally substantial redundant bogie vehicles of London & North Western and Caledonian origin, reappeared in Scotland in 1952* and for the 1953 season British Railways placed one each in the dock siding at Elie and in the siding adjacent to the platform at Lundin Links; for the 1954 season they were joined by a further coach at St Monance, which was tucked away in the goods yards. These must have proved popular for not only did they reappear each year but at each location the single coach was, in 1956, joined by another, the second coach being placed at Elie every summer until 1963, at Lundin Links until 1961. At the end of each season the coaches were sent to St Rollox works in Glasgow for overhaul before being returned to Elie, Lundin Links or St Monance for storage.

The 1963 season was the last one in which camping coaches were stationed in the area. As the coaches aged and their standards began to decline a number of ex-Pullman cars, with a superior standard of accommodation and an increased weekly rental of £15, began to arrive in Scotland and in 1963 one was placed at St Monance in place of the regular carriage. This, however, proved to be a swansong for the coaches did not appear in East Fife for the 1964, season, no doubt because, by then, the whole line was under a sentence of death.

* An earlier LNER camping coach had been stationed at Kingsbarns in 1938 but had been withdrawn when war broke out – see *The Anstruther & St Andrews Railway*.

Luckie Mucklebackit leaves Largo on a Crail to Thornton working in September 1958.
W.J.V. Anderson

'B1' class 4-6-0 No. 61140 with a down train leaving Largo on 1st August, 1959. *J.L. Stevenson*

Innovations and Improvements

On the passenger front, however, not all was doom and gloom for high summer services were still well patronized, particularly during the Glasgow and Edinburgh trades holidays and the revival of such institutions as Sunday train services on the southern part of the line and the reappearance of the 'Fife Coast Express' all helped to give an illusion that the line would continue to serve its traditional role well into the future. During the 1957 national bus strike there was a sudden influx of passengers and a typical effect was that noted by the *Leven Mail* of 31st July:

> Leven station was no place for the workshy or the comatose types last week particularly during the last few days of the week. Around 30,000 people boarded outward bound trains and a great many were holidaymakers returning to Glasgow, but just as many were daytrippers only going as far as Cameron or Kirkcaldy. Friday was the peak day for handling passengers and 7 extra trains were laid on.

The 'Fife Coast Express' ran for the last time in 1959 but a similar service continued in the following season, albeit without a name and by now composed of rather more mundane stock. However, it was recognised that traditional steam-hauled services were both expensive to operate and were becoming relatively unpopular with the general travelling public who, in an age of increasing sophistication, expected better. In 1959 the first diesel-multiple-units (dmus) were introduced on East Fife services, including on through services to Glasgow and Edinburgh. In May 1960 the majority of passenger services on the Thornton to Anstruther section of line were turned over to dmu operation and, although they did bring some of the necessary savings in expenditure and did something to boost public demand, they did not entirely supplant steam-hauled services. Many felt that an opportunity had not been taken to make further savings by eliminating steam-haulage altogether and by introducing conductor-guard working with the sale of tickets by the train crew and the consequent de-staffing of the passenger stations. On 1st April, 1960 further improvements took place when substantial cuts were made to journey times between Leven and Edinburgh and additional evening and morning services were provided. With the decline in goods workings and the advent of the dmus the small motive power depot at Anstruther was closed in the following month although its turntable, the only one on the whole line between Thornton and Leuchars, was retained so that visiting locomotives could still be turned when and if necessary.

What was not quite so apparent, however, was that, within the next few years, the private car would effectively supplant both the passenger train and the bus throughout the county and that the cheap foreign holiday would bring a gradual halt to the summer holiday trade. Although dieselization was a welcome advance on the life-expired passenger stock which had operated the line in the 1950s, traffic over the line in the winter months was dwindling almost to nothing and the bus and private car had, effectively, already won the battle.

Beeching and the Burghs

Passenger services along the coastal line continued although certain staff economies were put into effect and the signal box at Kilconquhar West, which latterly had only been in use at summer weekends, was closed altogether on 7th February, 1962. Then, in December 1962, letters were received from the Scottish Railway Development

A Swindon-built dmu on a Leven to Thornton service entering Cameron Bridge with the River Leven in the background. *Alan Goodwillie*

The 12.26 pm dmu from Crail picks up a single passenger at Pittenweem on 3rd October, 1959. *Roy Hamilton*

'B1' class 4-6-0 No. 61143 leaves St Monance with the 11.35 am empty coaching stock working from Crail to Thornton on 26th July, 1963. *Roy Hamilton*

'B1' class 4-6-0 No. 61133 at Largo with the 10.35 am Crail to Edinburgh Waverley service on 27th July, 1963, note the holidaymakers. *Roy Hamilton*

Grimy class 'J38' 0-6-0 No. 65916 at Kilconquhar on a Thornton-bound parcels working in 1964. *W.J.V. Anderson*

Association by the clerks of the various burghs and local authorities all along the line giving a warning that the rumours circulating in relation to the proposed closure of the Fife coast line were almost certainly based on fact and that the Association was prepared to offer what help they could if, and when, these proposals became a reality. The financial position of the newly-formed British Railways Board (BRB) was, by now, widely known to be extremely precarious and getting worse by the minute. It was therefore with little surprise that the BRB issued, in March 1963, their report on *The Reshaping of British Railways*, compiled under the aegis of their then Chairman, Dr Richard Beeching. Local fears were immediately confirmed – the whole of the section between Leven and St Andrews and all intermediate stations were listed for closure and the two stubs at either end, the Thornton to Leven and Leuchars to St Andrews lines, were somewhat ominously listed as 'not for development' and whose passenger services were to be kept under regular review.

The canny East Neuk folk had, however, already foreshadowed these conclusions and a public meeting had been held in Pittenweem on 19th February of that year to discuss the possible closure of their line. At that meeting a committee was formed, consisting of the provosts of the five East Neuk burghs (A.W. Scott of Elie & Earlsferry, the indomitable James Braid of St Monance,* J.D. Lawson of Pittenweem, John Armour of Anstruther and Tom Forsyth of Crail) with a remit to arrange meetings in Edinburgh with Sir John Gilmour, the Conservative and Unionist Member of Parliament for the area and with representatives of the Scottish Tourist Board, the Scottish Council for Development and Industry and the British Railways Board. And they proceeded to do this without delay. Once the Beeching plans were made public, a further meeting of interested parties was held in St Monance town hall, where it was presided over by Provost Braid, who became a leading light in the attempt to save the East Neuk line.

In September 1963 the British Railways Board formally intimated to the local authorities their intention to withdraw the passenger service between Leven and St Andrews and the stations at Crail, Anstruther, Pittenweem, St Monance, Elie, Kilconquhar, Largo and Lundin Links from a date to be announced. With the exception of the St Andrews Town Council, who seemed to have adopted a somewhat laconic and disinterested position, the response of the local authorities was swift and vociferous and the Five Burghs Committee resolved that they would fight the proposals all of the way and that 'every possible protest should be lodged by the people living between St Andrews and Leven'.

Public Protest, Private Grief

This protest did, in fact, take place and at the hearing held as a result of representations by the statutory body set up to consider passenger service withdrawals, the Transport Users' Consultative Committee (TUCC) one of the strongest arguments put forward by local objectors was that the tourist trade would be irreparably damaged by the withdrawal of services – a fact that was specially poignant given that the local councils and tourist board had been making great effort to publicize the attractions of the East Neuk towns to holidaymakers. Mr Ronald Prime, who was the then manager of the Anstruther Holiday Camp at Cellardyke† said that, during the 12 week summer season

* Jimmy Braid was something of a local hero whose dedication to his home town of St Monans was legendary!

† The Holiday Camp was based in the old buildings and site of RAF Anstruther, a post-war defence facility which, having failed to find any proper use in the Cold War, was now host to a flock of caravans – it continued in such use until the beginning of the present century and now is the site of the 'Silverdykes' housing estate.

Ex-LMS Stanier 'Black Five' 4-6-0 No. 45058 leaves the sylvan delights of Elie on 4th July, 1964.
C.C. Thornburn

'B1' class 4-6-0 No. 61342 enters a busy Elie station on 4th July, 1964. *C.C. Thornburn*

there, an estimated 3,500 of his customers came to Anstruther by train and that 'they really bring all the house with them. I doubt if they could ever get their luggage on a bus'. Another source of worry was what might happen to the hordes of schoolchildren who regularly used the train to travel to and from the Waid Academy at Anstruther and who, ironically, formed virtually the sole commuter traffic on the section east of Leven. The Fife County Council's education committee representative claimed that about 100 of the pupils of the school daily relied on the train and that they would be seriously inconvenienced by the closure. But the truth of the matter was, perhaps, otherwise. The East Fife coastal line had been built in an era when there were few rivals for its traffic and by the 1960s it still enjoyed heavy traffic on summer weekends from day-trippers and holidaymakers. The position in winter was, however, different and apart from the Waid Academy pupils, few locals used the train – hardly surprising, given the distance of several of the stations from the towns they purported to serve. The failure of the new dmus to stop the decline, notwithstanding their undoubted attraction for passengers could hardly go unnoticed. Indeed one of the authors remembers a weekday journey from Pittenweem at the height of the summer season when the train in both directions was virtually empty and, as was common at this time when people all over Britain were being extremely vociferous in their defence of their local railway lines, those who used the line least protested the most, oblivious of the maxim 'Use it, Don't Lose it!'

The debate continued but the British Railways Board held their ground and the incoming Labour government, strangely hostile to the plight of the BRB, ignored the representations of Sir John Gilmour. In February 1965, the Transport Minister, Tom Fraser, having considered the TUCC report 'was satisfied that if certain adjustments to existing bus and rail services were made to improve bus-rail interchange arrangements at Leven, any remaining hardship would be insufficient to justify the retention of the services'. Both Sir John and Provost Braid were, however, indomitable in their fight to prevent the East Neuk from losing its passenger services but the seemingly inevitable was now impossible to resist. Whether or not there was a case for keeping the line open as a social necessity was, apparently, never seriously considered by the government* and thus, on one level, the closure was politically motivated; on another it was more than justified economically and even the most ardent of railway enthusiasts would have struggled to present a good economic case for the retention of the service, certainly that running west of Crail. On 19th April, 1965 the East Neuk town councils received a letter from the Board stating that,

> After giving consideration to the various representations made regarding the effect on summer visitors to the Fife coast, it has been decided that the railway service should continue through June, July and August, and that the official closure notices will be published in the usual way, once details of the substitute bus and rail services have been finalised. In addition to extra buses, more trains would be provided between Leven and Edinburgh, connecting with buses to and from Crail.

In due course the closure date was announced as Monday 6th September, 1965, and replacement bus services were to be provided by W. Alexander & Sons (Fife) Ltd on a variety of routes, most of which gave a connection to the remaining railheads at Cupar, Leven or St Andrews.

One final attempt was made to save the passenger service between Leven and St Andrews and on 30th July a meeting was held in Glasgow between representatives of the

* Two contemporary reprieves on 'social' grounds (or, more cynically, grounds of political expediency) were the Far North line to Thurso and Wick and the Central Wales line from Shrewsbury to Swansea via Llandrindod Wells, both of which are still open today.

A 'J38' class 0-6-0 leaves the East Fife line at Thornton with a mixed freight in April 1965.
C.C. Thornburn

The new face of British Rail! Anstruther, 4th September, 1965. *C.C. Thornburn*

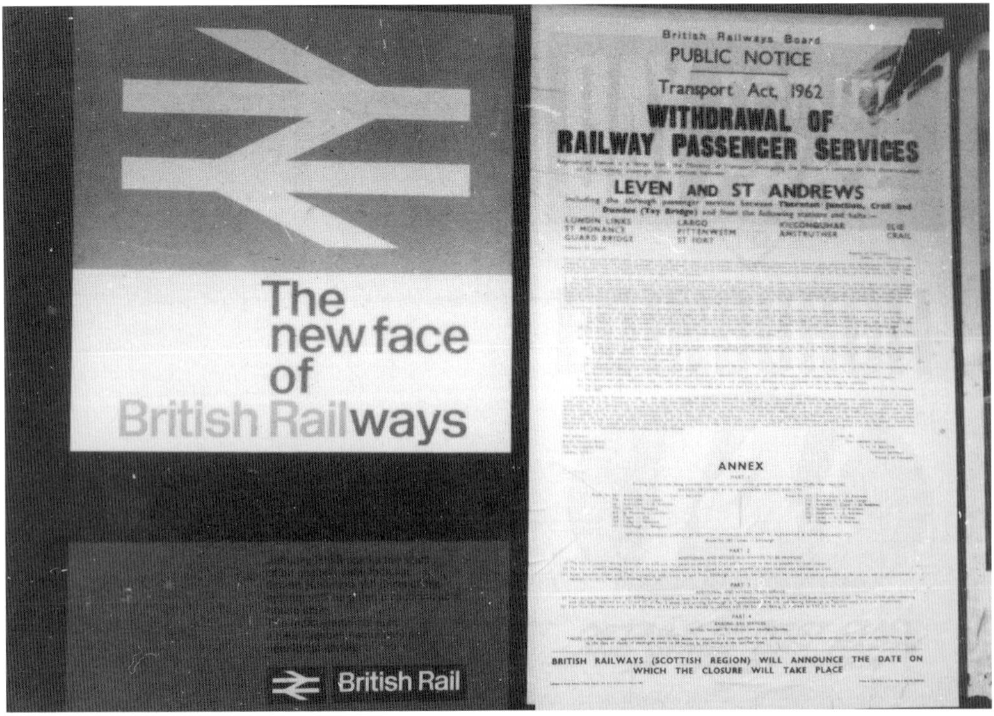

East Neuk burghs, Sir John Gilmour and the British Railways Board. Representations were, however, made in vain as the decision had already been taken and the BRB's hands were tied. With great prescience, Sir John roundly criticized the proposed alternative bus services, while expressing the view that Leven itself would only be a temporary railhead and that, within a couple of years, the station there would also be facing closure. He described the meeting with the Board as having been 'completely negative' and said that 'the possibility of continuation of the passenger service ... was now more remote than ever'. However, undaunted even at this late stage Provost Braid put forward the view that the line could be saved by de-manning stations, automating level crossings and by running four diesel trains each way per day between Dundee and Edinburgh via Crail on the principles advanced by Professor Hondelink, an academic whose views the Five Burghs Committee had sought. Such proposals were hardly radical,* but these further proposals fell on stony ground – the Board had resolved to withdraw the service, and given the dead hand of the government upon them, withdraw it they would.

In another final attempt Provost Braid wrote to the Secretary of State for Scotland and he said that,

> I am writing this to you before the closure of the East Fife railway line. In spite of several representations, you have chosen to hide behind the fact that this decision is that of the Minister of Transport and that this must be accepted. Surely, in view of the responsibility which your own office has over affairs in Scotland, it is proper that you should act against this empty policy. Perhaps you are not aware that our part of Fife has been classified as a development area. Perhaps your advisors have not made the position clear that this decision will wreck our tourist industry and completely jeopardise any chance we may have of further development. Surely you, sir, cannot isolate yourself on the slim pretext that it is a colleague's decision. Surely your office must be more than an empty figurehead not capable or allowable to make decisions that are vital to the economy of a part of our nation. Surely, sir, it is your duty to act now in this matter, or do you prefer the continuance of the bankrupt Tory policy?

Evidently the Minister did prefer the continuance of the previous administration's 'bankrupt policy' and, in foreshadowing the future, a Labour government once again was prepared to axe a further part of our national railway network.

Last Rites

Goods services were now firmly in a terminal decline and on 5th October, 1964 had been withdrawn between Crail and St Andrews. On the same day the siding at Silverburn was also formally closed although it is doubtful if this siding had actually handled much public traffic for many years. Then, with effect from 25th January, 1965, the once busy goods yard at Leven, situated in the old Leven Railway terminus, was closed to general traffic although the private sidings in the area all remained in use meanwhile. This left the yards and sidings at Anstruther, Pittenweem, St Monance, Elie, Kilconquhar, Largo and Lundin Links still nominally in operation although the only staple traffic which survived in any quantity was household coal brought by occasional trip workings from Kirkland and Thornton.

* De-manning, automatic or open crossings and conductor-guard working had been put into effect on the Central Wales and other rural lines and was widespread on the East Anglian lines where the 'Pay-train' concept was widespread – the authors have no explanation why similar measures were never tried out in Scotland in the 1960s and one might have thought that the East Fife lines were a prime candidate for such an experiment.

On the passenger front the last summer season of all was a quiet one although a slight influx of people making sentimental last journeys now that the fate of the line had been fixed did almost imperceptibly augment the figures. The few remaining goods services were still almost entirely steam hauled as were some of the seasonal through services from Glasgow and Edinburgh but otherwise all services were operated by dmus. The last public passenger service south of St Andrews that was operated by steam over the line was the 14.28 St Andrews to Glasgow summer Saturday-only service on 21st August, 1965 while the last steam-hauled passenger service of all was the 14.35 Crail to Thornton train, complete with its solitary fish van, which ran for the last time on Saturday 4th September. Thereafter it was up to the humble diesel multiple units to celebrate the last rites.

The honour of being the last passenger train between St Andrews and Leven fell to the 17.05 Dundee to Glasgow service which left St Andrews at 17.38 and served all of the local stations between Crail and Thornton. The final northbound service between Thornton and St Andrews via Crail ran later the same evening and was the 19.41 from Edinburgh Waverley to St Andrews, due at the latter station at 22.03 where it was welcomed by a large crowd who had gathered to see the last train over the former Anstruther & St Andrews Railway enter the town.

The final day of services over the East of Fife section – Sunday, 5th September, started in brilliant sunshine when the two morning dmu services from, respectively, Glasgow and Edinburgh served all of the coastal stations and brought the last handful of day-trippers by rail to enjoy the delights of the East Neuk. Excitement mounted all day amongst locals who were determined to give their local line a good send-off and Alexanders put on a special bus from Leven to take those who wished to travel on the last train, the 18.20 Crail to Glasgow, the last eastbound service having gone several hours before. Before 6 o'clock the ticket office at Crail had run out of tickets and paper certificates had to be issued in their place. The last ticket of all, No. 0599, was issued by the overwhelmed ticket clerk at the station to George Clacher, a coal merchant from Leven, and he had it signed by Jimmy Dobson of Eastfield, the driver of the last train. Provost Braid, in a short speech, remarked that he wished that there was an official from British Rail present to witness the interest shown by the folk of East Fife in their railway, adding that the closure was a tragedy and that the large crowd was present not because it was the last train but rather because they were interested in the continuance of the line – were that that was indeed the case!

Then, according to the *Fife Mail*,

> ... it was all aboard and with a final sounding of the two-tone horn, the last passenger train on the East of Fife line left Crail station seven minutes late. Among the passengers were a number of passengers with special reasons for travelling including Thomas Spinks, 72, a retired engine driver who had spent half of his long working life driving trains on the line and was wearing the watch presented to him on his retirement for the occasion, and W.Scott of Crail who had started working at the station in his home town 45 years before 'so I have seen more than half of its history'. Another passenger was Marjory Aitken of Braehead, St Monance, who had worked for the railway for the last 25 years mainly in the booking office at Elie and who now found herself out of a job. [Perhaps, most tellingly of all, the *Mail* reported] that two ladies from Lundin Links had made the journey to Crail to take their first and last journey over the line – a telling example of how many locals had ignored the railway to their peril. A little light relief was caused by a couple from Glasgow on a day-trip to Anstruther who recounted that they had not even realised that they would be on the last train until, enquiring that morning at Queen Street station as to the time of the return service were told that they would have to catch the 6.20 from Crail 'and that really is the last train – miss that and you'll have to walk!

All down the line people waved from the windows of houses and hotels and

> Sad though it may have been, none of the crowds waiting at the seven doomed stations along the route ... showed any signs of it. Dozens waited on each of the platforms and waved the train on its way. There were even a few balloons in sight and at Pittenweem there were detonators on the line to make sure that the train went with a bang. The approach of the home stretch of the East Neuk line between Lundin Links and Leven was the cue for the final rush to get that last photograph from the train and for young railway enthusiasts to make the final notes. As the train made its last run into Leven station, the clouds opened and the rain came down, as if weeping in sympathy. Once again there were dozens waiting on the platform, but this time huddled together under the covered section for shelter. And when the train drew up at the platform, the last tablet (which allows a train to pass from one station to another) was handed to the waiting porter, who was just a little surprised to see a large yellow balloon tied to it.

Passengers stepped off the train into torrential rain, but that didn't stop one young girl making the day for driver Dobson by giving him a farewell kiss before the train sped off for Glasgow Queen Street. Watching the train pull out, Provost Braid commented 'I am convinced that this is not the last train to run on the line. I feel sure that it will run again, whether in a private business-like manner or by British Railways in a non business-like manner.' And then it was all over and the only sound left was the splattering of rain on the lines which had carried the last train from the East Neuk, leaving behind it only anxiety in the minds of those in the coastal burghs who faced a future without a railway.

Going ... Going ... Gone!

On Monday 6th September the buses took over and although the stations at Crail, Anstruther, Pittenweem, St Monance, Kilconquhar and Largo remained open for goods traffic, Elie and Lundin Links having been closed to goods at the same time as to passengers, a general air of neglect began to set in as the folk of the East Neuk began to realize that they would miss the trains that they seldom used. In the Anstruther council minutes for 27th September, 1965, under the heading of 'Railway Signs – Anstruther' it was recorded that the council had remitted to Councillor Pickford that he was to make the best bargain that he could to purchase signs from the now closed railway station at Anstruther, with powers to spend up to £10 – a veritable bargain given their present value but the minutes do not reveal whether any signs were, in fact, purchased. Elsewhere the enamel 'totems' on each station rapidly found their way into private hands, several of those at Kilconquhar being given to the local minister, a life-long railway enthusiast who had worked for the Railway Clearing House in the 1920s. Seats, clocks and moveable items were all removed from the stations and as the weeds began to encroach on the deserted platforms a new concern began to arise, that of the total inadequacy of the replacement bus services which, not unsurprisingly, were hopeless. On 21st September, 1965 St Monance council noted via Provost Braid that, 'the interchange arrangements made by W. Alexander & Sons (Fife) Ltd were proving most unsatisfactory' and, despite widespread protests, British Railways and the bus company involved showed little interest in accommodating the former railway passengers. No effort was made to maintain through ticketing or proper connections and the very real fears that the tourist trade would suffer went unheeded. Little more was heard of the scheme to run the line as a private enterprise despite the offers of money and, in one case, of a locomotive and this is, in retrospect, hardly surprising for it was to be several years away that the first

Above: A poor quality newspaper image of Gresley 'A4' Pacific No. 60009 *Union of South Africa* on its journey over Largo viaduct.
Authors' Collection

Right: 350 hp diesel shunter and No. 60009 pass through Leven station in April 1967 en route to Lochty.
Alan Goodwillie

successful 'preserved' line in Scotland, the Strathspey line between Aviemore and Boat of Garten in the Highlands, was to open for business. And Provost Braid's fears that the Labour government would show no further interest was well-founded and it was to be a generation away into the future that a devolved coalition government in Holyrood would show a true interest in a by now sadly depleted railway system.

Strict economies were now carried out including the closure of the signal boxes at Crail, St Monans and Elie and their reduction to ground frames with effect from 5th October, 1965, while those at Anstruther and Largo were closed altogether. On 26th February, 1966 the Crail to Leven section was reduced to 'one engine in steam' status. The goods service continued to operate in a sporadic fashion between Crail and Leven but it was obvious that it was being run-down pending total closure. Within months Anstruther council were enquiring of the British Railways Board if they could have permission to use the goods yard in the town as a temporary car park but were informed that the yard would be in use until its scheduled closure date in April 1966 and that the Board were still considering possible disposals of the land. The end was, however, not long in coming and closure notices were posted in May 1966 informing the public, or at least the small proportion of the public who still cared, that goods services were to be withdrawn with effect from 18th July, 1966 and the stations at Crail, Pittenweem, St Monance, Kilconquhar and Largo were to be closed to all traffic. Thereafter all remaining wagons and moveables were collected and the line was officially closed with effect from 18th December 1966;* the grass-grown track was now left to await its fate at the hands of the demolition gangs.

A poorly used service

At the western end of the former coastal line, the remaining section from Leven to Thornton Junction seemed to have been granted a new lease of life following the closure of the line from Crail. Leven remained, at least nominally, as the railhead for the East of Fife line bus replacement services, notwithstanding the fact that the services latterly did not actually run up to the station and a transfer between the two modes of transport involved a walk. The timetable was revised, and the passenger service of through dmu trains between Leven and Edinburgh, obviating the need to change at the increasingly decrepit Thornton Junction station, consisted of eight trains per day from Leven between 6.44 am and 8.25 pm, with 10 regular journeys in the opposite direction, and was relatively well patronized. Goods services, however, continued to decline and the public freight facilities at Cameron Bridge station were withdrawn on 11th September, 1967; the majority of the private sidings on the line, however, were to continue in use albeit that they appeared by now to be fairly poorly used.

In view of the increasing losses being made by British Rail it was perhaps inevitable in an area already well served by buses that closure of the Leven to Thornton line to passengers would follow. In September 1967 a deputation from Fife County Council was sent to London to meet the Minister of Transport to put the case for various lines in Fife threatened with closure, namely the St Andrews, Newport and Leven branches. Provost Charles Gardner of Leven reported to the *Dundee Courier* that his burgh were 'trying to attract the family holidaymaker – the mum and dad with their four kids and all their

* In actual fact the last train on the line was one conveying a locomotive that would never have been permitted to travel over the line. In April 1967 the 'A4' Pacific *Union of South Africa* was hauled by a 350 hp diesel locomotive complete with match wagons to spread its axle weight and a brake van along to Crail for onward transmission to the Lochty Private Railway – the very first and last time such a mighty locomotive was seen on the line! Incidentally clearance restrictions required for the engine meant that a dozen platform edging slabs had to be removed at Kilconquhar.

No. 65918 returns to Thornton with a track-lifting train from the coast line. *Alan Goodwillie*

cases'. But the figures were not encouraging and in what was described as 'a representative week' in May 1968, a passenger census showed that 203 persons joined the trains every day at Leven and 193 alighted, whereas the respective figures for Cameron Bridge were 58 and 63 and for Thornton Junction 302 and 292, the latter being, of course, mainly railwaymen. The Leven service also provided the stops on the two main-line stations between Thornton and Kirkcaldy, namely Dysart (46 and 39 passengers) and Sinclairtown (235 and 166). In addition it was claimed by British Rail that the Leven service was running at a considerable loss and although something would be saved by de-manning the stations and selling tickets on the train, there was no possibility of the line breaking even. Accordingly in December 1968 closure notices were posted, the date being given for the withdrawal of the service as 6th January, 1969, the same date as the Leuchars-St Andrews service.

There having been formal objections to the closure, which also involved the stations at Thornton, Dysart and Sinclairtown on the main line, it was necessary to postpone the closure to allow the TUCC for Scotland to hold a public inquiry and this was done in the same month.

Complete betrayal

At a three-hour long hearing before about 30 members of the public and held in the Scoonie Hotel, Leven on 15th January, 1969, the TUCC Chairman, E.W. Craig, stated that the annual receipts for the branch line were given as £7,230 while the estimated direct expenses of operating the service was given as £56,640. Sir John Gilmour MP gave evidence first and castigated British Rail for the fact that the current public timetable was misleading, that bus connections were poor and that the Edinburgh-bound trains often managed to miss Glasgow trains at Haymarket by a matter of minutes. Thomas Murdoch, a daily commuter from Leven, stated that he currently caught the 7.34 train but that if the train service was withdrawn he would have to catch a bus to Kirkcaldy at 6.50 am in order to arrive at Edinburgh at the same time and that his working day would consequently be increased by over an hour. A further insult would be caused by the fact that he would have to read a tabloid newspaper as his usual broadsheet would not fit in the bus! Another commuter pointed out that it would cost £2 a week to drive his car from Leven to the new railhead at Kirkcaldy. Other local residents had fears that the buses would be unable to carry large quantities of luggage and this was a particular concern to a Pittenweem lady who had four sons away at English universities.

Further objections were raised in respect of longer and more expensive journey times by bus for National Union of Railwaymen members travelling to work at Thornton and an inability to take their bicycles with them, that 12 members of staff at Cameron Hospital would no longer be able to rely on the train to get to work and patients' visitors would also be affected and that a local farmer who would now have to take his livestock to Markinch to catch the train (although given that the hearing was dealing with the withdrawal of passenger services this objection seems to have been misplaced). The same farmer commented that, 'both the present and the past governments have condoned the sabotage of the railway system' and this was followed by a possible legal objection from an Elie solicitor, David Thomson, who said that the closure of Lundin Links station had been ultra vires in terms of the Leven & East of Fife Railway Act 1855 and that in closing a further section of the line British Rail was acting beyond it powers. A particular concern was expressed by David Reid, the Fife County Council traffic officer, who stated that since the Levenmouth area was now one of the five special development districts in

Scotland the absence of a railway connection would cause difficulties and further that Leven's status as a holiday resort would also be adversely affected. George Sharp, the chairman of Kirkcaldy District Council was more blunt when he said that, 'The decision to close Leven station is in our opinion a complete betrayal by British Rail of the underlying promise that was given when the East Fife branch line was closed. At that time it was indicated that if the East Fife line was closed there would be complete integration of the transport services in the area and that Leven station itself would ultimately become a bridge-head for the tourist requirements of the East Fife region'. Reid then queried the financial information which had been adduced on behalf of British Rail but this attempt to open up the validity of the figures produced was ruled out of order by Craig, the chairman, who also rejected any idea that British Rail had given any guarantees about the future of Leven station. A.B. Arundale, for British Rail, said that between 1964 and 1967 there had been a 24 per cent drop in the number of season tickets issued: at Cameron Bridge 15 per cent, at Thornton Junction 15 per cent, at Dysart 23 per cent and at Sinclairtown 20 per cent, partly explained by the fact that many commuters drove to Kirkcaldy to catch the better services from there. It was recorded that of those who held season tickets valid from Kirkcaldy six were held by residents of Leven, four from Lundin Links residents and one each from persons resident in Lower Largo and Crail. He continued, 'Let it not be said, and it has been said here today, that we have not made economies. They have been made in relation to the whole of the Fife train services of which the line under discussion was a part. Since 1963 there have been three major economy exercises. They had been based on computer techniques which in 1964, 1966 and 1968, resulted in the saving of many vehicles, men and miles ... without major reductions in the number of trains.'

He then gave further figures relating to the number of season ticket holders using the line stating that, in October 1968, the statistics were: Leven 32 (28 to Edinburgh, 4 to Kirkcaldy), Cameron Bridge 5 (all to Edinburgh), Thornton 9 (6 to Edinburgh, 2 to Cowdenbeath, 1 to Burntisland), Dysart 24 (14 to Edinburgh, 26 to Rosyth, 3 to Inverkeithing, 2 to Aberdour). This gave a total of 134 regular travellers, the Kirkcaldy season ticket holders including six Leven residents, four from Lundin Links and one each from Lower Largo and Crail. He then added that although the different cost of bus and rail travel via Kirkcaldy was not material he would concede that overall travelling times would be longer. There was nothing to stop local authorities from subsidizing local services if they so wished but, according to Mr Craig, that was a matter for themselves and the Minister.

The last witness, James Tweedie, commercial manager of the Scottish Bus Group, gave the show away when he admitted very candidly that, 'Bus services had been built up over the years to serve Fife and beyond and had not been designed as road-rail inter-connecting services. Their primary purpose had been the service of the communities'. And, in view of the fact that the so-called connecting services had already been routed away from Leven station and the company's unwillingness to provide better connections if the Leven line was to close, it appeared that the 'service of the communities' effectively meant that this bore a direct relation to the profits of the nationalized Scottish Bus Group and little to the environmental and social benefits which an integrated transport system would have brought to the country. Its privatized successors have been no better in either of these respects.

One body that did not object was the Levenmouth Trades Council who had already decided that they could not put forward a case for the saving of the passenger service but that they would fight to save the freight service – a fight that, too, was doomed.

The Loss of Leven

Given the way that the TUCC inquiry had been conducted and the willingness of the Labour government to go further than the Tories had dared, it was thus not surprising that in June 1969 the Minister of Transport announced that he had given his consent to the discontinuance of all railway passenger services between Thornton Junction and Leven but an assurance was given that such a closure would not be effected before the end of the holiday season.* Once again no social grant would be forthcoming and therefore on 2nd September British Rail formally announced that the service would be withdrawn and the stations at Leven, Cameron Bridge, Thornton Junction, Dysart and Sinclairtown closed with effect from Monday 6th October, 1969. Once again, there being no Sunday service, the last trains were to run on the previous Saturday.

According to the *East Fife Mail* of 8th October,

> The broken clock on the platform at Leven station signalled on Saturday evening that time had despairingly run out for the passenger train at Leven for at 8.25 pm the last passenger train left from a dark and dejected platform on its ultimate journey to Thornton. A sizeable crowd had gathered on the platform to catch a fleeting glimpse of the last diesel as it pulled slowly out of Leven station. Camera flash bulbs lit up the darkened station as some enthusiasts captured the last chance to picture a passenger train leaving Leven. About 100 people, young and old, had actually boarded the train to make a last sentimental journey. Most of these only travelled the short distance to Thornton or Kirkcaldy, but a few ventured further along the line. A crowd gathered at Thornton to give the train a cheer and a wave as it left on the journey to Edinburgh where it would be gobbled up in the hurly burly of the busy Waverley station.
>
> Driving the last train was Mr Andrew Low, a railwayman of 35 years service, from Dundee, who commented, 'It is never good when a line closes, but these things happen. If it had not been this line that closed, it would just have been some other.' Guard George A. Mair, who started in the railway as a porter in 1954 added 'Jobs have been lost over the closing of this station and this cannot be a good thing'. He added, 'I am both proud and sad to be on this last train journey'. Three railwaymen, with 134 years service among them, shared the last compartment of the six carriage train. They were Mr Hugh MacGregor, resplendent in kilt and bonnet, of Wellesley Road, Methil, brother Alex and William Davidson from Kirkcaldy. All three were former signalmen with the North British Railway and they started their railway career in Edinburgh. One said 'We all took the last carriage so that we could have a backview from the train as it pulled out of Leven station for the last time'.

And it was, indeed, a backview for, in the space of barely five years, East Fife had regressed by more than a century back to the era of the horse and trap and a time when the only railheads had been the newly-opened but distant stations at Kirkcaldy, Cupar and Leuchars. The government had spoken and the trains had vanished.

* This was in contrast to the decision, announced on 19th September, 1969, to reprieve the North Berwick branch line, a fact which was noted and commented on in East Fife.

Chapter Thirteen

East Neuk Derailed: From 1969 to the present day

'I would be willing to look at the proposition of a passenger/goods rail link between Leven and Kirkcaldy.'

Malcolm Rifkind, Secretary of State for Scotland, 1987

The Railway Vanishes

By 1969 the demolition gangs had removed most of the rails by lorry* and those structures which remained but were thought to have any real scrap value, such as girders and footbridges, were cut up on site and removed within the next year or so. With the end of any proper maintenance sections of the trackbed were becoming waterlogged and choked with weeds and in the former station gardens those plants that had not been removed for use elsewhere ran riot. Then, as part of a remarkably short-sighted view taken by the County Council and despite the early efforts of some local residents backed by the recommendation of a statutory body, the Countryside Commission for Scotland, the section of trackbed between St Monance and Leven was sold off in small chunks to whoever was willing to buy it. The eastward portion from the former place to Anstruther had been already disposed of and thus a potentially excellent route for cyclists, rides and ramblers disappeared for good. The former level crossing houses were nearly all sold off as private dwellings but the stations had a mixed fate. The by-now disused section of line between East Fife Central Junction and Leven station was declared out of use as from 12th October, 1969 and thereafter lay derelict until lifting operations began in March 1973 when the main station buildings at Leven were demolished; traces of the platform with its fence survived until the road alterations of relatively recent times. The Glenlyon Road bridge was demolished in 1990 and with this, and the removal of the level crossings that had once so bedevilled traffic, congestion problems in the town were alleviated. The trackbed to the east of Leven station was landscaped by the Leven Town Council in 1969-1970.

At Silverburn the site of the siding was incorporated into the Silverburn Country Park and the station at Lundin Links was bought by the local golf club and demolished in 1971. Largo station also disappeared within a short time – the site survives, however, as a car park and for many years the 'lion on the wheel' motif in the former station garden could be clearly seen. At Kilconquhar the station buildings were incorporated into a private house and still has the distinction of being the most recognizable Leven & East of Fife station to survive. Elie station was gutted by fire in 1968 (reputedly started by a disgruntled former railway employee) and for days half-burnt items of NBR paperwork littered the streets; the remains of the station were pulled down and replaced by a small development of houses appropriately named after William Baird. St Monance station disappeared when road alterations were undertaken although the gaunt footbridge survived until the late 1970s – the station yard is now an industrial estate where a local man, Ian Kirk, had a factory producing scale model railway wagons out of polystyrene.† Pittenweem station

* A BR 350 hp diesel locomotive had been hired out to the demolition contractors and was used for a time when the line was being lifted.

† The business expanded and subsequently moved to a site in Kirkcaldy.

building survives as an equestrian centre although an unsympathetic coat of harling and new windows have radically altered its looks; the goods yard was, after closure, used as a scrap yard but has a much tidier look nowadays in its new guise. Anstruther New station has disappeared and its cutting has been filled in but the site of Anstruther Old, where not built on, has survived as a public park and its layout is still quite recognisable. Other features remain including many of the stone under and over bridges and, of course, the two mighty viaducts at Largo and Anstruther. Parts of the trackbed remain but others have been swept away under the plough; other tangible assets include NBR houses and a plethora of 'station' and 'railway' road names.

In contrast the remaining section of the Leven & East of Fife Railway, that line from Leven Dock to Thornton, survives intact (apart from the track) and the platform at Cameron Bridge is still extant but of Thornton Junction, closed on the same day as the Leven branch, there is little to remind the present day traveller on the Aberdeen main line that, once upon a time, Thornton was a major railway centre.

When the line to Anstruther was closed, the local bus service was nominally revamped so that, as before, most local journeys would terminate at the bus station which had been built on the site of Leven Dock and thus passengers for Edinburgh and the West would require to change onto a train or another bus. With the closure of the Leven branch another lost opportunity ensued when the obvious step of continuing the coastal bus route from the bus station at Leven through East Wemyss to Kirkcaldy, where it could have provided connections at the railway station there, was not taken notwithstanding the Inter-City status of Kirkcaldy and the fact that, according to surveys, it was a more popular destination for shoppers from the East Neuk than any other. British Rail apparently did not care that they had lost any possible traffic from the towns between Largo and Crail while the Scottish Bus Group were not interested in providing an interchange – a disgraceful example of two nationalized concerns who had little regard for the real interests of the travelling public! For many years Fife Scottish provided a basic round-the-coast service until, on privatization, the Stagecoach group took over. Some short-lived local services were provided but the basic pattern remained of an hourly service between Dundee, Leuchars, St Andrews, Kingsbarns, Crail, Anstruther, Pittenweem, St Monance, Elie, Kilconquhar, Largo, Lundin Links and Leven. A few years ago this was replaced by a St Andrews to Leven via Crail service served, often, by double-deck buses. In addition an hourly service from St Andrews to Edinburgh service via Anstruther (by the direct road via Dunino) and then from Anstruher via same villages as the coast service to Leven before going on to Kirkcaldy and the Forth Road Bridge – this was dubbed an 'express' service by its operators but only 'express' in the same sense as the North British understood it! What the buses lack in comfort they make up in frequency but unfortunately many in the East Neuk have long forsaken public transport and it will take a lot more effort to persuade them otherwise.

Fading Away

Following this closure the line between Thornton Junction and East Fife Central Junction was singled and downgraded to goods standard only, the signal boxes at Cameron Bridge and East Fife Central Junction being closed on 8th March, 1970, the former being replaced by a ground frame to serve the distillery sidings. The whole of the line between Thornton and Methil East (i.e. the remaining sections of the

Two views of diesel-electric locomotive No. 26027 with CO_2 tanks at Cameron Bridge on 11th July, 1991. *(Both) Nicholas Walker*

Leven Railway and the Leven Dock branch) was singled in December 1972 and thereafter worked by the telephone and notice board system but traffic was continuing to decline and all the remaining sidings in the Leven area had closed between 1968 and 1971. The decline in the coal traffic resulted in Kirkland Yard ceasing to be worked on a 24-hour basis in September 1976 and coal shipments from Methil Dock ended when the *Sir John Snell* left the docks for the last time with a load on 18th May, 1977. Kirkland Yard was closed to all traffic in September 1977 and the public goods facilities at Methil followed in 1980 thus leaving the only remaining traffic over the Thornton to Leven Dock section as that serving the power station at Methil, the distillery at Cameron Bridge and a public coal siding at Leven Dock. At Cameron Bridge further track alterations were made when, in May 1975, the main line was slued to the eastbound side of the still-extant passenger island platform and the westbound line was converted into an east-facing siding known as the Platform siding. However, the transport of grain to Cameron Bridge distillery ceased by the end of 1978, apparently due to changes in railway freight tariffs which made it no longer cost effective for the Distillers Company Ltd (DCL) to use rail transport and in consequence this traffic was lost to road haulage.

For a brief period in the 1980s there was talk of a possible reopening of the Thornton to Leven line to passengers and the *East Fife Mail* of 11th January, 1984 reported that a Policy Charter had been drawn up between Fife Regional Council and British Rail which was stated to be 'a comprehensive feasibility study into improving rail access to communities remote from the network' with priority being given to the two largest non-rail served communities, Levenmouth and Glenrothes. Councillor Henry McLeish* stated that, 'There has been some pressure from the Levenmouth Community to see if a rail link would be a realistic proposition'. In March 1987 the *East Fife Mail* reported that in an interview 'Getting Levenmouth back on the rails is an idea that interests Secretary of State for Scotland Mr Malcolm Rifkind', Rifkind had told *East Fife Mail* editor Ian Paterson that, 'I would be willing to look at the proposition of a passenger/goods rail link between Leven and Kirkcaldy'. He requested that further details should be forwarded to the Scottish Office and the newspaper article stated that the present line could be an additional aid in fostering trade and tourism in the area.

In the event, however, Levenmouth did not get its station but, consequent upon the inauguration of a new Edinburgh-Kirkcaldy-Cowdenbeath-Dunfermline-Edinburgh 'Fife Circle' service in 1989, a new station named Glenrothes with Thornton was opened on 11th May, 1992 on the Cowdenbeath line to the west of Thornton village. Although this station did attract some custom the inclusion of the new town of Glenrothes in its title was somewhat optimistic and as a railhead it was rather less attractive than Kirkcaldy which, with its mixture of slow and fast services to Edinburgh, enjoys a far better service.

Out of use

Leven Dock coal sidings were closed on 1st May, 1986 and subsequently lifted. There was, however, some residual traffic from the Cameron Bridge distillery when, during the early 1990s, liquefied carbon dioxide (CO_2) was conveyed to a rail depot in North London from Cameron Bridge. It was then used in the drinks industry and in processing poultry. The distillery sidings continued to appear in official literature and indeed on 12th June, 1992 were renamed from the then-current DCL (Cereals)

* Later Henry McLeish was, briefly, to become First Minister of the devolved Scottish Parliament and lived in Cellardyke.

sidings to the even clumsier Cameron Bridge, UMGD sidings; the CO_2 traffic did not last beyond a couple of years and a proposal to lay a new siding into the bottling plant at Leven came to naught. Coal traffic to Methil power station was latterly reduced to two trains per week worked to Kirkland Yard and from there propelled down the line to the power station. The fly ash residue was taken away by lorry. All traffic to the power station ceased in 1999 and the last remaining remnant of the East Fife line became officially 'out of use' and the points leading to it were formally clipped at Thornton North Junction during November 2001. By now it seemed extremely unlikely that anything but a demolition train would ever be seen running over the original Leven Railway.

Surprisingly, however, this was not the case. On Friday 28th February, 2003 a trial train was run by Direct Rail Services from Grangemouth to Cameron Bridge consisting of a single large bogie van of empty bottles sandwiched between a class '37' and a class '20' diesel locomotive. At Cameron Bridge the bottles were unloaded and a consignment of bottles filled with Smirnoff Ice vodka was loaded, the train then returning to Grangemouth, these bottles having been delivered empty by road earlier on. The train arrived and departed late from Cameron Bridge, the unloading and reloading of the wagon having taken much longer than expected due to insufficient space for a fork-lift truck to manoeuvre efficiently. Whether, however, regular distillery traffic returns to the line is largely a matter of economics and the effectiveness or otherwise of the government's, or more likely the European Communities' policies relating to rail freight and the proper taxation of fuel.

Demolishing the Glenlyon Road bridge, Leven in 1990. *Ian Addison*

Towards a revival

However, all is not yet lost for in 2009 plans were afoot for a new siding at the Double Dykes level crossing to handle coal from a new opencast site at Mackies Mill close to Thornton; the planning permission granted for this new facility required that rail transport was used in preference to road. Construction of the new Earlseat siding began early in 2012 and on 22nd August the first coal train left from here (the first new railway facility in the area for more than 50 years!) hauled by English, Welsh & Scottish Railways (EWS) locomotive No. 66138 and bound for Hunterston.

As the track is still in place as far as the River Leven bridge at Methil there have, over the years, been attempts made to raise interest in the possibility of reviving a Leven to Edinburgh passenger service, operated by modern multiple-units and, possibly, serving the intermediate stations at Cameron Bridge, Dysart and Sinclairtown. In December 2004 the Levenmouth Regeneration Group expressed a long-term ambition of seeing the railway to Leven revived so as to improve the economic prospects of the area, which ironically is now regarded as one of the most deprived areas in Scotland. Whether this will ever happen must depend on political will and concerted local pressure the possibility of a new service starting close to the former site of Methil power station is not beyond hope. Certainly with the Scottish Parliament showing a clear interest in passenger railway revival schemes a second edition of this book might one day carry illustrations of the first train from a new Leven station.

Tail Lamp

And what of the area served by the Leven and East of Fife in the post-railway era? On the face of it there seems to has been little change – the towns and villages look much the same, apart from a creeping suburbanization on their fringes and an increase of traffic on the winding and largely unimproved country roads that link them together. But, as with all things, the changes are much more subtle than they first appear. The second agriculture revolution and the dictates of the European Community has wrought many changes on the landscape with mechanization, 'setaside', and the general industrialization of farming, the rural farmworker and his lifestyle are a thing of the past. Fishing on any significant scale has all but gone from local waters and those fishermen who have remained now go out to distant places in order to catch their quotas or have to content themselves with lobsters and partans. Although the fish market at Pittenweem survives and serves the boats now based there, the smaller harbour and the great Union Harbour at Anstruther now largely contain leisure craft. The once busy holiday trade has shifted away from its traditional genteel origins and the mass once a year boom during the Edinburgh and Glasgow trade holidays has given way to day trippers and up-market weekend breaks while farm cottages and fisherman's terraces alike have been transformed into smart second-homes. Manufacturing and virtually all heavy industry has deserted the area completely and the once busy workshops and factories of the area are silent and East Fifers now often have to commute long distances to find work. Some, no doubt, say that the area has lost much of its character and that incomers and changing tastes have diluted the individualism of what was once a remote and quirky corner of the world. But despite all of these reservations the area is still very much alive and its beaches, golf courses, historic towns and quaint villages, still attract locals and visitors alike. The beggar's mantle may no longer be embroidered by a ring of steel rail, but its fringe of gold remains.

Chapter Fourteen

Of Humans and Hens: An East of Fife Miscellany

'Our compartment was invaded by three women, with a baby and a box of oranges'

East of Fife Record

Travellers woes

Much of the flavour of the railway in East Fife, its passengers and staff, can be gathered from the pages of the local press over the century or so during which the railway was open to the public. We begin with the *Scotsman* of 18th September, 1860 which related to the state of a fellow traveller on the late train to Leven:

> Sir – when travelling by the above line by the last train on Saturday evening I experienced a remarkable instance of what is but too common, the great difference between railway regulations and practices. Before we started from Thornton Junction a passenger in the last stage of intoxication was thrust into a third-class carriage, which was also imperfectly lighted. In consequence of this circumstance the rest of the passengers were subjected to grievous annoyances. The writer, and a respectable female, between whom the individual was placed, had their full share. We were compelled to listen to improper language of every description, as well as to support the head of the inebriate on our shoulder from time to time. I need barely to add that this was at once a most dangerous companion, and utterly incapable of attending to his own safety. Through your columns I beg to protest against the repetition of such abominable circumstances. Surely sober and respectable third-class passengers have the right as well as those who can afford to pay a higher fare. I have only to add that the circumstances complained of was not unknown to the servants of this company. Before the train started there was a lengthened altercation between the intoxicated passenger and one of the porters, in respect of the ticket, which had gone amissing.

That this Saturday evening experience was far from uncommon is evidenced by the account of a Mr J. Stevenson of Elie who was a passenger travelling from Edinburgh in 1904:

> I left Edinburgh by the 7.12 pm train with three ladies travelling first class. On arriving at Haymarket our troubles began, for our compartment was invaded by three women, with a baby and a box of oranges, with third class tickets. On my objecting to such an invasion the only answer that I got was that there was no accommodation elsewhere. This, I don't suppose was true, but as there was no one to appeal to, we bore our troubles to Queensferry, where on seeing some passengers get out of the next first-class compartment we got in there. At Inverkeithing we had a long wait but the biggest disgrace was at Thornton Junction where we kept for about 45 minutes, although we arrived there close on 20 minutes late. Here it was only with the aid of a friendly porter, who had locked the doors for us on both sides, that we and four others were able to prevent a lot of drunken roughs from invading our carriage. Finally we reached Elie at about quarter to eleven or an hour late after occupying three and a half hours to do a distance of 45 miles which surely must be a record for slowness. I would add that not at any place en route was there any checking of tickets, and it really seems an absurdity for anyone to pay first class fare, when apparently anyone can travel with third class tickets.

Once again an experience that could be replicated in the present day by Saturday evening passengers on trains bound for Fife but the relevance of the box of oranges seems to be less apparent to modern travellers.

A hen on holiday

On a lighter note, and proof of the fact that some passengers were less troublesome than others, It was reported on 9th January, 1892 that,

> On the arrival of the East of Fife train due at Thornton at 4.52 on Friday, the engine driver on alighting was amazed to find a Spanish black hen firmly perched on the buffers. How the bird came to be there, and by what means it managed to find that strange roosting place, is a mystery. When it was removed to the luggage room it seemed little the worse for its cold ride.

A boy's first ride on the rail

An item of news from Kilconquhar appeared in the local press on 20th September, 1862:

> On Saturday morning early, a boy residing in the northern part of this parish, took a *fourth* class ticket from the station here to Cameron Bridge, and it, being the first time that he had been on a railway, or at least had travelled alone by such a mode of conveyance, he deemed that the *fourth* carriage in the train as the one indicated on the ticket. Accordingly he entered it, and was the only passenger in it that morning, it being a first class carriage, and where the little fellow was as grandly accommodated and cushioned as if he had been a minister of state or a peer of the realm. Hurrying along the shore of Largo Bay and the banks of the Leven, he at length arrived at Cameron Bridge Station, the place of his destination, but failing to have made known his situation to the officials there, he could get no egress out; and the train again starting, he was hurried away through the vale of the Orr to Thornton, where he got out.; and fearing that some other mischance might befall, and that if he had again trusted to the steam steed he might be taken still further , he did not wait for the return of the train, but hurried back on 'Shanks naigie' – walked and ran along the line to Cameron Bridge – where he arrived safely, and told of his morning's adventures with much naivety – his first ride on the rail – as an incident in his early experience, and an interesting chapter in the travels of boyhood.

Time and the East Neuk

Timekeeping on the local lines had often been the subject of adverse comment and on 6th June, 1873 a letter appeared in the *Record* asking one simple question, namely that of which of the East Neuk clocks was to be regarded as reliable as apparently,

> ... each one contradicts its neighbour. The railway clock at Anstruther ought to be the centre of authority. It is either a poor uncontrollable piece of mechanism or requires cleaning or more attention. It has been tested by good house clocks and watches for weeks together and has been found to vary for two or four minutes a week.

The writer ended by concluding that, 'Reform and regulation are loudly called for'. However, in 1899 the Elie station master in a speech on his retirement remarked that the Leven and East of Fife,

> ... was an innocent railway and not particular about a matter of minutes and when intending passengers gave him notice that they intended to catch a particular train the would ensure that the signals were left at danger for it and instruct the driver to sound the whistle repeatedly to let the missing passenger know that the train was waiting.

The sheriff at Dunfermline was, however, less careless with time and the *Record* in 1909 reported the Court proceedings in which William Bothron, described as a miner of Rosebank, Markinch, was the pursuer:

> The pursuer was one of a party who proceeded to take to their work at Wellsgreen Colliery in a brake on 29th January. The brake was held up at the level crossing at Cameron Bridge for 15 minutes, and in consequence the pursuer did not reach the colliery until 10 minutes to seven o'clock in the morning, by which time it was too late to descend the pit. The amount of his claim, *7s. 0d.*, represented his day's wages. In giving the decree with expenses the Sheriff finds that the gates at the level crossing were closed for an unreasonable period, and he adds that in the circumstances there was nothing unusual nor unforseen in such a claim being made.

How the North British treated East Fife

In the *Glasgow Herald* of 4th June, 1906 the following letter appeared:

> I have gone to the shores of Fife for the last ten or twelve years for a holiday and have been the means of inducing a number of Glasgow people to go there also. As time passes the North British Railway Company , instead of giving an improved service, appear to be making it worse, and out of curiosity I have looked over their time-tables just issued and find, for instance, that to Elie by the first train leaving Queen Street station at 6.35 am, passengers are allowed to cool their heels on the Dunfermline platform for 24 minutes, and this not being sufficiently aggravating, when they reach Thornton , the coldest and windiest place on the face of the earth, they are laid by the heels for another 51 minutes, and finally the train is is due to arrive at Elie at 10.29 am. Then taking the last train, 5.28 pm, there is a wait for two solid hours at Thornton, and the train is due at Elie at 9.47 pm. Not only is it difficult to get into Fife by rail, but it seems that the ingenuity of the North British Railway officials is exhausted in trying to keep people in Fife once they are there. For instance, there is no possibility of businessmen getting into town before 10.47 am, and that in our experience means 11.15 and even with that early start and long delay, 53 minutes are spent waiting in Thornton!

A week later similar sentiments were expressed at a meeting of the Pittenweem Town Council when they discussed the outcome of a deputation which had been sent by them to the NBR in Edinburgh and it was emphasized that they wanted not more trains for Pittenweem but that the trains kept better time. As a speaker emphasised:

> He [Mr Birrell] was very strong about the practice of shunting passenger trains to allow goods trains to pass. He also pressed for a double line from Thornton along the coast ... He also asked for better accommodation at the stations, and especially to provide a room

> for smokers. He also wanted covered-in sheds at stations for goods to prevent them getting wet, and obviate the claims for damages. Another thing he asked for was a reduction of fares on Wednesdays to enable the shopkeepers to have the same privilege as other classes had on the Saturdays and at the weekend. The whole of the deputation were strong for the double line. Another thing spoken of was the long wait at Thornton by the 5.35 from Glasgow to the East of Fife, where passengers often had to wait for two hours for the connection. Of course they did not get any promise that all the suggestions would be carried out, but they promised to consider them and let them know their decision.

This was certainly how the North British treated its customers in the East of Fife and although some efforts were made to remedy complaints they were too little and too late. By the time that the LNER sought to improve matters the railways had already lost out to the internal combustion engine.

Refreshments at Thornton

One advantage of the need to change trains at Thornton Junction was the facilities available before the station began to collapse. The North British Railway public timetable for 1919 states that at the company's station refreshment rooms, including those at Thornton Junction, breakfast, luncheon and tea baskets can be obtained. The breakfast basket contained a pot of tea, coffee or cocoa, fish or eggs, toast and butter at a charge of 2*s*. 6*d*. The luncheon basket contained roast fowl with ham or any cold meat in season, cheese, butter, bread, biscuits and salad at a cost of 3*s*. but a hot luncheon could be obtained if passengers notified their wants to the station-master at the preceding stopping station. The tea basket contained a pot of tea, one slice of bread and butter, one biscuit and one small slice of cake for a modest 1*s*. By 1960 the equivalent of the luncheon basket, the 'compact meal', consisted of a pork pie, egg roll, cheese and biscuits, a piece of fruit cake and a chocolate wafer biscuit and cost 3*s*. 6*d*. but, by then, the Thornton refreshment room had long gone!

For those in peril

For a seafaring community Anstruther relied on the railway to transport its fish, its fish buyers and the coal and later oil needed to keep the vessels running but it is perhaps less well known that its first three lifeboats also used the railway's facilities. After much agitation on the part of the town's inhabitants, Anstruther finally received its first lifeboat in the shape of the *Admiral Fitzroy*, a 31 ft open rowing vessel built at Limehouse on the Thames and paid for by a Miss Hannah Harvie of Cheltenham. The boat was brought by rail, arriving at the goods yard in the town on Friday 17th November, 1865 and was then hauled to the harbour by a team of six horses and accompanied by a large congregation of local people. On 2nd February, 1888 it was replaced by the *Royal Stuart* which once again had arrived by rail from Shadwell Dock in London and the *Admiral Fitzroy* was retired from service and left Anstruther by rail for a new destination, namely Kinsale in County Cork. The third lifeboat destined for Anstruther also arrived by rail and on 30th July, 1904 the *James and Mary Walker* was conveyed by rail from Canning Town in London to Anstruther and hauled from the goods yard there to the harbour amongst great ceremony. The

The *James and Mary Walker* being taken from the station to the harbour to become Anstruther's third lifeboat in July 1904; a century later it has returned to the town but, unfortunately, not by rail! *Scottish Fisheries Museum Collection*

era of the non-powered lifeboats eventually came to an end and on 24th May, 1933 the motor vessel *Nellie and Charlie* arrived under its own power in Anstruther and its predecessor sailed off to enjoy a long retirement elsewhere in Fife. The *James and Mary Walker*, found languishing in a boatyard in Anglesey, has been returned from Wales (although sadly not by rail) to Anstruther in 2010 for eventual restoration and preservation.

A female employee!

Although the employment of women on the railways in Scotland was not unknown, and indeed female booking clerks had been employed by the North British in Edinburgh as far back as 1859, they were a rarity in East Fife until the advent of World War I and the general shortage of labour caused by mobilization. The women so employed were largely made redundant at the end of the war but a few worked on and this was regarded as so unusual that it was worthy of comment in the *Railway Magazine* which in March 1935 could comment that at 'Lundin Links, on the East of Fife Section of the LNER, still boasts a station-mistress. It would be interesting to learn if any other examples can be cited in Great Britain of similar feminine control of railway operation.'* Women returned again in 1940 and several remained on the line after the war including female booking clerks and signalwomen in the East Neuk area.

* Other examples might have included the female station masters employed on the North Wales narrow gauge lines and the numerous clerks, secretaries and women employed in administrative and operational activities throughout the LNER system, the existence of which could hardly have been unknown to the editor of the company's own staff magazine!

Chapter Fifteen

Thornton to Anstruther: The Line Described

'The world has changed; and with it the Fringe of Fife'

John Geddie, 'The Fringes of Fife'

In this chapter the main physical features of the Leven and East of Fife lines are described on a topographical basis starting with the junction of the main line at Thornton. It should be borne in mind that the all of the features described may not necessarily have been present simultaneously or throughout the entire and lengthy history of the lines; when in doubt the description relates to the period immediately before World War I. The mileages given are the official mileages (including chains) from Thornton, for the Muiredge branch from Cameron Bridge and for the Leven Dock line from East Fife Central Junction all as reflected in the working timetables.

Thornton to Cameron Bridge

The western portion of the coastal route was a six mile stretch opened in 1854 by the Leven Railway as a cheaply-built single-line and was operated initially by the Edinburgh, Perth & Dundee Railway until 1855 when the owning company undertook to operate the line itself. Amalgamating with the East of Fife Railway in 1863, the line was acquired by the North British in 1877 and this section was doubled by the latter company in 1910. Closed to passengers in 1969, the section between Thornton and Leven Dock is still *in situ*, although rarely used in recent years.

Thornton Junction (00.00) was a somewhat isolated place, lying on the Edinburgh to Dundee main line nearly five miles north of Kirkcaldy and half a mile or so west of the small village of Thornton situated on the Kirkcaldy to Cupar main road (A92) at the point where it crossed the River Ore. Travelling northwards, the first junction encountered was Thornton South, immediately north of the bridge carrying the main line over the by-road to the Ore Mills. Here the loop line, which connected with the Cowdenbeath and Dunfermline line, departed on the down side,* and the main line then crossed in turn the River Orr and the single line which gave a direct connection between the Cowdenbeath line and the Methil branch before entering Thornton Junction station.

Originally the station consisted of a tall gabled sandstone building lying on the down side but this was replaced by a broad island platform to the east, situated between the up and down main lines with a separate island platform for Methil branch trains situated to the east and connected to the main platform at its northern end by a 120 ft-long iron footbridge which also carried a right-of-way. The main island platform, which was almost 300 ft in length, had two bays, one south-facing and one north-facing and used, respectively, by down trains terminating at Thornton and by East Fife trains. Between the two bays were the main station buildings constructed in 1885. This was a handsome structure with well-appointed waiting rooms, useful in an age when connections were often poor or missed, the

* From 1st January, 1868 all southbound trains on the North British system were designated 'up' trains and all northbound trains 'down'. Thus all East Fife trains travelling to Edinburgh via Leven were up trains and vice-versa.

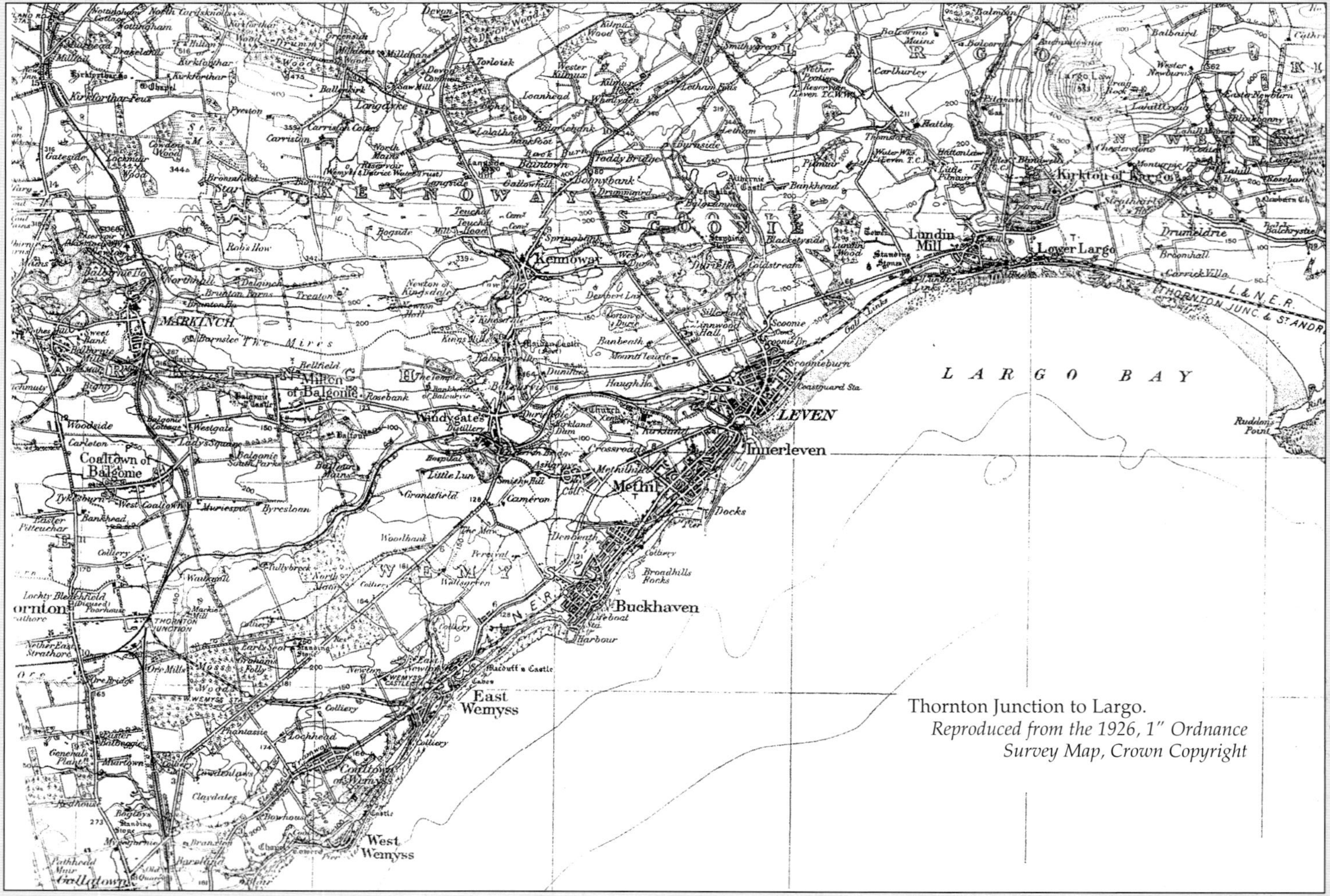

Thornton Junction to Largo.
Reproduced from the 1926, 1" Ordnance Survey Map, Crown Copyright

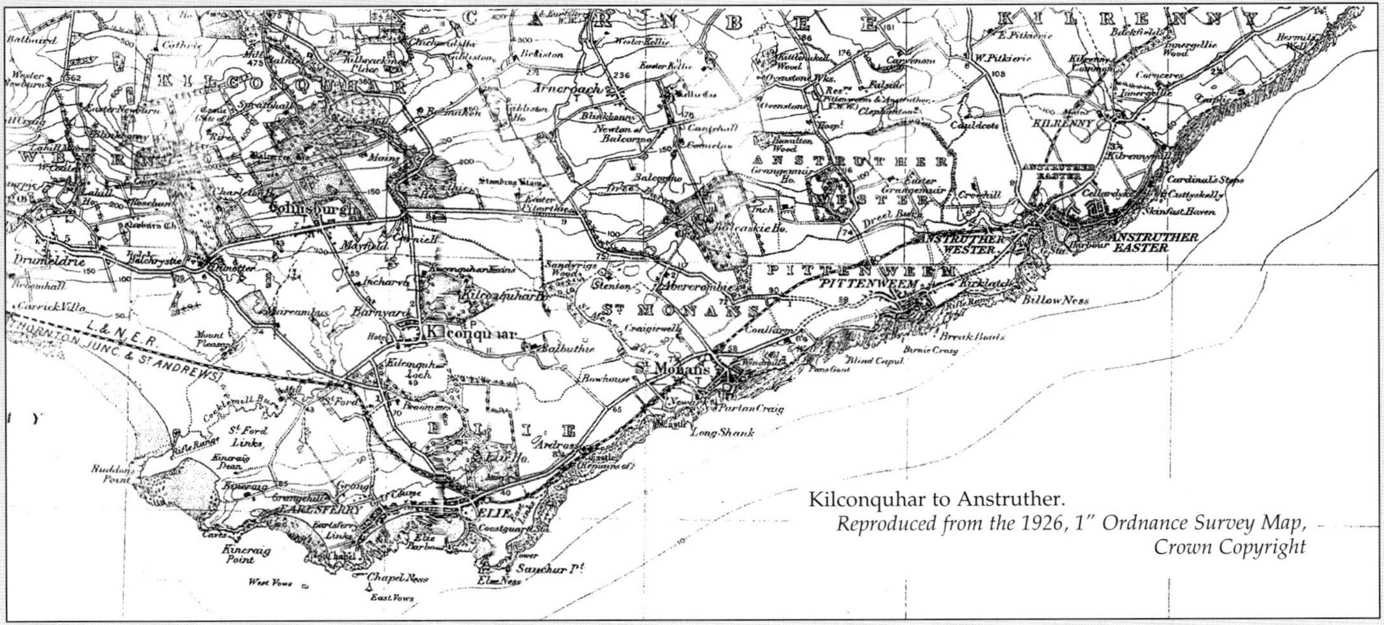

Kilconquhar to Anstruther.
Reproduced from the 1926, 1" Ordnance Survey Map, Crown Copyright

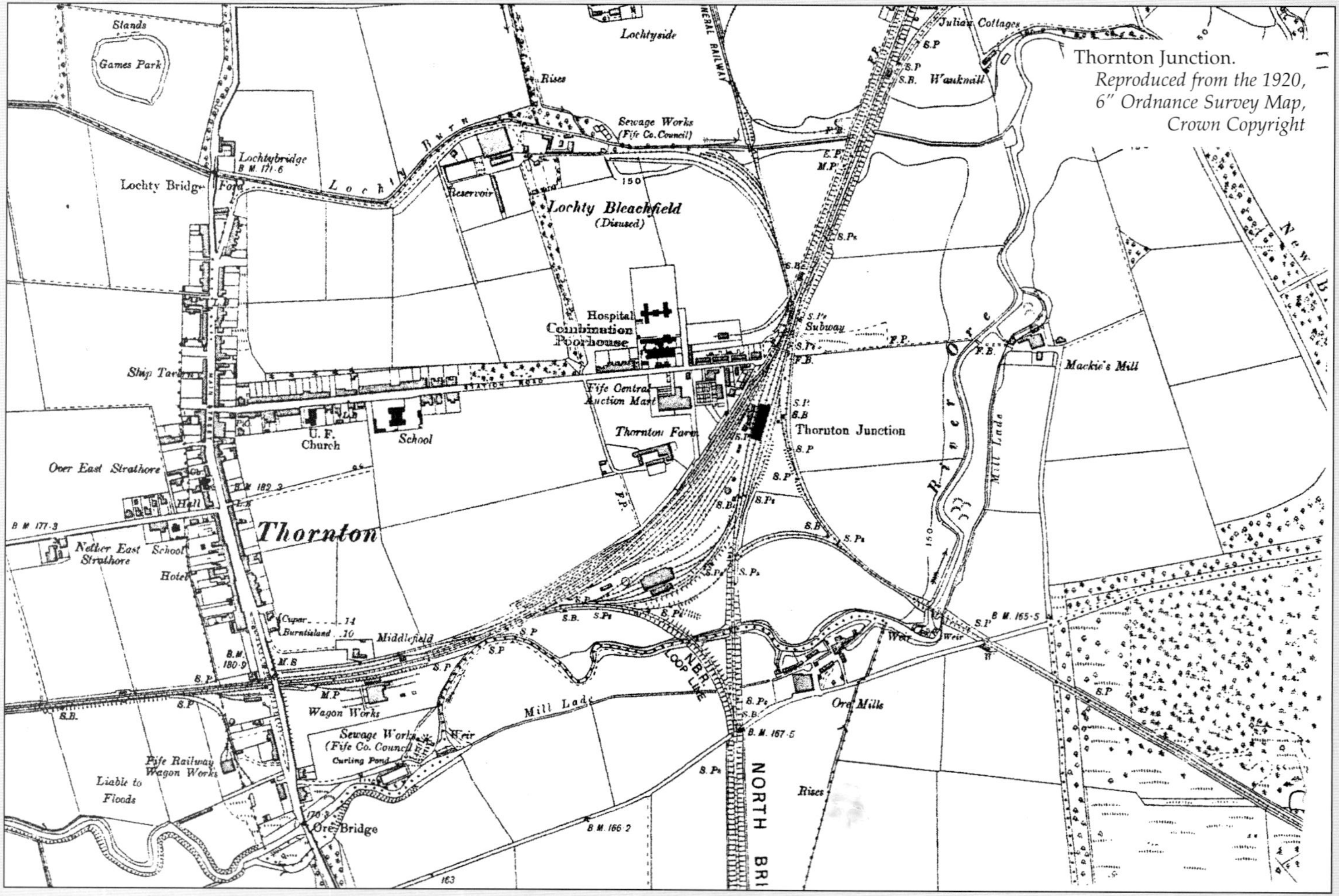

Thornton Junction.
Reproduced from the 1920,
6″ Ordnance Survey Map,
Crown Copyright

Holmes 'M' class 4-4-0 No. 636 on a Crail train at Thornton *circa* 1900.
NBRSG, Hennigan Collection

Thornton Junction looking north in 1969, with the LEoF line going down to the right and the removal of the Balgonie mine waste going on in the background. *G. Hume*

Thornton Junction for Leven, Buckhaven and Methil. *R.W. Lynn Collection*

Greetings are exchanged at Thornton Junction. The view from a Leven-Edinburgh dmu in the bay platform. Note the closure notices are evident and the station is clearly on its last legs.

Norman Turnbull

usual offices for the staff and a wide glass and iron veranda which gave adequate protection from the elements. A particular feature of the station were the refreshment rooms for each class of passenger, the first-class one being particularly ornate with mock-Gothic seating and a marble bar counter. Not only were they licensed but also provided breakfast, luncheon and tea baskets for hungry passengers; the second class refreshment room could be lively on a Friday or Saturday evening according to local press reports. Unfortunately these facilities were later withdrawn when subsidence, caused by the fact that the land upon which the station stood subsided due to mining, it led to the demolition of these fine Victorian buildings in the early 1930s. They had been constantly underpinned and held up with large wooden props and were replaced by somewhat makeshift buildings and platforms constructed of wood which, in their latter days, were wind-swept and unattractive despite the efforts of the staff. South-west of the station lay the goods depot, extensive stabling sidings, an engine shed built in 1933 to replace the original shed and, to the south side of the Cowdenbeath line, two wagon repair works. These were the Fife Railway Wagon Works owned by the Motherwell Wagon & Rolling Stock Co. and the works of R. & Y. Pickering Ltd (later owned by Wagon Repairs Ltd. There were, of course, a large number of wooden-bodied coal wagons in Fife, all of which required regular maintenance and repair and so Thornton was an ideal location for this. In 1957 a large new mechanized marshalling yard was brought into use at Redford, to the west of the junction with the Dunfermline line.

To the immediate north of the station footbridge was a mineral line serving a factory and the Lochtyside and Julian pits of the Balgonie Colliery of the Balgonie Colliery Company Ltd, whose huge coal bing dominated the view – Lochtyside pit lay half a mile north-west of Thornton Junction station on the down side of the main line but the Julian pit lay to the north-east and on the up side, crossing under the main line close to Julian Cottages and adjacent to the Leven line. On the down side immediately to the north of the station lay the point where the Leven line physically left the main-line at Thornton Junction signal box from where the Leven line paralleled the main line for 21 chains on a slight falling gradient of 1 in 250, before turning east and passing over, at Julian Cottages, a minor road leading to the Waulkmill on the north bank of the River Ore. A short climb took the line past the Balgonie Colliery Julian pit (where there was a manned public level crossing but no direct railway communication with the Leven line) before reaching the manned **Double Dykes level crossing** (00.61); in 2012 a loop and **Earlseat siding** were built on the south side of the crossing in connection with a nearby open cast mining at Mackie's Mill. The line now began to fall all the way towards Leven on a ruling gradient of 1 in 100 and running on the north bank of the River Ore, with which it kept company for a couple of miles. At **Tullybreck level crossing** (01.60) the line crossed a minor track used by pedestrians which led to a bridge and the farm of that name; the crossing was manned and protected by signals. The line continued to follow the river in a series of reverse curves over which there was a 40 mph speed restriction. The line with Wemyss Wood on the south bank generally took a meandering north-easterly direction through open countryside for three-quarters of a mile until crossing the river; like all other bridges on the route as far as Leven, this structure had originally 'a substantial but not very elegant bridge between stone pillars and wood flooring' but replaced in turn with an iron bridge and the present steel girder bridge.

A mile further on the line again crossed the river although by this time it was the River Leven for the upstream confluence of the Ore and Leven lay a short distance

'B1' class 4-6-0 No. 61133 approaches Thornton from the East of Fife line on 3rd April, 1965.
J.L. Stevenson

Beside the Ore - the view from the train window between Cameron Bridge and Thornton on 3rd April, 1965.
J.L. Stevenson

to the north and then reached **Haughmill siding** (03.25), a short west-facing siding with a connecting horse-worked link to the flax mill and bleaching works of that name. Then followed the manned **Haughmill level crossing** before the river was crossed twice and the short-lived **Drumcaldie Distillery siding** (03.45), leading off on the north side of the line, was reached. This led off to the north on the down side of the line and originally serving a small independent malt whisky distillery of that name whose premises were later taken over by the Distillers Co. Ltd.

Cameron Bridge to Leven

By now the line was taking an easterly route again and shortly after the second river crossing the **Cameron Bridge Distillery** was reached. This lay on the up side of the line and consisted of an extensive series of buildings; a connection left the line at a trailing junction on the up side and crossed the River Leven on its own bridge before entering the extensive Cameron Bridge Distillery which was served by a number of sidings on the up side which included their own bridge over the river to the main buildings on the west bank. The original **Cameron Bridge station** (03.62) for passengers was on the down side of the line and immediately east of a level crossing carrying the Kirkcaldy to St Andrews road across the railway. The main station building was of stone and predated the line; it was adapted for use as a station house. The small goods yard was immediately north of the passenger station. On the doubling and rebuilding of the Thornton to Leven line in 1910 a new island platform was constructed between the up and down lines and the level crossing was replaced by a footbridge; the main road (the present A915) was realigned to run over a girder bridge at the Leven end of the platform, from which the main access to the station was gained by a flight of steps. The station offices and waiting room were provided in a small brick and wood building on the platform and a canopy that extended over both platforms; a small corrugated iron lamp hut was also provided. The brick and timber signal box was on the up side close to the site of the level crossing and replaced the original signal box; a water column was a feature of this station. At the east end of the site the **Muiredge branch** left the Leven line at a trailing junction on the up side.

The line now passed to the south of Cameron Bridge House and clung to the river with farmland to the north and, latterly, the outskirts of Methilhill to the south, before reaching the junction with the Lochty line. The Lochty joined the Leven line at a trailing junction on its the down side at the eponymous **East Fife Central Junction** (04.41) where a signal box was installed on the down side for the opening of that goods-only line in 1898. A short distance beyond lay a weir and sluice on the river where the Burn Mill lade left the river and ran parallel to the railway almost as far as the original Leven station. Less than a quarter of a mile further on the **Kirkland branch**, also known as the Kirkland siding, joined the line by a trailing junction on the up side. This was the first branch line to be built on the Leven Railway and ran for seven chains southwards before crossing the River Leven and proceeding for another 10 chains to the Kirkland Works. On the closure of these works the branch lay derelict for some time and then was lifted, the bridge over the river being demolished.

When the line was reconstructed in the first decade of the 20th century the new access to the **Leven Dock branch** and the **Kirkland Yard** was seven chains east of East Fife Central Junction signal box and when the Kirkland branch was re-opened

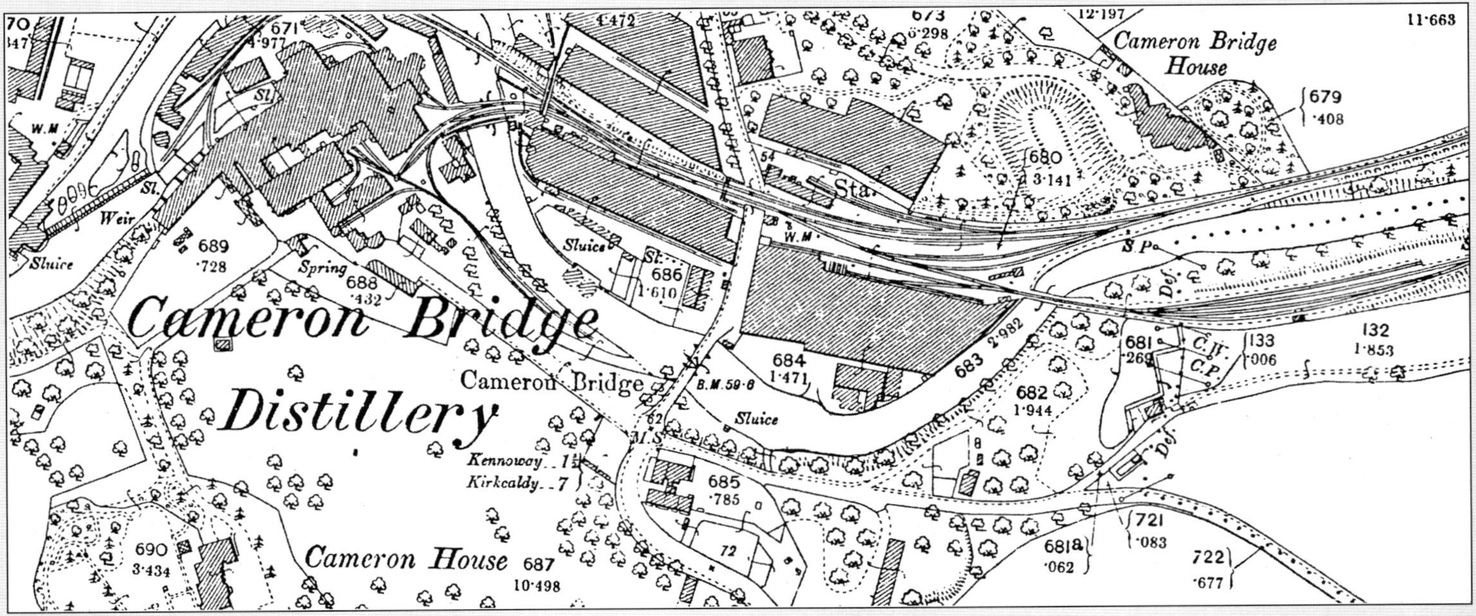

Cameron Bridge station.

Reproduced from the 1894, 25″ Ordnance Survey Map, Crown Copyright

A panorama of Cameron Bridge taken from the remnant of the Muiredge branch in the 1960s.
P. Westwater

Cameron Bridge distillery; an illustration from *Barnard's Whisky Distilleries of the United Kingdom.*

Cameron Bridge station before World War I. *Lens of Sutton Collection*

Cameron Bridge station looking towards Leven in the late 1940s. *R.W. Lynn Collection*

Cameron Bridge with a Leven-bound dmu in 1969. *Hamish Stevenson*

Helen, Teddy and the NBR footbridge at Cameron Bridge in September 1989. *Hamish Stevenson*

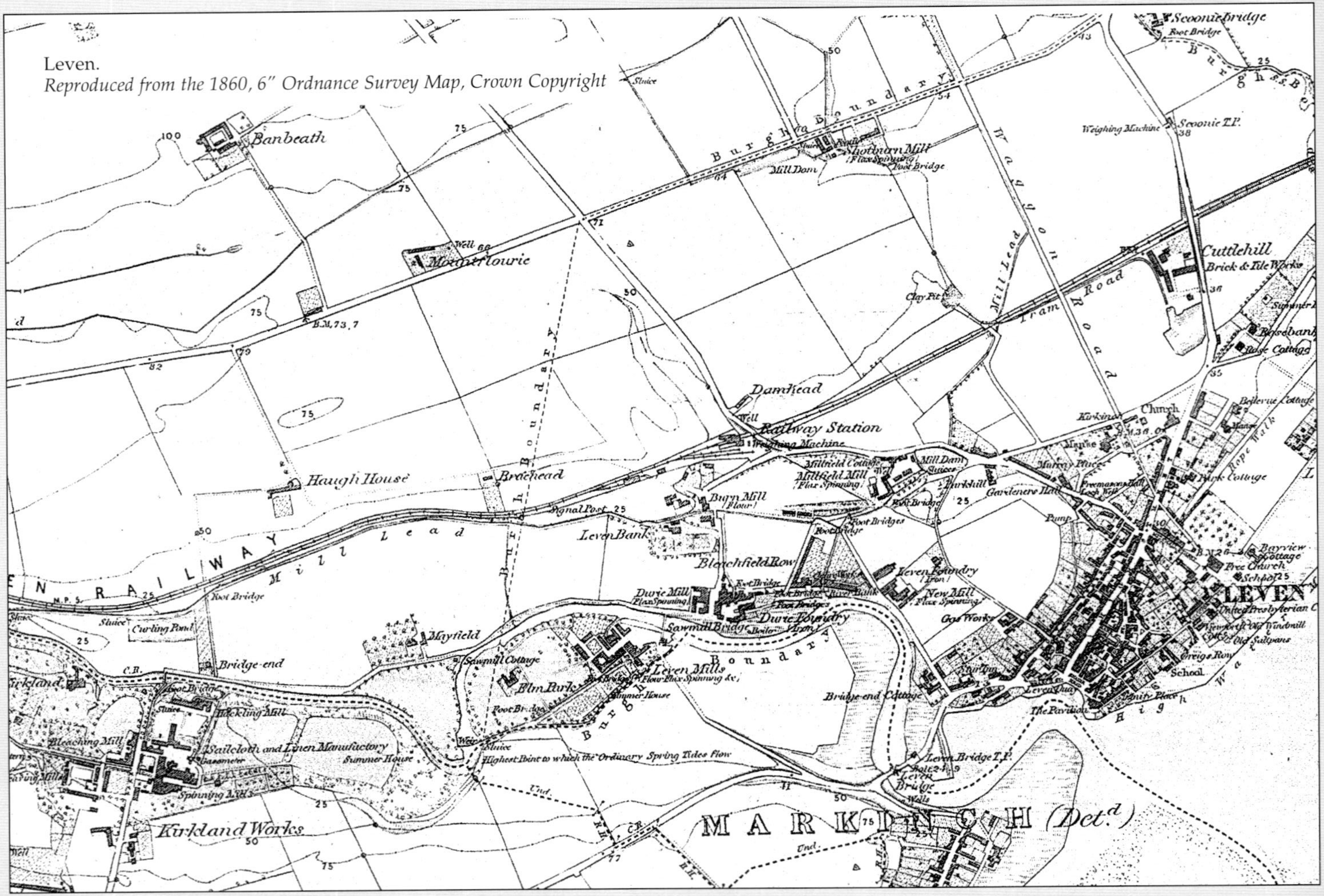

Leven.
Reproduced from the 1860, 6" Ordnance Survey Map, Crown Copyright

to serve the National Steel Foundry it was realigned and now led off the Leven Dock branch. The Leven line now proceeded in an east-north-easterly direction for another quarter-mile or so to the point where the original alignment of the Leven Dock line came in on the up side and ran parallel to the Leven line for a short distance; both lines then proceeded eastwards, passing over the **Burnmill level crossing,** originally a private occupation crossing which later became public and where there was a crossing keeper's hut, and **Burnmill siding** before there was a physical junction with the Leven Dock before the entering the original **Leven (Old) station** (05.57). The first station line here was a terminus entered from Burnmill Road and consisted of a single passenger platform and a number of sidings and the original Leven Railway engine shed situated near to the level crossing and latterly used as a shed for the railway carters. In 1859, when the line was extended to Kilconquhar, a second passenger station was built on the north side of the line adjacent and on the up side of the **Glenlyon Road level crossing**. The original station, became a goods station and remained as such until the closure of the line; the yard possessed a 5 ton crane. The works of the Leven & East of Fife company were also situated here. The Glenlyon Road level crossing was replaced by a two-span bridge in 1910, which carried the present B933 road over the line.

Leven to Largo

Continuing eastwards over the line opened by the East of Fife Railway in 1857, the route originally lay on the northern boundary of the built-up area of the burgh until the new **Leven passenger station** (05.77) was reached. This consisted of a tall brick two-storey building, dating from 1887, housing the ticket office, offices and waiting rooms on the ground floor and accommodation for the station master and his family on the upper storey. With the doubling of the line from Thornton to this point in 1910 a down platform with a standard North British brick and timber building was added on the north side of the line. On the up platform was a plain brick-built signal box and travelling eastwards between the houses the line crossed two level crossings in rapid progression, the first of these being **Aithernie Road level crossing** (06.06), a private unmanned pedestrian crossing with wicket gates which was also known as **Laundry level crossing** and formerly led to the Fever Hospital. When road traffic required the road gates to be opened this was done by an employee of Leven Town Council rather than by a railwayman. At this level crossing there was a crossover from the down loop line onto what was the up loop west of this point and the single main line to the east; the crossover known misleadingly as the **Leven Brickworks crossing** was subject to a 4 mph speed limit and the warning was given that 'Drivers must have their trains under such control when approaching that they will be able to stop clear of the crossing'. Then following the point where the Leven Brickworks tramway crossed the line was **Waggon Road level crossing** (06.12) which was a manned crossing marking the point where the route of the early Leven horse tramway ran. In later years all three level crossings in Leven were notorious for holding up traffic and pedestrians and the Wagon Road crossing was the scene of a fatal accident in the 1950s when a horse-drawn Co-op milk float crashed into the crossing gates after the horse bolted. The original brickworks tramway was crossed at this point before the **Leven Council siding** was reached on the down side followed by **Leven Brickworks siding** (06.18) on the up side after which the line now passed under Scoonie Road (A955).

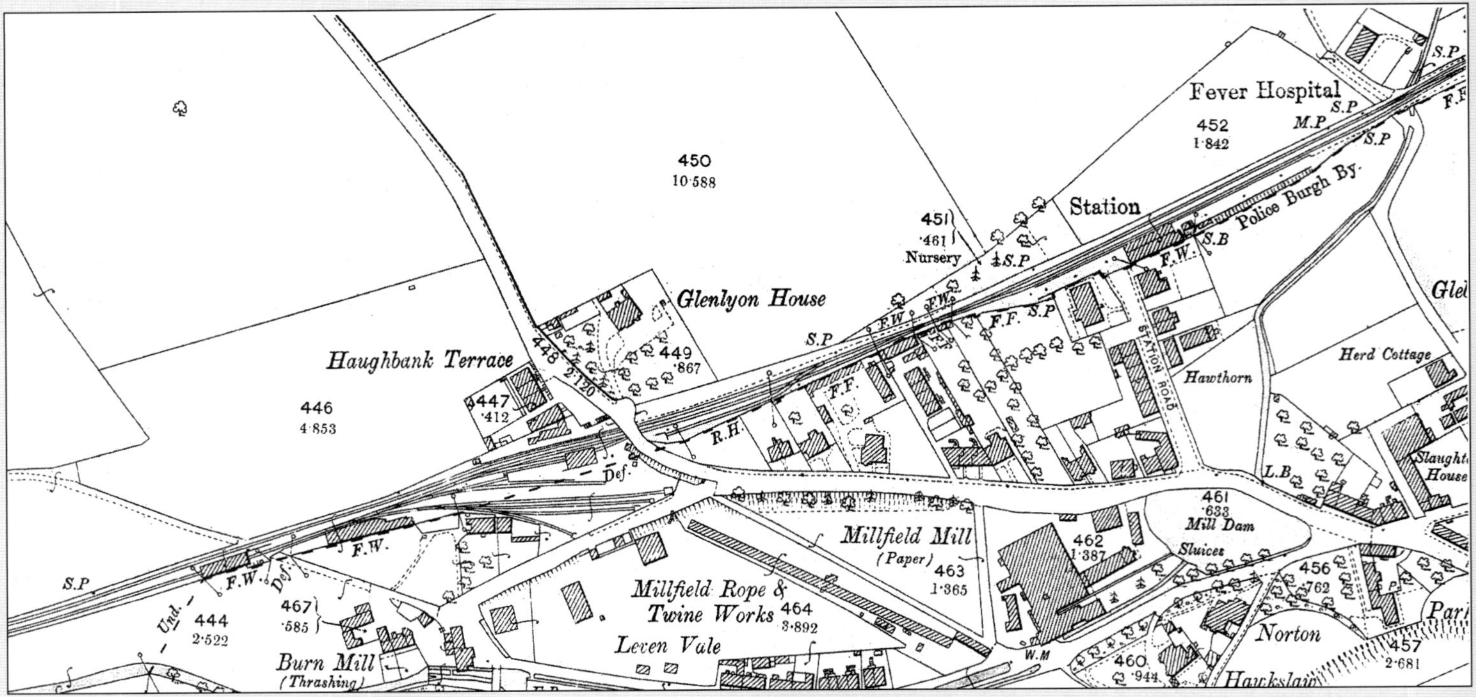

Leven showing the original Leven Railway terminus and works and the replacement station with a single platform.

Reproduced from the 1894, 25″ Ordnance Survey Map, Crown Copyright

No. 62492 *Glen Garvin* on a train arriving from the coast at Leven. *J.L. Stevenson*

Manoeuvres at Leven, looking towards Largo, in 1961. *M.B. Smith*

'B1' class 4-6-0 No. 61081 on the Aithernie Road level crossing on 1st August, 1959.
J.L Stevenson

'B1' class 4-6-0 No. 61324 at Brickworks crossing with the 8.40 am Edinburgh (Waverley) to Crail service on 27th July, 1963. *Roy Hamilton*

After crossing the Scoonie Burn there followed on the down side the topographical divergence point of the **Durie siding** (known when it first opened as the **Durie Colliery siding**) which, having run parallel to the main running line for some distance, then ran for a quarter of a mile in the northward direction. The line now crossed the Scoonie Links with seaward views over Largo bay and on the down side was the long-lived **Silverburn siding** (07.16). until amidst the greens of the eponymous golf course we reach **Lundin Links station** (07.60). This station had but a single platform on the down side and no passing loop or signal box but a small goods yard, consisting of two sidings controlled from a ground frame and entered from the Leven direction; the yard had a 1½ ton crane. The original unique station building and the later NBR building stood side by side on the platform, the latter housing the ticket office and waiting rooms, and a camping coach was parked in the dock immediately behind the passenger platform. The line now passed under a footbridge leading from the foot of Victoria Road and at **Drummochie** the line entered a short cutting on a gentle up gradient of 1 in 1100 passing under Emsdorf Road, which had been diverted to cross over the line on a bridge. At the end of the cutting the line emerged to cross the impressive **Largo viaduct** (08.45) from where fine views were to be had from the train of the harbour and the Robinson Crusoe Hotel. Then followed **Largo station** (08.60), constructed on the raised beach above Lower Largo (or Seatown of Largo) and originally consisting of a single platform situated on the down side of the line with a standard East of Fife Railway rendered brick single-storey building similar to Elie and other stations on the line. This housed the ticket office, waiting room and all of the usual station offices. When a passing loop was added in 1894, a new up platform was provided with a brick-built North British station building and a brick signal box (similar to those at Leven, Elie and St Monance). The goods yard included a 1 ton crane and a paraffin shed which wayward wagons could strike with unfortunate results. A tall footbridge at the west end of the station connected the platforms and carried a footpath over the line.

Largo to Kilconquhar

The line now passed behind Lower Largo on an embankment, passing over **Cardie level crossing** before leaving the burgh behind at Temple and entering what was probably the loneliest and bleakest section of the line, albeit one which rewarded passengers and crew with superb sea views. For quarter of a mile the line followed the shoreline and was particularly subject to slipping – indeed much of the trackbed had to be reconstructed in 1937 after a particularly bad fall. At **Viewforth level crossing** (09.34) the line crossed a minor road from Kirkton of Largo leading to the sea while a short distance further on was the facing junction on the up side where **Strathairly siding** (09.45) led off. This siding literally led to the beach and was situated just above the high water mark and ideally placed to allow sand to be loaded here. At Carrick Villa a small burn was crossed and shortly thereafter **Serpentine level crossing,** carrying a minor lane leading to the beach, crossed the line. Thereafter the line continued on a straight easterly course but the coast turned away to the south, leaving the railway to cross the windswept Dumbarnie Links, grazed by sheep but devoid of human habitation. **Kilconquhar West** (11.50) was an intermediate block post and loop capable of holding 55 four-wheeled wagons and was situated in a lonely location on the links. The brick and timber signal box, which lay between the running line and the loop, was opened in 1907, and became part-time in 1925 and was closed in 1962.

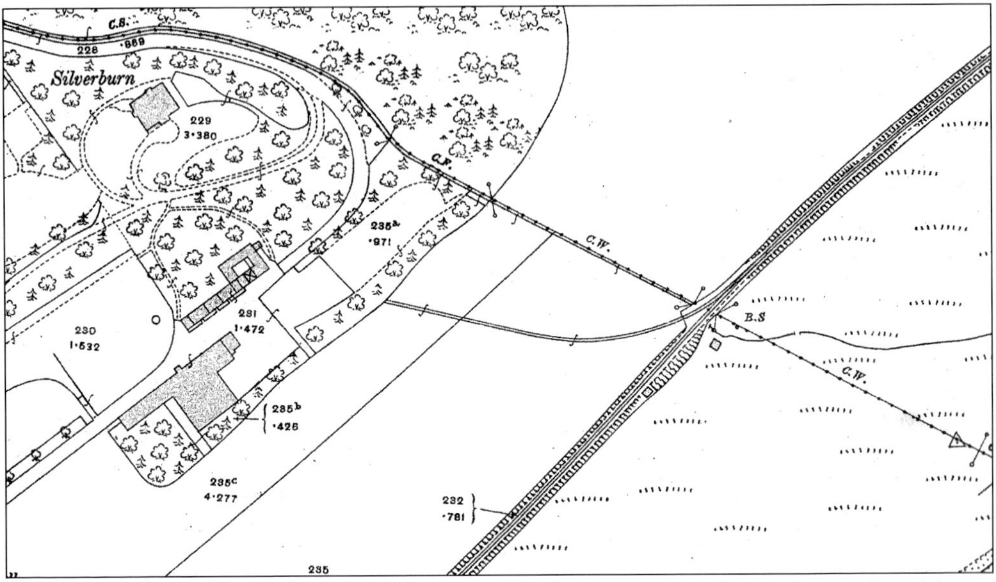

Silverburn siding. *Reproduced from the 1912, 25" Ordnance Survey Map, Crown Copyright*

Lundin Links before the NBR building was added; the golf club now occupies the station site. Sunnybraes predated both the railway and Standard Life and still stands today.
Reproduced from the 1894, 25" Ordnance Survey Map, Crown Copyright

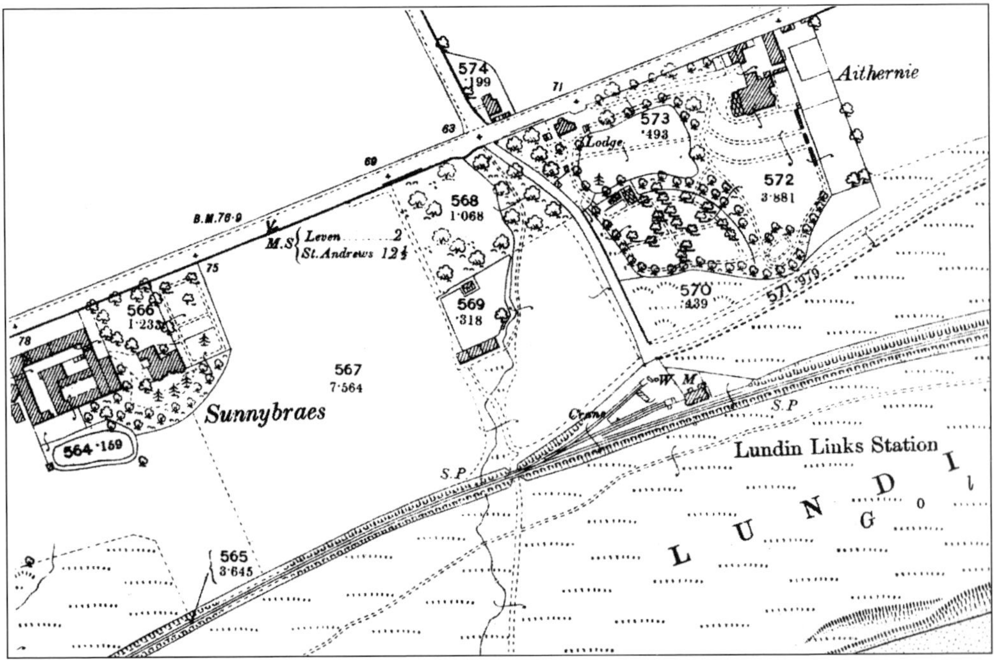

The goods sidings at Lundin Links on 18th July, 1959, with the camping coach in the right-hand siding *J.L. Stevenson*

Lundin Links station. *J. Hurst Collection*

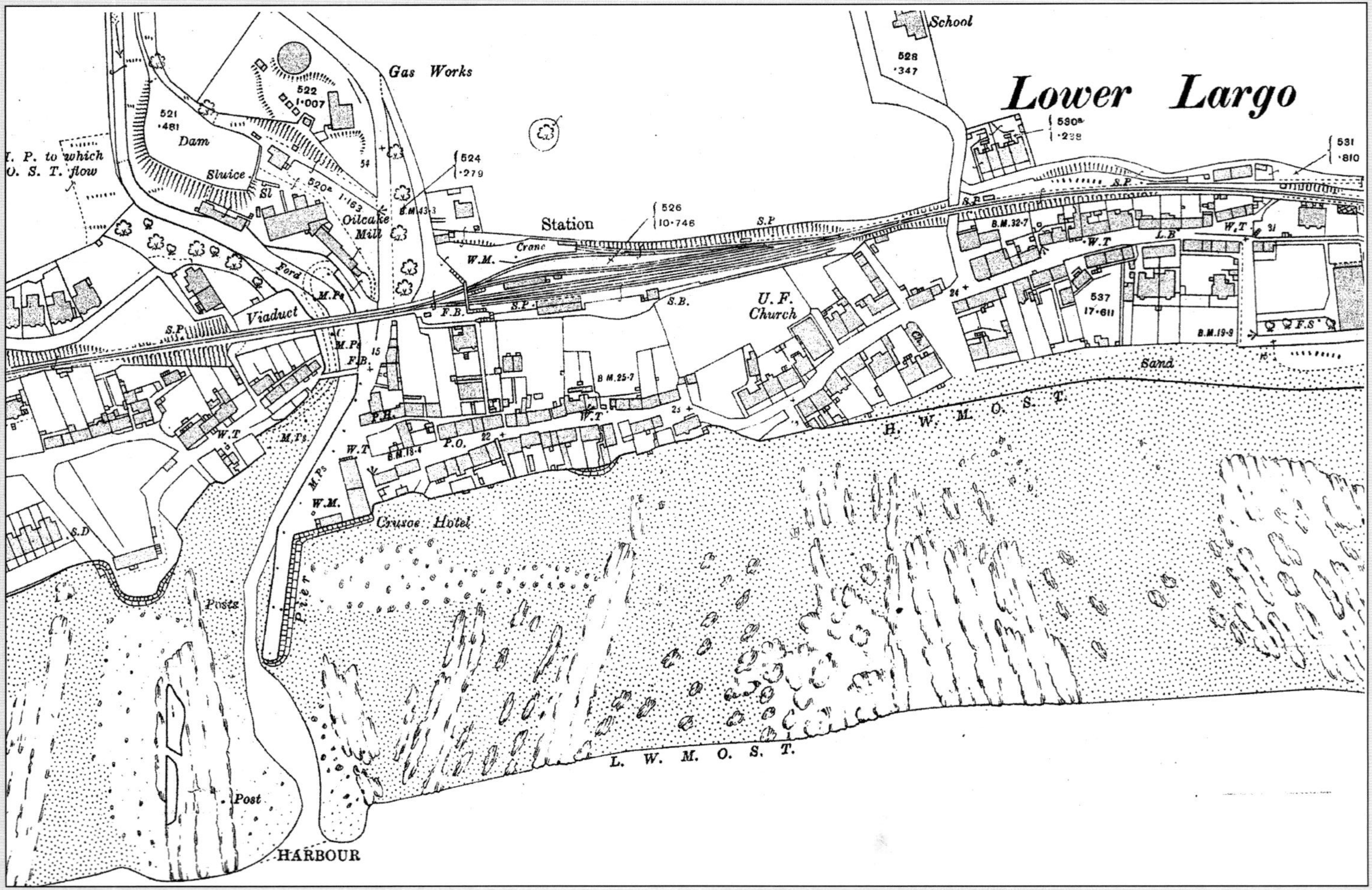

Largo station.

Reproduced from the 1914, 25″ Ordnance Survey Map, Crown Copyright

'B1' class 4-6-0 No. 61133 on the 2.35 pm Crail to Thornton service passes a dmu at Largo on 3rd April, 1965. *J.L. Stevenson*

Largo station looking east in LNER days with the original East of Fife Railway buildings in the foreground. *R.W. Lynn Collection*

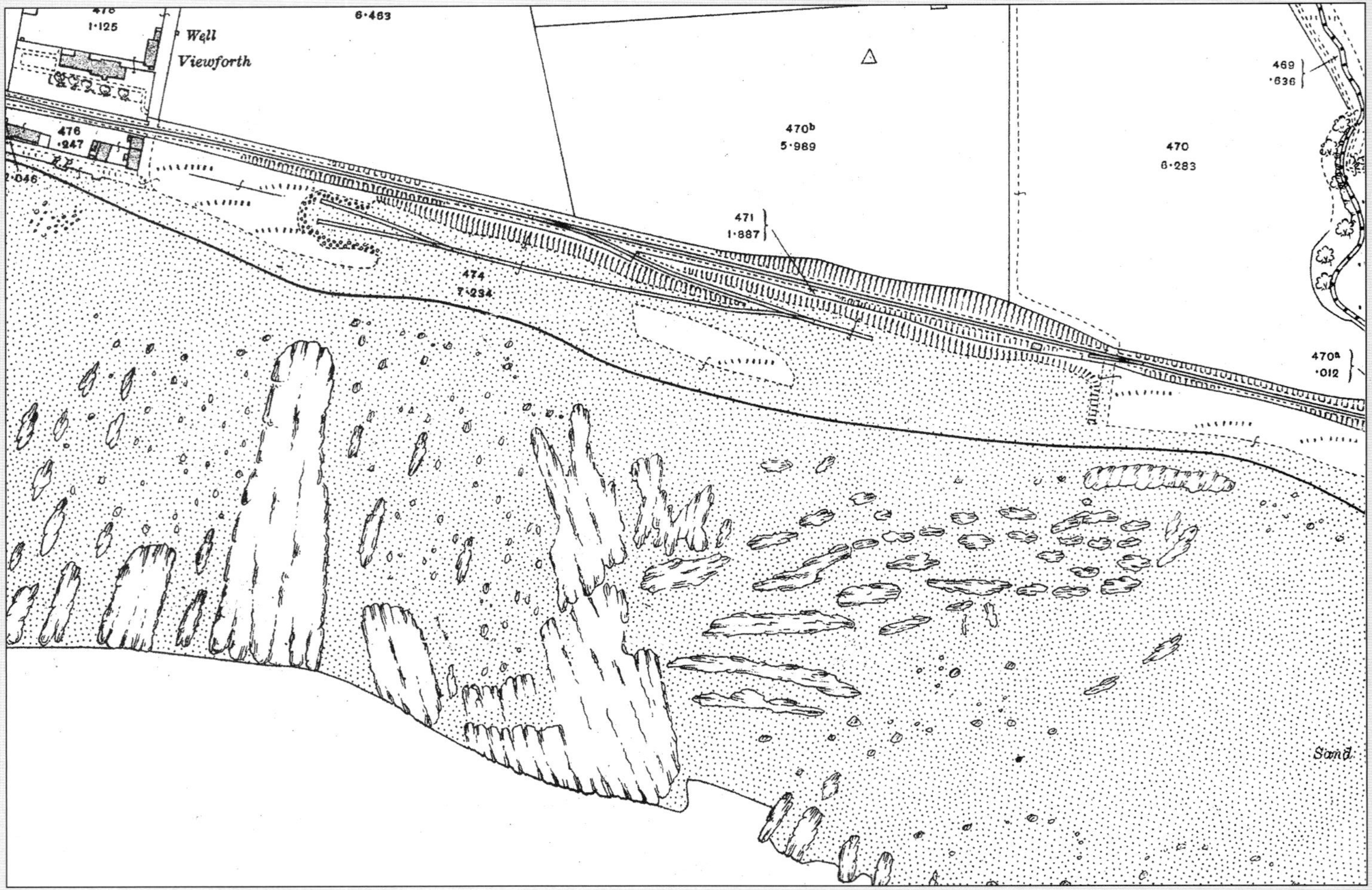

Strathairly with the sand sidings, Viewforth level crossing and in the foreground the beach. *Reproduced from the 1914, 25″ Ordnance Survey Map, Crown Copyright*

Another straight stretch over grazing land led past West Muircambus and over the Cocklemill Burn by a single-arch masonry bridge to **Kilconquhar level crossing**, carrying the by-road to Shell Bay and Kincraig across the line. Immediately thereafter was **Kilconquhar station** (12.39), the original terminus of the East of Fife Railway and situated on a gentle curve with the sole passenger platform on the down side. The main station building (originally 'Kilconquhar and Elie') was the original dating from 1857 and was always well kept – indeed the whole station had a somewhat antiquated but pleasing air right up to its final closure. The sidings were on the up side and were controlled by a ground frame situated in a wooden hut (rather like a large wardrobe or press) at the east end; the crossing gates were operated by the station staff. The former engine shed was converted into the station master's house and the inspection pit was boarded over. There was a 1 ton goods crane here. The station was in a picturesque but quiet setting, half a mile from Kilconquhar village and 1½ miles from Colinsburgh, which it also purported to serve.

Kilconquhar to St Monance

This section was opened by the Leven & East of Fife Railway in 1863 and closed to passengers in 1965 and to goods in the following year. Leaving Kilconquhar the line now abruptly turned south, passing at St Ford under the Broomlees to Earlsferry minor road before skirting the golf course and passing under the Largo to Elie road (the A917) at Park Place on the edge of the burgh of Elie (the bridge had its girders replaced in 1915). It then ran for a short distance to the north of the town, passing under the A917 again, before entering **Elie station** (13.70). Like Kilconquhar, Elie was situated on a curve and the original platform, on the down side, contained a long single-storey station building dating from the opening of the Leven & East of Fife line in 1863 and of a similar pattern to those at Largo, Kilconquhar, St Monance, Pittenweem and Anstruther (Old); a wooden lamp hut was also provided. When a loop (capable of holding 30 wagons) was added in 1898 and the station became a crossing place, a new up platform was provided along with a brick signal box and North British-pattern brick-built station building. A footbridge, originally of wooden construction but later replaced with an iron lattice structure, linked the platforms. On the up side a small dock was later used for camping coaches and the goods yard, with four sidings and a 3-ton crane, lay on the same side of the line but at the east end of the station. A large water tank was situated on the down platform; this was the sole watering point between Cameron Bridge and Anstruther and had been moved from its original position slightly to the west in 1900.

The line now crossed the links and turned north-east to follow the coast passing, in turn, the remains of Ardross and Newark Castles and the ancient chapel of St Monan, later the parish church, before reaching **St Monance station** (15.78) and the Inverie burn. Situated at the back of the town and away from the harbour, the original station consisted of a platform on the down side of the line, complete with a standard Leven & East of Fife building. In 1900 a loop (capable of holding 29 wagons) and up platform were added together with a small North British shelter on that platform and a brick-built signal box, which was situated at the east end of the down platform adjacent to a long footbridge which connected the platforms to the town. The goods yard was situated on the up side, facing west, had five sidings, long loading bays, a 2 ton crane and, latterly, storage tanks for diesel fuel. At the east end

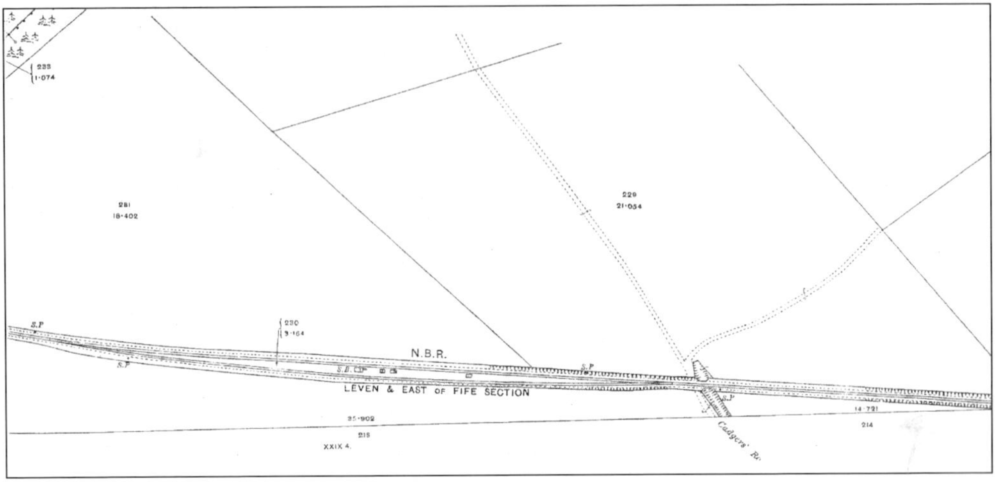

Kilconquhar West showing the isolated position of the loop and signal box.
Reproduced from the 1914, 25" Ordnance Survey Map, Crown Copyright

Kilconquhar; the two roads shown are the Largo to Elie main road and (over the level crossing) the Kilconquhar to Shell Bay lane.
Reproduced from the 1894, 25" Ordnance Survey Map, Crown Copyright

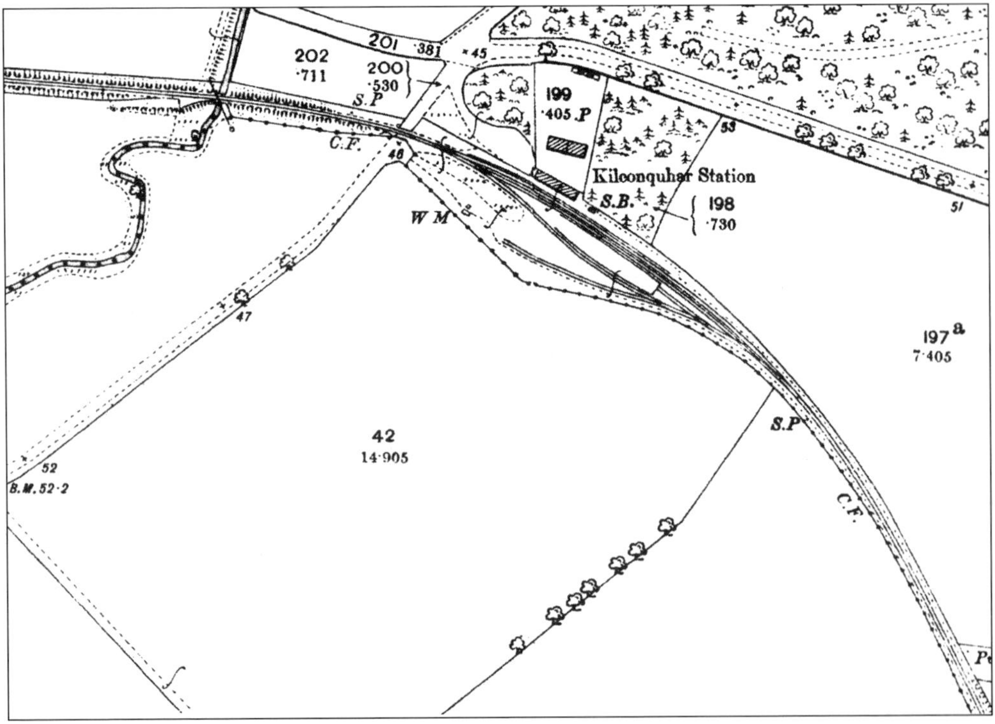

Kilconquhar with the East of Fife Railway's former terminus and the 'wardrobe' ground frame in June 1953. *J.L. Stevenson*

'B1' class 4-6-0 No. 61404 arrives at Kilconquhar with the 12.17 pm Thornton Junction to Crail service on 27th July, 1963. *Roy Hamilton*

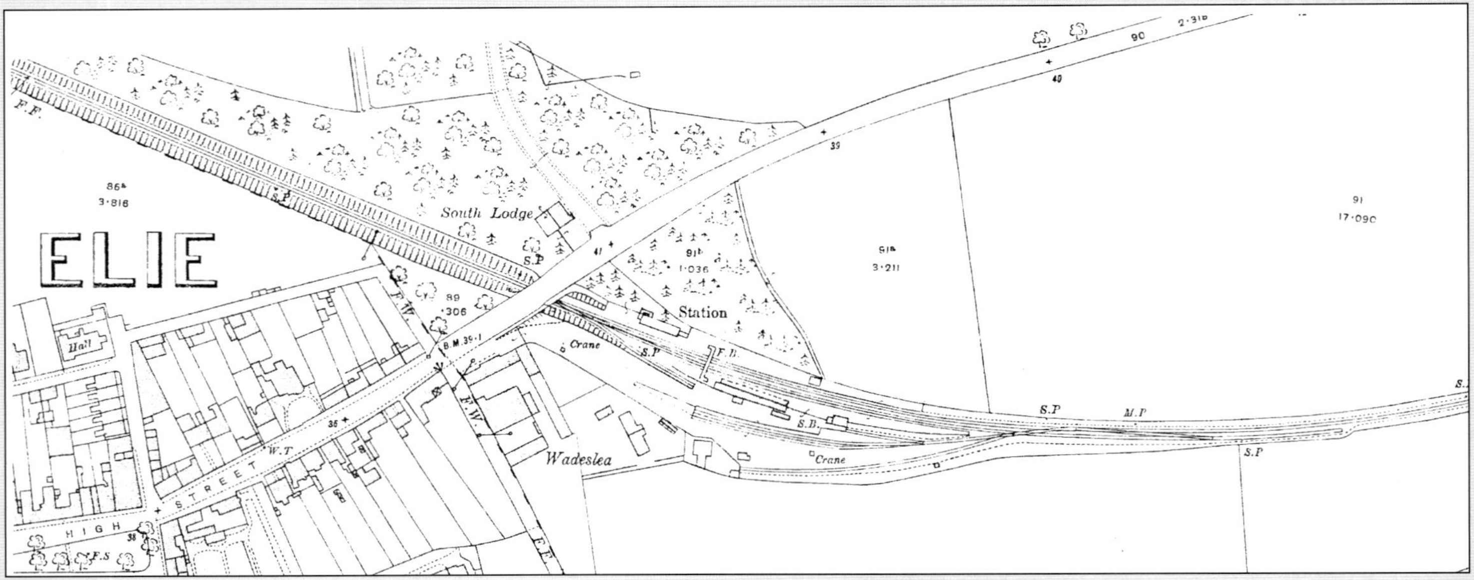

Elie station.

Reproduced from the 1912, 25″ Ordnance Survey Map, Crown Copyright

'B1' class 4-6-0 No. 61146 on a down train at Elie on 10th August, 1963. Note the camping coach in the dock. *C.C. Thornburn*

The impressive NBR water tower at Elie on 8th September, 1955. *R.M. Casserley*

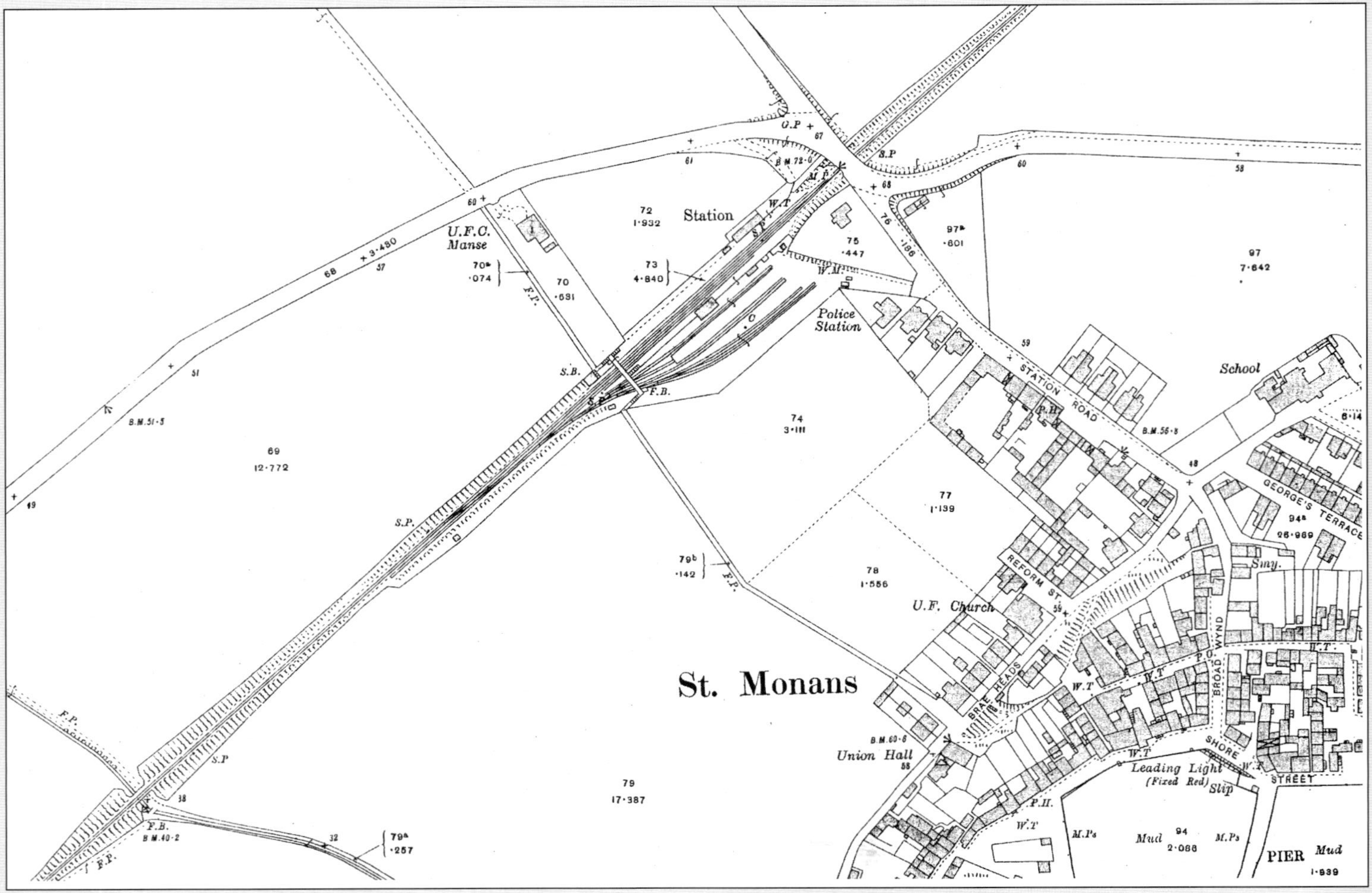

St Monance station,goods yard and the road leading down to the harbour.

Reproduced from the 1914, 25" Ordnance Survey Map, Crown Copyright

St Monance station from the carriage window, 13th April, 1953. *J.L. Stevenson*

The goods yard at St Monance with the Bass Rock Oil Co. storage tanks clearly visible, July 1953. *A.G. Ellis*

The 1.40 pm Edinburgh (Waverley) to Anstruther dmu service enters Pittenweem station on 14th July, 1964. *Hamish Stevenson*

Pittenweem station with the station master's house and the long walk to the town.
Reproduced from the 1914, 25" Ordnance Survey Map, Crown Copyright

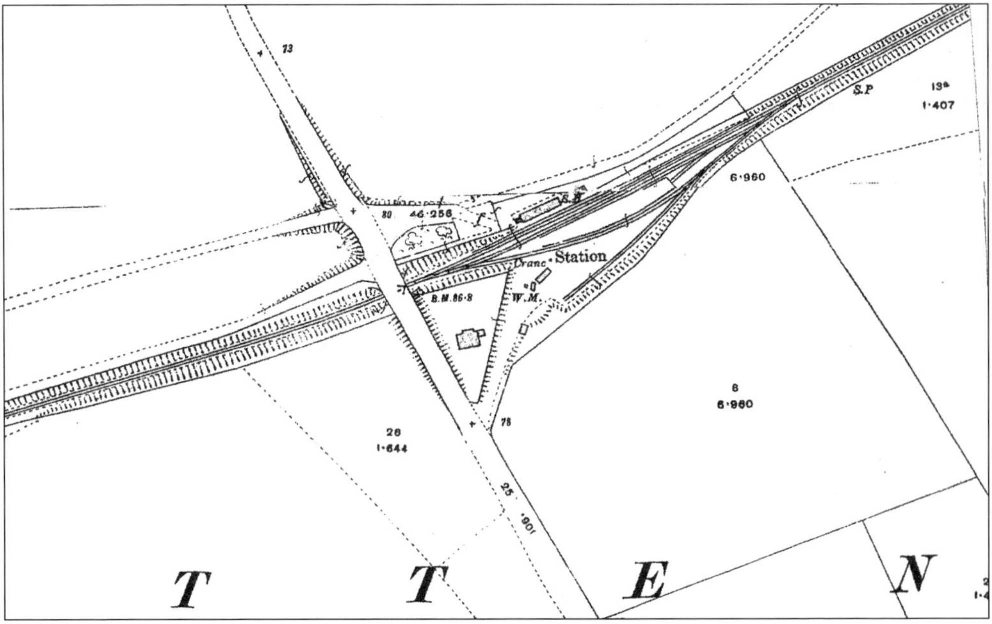

of the station the line was crossed by the main coast road (A917); since closure the bridge has been demolished and the road system realigned. A separate station master's house was situated next to the east end of the goods yard.

St Monance to Anstruther

The line now passed inland behind Coal Farm and, following the route of the long-vanished Pittenweem coal tramway, across the fields to **Waterless bridge**, where the Colinsburgh to Pittenweem road (the B942) went over the railway. Three-quarters of a mile further on, and immediately west of the bridge carrying the Carnbee to Pittenweem road over the line was **Pittenweem station** (17.42), half a mile from the edge of the burgh when first built and a good mile from the harbour. This was not a passing place and had a sole platform situated on the down side on which was placed the original Leven & East of Fife single-storey building. For many years this was a well-kept station with a small garden with a rustic fence. A small shed, similar to that at Kilconquhar, and situated on the platform to the east of the main station building, housed a ground frame. The goods sidings, complete with a non-passenger loop and two sidings with a 1½ ton crane, were placed on the up side of the line immediately opposite the passenger platform

The line now swung to the east and after passing under a minor road leading to Milton Mill reached **Anstruther Junction** (18.36), where a signal box situated on the down side marked the junction between the Leven & East of Fife and Anstruther & St Andrews companies. The line to Crail diverged on the down side while on the up side and on the edge of Anstruther Wester the terminus of the Leven & East of Fife was reached at **Anstruther (Old)**, latterly the goods station for Anstruther. The former passenger platform, with its original building, and later used to load the fish trains which were such a feature of this station, was flanked on the north side by four further sidings used by fish traffic and a 50 ft locomotive turntable, rather surprisingly the only turntable on the line. To the south lay further sidings, a small brick-built two-road engine shed and a water column. A 1½ ton crane and further sidings lay to the south.

From **Anstruther Junction** the line travelling eastwards was operated as a double track and crossed the Dreel Burn, which marked the boundary between the twin burghs of Anstruther Wester and Anstruther Easter, on a stone viaduct of two arches each with a span of 35 ft, the western arch carrying the line over the burn and the eastern arch over a mill lade. The parapet was an open iron lattice and the deck also carried on the up side a footpath which ran between the Old and New stations for the convenience of railway staff and passengers wishing to directly access Anstruther Wester; the pathway was divided from the track by a painted wooden paling fence. **Anstruther (New) station** (18.52), usually referred to merely as Anstruther, consisted of two platforms, the up containing the main building being stone-built, 110 ft in length and with a shallow canopy extending over the platform. The principal offices were on this side as was Anstruther Station signal box, which was situated to the west of the station building. The down platform had a smaller brick-built building with a wide canopy of standard North British design and was linked to the up platform with a lattice footbridge. The station was on a north-easterly curve and after the station entered into a cutting where the down loop line rejoined the up line and a single track section commenced. In 1926 the signal box at Anstruther station was closed and the down loop truncated at the east end of the

The afternoon train at Pittenweem taking the Waid Academy pupils back home for tea.
H.C. Casserley

Ex-LMS 'Black Five' 4-6-0 No. 44704 makes a smokey exit from Pittenweem with a Glasgow (Queen Street) train on 27th July, 1963. *Roy Hamilton*

The original LEoFR terminus at Anstruther which later became the goods depot, seen on 21st August, 1958. *A.G. Ellis*

Anstruther with 'D11' class 4-4-0 No. 62691 on a working from Crail. Here the pupils from the Waid Academy, seen in the background, boarded their homeward trains. *Authors' Collection*

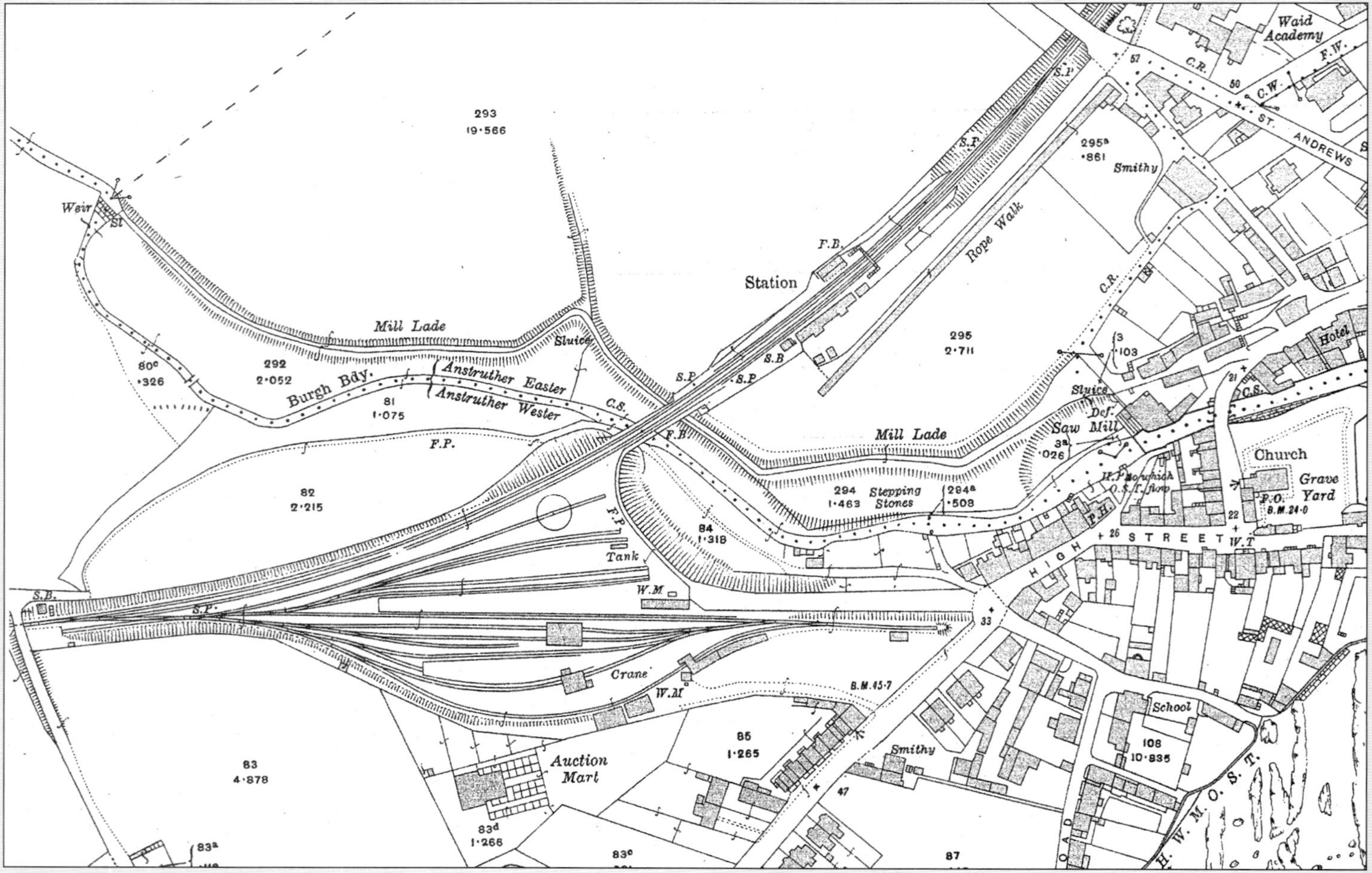

Anstruther with (*left to right*) the Junction signal box, goods yard, turntable, original LEoFR passenger station, the viaduct over the Dreel Burn, the NBR station and (*top right*) the Waid Academy.

Reproduced from the 1914, 25″ Ordnance Survey Map, Crown Copyright

'D34' class 4-4-0 No. 62467 *Glenfinnan* entering Anstruther with the 5.40 pm from Thornton Junction in the late 1950s. *W.J.V. Anderson*

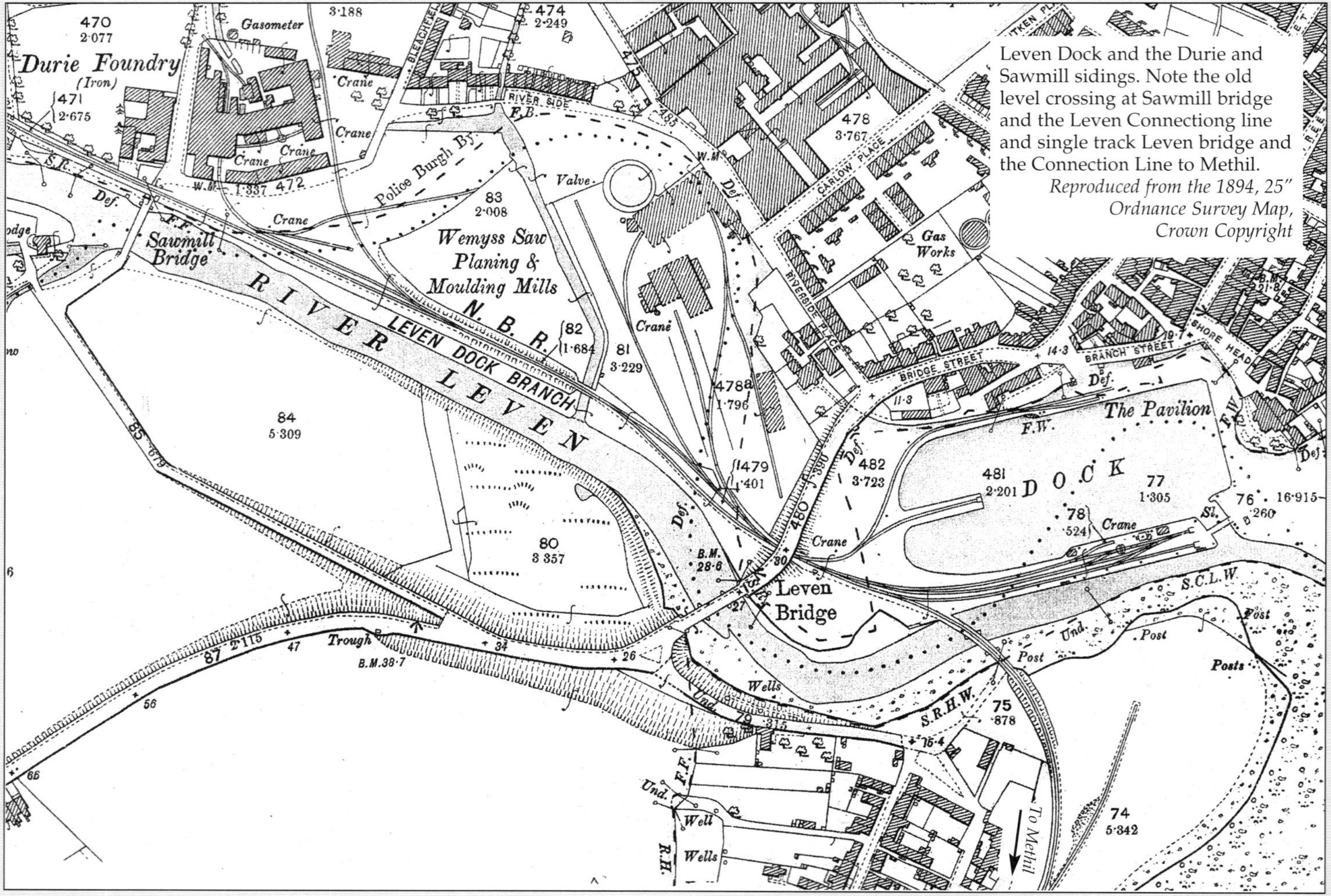

Leven Dock and the Durie and Sawmill sidings. Note the old level crossing at Sawmill bridge and the Leven Connectiong line and single track Leven bridge and the Connection Line to Methil.

Reproduced from the 1894, 25" Ordnance Survey Map, Crown Copyright

station, making the former down line as a dead-end line and capable only of catering for trains from the Leven direction which were terminating at or starting from Anstruther.

The Muiredge Branch

The Muiredge branch was single track throughout and left the main line at the eastern end of Cameron Bridge station and crossed the River Leven on a single-span metal bridge before running on an embankment along its southern bank for a short distance after which it entered a cutting and swung south-eastwards on a ruling gradient of 1 in 56 on the climb towards Methilhill. The cutting gave way to an embankment and **Pirnie level crossing** was reached on the Cameron Bridge to Methil road (the present B932). The line continued southwards to **Pirnie Junction** (0.69) where a long private mineral branch of the Fife Coal Company led off to the Leven Nos. 1 and 2 pits at Aberhill (from where a steep connection led to Methil Dock) and the Leven Nos. 3 and 4 ('Klondyke') pits. (Despite their names none of the pits were in Scoonie parish (Leven) but were in the adjacent Wemyss parish.) **Cameron Pit sidings** (0.76) were then reached where there was a connection with the Muiredge, Cameron and Rosie pits of Bowman & Co. (later the Weymss Coal Co. (WCC)). The branch then terminated at **Muiredge siding/Buckhaven (Old)** where there was a goods depot on the north side of the Kirkcaldy to Methil public road. When the Wemyss and Buckhaven Railway was built in 1881 the Muiredge branch was then continued across the road to make a connection with it. When the Wemyss Private Railway was opened in December 1900 it crossed the track of the Muiredge branch at **The Plunks** and the site of Cameron Junction and this led to the branch being operated in two sections, namely from Cameron Bridge to the Plunks with a west-facing connection to the WCC line and from the Plunks in an east-facing connection to the NBR Wemyss and Buckhaven line; the former Buckhaven (Old) goods depot was closed.

The original Leven Dock Branch

Leaving the Leven & East of Fife line just before Burnmill and heading south-east to cross the Burnmill mill lade on a short bridge this passed Leven Bank House (home of Henry Balfour, founder of the Durie Foundry), passing over an ungated level crossing, and then ran along the east bank of the River Leven. The Sawmill bridge, carrying a minor public road over the river, was then crossed by a gated level crossing taking the road in to Leven. The line carried a parallel long siding serving the **Durie Foundry siding** on the down side and, after crossing a mill lade, was joined in a trailing junction by the **Wemyss Saw Planing and Moulding Mills sidings** of Messrs Donaldson's. The branch then ran under the public road leading to the Bawbee or Leven bridge to reach the **Leven Dock sidings** serving the quaysides while the branch then swung off to the south side and crossed the River Leven on a single track girder bridge of three spans to form the Leven Connection Railway which led to Methil Docks.

The Leven Dock branch with Donaldson's sidings to the right; this view was taken at the time of the reconstruction of the branch in 1909-10. *Alan Brotchie Collection*

A Crail to Thornton train passing Kirkland Yard in 1965. *W.A.C. Smith*

Inside the creosote sidings at Leven in the 1960s. *P. Westwater*

The new Leven Harbour Branch

The branch was extensively rebuilt in the 1908-1910 period and became known as the Leven Harbour line or, by the name it was known in later years, as the Methil Dock branch. The branch left the 'main' line at **East Fife Central Junction** and followed the same path as the earlier Leven Dock branch line was quadrupled between the east end of **Kirkland Yard** and Methil East signal box. The two sets of rails on the west side of the branch, which were paralleled by a retaining wall on the river, were the principal up and down running lines while the third rail formed an additional ingoing line only as far as Methil East and the fourth line (furthest away from the river) gave access to the various sidings. Methil Docks themselves* were built in the period before World War I and transformed the Leven Harbour branch; they became the single largest coal exporting docks in Scotland reaching a peak year for coal exports in 1923 when about 3,400,000 tons were exported. The docks were owned, successively, by the North British, the LNER, the British Transport Commission and by the Forth Ports Authority.

The first sidings reached were the **Creosote Works sidings** (0.47) which led in on the up side and were parallel but to the south of Kirkland yard followed by **Kirkland Yard Junction** (0.60) where the lines from the yard joined the branch.† Immediately to the south and on the up side of the line the single track 10 chains-long **Leven Oilcake Mills siding**, which crossed the river on a single-span girder bridge, joined the branch. The **Balfour Bridge hut**, which contained a ground frame controlling the signals in this area, was situated on the up side at the junction of this siding and immediately thereafter the rebuilt Sawmill bridge, replacing the original level crossing, crossed the line. Thereafter the **Durie Foundry siding** (0.69) and **Donaldson's siding** (0.74) joined the eastern set of rails followed, after the overbridge carrying the Leven to Methil public road (and also the tram tracks to Kirkcaldy), by **Leven Dock siding** (0.76), also known as the Shorehead sidings, on the filled-in basis of the former Leven harbour. The line passed **Methil East signal box** (0.79) on the down side and crossed the river by a four-tracked girder bridge before the lines to the west continued on to Methil Docks and the lines to the east to the power station at Methil.

* The Docks are dealt with in greater detail in Alan Brotchie's magisterial *The Wemyss Private Railway* (Oakwood Press, 1998).

† These two sidings are now the site of the Kingdom of Fife Railway Preservation Society's Kirkland Yard depot and will be covered in the authors' forthcoming *East of Fife Central Railway (The Lochty Branch)* volume.

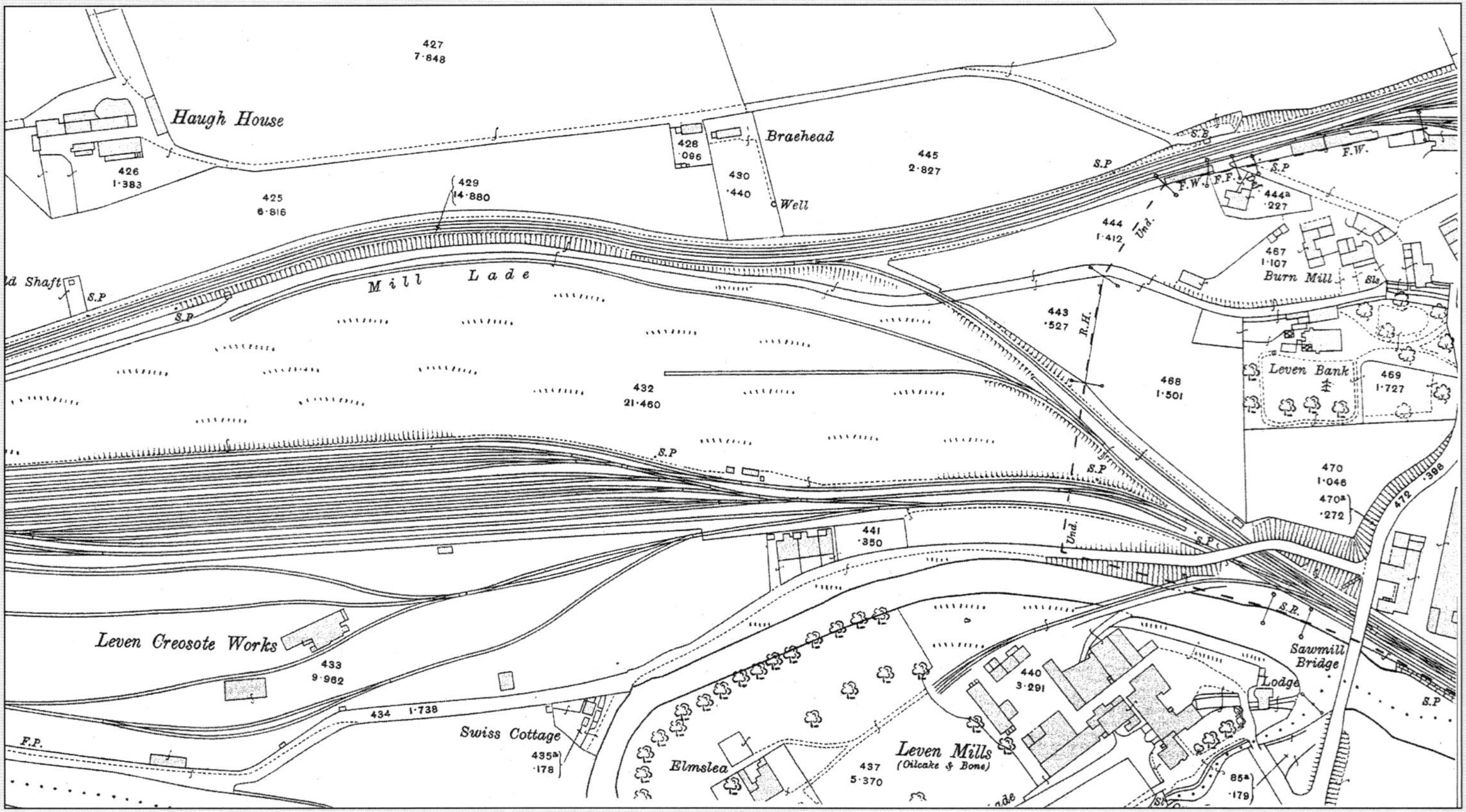

The Creosote works sidings. Kirkland Yard and the Leven Mills siding branch. *Reproduced from the 1914, 25" Ordnance Survey Map, Crown Copyright*

Chapter Sixteen

Fish Suppers and General Merchandise: Goods traffic on the Line

> *'All trains must , unless otherwise specially ordered, both lift and leave Traffic at the places where they are timed to call'*
>
> *NBR Rules and Regulations for Goods Traffic*

A General Survey

The East Fife railways did not carry the heavy, long-distance traffic of the main line but were in no way a sleepy rural backwater for there was a considerable range of traffic over the 20 miles of line between Thornton and Anstruther. Over most of the region the predominant industries were agriculture and fishing but there were pockets of other commercial activity in the Leven and Cameron Bridge areas. Coal, both inward and outward, remained the single most important traffic on the line and it was extensively used for both domestic and industrial purposes. For many years Methil, reached via the Leven Harbour branch, was the largest coal-exporting port in Scotland. Until well after World War I the railway used to bring in the greater part of all the of the raw materials and household necessities consumed in the region and to take out local produce, manufactured goods and minerals, although coastal shipping still had a part to play, particularly in relation to coal and potatoes. From the 1920s onwards the motor lorry began to eat in to the traffic and to cream off short distance and high value trade, while the railway was left in the main to carry heavy and bulky items which attracted lower rates than more profitable traffics. This decline continued unabated after 1945 and was exacerbated by a national railway footplatemen's strike in 1955 which caused some of the larger industrial concerns to reduce their dependence on rail traffic. Towards the end of that decade traffic began to dwindle in such an alarming manner that within a few years it had all but disappeared.

In this chapter the goods traffic which ran over the Leven & East of Fife line is dealt with in some detail on a geographical basis, but we begin with a survey of one of the principal local industries, namely fishing.

Fishing

The fishing ports served by the Leven & East of Fife Railway were Largo, Elie, St Monance, Pittenweem, Anstruther and Cellardyke and it is interesting to note that none of these ports, most remarkably Anstruther, were served by direct lines running to the quaysides. Before World War I some 3,000 persons were employed in the fishing industry locally and the annual landings were worth some £700,000. Herring was the most important catch followed by cod, haddock, plaice and dabs while Crail specialized in shellfish and crabs. In 1862 it was said that Anstruther was one of the best fishing stations in Scotland and that upwards of 50,000 barrels of herring had been caught in one year, 'all of which were either cured on the spot or despatched by cart, rail and steam boat to the inland towns'. One feature of the herring trade was its seasonal nature – originally the season for herring ('the drave') was in the summer but due to the mysterious movement of the herring local

'J37' 0-6-0 No. 64606 with the 'Coast Goods' between St Monance and Elie. *W.J.V. Anderson*

An NBR open wagon as used on the Anstruther fish specials. *NBRSG, Hennigan Collection*

'B1' class 4-6-0 No. 61401 with the 2.30 pm train with attached fish van leaving Leven for Thornton in 1964. *Author's Collection*

landings became concentrated between January and April, with an emphasis on February and March; in those two months alone, 83 per cent of the annual catch was landed. This meant that the railway had a sudden but welcome influx of traffic since the rival East Anglian and Northern Scottish ports which had summer seasons could not compete and thus East Neuk fish enjoyed better market prices than it might otherwise have done. The railways found that it filled a welcome gap in which fish vans, which would otherwise have seen little use at that time of year, were used to capacity. Local boats migrated with their crews to Fraserburgh, Peterhead, Lerwick, Yarmouth and Lowestoft in the summer season and the 'fisher lassies', their wives, daughters and girlfriends involved in the gutting and preparation of the catches, often followed by rail.

The principal home markets for herring and white fish were London, which took the lion's share, as well as Grimsby, Lowestoft, Great Yarmouth, Birmingham, Liverpool, Manchester and Glasgow, and special overnight rail services were run to service these towns. By late Victorian times the majority of the catch was no longer being salted and cured locally but was being sold fresh, a trend helped by the absence of fresh winter-caught fish from other east coast ports and improvements in the storage and refrigeration. Herring were also exported, via Methil and Leith Docks to Russia (a traffic lost after the revolution but regained in the 1920s), Latvia (Libau, Riga, Windau and Ventspils), Konigsberg in Germany (now Kaliningrad in Russia) and the then-German ports of Danzig, Stettin, Hamburg and Altona. This trade was known as 'Klondyking', after the boom in trade in salted goods to the Californian and Yukon gold miners, and disappeared for ever in 1939.

For the first 30 years or so after the railway reached the district fishing vessels were sail-powered but steam gained an early introduction to the Anstruther District* and by 1896 five-sixths of the entire Scottish steam-driven fishing fleet was shared between the Aberdeen and Anstruther fishing districts. In the years immediately prior to 1914 the motor boat began to appear in Fife and by then the larger sailing vessels were doomed, no further examples being built. The number of steam vessels operating out of Anstruther harbour rose to 58 in 1924 but this was a peak and after that they began to be replaced by diesel-powered craft. By 1938 there were only 19 steam drifters left operating out of Anstruther; seven years previously Anstruther had 120 motor boats and 53 steam drifters. At this time the fleet was still largely concerned with herring fishing and in the period 1930-1939 the total value of such landings in the Anstruther District was £563,029 compared with £196,764 for white fish and £47,654 for shellfish. The highest single year for herring fishing in the area was 1936 when 13,000 tons were landed, a figure which was to remain unchallenged. Towards the end of World War II herring deserted the Firth of Forth† and the fishing fleet now had to go after white fish or to move elsewhere. After 1939 the railway lost most of the remaining fish traffic to motor vehicles, one of the major reasons for this being the absence of any harbour railway branches, so that fish had to be transhipped between the boats and stations, and the other being the flexibility of the lorry in servicing the markets, with a guaranteed overnight delivery. By the late 1940s Pittenweem overtook Anstruther as the major East Fife fishing port and remains so to this day, albeit that the fishing industry is nowadays a pale shadow of what it once was. Associated with fishing were certain ancillary industries all of

* The Anstruther District included all of the East and North Fife ports from Buckhaven to Newport-on-Tay but was dominated by Buckhaven and the three East Neuk ports.

† Herring are notoriously sensitive to slight temperature changes and a possible explanation for this desertion was that there had been a slight, but permanent, change in the water temperature in the Forth at this time.

which depended to a greater or lesser extent on the railway for bringing in raw materials and for exporting the finished product – these industries included fish processing (gutting, salting and other fish preparation), cooperages which made herring barrels, fish boxes and casks, the manufacture of fishing nets and associated paraphernalia, the making of sou'westers and other oilproof clothing and, last but not least, the building of sea-going vessels at St Monance.

Fish was originally transferred by rail in open wagons although closed vans were in use from the beginning of the 20th century and later refrigerated wagons were used. In BR times the last fish traffic on the line was the van attached to the 2.00 pm Crail to Thornton – the wagon tended to be an ex-LNER ventilated fish van but ex-LMS six-wheelers and ex-GWR vehicles were also used.

Coal and Other Minerals

Leven lies at the edge of the Fife coalfield and, as one travels eastwards, isolated outcrops of coal continue to appear as far away as Elie and Pittenweem. Apart from the product of the West Fife coal fields which travelled over the line between Thornton Junction and Leven Dock and the products of the Leven coalfields which used the Muiredge branch, other outward sources of coal traffic included the Durie mine (reached via its own short branch line) and the coal mined in the Lochty and Largoward areas which travelled via the Lochty branch on to the line of the Leven Railway. The isolated pits in the Elie Grange and Pittenweem areas appear to have ceased any coal production before the railway arrived but the plan in the 1890s to develop large scale mines in the Pittenweem area, which would have brought a considerable coal traffic over the line, came to naught. The inward transit of coal was widespread over the area, both for industrial and domestic use. Industrial users included the boilers of the Cameron Bridge distilleries, the various works in the Leven area, the flax-mill at Silverburn, the net works at Largo and the miscellaneous business concerns at Anstruther. In addition the gas works at Leven, Elie and Anstruther all used rail-borne coal, even though none of them were directly rail-served. Other major users included hotels and other residential establishments and, most critically, the steam trawlers based in the fishing ports, although the absence of direct rail connection tended to result in the trawler owners bringing supplies of coal by sea from Methil Dock. Domestic coal was delivered by the wagon load to all of the local goods sidings where a number of coal merchants had their offices and the coal was then delivered by road to the end users. In certain cases the local station master also acted as the coal agent. Other minerals that were carried over the line included china clay, salt, coke and, for use as fertilizer, lime.

Earlseat Siding

Opened in August 2012 and lying on the up side of the line, this siding serves the Mackie's Mill extension of the Earlseat open-cast coal mine. Coal from here is taken via Cardenden, Dunfermline and Alloa to Hunterston Low Level in Ayrshire where it is then blended with lower-grade imported coal for onward transmission to various rail-served power stations in England. Up to 30 trains of 20 wagons each are expected to be run to and from Earlseat siding every week.

Haughmill Siding

The next goods facility east of Thornton Junction was the Haughmill siding, a short siding on the south side of the line which served the Haugh Mill, a flax and linen mill operated by G. & W. Beveridge and situated on the north bank of the River Leven, west of Cameron Bridge station. In addition it served the Haugh Bleaching Company's associated cloth bleaching works. The siding, which ran parallel to the line on the up side and faced west, would have been used for bringing in the raw materials for linen production and for taking out the finished product but it is notable that the siding only appears in one edition of the North British Railway's *List of Sidings*, that for 1896, and appears to have been lifted by about 1904.

Drumcaldie Distillery Siding

A single siding was provided to the west of Cameron Bridge for a small malt whisky distillery set up in 1896 by the Fife Distillery Co. Ltd. The business was, however, short-lived and failed in 1903,* the buildings being acquired by the Distillers Company Ltd, who incorporated them into their adjacent Cameron Bridge distillery when the siding was lifted.

Cameron Bridge

The main goods traffic, however, on the Thornton to Leven section was from the Cameron Bridge Distillery which dominated the whole area and had its own sidings from the opening of the line. Opened by William Haig, the distillery was merged with other Scottish grain whisky distilleries to form the Distillers Co. Ltd, which was to become a major international company and the biggest single producer of Scotch whisky in the world. The company was acquired by Guinness PLC in 1986 which later merged with Grand Metropolitan PLC to form Diageo PLC. The railway was used to bring in grain and coal supplies from Fife and further afield – in 1862 Egyptian grain was imported via Burntisland and in later years grain came from East Anglia and the north-east of Scotland. Outward traffic principally consisted of casked whisky which was taken from the bonded warehouses to shippers or blending and bottling plants in Leith and Glasgow although a small quantity was sold as a single grain malt whisky. Until 1924 bakers' yeast was also manufactured here and this, too, was taken by rail. From about the beginning of the 20th century, the Distillers Co. had special grain vans built for their grain traffic which came both from inland grain merchants and from ports, principally Leith. These vans were wooden-bodied, with peaked roofs (and thus looking rather like dog kennels on wheels!) and were unloaded quickly by bottom discharge from the hopper-shaped interior of the vehicle, into a pit in between the running rails of the siding. These wooden-bodied wagons were gradually replaced by larger all-steel grain wagons from the late 1930s. The new wagons† were four-wheeled and of 20-ton capacity and discharged from the bottom. They were a familiar sight at Cameron Bridge and were generally lettered 'S.G.D.', which stood for Scottish Grain Distillers, a subsidiary

* Brian Townsend in 'Scotch Missed' (1997), memorably described Drumcaldie as being 'the shortest lived major distillery built on Scottish soil … a white elephant from the word go.'
† Hurst, Nelson built a number of these to LMS dia. D1689 in 1937 – see G. Gamble, *British Railway Private Owner Wagons, No. 9 Opens and Hoppers*, Cheona Publications, 1999.

No. 65913 hauling grain wagons at Cameron Bridge on 1st August, 1961. *Hamish Stevenson*

Distillers 10 ton grain wagon. *Historical Model Railway Society*

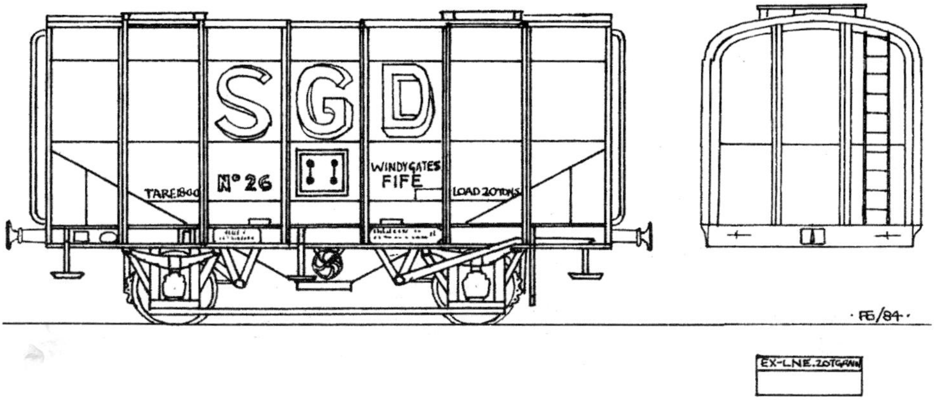

Scottish Grain Distillers 20 ton grain wagon. The body and solebar were grey, with a black underframe. The lettering was white with black shading. *Alan Goodwillie*

A DCL grain wagon beneath the road at Cameron Bridge, 1964. *C.C. Thornburn*

The DCL shunter performs maneouvres at Cameron Bridge under the gaze of the signalman, 14th July, 1964. *C.C. Thornburn*

Shunting at Cameron Bridge in 1986. *Jim Page*

company of the Distillers Co. Ltd. A by-product of the distilling process was draff, i.e. the husk and residue of the grain used. This was used as cattle feed and was loaded into railway wagons at Cameron Bridge for dispatch to farmers via their local station; one favourite East Fife destination was Mount Melville. The transport of grain to Cameron Bridge finally ceased by 1990 and the last use of rail by the distillery was the outward transit of liquefied carbon dioxide, another by-product of the distilling industry, in the early 1990s when this was dispatched in special railway tank wagons from Cameron Bridge to another Diageo site in North London; up to 400 tonnes of this substance was loaded each week. There is currently no traffic using the still-extant distillery sidings.

The Kirkland Branch

A short branch line, known variously as the Kirkland siding or Kirkland branch, led to the south bank of the River Leven to serve the Kirkland Works. This was a large spinning mill which at one time employed 800 persons, spun bleached and wove flax, hemp and jute and, by the time that the railway opened, produced starching warps for use in the rapidly expanding Kirkcaldy linoleum trade. The short railway connection was used to receive raw materials and coal and to dispatch finished goods and for many years was busy with traffic – the tonnage of flax, hemp and jute received by rail in 1864 was in the region of 1,500 tons. However, foreign competition, at its height in the 1880s, caused the demise of many spinning mills and Kirkland was no exception. Work was suspended towards the end of that decade and never resumed so that the mill and its associated railway lay derelict by 1893; the bridge over the River Leven having been dismantled. For a number of years the site remained derelict until, in 1896, it was purchased by a firm of chemical manufacturers, the Scottish Cyanide Co. Ltd. This concern was formed to manufacture cyanide, which was at that time being used in large quantities in the process of recovering gold from gold-bearing rock, the major market being the Rand area of South Africa. The principal raw material used in the manufacture of cyanide of sodium was coal, of which there was a plentiful supply locally and the branch line was revived, so that coal could be delivered by rail. Unfortunately the plant, with its new machinery and powerful furnaces, had a short life because of a sudden fall in the price of cyanide which, in 1899, had been sold for 1*s.* 2½*d.* per lb. During the Boer War exports ceased and the market suddenly became glutted, the price falling to a mere 6½*d.* per lb. For three years the works were selling from their stockpile and the price barely recovered and in 1905 the company closed the works down.

In 1910 the site was acquired by the National Steel Foundry Ltd. This company originally conducted its business on a fixed contract basis and, with the rise of costs associated with the advent of World War I, could no longer complete. Going into members' voluntary liquidation the business was acquired by a new company, National Steel Foundry (1914) Ltd who continued to run the works, albeit on a more sound financial basis. The works, which was a sizeable metal casting and machining concern, was served by the Kirkland branch, but this had to be realigned because of the construction of the Kirkland Yard in the interim so that it now had a westwards-facing junction with the main line, situated some 100 yards or so west of the original junction. The company produced steel castings for a number of customers, with the transport market being the major one. Lorry hubs and axles were produced for Scammell lorries, railway rolling stock axle boxes were produced for Timkin and

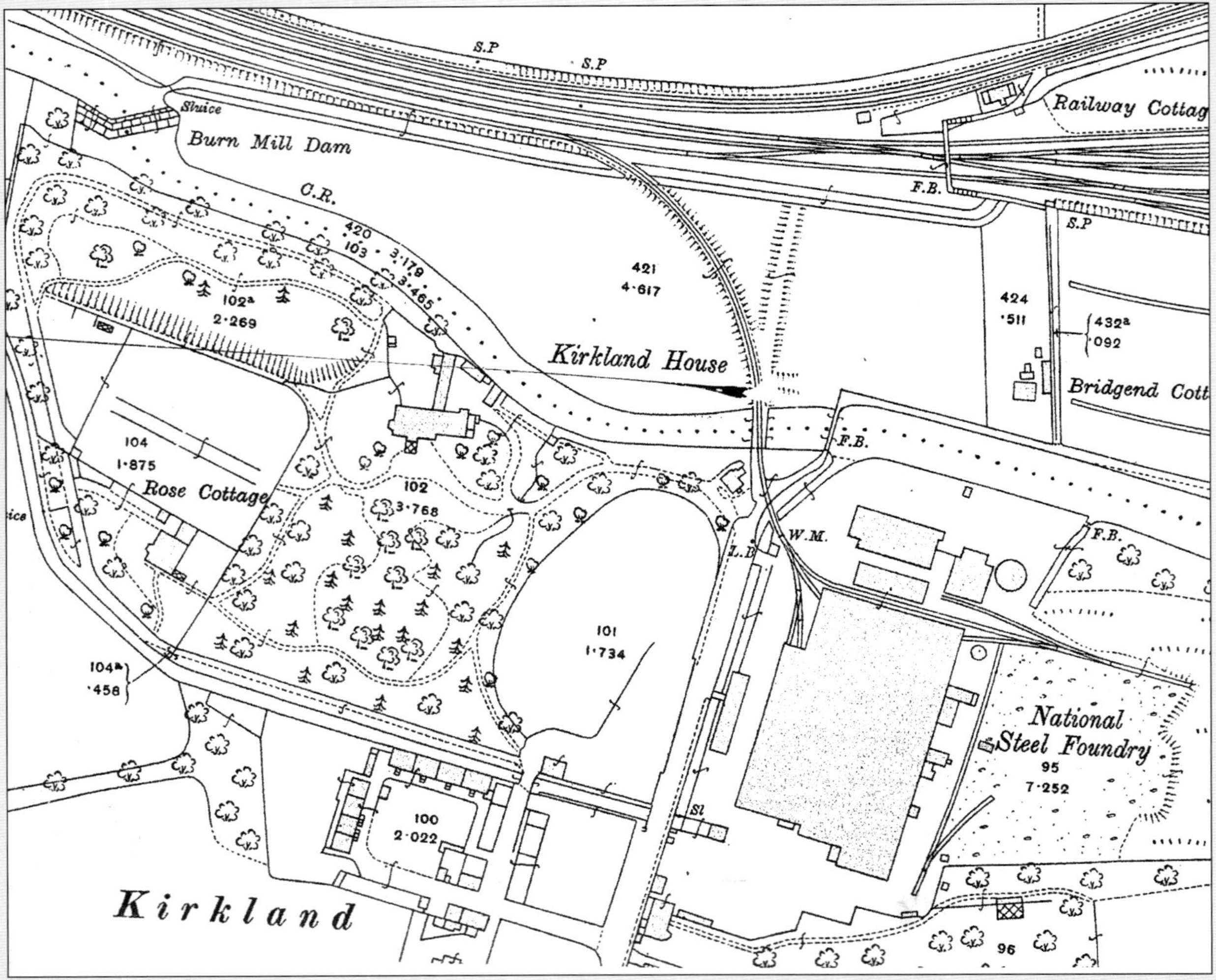

The Kirkland branch as rebuilt.

Reproduced from the 1914, 25″ Ordnance Survey Map, Crown Copyright

No. 64616 enters Kirkland Yard with a long coal train. *Alan Goodwillie*

'B1' class 4-6-0 No. 61133 starts off with a load of empties for Thornton on a frosty Saturday morning at Kirkland Yard. *Alan Goodwillie*

SKF and railway wagon wheels, couplings and buffers were also made. The works also produced parts for Anderson Boyes coal-cutting machinery as well as pipes for pipelines and wellhead valves for the oil industry; by the early 1960s the company had around 550 employees. Inward rail traffic consisted of steel ingots for melting and subsequent casting, steel plate for punching, foundry sand for use on the moulding shop, coke and coal for the furnaces and scrap metal for melting while the outward rail traffic consisted of the finished castings and forgings. After the cessation of rail traffic the company went into receivership and the business was acquired by Glencast Ltd who continued in business until the plant was finally closed in 2001.

Burnmill Siding

This was built in 1955 and used in connection with Donaldson's timber business for storing timber imported through Methil; the siding finally went out of use before 1964.

Leven Goods

The goods station at Leven was a busy one and in the late 1930s there were six goods clerks and a goods manager employed there. Traffic included timber for the Donaldson's Wemyss Saw Mills, coal, fruit, vegetables and groceries. Other local industries which were not directly rail served but which used the railway were the Millfield Rope & Twine Works, the Glebefield Aerated Water Works and the Leven Steam Laundry. A major railway user was the Boase or Hawkslaw Spinning Mills, a substantial concern which employed 240 persons in the 1950s and which produced yarn for medium and heavy canvas and also heavier yarns for rope and twine manufacturers. The mill was part of a group of companies based in Dundee and at one time half of the Leven mill's production was sent by rail to the company's spinning mills close to the Fairmuir goods yard of the Caledonian Railway. Inward traffic to the mill consisted of hemp and yarns and coal for the boiler house and outward traffic included canvas and cloth. The mill closed in 1982. Another major user of Leven goods yard were the Fife Paper Mills Ltd whose Millfield Mills were close to the goods yard. Started by Grossett & Co. in 1880, this mill produced biscuit caps and envelope papers and, after takeover by Fife Paper Mills Ltd, it specialized in manilla and envelope papers and, later on, paper bags, glazed and kraft papers. Inward rail traffic consisted of coal, woodpulp, rags, china clay, waste paper and paper maker's chemicals, wood pulp was also brought in via the Leven Dock branch from Methil Docks. The mill was scheduled to close in March 1965 but was transformed into a plant producing multiwall paper sacks, refuse sacks and metal refuse bin holders and the works finally closed in 1979 and were demolished shortly thereafter. Other general traffic handled at Leven, including parcels sent by passenger train, were shoes and other goods for the Leven co-op and, after the war, fish from Aberdeen. The Leven goods yard was finally closed to all traffic on 25th January, 1965. During the LNER period six or seven horses were kept in railway stables at nearby Burnmill for use by the railway carters; during BR days there were a couple of Scammell mechanical horses based there making local parcel deliveries.

LEVEN DOCK BRANCH.

WEEK-DAYS.

Stations and Sidings.		Distance from Leven Goods Station. Miles.	Chns.	1 Goods	2	3	4 Goods	5	6	7 Goods	8	9	10
				a.m.			a.m.			p.m.			
Leven Goods Station	depart	...	...	8 0	...	...	11 30	...	...	3 30	...	...	...
Durie Foundry Siding	,,	0	46	8 10	......	......	......	......	......	3 40	......	......	......
Leven Dock	,,	0	57	8 45	...	..	12 0	...	...	4 10	...	...	...
Methil Dock	arrive	1	50	8 50	......	......	12 5	......	......	4 15	......	......	......

Stations and Sidings.		Distance from Methil Dock. Miles.	Chns.	11 Goods	12	13	14 Goods	15	16	17 Goods	18	19	20
				a.m.			a.m.			p.m.			
Methil Dock	depart	...	...	7 0	...	...	10 0	...	...	2 0	...	...	...
Leven Dock	,,	0	53	......	......	......	10 30	......	......	2 30	......	......	......
Durie Foundry Siding	,,	0	64	...	...	...	...	...	...	2 40	...	...	...
Leven Goods Station	arrive	1	50	7 20	......	......	10 50	......	......	3 0	......	......	......

Nos. 1, 4, 7, 11, 14 and 17.—Work other Sidings on Leven Dock Branch as required.

Working timetable for the Leven Dock branch from 20th September, 1926.

Leven Council Siding

This short-lived siding was opened in 1920 to serve the post-war council house-building requirements of the Leven Town Council and was in operation for a relatively short period, being closed in about 1926.

Leven Brickworks Siding

In use by 1859, this siding situated on the northern side of the line, served, via a connecting tramway, the Leven Brick, Tile and Ochre works of John White & Son and principally used for dispatching the finished products from the works as well as bringing in certain of the raw materials. In 1904 the siding is listed as being operated by Wilkie & Gibb and in 1921 it was used by D. Gordon for coal and timber, J. Lawson for cement and A. & J. Howie, plasterers. The siding was still in use in 1937 but became disused after the beginning of the war.

Durie Colliery Siding

This pit, lying between Leven and Lundin Links, was situated north of the railway and linked to it by a private siding. The most easterly of the Fife Coal Company's collieries, Durie was sunk in 1888-1890 and had a relatively brief life, being abandoned on 19th January, 1903. Durie Colliery Siding, opened to traffic in April 1888, remained in use for a few years after that, presumably to assist with the removal of stockpiled coal and in the demolition of the pithead buildings and other structures; by December 1906 it was listed as 'now being closed'. However, a short length of it remained in use as Durie siding which, in 1921, is shown as a public siding and it was still shown as in use as late as 1956. Its purpose by then appears primarily to have been for wagon storage and during the winter months for the storage of surplus carriages.

Silverburn Siding

For many years there was a flax retting mill at Silverburn, lying between the railway and the shore, and this was served by the only recorded siding on the East of Fife Railway, being in use by 1856. Retting consists of the steeping of flax stems in water until they are soft and the softened stems are then teased out by machinery in order to obtain the fibres from which linen is made. There were many factories producing linen in Fife at one time and the Silverburn mill probably supplied those situated in Leven, Kirkcaldy, Dysart and East Wemyss with raw material. The linen trade was open to fluctuations in its fortune, caused by the rise of the Lancashire cotton industry and competition from Ireland and elsewhere. The siding seems to have been disconnected at some time as it is shown in North British Railway records as having been reinstated and reopened for traffic again on 12th June, 1888. By 1893 the mill is shown as being 'disused' but the siding is still in place. In 1914 the siding was extant but all traces of the mill or other industrial premises had gone; by 1921 the firm using the siding is shown as 'vacant'. The Silverburn siding was used intermittently for the delivery of single wagons of coal for use on the estate after the war and still existed in 1956 as a stub of the original siding and was, presumably, used as a ballast or sand siding.

Lundin Links

There was only a modest freight traffic at this station, consisting largely of inward traffic of coal from the Fife Coal company and the Wemyss Coal Co. through merchants such as Thomson & Small and an outward traffic of potatoes from merchants such as John A.D. Steins and Isaac Poad & Sons Ltd. Until World War I there was a regular traffic in horses and horse-drawn carriages destined for the large houses in the village. Other traders who used the small goods yard in the years before the World War I included D.M. Patrick, golf club and golf ball manufacturers, and W. Dick, coach builders. Despite the lack of traffic apart from coal in later years, Lundin Links retained its goods yard until the complete closure of the station on 6th September, 1965.

Largo

Largo station had a small goods yard which handled mainly coal and agricultural produce. Inwards traffic included coal and fertilizers and outward traffic included grain, potatoes, sugar beet and livestock, principally sheep. There was also some fish traffic at Largo, although hardly of the scale at Anstruther. Coal traffic was destined for local coal merchants such as J. Elder and for the Largo works of the Largo & Lundin Links Gas Co. Ltd. Other traffic included that originating from the Largo Oil Works of D. Russell & Co. the oil mills of Alex. Philip & Co. and the Teasses Limeworks of A. Whittaker. Between 1868 and 1886 a fishing-net factory known as the Cardy Net Factory of David Gillies was in operation and the railway was used to bring in raw materials and coal and to distribute the finished nets. Latterly coal was the only ingoing traffic and a seasonal traffic in beet only that outgoing. Goods facilities at Largo were withdrawn on 20th April, 1965, six months before the withdrawal of passenger services.

Kilconquhar

Kilconquhar was a busy place for freight traffic and consisted mainly of agricultural produce from the various farms and landed estates in the area, together with an inwards traffic in coal. The station was also the railhead for Colinsburgh and Newburn and at the former place the small gasworks there also received coal. Another traffic was that in horses and this horsebox traffic included bloodstock for racehorse-owning landowners such as Lord Lindsay and Baroness Bonde. There was also occasional horse traffic for the inhabitants of Kilconquhar, Charleton and Balcarres Houses. In 1918 there was a short-lived traffic in aviation spirits and miscellaneous stores in connection with the wartime landing ground at Kilconquhar. There was an outgoing traffic in sugar beet and a small ingoing traffic in coal in later years. Goods facilities at Kilconquhar were withdrawn on 18th July, 1966.

Elie

Elie yard was used mainly for agricultural purposes, sundries and coal and, at one time, there was a small railborne traffic in salmon caught in staked nets ('fixed engines') placed in the sea at places such as Shell Bay. There were few local industries apart from golf-club making and tourism. There were two local coal merchants (in the 1920s they were J. M. Allan and J. Bell & Son) and the wagons of the Fife Coal Co. and the Wemyss Coal Co. were often seen in the yard. A local user and importer of coal was the Elie & Earlsferry Gas Co. who carted coal from the goods yard to their works at Williamsburgh. Elie goods yard was closed on 5th October, 1964, two years before the final closure of the line.

St Monance

There was a reasonable sized goods yard at St Monance and traffic handled here comprised livestock, fish, coal and various agricultural produce; there was also an oil depot at this station. A livestock special was run from this station to Thornton market every Monday morning in the period between 1920 and 1939. There was also some freight traffic for the boat-building yard of James Miller & Sons Ltd, a major employer in the burgh. At one time there were six fish curers in the town who used rail to send their products to market. The goods yard at St Monance was closed on 18th July, 1966.

Pittenweem

The station and goods yard here were inconveniently sited for the inhabitants of the fishing town and thus were little used for fish traffic, traffic from the harbour at Pittenweem being dispatched via the neighbouring goods yard at Anstruther. However, there were a number of farms and landed estates such as Balcaskie in the vicinity and these gave traffic in the form of agricultural produce, fertilisers and livestock. A small amount of milk in churns was sent from Pittenweem by rail. At the turn of the century a small coal pit at Grangemuir was in operation near to the station and some extra traffic was generated. The station also saw a steady inward traffic in coal for domestic use and for the local gasworks and there were a number of Pittenweem coal merchants, including Fyall and Wilson & Brodie, who used railborne coal which they then distributed through the town with their Commer lorries. A regular user of the goods yard was J.L. Burnett & Co. of Ovenstone, a local agricultural dealer who often had new agricultural machinery brought in by rail from manufacturers including New Holland; their showroom and workshops lay up the road from the station. The goods facilities at Pittenweem were closed as from 18th July, 1966.

Anstruther

Situated in the old station, the goods yard at Anstruther was notable for being the main loading place for the fish traffic. The railway itself did not run down to the harbour so the fish was transported in wooden boxes which were carried mainly in horse-drawn lorries up the hill to the railway goods yard for loading the wagons. During the winter herring season the fish traffic was extensive and extra labour was required to help in the loading of the fish trains – this extra labour was mostly local casual labour and during the season there could be three or four special fish trains

Thornton Trip Engines

No. B.126

Class 5F (J.37) Engine.

		On	Off
Locomen	SX	3.15pm	11.15pm
Guard	SX	3. 0pm	11. 0pm

	J	J
	SX	SX
	p.m.	p.m.
Thornton E.S.		3.30LE
Thornton Yard	3.40	3.50
Cameron Bridge	4.20	4.45
Leven		5.15
Largo	5.27	5.45
Lundin Links		6. 0
Leven		6.25
Cameron Bridge		7. 5
Thornton Pass.Stn	7.20	7.30
Thornton Yard	7.45	

Works Rothes Colliery.

Thornton Yard		- LE
Thornton E.S.	-	

		On	Off
Locomen	SO	12.25pm	8.25pm
Guard	SO	12.40pm	8.40pm

	SO	SO
	p.m.	p.m.
Thornton E.S.		12.40LE
Thornton Yard	12.50	1. 0Van

Conditional working.

Thornton Yard		8. 5LE
Thornton E.S.	8.15	

No. B.110

Class 5F (J.37) Engine.

	On	Off
Locomen	4.40am	1. 5pm
Guard	5. 0am	1. 0pm

	J	J
	arr	dep
	a.m.	a.m.
Thornton E.S.		5.25LE
Thornton Yard	5.35	5.50/
Kirkland Yard	6.25	6.45
Largo		7.20
Kilconquhar		7.40
Elie		7.55
St. Monance		8.10
Pittenweem		8.25
Anstruther	8.30	

Shunt as required.

Anstruther		9.45
Crail	10. 0	10.15EBV
Kirkland Yard	11. 3	11.15K
Cameron Bridge	11.22	12P 5
Thornton Yard	12.35	12.40LE
Thornton E.S.	12.50	

/ Conveys Leven and Cameron Bridge traffic to Kirkland Yard along with extra brakevan.

No. B.127

Class 5F (J.37) Engine.

	On	Off
Locomen	1.35pm	9.35pm
Guard	1.20pm	9.20pm

		J	J
		p.m.	p.m.
Thornton E.S.			2.20LE
Anstruther		3. 0	4. 0LE
Crail		4. 5	4.15Van
Kingsbarns	QSX		(4.21)
Boarhills	QSX	4.26	4/35
Kingsbarns	QSX	4.41	5Ø 0
Crail		5.10	5.25
Anstruther		5.37	6.20
Pittenweem			R
St.Monance			R
Elie			R*
Kilconquhar			R*
Largo			*
Lundin Links			*
Leven			pass
Thornton Pass.Stn		7.52	8. 0
Thornton West		-	-
Thornton Yard		-	9.10LE
Thornton E.S.		9.20	

/ Propels Boarhills to Kingsbarns
Ø Rounds train at Kingsbarns
R Calls when required to attach or detach freight traffic.
* Uplifts passenger rated traffic for detachment at Thornton.

No. B. 91

Methil No. 4 Pilot.

Class 204 H.P. Diesel/ Mechanical Loco.

6.40am to 8.50pm SX
6.40am to 1.30pm SO

		On	Off
Locomen			
1st shift		5.45am	1.45pm
2nd shift	SX	1.15pm	9.15pm
Guard			
1st shift		6. 0am	2. 0pm
2nd shift	SX	1.15pm	9.15pm

	arr	dep
	a.m.	a.m.
Methil E.S.		6.30LE
Kirkland Yard	6.40	

Works traffic for B.108 from Kirkland Yard to Leven Goods Station, shunts Leven Goods Station and sidings on the Leven Dock Branch and returns to Kirkland Yard to work to orders.

		p.m.	p.m.
Methil East	SX	1.30	
Methil E.S.	SO	1.30	
Methil East	SX		1.35LE

Shunts and trip as required. On completion of work in Leven Dock area to proceed to Methil Goods and shunt rail head, and convey outgoing traffic to Leven Goods Station to connect with B.125.

Methil East	SX		8.50LE
Methil E.S.	SX	8.55	

BR tripworking notice, 1962 - note how the faithful 'J37s' have now been augmented by a diesel!

per day from Anstruther with the largest number in a single day being seven. Fish trains often had to be run at short notice owing to the tides and the fact that the size of the catch could not be predicted on shore, there being no ship to shore radios in use for most of that era. One telegraphic code used in LNER days was 'A.N.F.I.', which stood for 'Anstruther to Kings Cross Fish Train Runs Today'. Empty fish vans were worked to Anstruther from Thornton Junction, usually by Thornton-based locomotives and the vans were then loaded in Anstruther goods yard before being dispatched by the specials. On occasions it was also common for fish vans to be attached to Edinburgh-bound passenger trains where they would be detached and added to other similar vans which had travelled down from Aberdeen, Peterhead and Fraserburgh for working to London. Other fish destinations included Dundee and Aberdeen and, in respect of fish for export, Leith and Methil docks. Fish merchants who used rail from Anstruther included Burgon & Co., Bonthrone, MacFisheries and various railway canvassers. The fishing boats themselves, if coal-fired, tended to be coaled at Methil docks and not their home port, the handling facilities being better there and the price being cheaper. Diesel fuel was delivered in drums by rail and then sold by local chandlers such as Cunningham & Co., who delivered it to the quayside; rail tank wagons were seldom seen at Anstruther goods yard. Other locally based ancillary industries that received supplies by rail and sent goods by rail from Anstruther included coopers making the fish barrels and fish curers. Coal was delivered by rail to Anstruther and there was a large local coal merchant and colliery agent at the station, namely W.G. Readdie & Co., who had its own fleet of private trader wagons. Another source of coal traffic was the Anstruther gasworks, opened in 1841 and, by the time of the gas industry nationalization in 1949, owned by the St Andrews Gas Co. Ltd; it was closed in 1958. Other traffic handled at the yard included cattle from the local cattle market, materials for local boatyards and materials used by the local oilskin clothing factories of Martin & Co. and Watson & Co., received by both goods and passenger train, and of linseed oil, cloth and canvas. Outward traffic included farm produce, especially potatoes, turnips and sugar beet and also cattle and sheep being sent to market; oilskin clothing was also dispatched by rail, usually by passenger train. The goods yard at Anstruther closed to all traffic with effect from 18th July, 1966

The Muiredge Branch

The Muiredge branch (also known as the Cameron Pits branch) was built by the former Leven & East of Fife Railway to serve the coal mines lying to the south of Cameron Bridge. The branch was fed with traffic from the private mineral branches connected to it. These private lines were owned by coalmasters who initially were the Fife Coal Co., owners of Leven Nos. 1, 2 and 4 pits and the Pirnie Pit (or Leven No.3), and Bowman & Co. who worked the Muiredge Pit and the Cameron Pit and there was also a public goods facility known as Buckhaven (Old). From the beginning of the 20th century the Wemyss Coal Co. began to use its own private line to reach Methil Docks and all coal traffic began to travel southwards, rendering the northern section of the branch something of an anachronism. The branch was closed to all traffic in 1936, although its trackbed was in places used by the Wemyss company for its own railway.

The Leven Dock Branch

The Creosote Siding

There were a number of industrial concerns served by the Leven Dock branch the first of these, geographically, being Alexander Bruce & Co., who owned the Leven Creosote Works which were joined to the branch by private sidings lying to the south of Kirkland Yard. These works produced railway sleepers and telegraph and telephone poles – at one time they were the only telegraph pole depot in Scotland. Rail traffic in the inward direction consisted of railway sleepers (mainly imported from Russia), poles (imported from Norway) and creosote, a coal-tar derivitive conveyed in tank wagons. Outward traffic consisted of preserved and creosote impregnated poles and sleepers for consignment to the railway companies and the General Post Office. Latterly the yard was operated by a firm called Jones, Jones & James and they continued to use rail transport until the 1960s.

Kirkland Yard

This was used primarily for the marshalling and sorting of coal trains from Fife which were bound for Methil Docks and by the 1950s came from Fife pits such as Aitken, Glencraig and Bowhill for seasale coal exports and unscreened navigation coals for ships bunkers from Valleyfield and Kinglassie pits. The wagons were sorted out at Kirkland according to the various types of coal, its calorific value, sulphur content and clinker value and trains bound for Methil Docks were taken from the east end of the yard depending on whether it was seasale or bunkering coal. Coal intended for domestic use was taken out of the western end of the yard for Thornton and beyond. Export coal was taken in 16 ton wagons and the length of the train depended on where in the docks it was to be taken. Kirkland yard regularly handled loaded coal trains of 30 or 40 wagons in length and trains of empty wagons up to 60. Smaller amount of pulp and timber was held in the yard for onward transmission to local paper mills. Other cargoes handled included raw materials from Motherwell for oil platform construction at Methil in the early 1970s and coke from various gas works in Dundee and Fife. The yard foreman's offices at Kirkland were at the lower end of the yard and there were bothies for the shunters, pointsmen and chargehands.

Leven Mill Siding

John Balfour's Leven Mills were situated south of the River Leven and served by a siding opened in 1910. The mills consisted of a bone crushing mills used to manufacture fertilisers and a oilseed crushing mill used to produce cattle food. Inward traffic consisted of coal and materials for processing – these materials came in by ship from Methil docks and were worked the short distance from there up to the Leven Mills private siding. The finished products were distributed by rail to agricultural merchants throughout Fife and eastern Scotland. After the works closed the site was acquired in 1955 by Donaldson's, the timber merchants, for additional space for stacking timber and a siding was used for bringing in timber by rail until it finally went out of use in 1964.

Durie Foundry Siding

The Durie Foundry of Henry Balfour & Co. Ltd, situated north of the River Leven and connected by a private siding (opened in March 1880) to the Leven Dock line, was at one time the largest local employer, having a workforce of about 800. The company carried on the business of gas and chemical engineers and boilermakers, originally making gasworks apparatus, steel structures, roofing and contractors' plant and 'having a splendid reputation at collieries in Fife for turning out machinery of the best type'. They went on make gas works and plant for concerns all around the world and cast- and wrought-iron tanks for water storage in towns, distilleries, factories and railways and mining equipment that was used in every continent. In World War II the foundry produced the wings for Hurricane fighter aircraft, gun turrets for bombers, bombcasings, floats for boom defences, anti-aircraft transporters and landing craft used in the Normandy invasion; much of this traffic left by rail. In the post-war period the foundry employed some 700 persons making large tanks for the gas, chemical and beverages industries and large items of plant for the paper industry. Inward rail traffic consisted of wagons of metal plates, coal and coke, foundry sand and glass – the latter was used in the manufacture of glass-lined tanks made by the company for the food industry which was made in Leven by an associated company called Enamelled Metal Products Ltd. The majority of their products were exported by rail although one item that defeated British Railways were the digestors for the Corpach pulp mill near Fort William. These were so large that they had to be towed by sea via Inverness and the Caledonian Canal. In the early 1950s a second siding was added to the north of the original railway entry to the foundry to serve the plate yard behind the press shop. The sidings went out of use in the mid-1960s and were finally closed by 1968/1969.

Donaldson's Siding

Donaldson's was a firm originally based in Tayport which, in 1887, came to Leven and set up what became one of the largest woodyards in the country, occupying five acres on the northern bank of the River Leven adjoining the Durie Foundry. This yard, known as the Wemyss Saw, Planing and Moulding Mills, at one time employed a staff of 75. Timber was imported via Methil Dock and the firm produced a wide variety of goods such as mouldings and finishings for the construction trade and specialized at one time in the making of a heavy timber work for colliery use, all of which was sent out by rail via the company's siding, known as Wemyss Sawmill siding (or, more simply, Sawmill siding) leading to the Leven Dock branch. Traffic ceased to use the Sawmill siding in the summer of 1959. The firm is still in existence but has relocated to Muiredge; the site of the sawmills and the siding are now occupied by Sainsbury's Leven store.

Leven Dock Siding

Leven Dock itself was opened to traffic in March 1880 and had a brief life as a shipping port being used by coalmasters such as the Fife Coal Co., the Denend Coal Co. of Cardenden, the Balgonie Coal Co. and Bowman & Co. (also known at one time as Bowman & Cairns). After closure of the dock in 1910 it was filled in and replaced by the Shorehead sidings known as the Leven Dock sidings. These sidings dealt with coal traffic from the Wemyss Coal Co. destined for the Leven gas works which were opened in 1838 and closed in 1961. Situated on Riverside Place and not directly rail-served, the gasworks received coal delivered to the Leven Dock sidings and taken by cart (or, later by motor lorry) to the nearby works; return traffic included tar and amonia. Another user of coal via the Dock siding was the Fife Paper Mills Ltd which also used the sidings for woodpulp traffic.* The latter was brought in from Methil dock and kept in the storage sidings at Leven Dock – in the 1920s this consisted of eight wagons of woodpulp a day. From here it was carted to the mill by J.P. Cameron, the LNER's carters in Scotland. Other traffic included packed manure for various consignees and rock salt from Methil Dock which was sent by rail the short distance to Leven Dock and then conveyed by lorry the quarter mile or so to Messrs R. Gerrett & Son's salt works at Leven. However, the majority of the large manufacturing concerns in the vicinity of Leven relied on their own private sidings rather than on the Leven Docks siding and consequently traffic at Leven Dock was considerably less than might have been anticipated. The sidings did, however, contain a coal depot and in LNER days the tenants were W.A. Lawson & Co., coal factors and colliery agents, James Thompson & Co., coal agents, and the coal merchant department of the Leven Reform Co-operative Society. By the 1950s Lawson & Co. were using the sidings as a distribution point for loading coal into motor lorries for distribution to large-scale customers including the linoleum works at Newburgh in North Fife and to the Fife County Council Education Board for schools and colleges throughout the county. Coal was also taken by Lawson's to Aberdeen from here by road. Latterly most of the coal was imported from the Yorkshire and Nottinghamshire coalfield, bought in bulk at low prices. Leven Dock siding finally closed in mid-1986, 76 years after the eponymous dock had been filled in.

Methil Docks

After the closure of Leven Docks the branch was used as the main route for 'seasale' coal to Methil Docks. Seasale refers to coal which was being exported, whether to other countries or to parts of the UK by coastal shipping, as opposed to landsale coal which was for inland consumption. The importance of Methil Docks lay in the fact that it was the largest coal exporting port in Scotland and, in its peak year for shipment, 1923, a total of 3,368,300 tons of coal were shipped. Seasale coal from the Fife area was taken by rail to the docks although not all of it travelled over the Leven Dock branch; the alternative public route to the docks was the Methil branch of the North British Railway, which was less attractive to coal traffic having a steep descent into Methil itself. The main coalmasters that sent coal over the line were the Fife Coal Co. (Valleyfield, Aitken, Lindsay, Benarty, Lassodie Mill, Mary at Lochore, Dalbeath, Lumphinnans, Donibristle, Kinglassie, Bowhill, Dunnikier and Wellsgreen pits) the Balgonie Colliery Co., the Earl of Rosslyn's Collieries Ltd (the Frances, Randolph and Lady Blanche pits at Dysart), the Lochgelly Iron & Coal Co. Ltd, Wilsons & Clyde Coal Co. Ltd (Glencraig and Lethans pits), Henry Ness & Co.

* Contemporary details of this and the other traffic using the Leven Dock Sidings can be found in the evidence of the Leven station master included in the file dealing with the little-known 1926 dispute over woodpulp carriage charges which culminated in the case of *Fife Paper Mills Ltd v LNER* – see NAS file No. BR/RRT (S)/2/5.

(Muircockhall and Muirbeath pits near Townhill), Oakley Collieries Ltd and Thomas Spowart & Co. (pits at Lassodie and Wellwood). There were two private railway systems which also served the docks namely the Wemyss Private Railway which carried the entire seasale coal traffic from the Wemyss Coal Company's collieries of Michael, Muiredge, Wellesley, Rosie, Cameron, Lochead and Earlseat, and the Fife Coal Company's private line which connected at the western end with the Muiredge branch and carried coal from the Pirnie and Leven Nos. 1, 2 and 4 pits.

Coal was exported from Methil Dock in the period before World War I to Sweden, Denmark, Norway, the Netherlands, Germany and Imperial Russia; there was also a sizeable coastal trade to London and Aberdeen. After the war much of the export trade vanished, along with the demand for coal used by shipping until oil-firing began to supplant coal at this time. With the rise of the electrical generating industry much coal was shipped to power stations on the Thames, Medway and south coast of England where Fife coal was much appreciated for its property of quickly releasing heat so that stations could be made operational at short notice and switched in to the national grid to meet peak demands. Although Methil was principally an export port for coal there was an import trade in timber for Donaldson's and other merchants and wood pulp and esparto grass used in the paper industry and dispatched by rail to Leven for the Fife Paper Mills Ltd Millfield site, Glenrothes for Tullis Russel's Auchmuty Mills and Leslie for Smith Anderson's Fettykil mills.

Methil Power Station

The Methil electricity generating station provided much traffic to the line for over 30 years. At full capacity the power station used about 1,000 tonnes of slurry per day, all of which was delivered by rail and the slurry trains travelled via Thornton, Kirkland Yard and the Leven Dock branch via the spur to Methil harbour. In the early years the slurry was sourced from Fife, principally from the washeries at Bowhill, Denbeath, Valleyfield, Blairhall and other pits in the Kelty and Cowdenbeath areas. However, once these local supplies were all used up, slurry was latterly brought in from Ayrshire. During the early 1990s slurry was received from the Westfield open cast complex near Kinglassie in Fife, and from Killoch in Ayrshire and it was not uncommon to see seven trains a week arriving at the power station sidings. Originally 16 ton steel-bodied mineral wagons were used, being replaced by 20 ton wagons and, latterly, 38/39 ton wagons and large steel-bodied wagons which had been built for scrap metal traffic. They were unloaded by means of two overhead-mounted grab cranes which unloaded the slurry and placed it into coal bunkers. Fly ash from the power station was sent by rail to Cadder Yard on the outskirts of Glasgow for use in making breeze blocks for building. All traffic from the power station ceased in 2000 and the building itself was demolished in early 2011; the line was severed at the north end of the river bridge.

Goods services

In the early days the Leven Railway and the East of Fife Railway operated a number of mixed trains over their lines but by the time that the North British acquired the system separate goods services were provided. From Anstruther westwards general goods were conveyed in a pick-up service to Thornton, initially worked as an extension of the goods service southwards from St Andrews with additional workings over the Leven Dock branch. Dedicated workings to Methil Docks over the extension line from Leven Harbour were worked generally from Thornton. Latterly a single goods service was operated from Crail to Thornton with additional trip workings over the Leven Dock line by the Methil or Thornton pilot engine. All services including those over the Muiredge line were operated by North British locomotives with the exception of workings over the Durie Colliery line, which were worked by the Fife Coal Company's own locomotives.

Private Owner Wagons

A number of private owner wagons were based on the Leven and East of Fife line and these, along with numerous assorted colliery wagons, were seen on the system. The local wagons consisted of those owned by the following coal merchants:

W.D. Matthew of 22, Shore Road, Anstruther	One Pickering 10 ton sprung wagon of December 1903 painted in brown oxide and lettered 'empty to Bowhill Coal Co, Cardenden'.
Alex. Smith & Son of Cellardyke	One Pickering 10 ton sprung wagon of March 1909, livery unknown.
W.G. Readdie of Anstruther	Four 8 ton wagons, four 10 ton wagons all of 1900 and origin unknown, two 10 ton wagons built by Pickering in 1899; four 10 ton wagons of July 1912: the livery was grey and the latter wagons were acquired by Alexander Benzie of St Andrews and Readdie, the largest coal merchants in the East Neuk, later were taken over by the nationalized gas industry.
R. Given of Elie	One 8 ton sprung Pickering wagon built in 1903 in brown oxide with white lettering with black shading. The wagon was later sold to William Fleming, coal merchant of Friockheim.
James Elder of Lower Largo	One Hurst, Nelson 8 ton wagon of 1900.
A. Lawson, Colliery Agents, Leven and Methil	Fifteen 8 ton wagons and two 10 ton wagons, livery unknown.

Other private wagons were the oil tankers of Shell-Mex, Regent and the Scottish Oil Agency which were found at Leven Dock yard and Anstruther goods depot.

The Distillers Co. Ltd used its own grain (barley) wagons to transport grain from Leith and elsewhere to Cameron Bridge and these were all painted in a distinctive grey livery and lettered with the company's 'S.G.D.' subsidiary initials (Scottish Grain Distillers). The first type to be used were substantial wooden-bodied vans with a peaked roof like a dog-kennel and were of 10 ton capacity emanating from Pickerings and Hurst, Nelson. In the late 1930s higher-capacity 20 ton steel wagons began to replace the wooden wagons, although the older wagons were still in use up to the 1960s. The DCL grain wagons rarely worked east of Cameron Bridge.

Chapter Seventeen

All Tickets Must be Shown: Passenger Traffic on the Line

'No passenger will be permitted to take his seat unless he has a Ticket'
NBR Regulations as to Passenger Traffic

Mixed and other trains

From the very opening of the Leven Railway passengers were carried in four separate classes although the fourth and subsequently second class were eventually abolished and third class became, in BR days, reclassified as second. In the early days mixed passenger and goods trains were operated but, as the *East of Fife Record* reported in 1869:

> Travellers have a claim on the railway company for a comfortable transit, and this claim ought to be attended to. It can never be attended to until while goods and passengers are carried by the one and same locomotive. The time thereby put off at many stations is sometimes very considerable and the delay especially in cold weather is most intolerable to the passengers and causes exceeding discomfort. The Leven & East of Fife Railway Co really do owe it to the public that this change should be made.

It eventually was and by the start of the North British era delays caused by shunting of goods wagons were reduced to a minimum and mixed trains became a thing of the past. Passenger coaches on the line were initially four-wheeled closed compartment stock and although the first class was comfortable and of a good standard the other classes were of a more variable standard. The original stock was superseded by standard North British four- and six-wheel stock in the late 1870s but such short and often rough-riding carriages became the usual fare until the gradual appearance of bogie stock at the turn of the century, initially on through trains to Glasgow and Edinburgh and later by the gradual transfer to East Fife of other stock. In the 1930s only the Leven Dock workmen's trains were still four-wheelers and LNER Gresley-designed teak finished stock became commonplace. At the end of the war Thompson corridor stock appeared along with the Gresley stock and this became mixed with, and later largely supplanted by, the BR standard Mark I coaches which were, on the Thornton to Leven section, subject to a 25 mph speed limit. The 'Fife Coast Express' stock was composed of a streamlined Gresley pre-war twin first and third triplet which was withdrawn upon dieselization of many local services in 1959. Other more exotic stock seen on local trains included the 'Junior Scotsman' Thompson stock of 1946 and, on workings from Glasgow Buchanan Street, ex-LMS stock and on one occasion a railtour brought Bulleid ex-Southern Railway stock. From 1959 onwards diesel multiple units, principally of the Metro-Cammell and Derby variety subsequently known as the '101' and '107' classes, became regular performers on the line.

The basic pattern of passenger services was for four trains per day each way between Leven, and later Kilconquhar, and Thornton. Services were increased by the opening, in stages, of the line to Anstruther and later on by the extension from Anstruther over the Anstruther & St Andrews line to Boarhills and St Andrews and especially by the opening of the Forth Bridge. By 1896 the down passenger service consisted of:

A westbound train crosses Largo viaduct at low tide in the 1930s; the station footbridge can be seen over the houses to the right. *Author's Collection*

Innocent pleasures at Elie. *P. Westwater Collection*

am	
7.47	Thornton to Leuchars
8.15	Thornton to Anstruther
9.49	Thornton to Anstruther stopped at Kilconquhar Weds only and omitted St Monance
10.40	Thornton to Leuchars
11.25	Thornton to Leven (extended to Elie on Thursdays)
pm	
1.20	Thornton to Leven
1.35	Edinburgh to Kingsbarns Saturdays only and omitted Thornton
5.47	Thornton to Leuchars
8.50	Thornton to Anstruther

This same basic pattern survived with subsequent alterations until 1965 although more trains ran through from Edinburgh and Glasgow to Dundee via Leuchars and dmu workings were extended at each end to occasionally start in Dunfermline and terminate at Arbroath. Sunday services commenced after World War I but were relatively sparse with no local trains run and only a couple of trains running to and from Glasgow and Edinburgh. Between 1965 and 1969 a relatively frequent service of dmus operated between Leven and Thornton and Kirkcaldy.

Excursion and summer traffic

On the Leven & East of Fife there was a good deal of excursion traffic both to and from the Fife coast. Much of the inward traffic was by daytrippers, summer holidaymakers, golfers, artists and walkers who all arrived on scheduled services although there were special trains run from various locations throughout Scotland, particularly in the NBR and LNER eras. The annual Glasgow and Edinburgh fair and trades holidays brought an influx of tourists and complaints were often made of unauthorized travel in first class carriages at these times and an absence of any visible traffic inspectors. Like all seaside areas the heaviest traffic was in the summer months and there was a notable lack of pleasure traffic in the winter months. Up to the 1950s there were a notable number of middle-class families who decamped by rail to Largo, Elie and Pittenweem for a month at a time with all their luggage and camp followers (including, at least in the early days, servants). Outward traffic included excursions from St Monance, Leven, Anstruther and other East Neuk stations organized by merchants and trade organizations, schools, church organizations, and even on occasions by individuals. Specific events attended, apart from sightseeing, shopping and what BR later referred to as 'awaydays', included football matches, exhibitions such as the 1908 Scottish Exhibition at Gorgie near Edinburgh and the 1938 Empire Exhibition in Glasgow. The Anstruther Merchants Association were particularly resourceful and in the years before World War I organized rail excursions to London for the Anglo-French Exhibition at Shepherd's Bush and Dublin and 'doubtless their efforts will be heartily encouraged by a good number of the general public'. In 1908 a contingent of over a hundred old and young people took advantage of the cheap fare given by the railway company for the excursion to Aberdeen on Wednesday'. The stock used was the same used as on everyday services but in the 1930s the LNER started using its new open tourist stock. A typically eventful excursion was that of the Anstruther Merchants Association to Loch Lomond in 1906 when it was recorded that,

The 'Fife Coast Express' at Craigentinny carriage sidings, Edinburgh with driver John Lawson.
T.G. Hepburn; NBRSG, Hennigan Collection

An NBR 4-4-0 in fine form close to Thornton. *W.D. Yuill Collection*

LEVEN

(FIFE)

for the complete family holiday

We'd need a book to tell you all about our town. But we don't need more than a few lines to say that this is the place to spend your complete family holiday.

CHILDREN'S PLAYGROUNDS. MILE-LONG SAFE SANDY BEACH. IDEALLY SITUATED CARAVAN SITE ON LARGO BAY. TENNIS. ANGLING. TWO 18-Hole GOLF COURSES. (One Sunday Golf). PUTTING GREENS. BOWLING GREENS. BEACH PADDLING POOL. CONCERT HALL and OPEN-AIR ENTERTAINMENT with DANCING IN ATTRACTIVE GLEN

Our Guide Book will prove our point.

Write to Town Clerk for a copy.

We'll be pleased to welcome you to

LEVEN

Please mention "Holiday Haunts" when replying to Advertisers.

The summer tourist trade in full swing. *From BR (Scotland) Holiday Haunts 1960 edition*

EXPRESS SERVICE

GLASGOW and EAST FIFE

Daily (Except Sundays)

THE FIFE COAST EXPRESS

		p.m.
GLASGOW (Queen Street)	lev.	4 7
BURNTISLAND	arr.	5 14
KIRKCALDY	,,	5 29
LEVEN	,,	5 54
ELIE	,,	6 10
ANSTRUTHER	,,	6 21
ST. ANDREWS	,,	6 50

		a.m.
ST. ANDREWS	lev.	7 14
ANSTRUTHER	,,	7 44
ELIE	,,	7 59
LEVEN	,,	8 14
KIRKCALDY	,,	8 37
GLASGOW (Queen Street)	arr.	9 50

For other Services between Glasgow and St. Andrews, etc.—
See Tables 95, 101, 102

'Fife Coast Express' timetable, 1950.

BRITISH RAILWAYS

B. 26846

CHEAP EXCURSIONS
FROM
LINLITHGOW
EVERY SUNDAY
21st June to 13th September, 1959

OUTWARD			RETURN		
		a.m.			p.m.
Linlithgow	leave	11 20	Crail	leave	6 8
Inverkeithing	arrive	11 43	Anstruther	,,	6 17
Aberdour	,,	11 52	Pittenweem	,,	6 21
Burntisland	,,	11 59	St. Monance	,,	6 26
Kinghorn	,,	12 6p	Elie	,,	6 34
Kirkcaldy	,,	12 12	Kilconquhar	,,	6 39
Thornton Junction	,,	12 26	Largo	,,	6 46
Leven	,,	12 44	Lundin Links	,,	6 49
Lundin Links	,,	12 51	Leven	,,	6 54
Largo	,,	12 55	Thornton Junction	,,	7 13
Kilconquhar	,,	1 2	Kirkcaldy	,,	7 26
Elie	,,	1 7	Kinghorn	,,	7 33
St. Monance	,,	1 13	Burntisland	,,	7 39
Pittenweem	,,	1 18	Aberdour	,,	7 46
Anstruther	,,	1 23	Inverkeithing	,,	7 59
Crail	,,	1 31	Linlithgow	arrive	8 18

Second Class Return Fares To

Inverkeithing 2/9	Aberdour 3/8	Burntisland 4/1	Kinghorn 4/8
Kirkcaldy 5/1	Thornton Jct. 6/3	Leven 7/-	Lundin Links 7/3
Largo 7/6	Kilconquhar 8/-	Elie 8/3	St. Monance 8/9
Pittenweem 9/-	Anstruther 9/3	Crail 9/9	

The tickets are valid on the date for which issued and by the services specified

(over)

Excursions from Linlithgow, 1959.

> This popular outing took place on Wednesday and was largely patronized, nearly 600 taking advantage of it. The run to Balloch was accomplished almost to time. Notwithstanding that several of the mountain tops were enveloped in mist the sail of over twenty miles was greatly enjoyed. Just as the steamer was leaving Ardlui on the homeward trip rain began to fall making the sail to Balloch rather unpleasant. By an unfortunate accident to the engine the run home was very protracted Anstruther not being reached until the 'wee short oor ayont the twal'. We trust that the Railway Company will endeavour to trace miscreants who tampered with the communication cord on the outward and home journey causing the train to be stopped unnecessarily on both occasions.

The excursion trade began to suffer from competition with the charabanc and later 'luxury coach' offerings of local bus proprietors in the 1920s and few specials ran after 1939. The holiday trade was strictly organized on Saturday to Saturday letting schedules resulting in weekday trains being little patronized with the onset of local buses and, more importantly, by the family car being used in place of the train. By the time the line closed inroads were being made into be the local holiday trade by cheap holidays abroad but even after 1965 the traditional summer trade to the East Neuk still suffered a notable decline with the closure of the line.

Schools traffic

Pupils from Crail, Elie, Pittenweem and St Monance attended the Waid Academy, the principal secondary school for all East Neuk children and situated close to the station at Anstruther. All originally travelled to school by train, in the case of those from the west of Anstruther by the 8.39 am from Elie arriving at Anstruther at 8.54 and those from Crail by the 7.54 am arriving at Anstruther at 8.04 am; the return services left Anstruther at 4.00 pm and 3.58 pm respectively. By the 1930s pupils from Crail and Pittenweem were using the buses whose timings (and the location of the bus-stops) was more convenient but those pupils from Elie and St Monance continued to use the train. After the war all Elie pupils travelled by rail but those from St Monance who were in the upper stream at the Waid (the 'language' pupils who stayed on until the fifth and sixth years) travelled by train but the remainder now had to use the bus; the train timings had altered little over the intervening years for passengers from Elie and St Monance. One advantage of travelling by train was recalled by a former pupil who wrote that, 'Detention was rarely given – many children travelled by train, and if they missed the school train they might have to wait more than two hours for the next'.* The school train was frequently the scene of exuberant and high-spirited behavior on the part of those in the familiar black and red blazers. Pranks such as the pupils hanging out of windows and missiles being launched at station staff were not unknown. Latterly the school trains were dmus which tended to put paid to much of the hilarity that had taken place in the compartment stock† but it was with a real sense of regret that the school trains ceased to run in the autumn term of 1965.

* The *Waid Academy Centenary Magazine*, 1986.

† The school trains feature in a racy but fictionalized account in *Last Lesson of the Afternoon* by St Monance-born author Christopher Rush (Canongate Press, 1994).

'B1' class 4-6-0s Nos. 61398 and 61358 double-head a Glasgow to Dundee train at Elie on 18th July, 1959. Not a common occurrence on the coast line. *J.L. Stevenson*

A busy moment at St Monance on 10th August, 1963. The train engine is 'B1' class 4-6-0 No. 61133 and the stock is made up of smart Thompson-era carriages. *C.C. Thornburn*

Railway Workmen's Trains.

		1	2	3	4	5	6
		MO	‡ MX	‡	‡	Suns. only.	
		a.m.	a.m.	a.m.	a.m.	a.m.	
Thornton Junc.	depart	12 15	1 30	3 5	4 35	5 45	...
Kirkland Yard ...	,,	12 30	1 45	3 20	4 50	6 0	......
Methil (East) ...	arrive	12 32	1 47	3 22	4 52	...	...

		7	8	9	10	11	12
		MO	‡ MX	‡	‡	Suns. only.	
		a.m.	a.m.	a.m.	a.m.	a.m.	
Methil (East)	depart	12 40	1 55	3 53	5 20	...	...
Kirkland Yard	,,	12 42	1 57	3 55	5 22	6 8	......
Thornton Junc.	arrive	12 57	2 12	4 10	5 37	6 18	...

‡ **Nos. 2, 3, 4, 8, 9, 10.**—These trains also run on Sundays.

Note.—All the trains working between Thornton Junction and Methil, and *vice versa*, will call at Cameron Bridge, if required.

Commences week's work with 12-15 a.m. train, Thornton Junction to Methil Finishes at 7-45 a.m. Sundays Works at Passenger Station as required.

Railway Workmen's train timetable commencing 20th September, 1926.

Workmen's services

The Leven and East of Fife line also saw a number of regular workings which were strictly for railwaymen only. From about 1910 until after World War II a regular service of railway workmen's trains was operated from Thornton Junction to Cameron Bridge, Kirkland Yard and Methil East for the docks. These trains, which were third class only, ran in the early mornings only for shift workers at Kirkland yard and Methil and were operated as four services between midnight and 5.00 am every night with a modified service on Mondays; the journey time from Thornton to Methil occupied 18 minutes and these were the only passenger services on the Leven Dock branch. No details have emerged of the stock used but the same carriages were apparently used on other workmen's services between Thornton and Kirkcaldy later in the day. A short-lived workmen's service, for those working pits on the Lochty branch, operated from Leven prior to World War I* to a temporary station on the Lochty branch for a short period. Towards the end of that war a daily service operated from Thornton Junction to Crail for the benefit of John Laing employees engaged on the construction of Crail airfield.†

Marching as if to war

In the years before World War I a number of special trains were run in connection with army training exercises. The Black Watch and the Argyll and Sutherland Highlanders both had summer training exercises at Balcarres reached via Largoward on the Lochty branch but there were also a number of shorter training exercises where the Anstruther Territorials reached local venues by train. In 1906 it was reported that one such exercise took place at Kincraig close to Elie:

> At Kilconquhar station the company was divided into two portions … and Captain Murray, who was incapacitated from active participation in the fight, drove along and witnessed the movements which were being carried out … The defenders opposed the advance of the attacking party by a rallying fire of blank ammunition which was replied

* For details of these services see the present authors' forthcoming *The East of Fife Central Railway (The Lochty Branch)*.

† These are covered in the companion volume, *The Anstruther & St Andrews Railway*, (Oakwood Press, 2009).

An animated scene at St Monance as a 'whiskered' Metro-Cammell dmu pauses with the 12.52 pm Crail-Thornton Junction service on 3rd October, 1959. *Roy Hamilton*

The arrival of the 5.05 pm Dundee (Tay Bridge) to Glasgow (Queen Street) at Lundin Links on 27th July, 1963. *Roy Hamilton*

> to with equal vigour by the gallant attackers. With completion of the flank movement on the part of the attacking force, the defenders were exposed to a devastating fire, but the whistle 'ceasefire' saved them from annihilation. The men then formed up and marched with marvellous willingness back to Kilconquhar station, where a reward in the shape of a pie and a bottle of lemonade or beer awaited them.

Eight years later the same territorials marched to local stations and were again exposed to devastating fire but this time it was for real.

Individual stations

Virtually all local stations reached a peak for passenger numbers round about 1920 and a sharp or gradual decline from 1926 onwards depending on the extent and effect of bus competition. As well as being a major passenger interchange point with the main Edinburgh to Dundee and Aberdeen main line, **Thornton** was also the junction for the West Fife line to Dunfermline and the Buckhaven and Methil branch. There was also local traffic in connection with the village of Thornton a quarter of a mile to the east, the nearby mines, the wagon workshops and, for railwaymen, the locomotive sheds and marshalling yard. **Cameron Bridge** had a considerable passenger traffic in connection with the nearby pits, the employees at the distillery, the staff at the nearby Cameron Hospital and the inhabitants of Windygates to the immediate north of the station. **Leven** had by far the greatest number of passsengers and more than double those of the next busiest station on the line, Anstruther. There were an enormous number of holidaymakers using the station in summer months after about 1938 and apart from locals, employees at the major industrial plants in the area, bus passengers travelling onwards and commuters to Kirkcaldy and Edinburgh, this traffic in common with the East Neuk stations was concentrated in July and August. **Lundin Links** had a certain amount of residential traffic with day-trippers and golfers in the summer months and a number of holidaymakers. **Largo** served both Upper and Lower Largo and was a busy station especially in summer when it was a popular spot for those wishing to spend their holidays by the seaside and there were also day tourists coming to enjoy the associations with Robinson Crusoe. **Kilconquhar** served the villages of Kilconquhar and Colinsburgh, but not being particularly close to either suffered considerably once bus services had been established. In early days the East Fife Agricultural Society's annual shows were held in the vicinity and attracted much traffic and in later years the Shell Bay caravan site gave the line some traffic.

Elie was always busy in summer but less so in winter although even then passengers were found in reasonable number. As with all the East Neuk resorts, July was the month associated with Glasgow holidaymakers and August with Edinburgh ones and the more genteel visitors (in which trade Elie excelled) tended either to stay for a complete month or to have their own second or holiday homes in the town or to stay in one of Elie's 'select' hotels. Along with Largo the 'Fife Coast Express' brought in summer commuters who worked in the city while their families holidayed. The station was said to have attracted the highest number of first-class ticket holders of any station on the line and the quantity of luggage that they brought (and had transported to their lodgings by children, carriers or local fishermen) was said to have exceeded even that at Largo. Elie traffic remained heavy to the very end of the line's existence. **St Monance** like Elie had a number of regular schoolchildren 'commuters' and like Elie a number of locals who travelled from there to Anstruther to shop. Holiday traffic mainly consisted of visitors lodging in fishermen's houses and particular emphasis was given to holidaymakers with an artistic temperament. **Pittenweem** was unfortunate in that its station was some distance from the town but until the 1930s managed to attract a good level of custom and, like St Monance, attracted holidaymakers who enjoyed the local atmosphere and golf courses. **Anstruther**, the second-busiest station on the line, had good all year round passenger numbers with local tradesmen and commercial travellers, fishermen and their families, school pupils attending the Waid and locals who came to Anstruther to shop and buy their weekly provisions. Although traffic to St Andrews fell off somewhat when the quicker and cheaper direct bus service to that town was established, day trips to and from Anstruther flourished until well after the war. The town was a popular summer resort particularly in the Glasgow Fair and Edinburgh Trades holidays with the inhabitants of the former city enjoying the modest amusements of the town and staying, from the 1950s, in the holiday camp and caravan park. As with all the towns in the East Neuk which had a holiday trade, one noticeable trend that occurred once local residents had virtually abandoned the railway in favour of the bus (and later private car) was how the line increasingly depended on tourists for its summer passengers, and even this tended to be concentrated on Saturdays so that the stations were deserted for long periods during the weekdays. Summer Sunday services, inaugurated after the war, tended to bring day-trippers who visited the towns for the beaches, walking and that old East Neuk delicacy of fish and chips.

Anstruther Junction with a rare diesel locomotive-hauled excursion train; all is now history except for the bridge which still survives. *Jim Stormonth*

Chapter Eighteen

Observing the Instructions: Locomotives, Signalling and Staff

'Employees supplied with this book ... will be held responsible for the observation of all instructions contained therein...'

LNER General Appendix, 1947

Locomotives

Steam Locomotives

The Leven & East of Fife Railway ran its services using its own locomotives, the three Hawthorn 0-4-0s and the later Black, Hawthorn engines, throughout the whole of its independent existence with the latter locomotives being used on the Muiredge branch as well as the main line. These were all housed at the shed close to the LEoFR works and at the shed adjoining Kilconquhar station until 1863, when the Kilconquhar shed was replaced by a new shed at Anstruther. When the North British acquired the LEoFR in 1877, the two remaining Hawthorn locomotives and the Black, Hawthorn engines were transferred away to other lines and a number of NBR standard locomotives were drafted in, namely Hurst 0-6-0s and a variety of Drummond and Holmes engines. With the exception of the LEoFR branch lines no tank engines were scheduled to operate either passenger or goods trains and this remained the position until closure. These tender locomotives included examples of the following classes: 'J35', NBR Holmes Reid class 'C' (LNER 'J36'), NBR Reid 'B' and 'S' ('J37') and Gresley 'J38' 0-6-0s; 4-4-0 locomotives of NBR Reid class 'K' 'Glens' ('D34') and Great Central/LNER 'D11/2' ('Scottish Directors'). After World War II the ubiquitous Thomson 4-6-0 'B1s' appeared on the line and after nationalization BR Standard '5MT' 4-6-0s , 'WD' 2-8-0s, and LMS Stanier 'Black Five' 4-6-0s were seen on the line. On Thornton to Leven trains more exotic locomotives could sometimes be seen on 'running-in' duties from Thornton shed.* The route availability between Thornton and Kirkland Yard was 7 and eastwards of East Fife Central Junction was 6.

Leven Dock engines

From the opening of the Leven Dock line the main motive power was provided by members of the NBR 'G' class Neilson & Co. 0-4-0 saddle tank 'pugs' (LNER 'Y9' class) until they were gradually supplanted by the NBR Reid 'F' class 0-6-0T locomotives ('J88s') which had a virtual monopoly on local workings. In about 1960 they were replaced by Hunslet 204 hp diesel-mechanical locomotives and 350 hp English Electric class '08' diesel-electric locomotives. The 'Y9', 'J88' and diesel shunters in turn worked the various sidings on the line including the Kirkland branch for the National Steel Foundry, the Creosote works, Sawmill, Durie Foundry and Leven Dock lines and Kirkland Yard and Methil Docks were worked by the NBR 'A' class 0-6-2 tank locomotives (LNER class 'N15'; the latter were to marshal in Kirkland Yard and to take them on to the coal hoists at Methil Docks. Other locomotives seen working on the branch in BR days included examples of the NER 'J72' class 0-6-0Ts including BR-built examples and a fleet of five NBR 'F' class 'J88' 0-6-0Ts.

* An account of these is given by Alan Goodwillie in Chapter Nineteen . Appendix Three contains further details of individual locomotives seen on the line.

NBR 'G' class 0-4-0 (later LNER 'Y9' class) No. 310 is seen with driver John Allen and fireman John Key. Members of this class worked the Leven Dock branch. *NBRSG, Hennigan Collection*

LNER No. 10426, formerly NBR Drummond 4-4-0T No. 101 *Anstruther*, at Stirling shed, in 1926. *NBRSG, Hennigan Collection*

'D30' class 4-4-0 No. 62418 *The Pirate* at Thornton shed in August 1959. This was a regular engine on the afternoon train to Crail. *Alan Goodwillie Collection*

No. 62467 *Glenfinnan* waits for the 'Right away' with a train heading for the coast at Thornton in August 1959. *Alan Goodwillie Collection*

'N15' class 0-6-2T No. 69223 was a regular performer in Kirkland Yard and on the Leven Dock branch. It is seen here on 13th April, 1952. *A.G. Ellis*

'J37' 0-6-0 No. 64629 on the turntable at Anstruther in 1956. *Rex Conway Collection*

Diesel locomotives

In diesel days examples of the following locomotives were seen west of Leven: English Electric type '1' class '20', North British Locomotive Co. type '2' classes '21' and '27', Derby/Sulzer class '26' and '27' engines, Birmingham Railway Carriage & Wagon Co. type '2' classes '26' and '27' usually working in pairs, English Electric type '3' class '37', Brush type '4' class '47' and class '56' (these three classes usually working alone to Methil power station). Passenger services were only worked by diesel engines on rare occasions and in latter years were normally worked by 'B1' class steam locomotives and Derby and Metro-Cammell dmus.

Engine sheds

When the NBR took over the running of the LEoFR Thornton became the main point for keeping the locomotives working over the line. Here the motive power depot, rebuilt in the 1930s, was a large shed with six through roads situated at the west of the station area to the south side of the Dunfermline to Thornton line. The shed provided all the motive power for an extensive area of central and eastern Fife including the coast line and the Leven Dock branch and was extremely busy until the gradual run down of the Fife coal field in the late 1950s onwards. In BR days the shed was allocated the number 62A and it finally closed in April 1967. The allocation of locomotives to Thornton in 1950 consisted of 113 engines from the following classes: six 'B1' 4-6-0s, two 'D29' 4-4-0s, six 'D30' 4-4-0s, five 'D34' 4-4-0s, five 'D49' 4-4-0s, 11 'J35' 0-6-0s, 14 'J37' 0-6-0s, three 'J36' 0-6-0s, 13 'J38' 0-6-0s, two 'C15' 0-6-2Ts, eight 'J88' 0-6-0Ts, six 'J83' 0-6-0Ts, four 'J83' 0-6-0Ts, four 'J69' 0-6-0Ts, six 'N15' 0-6-2Ts and 22 'WD' 2-8-0s.

There was a small sub-shed at Anstruther (also 62A). This was situated next to the goods shed and was a two-road brick-built shed; it usually housed two locomotives and all the necessary coaling and watering facilities but in LNER days and later engines were not kept there overnight. In addition there was a turntable at Anstruther, the only one on the coast line and locomotives on trains terminating at Anstruther and Crail were turned here. The turntable was extended by two feet in 1946 to hold the new 'B1' locomotives working the line. The shed at Anstruther was closed in December 1960 but the hand-worked turntable remained in use until closure of the line in 1966. There was also a motive power depot at Methil where pilot engines and shunters were kept.

Private Locomotives

Both the Cameron Bridge Distillery and the Methil power station sidings were operated with privately-owned locomotives which ran up to the exchange sidings with the North British lines. At the distillery there was a standard gauge connection over which two locomotives were operated, namely an 0-4-0 saddle tank later replaced by a four-wheel diesel-mechanical locomotive. The steam engine was built by Andrew Barclay in 1892 (Works No. 726) and was supplied new to the Distillers Co. Ltd to work the line. It was scrapped in about 1952 and replaced by a new diesel, Ruston & Hornsby No. 321733. As well as having its own locomotive, it is known that on at least one occasion during the 1950s an elderly NBR 'Y9' class 0-4-0 saddle tank was hired from BR for use as a shunter while the resident locomotive was undergoing an overhaul. For a time in the 1990s another four-wheel diesel with black and yellow warning stripes was also seen in

Left: The three Hunslet diesel shunters travel in convoy to refuel at Thornton.
Alan Goodwillie

Below: A 350 hp diesel shunter (later class'08') at Leven in 1961. Note the configuration of the line to the east.
M.B. Smith

A panoramic view of Thornton shed *circa* 1960. *P. Westwater*

No. 64569 inside the shed at Thornton. *NBRSG, Hennigan Collection*

Anstruther engine shed on 17th June, 1936. *NBRSG, Hennigan Collection*

Anstruther engine shed in the 1950s. *G.A. Lyall*

the distillery sidings. Distillers engines were permitted to work over their sidings and the main line. At the power station a diesel-hydraulic locomotive was used for shunting purposes, Ruston & Hornsby 0-4-0 No. 506399 of 1964, transferred there from Braehead power station at Renfrew in 1966. When Durie Colliery was in operation the Fife Coal Co. locomotives (likely to have been a Barclay 0-4-0 or 0-6-0ST) was authorized to work between the sidings and Leven station. For a period before its final closure Fife Coal Co. locomotives were permitted to work south of Cameron Bridge on the Muiredge branch.

Signalling

Leven Railway

The Leven Railway was worked on the 'one engine in steam' principle with a staff. A reference in the company minutes to the consulting engineer Thomas Bouch having installed his own-pattern signals is of some interest but subsequently these were replaced by disc signals, Bouch's having proved unsatisfactory. These signals were essentially of a warning nature and would have been provided at stations, where they would have been worked by the staff there, and at level crossings, where the crossing keepers would have worked them. On 12th August, 1863 John Haig and Andrew Wilkie confirmed to the Board of Trade that on the opening of the line to Anstruther the Train Staff & Ticket system would be adopted:

> We hereby certify that in working the Leven and East of Fife Railway the mode of working by a train staff will be adopted. In working the line between Thornton and Leven a train-staff or train-ticket square and coloured red will be carried to and fro with each engine. Betwixt Leven and Kilconquhar a train-staff or train-ticket round and coloured blue will be carried to and fro with each engine. Betwixt Kilconquhar and Anstruther a train-staff or train-ticket triangular and coloured white will be carried to and fro with each engine.

The 1866 edition of the North British Rule Book gives instruction on the signals at the junction with the Leven Railway at Thornton Junction:

> They are 'Danger' except when allowing a train to pass within them. At the east side of the railway, and at the south end of the railway, is erected a semaphore signal. This signal has two arms; a higher and a lower arm with signal lamps to correspond and it is called the 'Leven Junction Signal'. The use of this signal is to regulate the passage of engines and trains coming from the Leven railway on to the North British Railway. The upper arm and lamp are worked by means of a wire, by the pointsman in charge of the distant signal covering the up main line of the North British Railway. The lower arm and lamp are worked by the signalman of the Leven Railway Company. Except when allowing an engine to leave the Leven Railway and enter upon the North British main line, as hereinafter explained, these signals must be kept at Danger.
>
> An engineman wishing to take his engine from the Leven Railway on to the North British main-line will give three distinct whistles, on which the signalman of the Leven Railway Company will set the lower arm of the Leven Junction Signal to caution, which will indicate to the pointsman in charge of the Up Main Line Signal that an engineman wishes to leave the Leven Railway and enter upon the North British main-line. He will lower the upper arm of the Leven Junction Signal to caution, whereupon the Leven Railway Signalman will drop the lower arm into the sheath of the post showing All Right, on which, but not before, the engineman may leave the Leven Railway and enter upon the North British main line. Immediately on the engine leaving the Leven Railway, the twin arms of the Leven Junction Signal must be set at Danger.

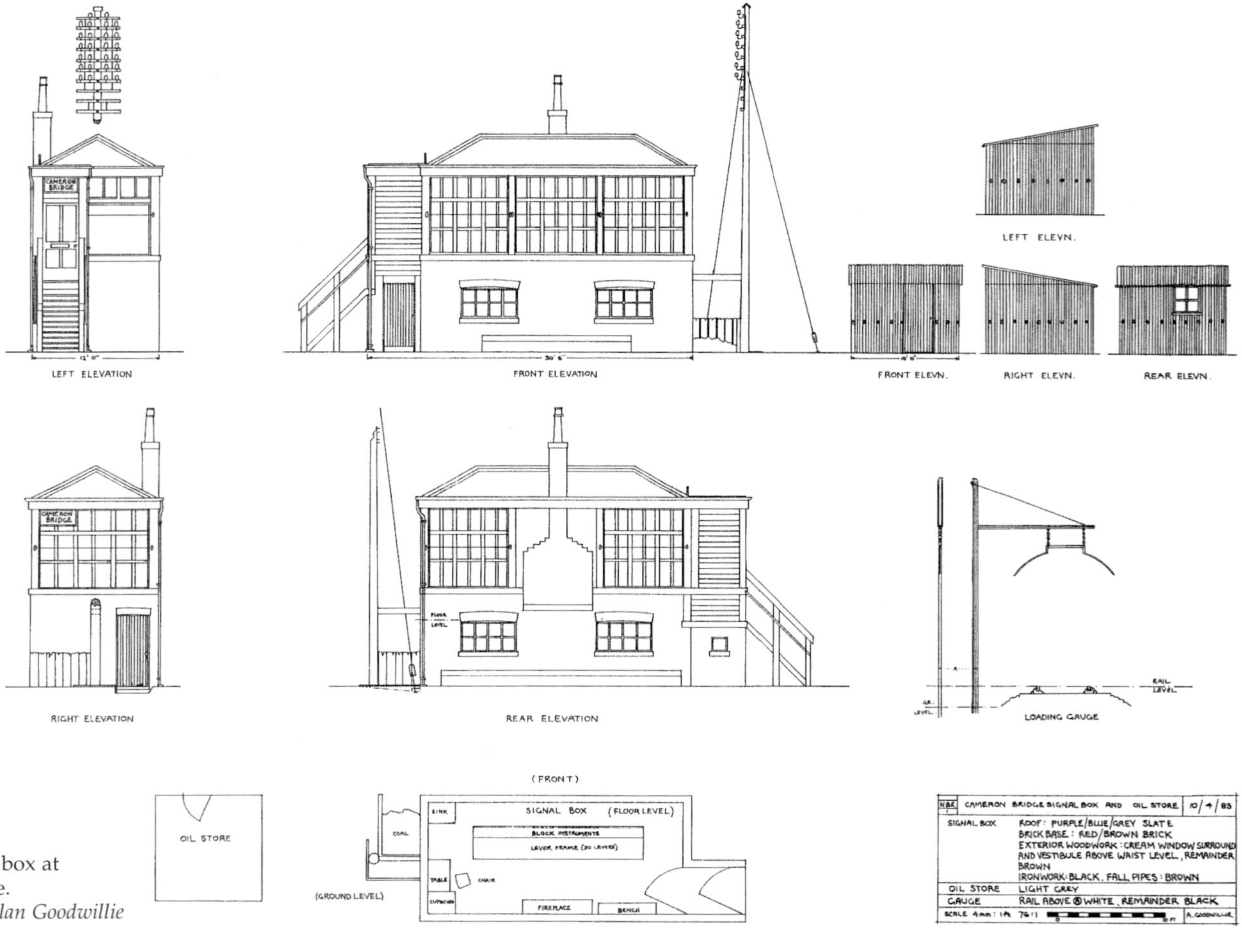

The 1910 signal box at Cameron Bridge.
Drawn by Alan Goodwillie

Prior to 1893 home signals only had one spectacle glass: red for danger and when the signal was set at 'all clear', there was in fact no spectacle glass shown in front of the lamp which would of course display a white light. The two aspect spectacle then introduced showed red for stop and green for all clear. In NBR days the green glass was emerald in colour but later changed to blue-green which showed green when lit by a yellow paraffin oil flame.

North British Railway

The North British period saw many changes to the signalling on the line including the gradual installation of fully interlocked points and signals (made compulsory by the Regulation of Railways Act 1889), the installation of semaphore signalling all along the line and the installation, by the late 1890s, of the Tyers electric tablet instruments at each signal cabin; this replaced the older train staff system for controlling single lines although the train staff was retained for the working of the goods-only lines. The electric token block system was described thus in the LNER *General Appendix of 1947*:

> The objective of the electric token block system of signalling is to prevent more than one train being in a block section between two token stations at the same time, and when no train is in the section between two token stations, to admit of a train entering the section from either end. This is accomplished by every train carrying a token, one token only being obtainable from the token instrument of the same section at the same time.

North British signals were supplied by Stevens & Sons of Glasgow and London, a major firm of contractors who supplied signals to many of the major British railway companies. Their signals had distinctive egg-shaped spectacle glasses and many Stevens signals survived on the East Fife line until its closure.

The 1922 North British *General Appendix* lists the method of working of the line as:

> Thornton Station and Leven Station – block telegraph [double line], Leven and Anstruther Junction – tablet No. 6, Anstruther Junction and Anstruther Station – block telegraph [double line]. The block sections were as follows: Thornton North to Cameron Bridge (3 m. 53 ch.), Cameron Bridge to East Fife Central Junction (0 m. 77 ch.), East Fife Central Junction to Leven (1 m. 16 ch.), Leven to Largo (2 m. 55 ch.), Largo to Kilconquhar West (3m. 9ch.), Kilconquhar West to Elie (2 m. 12 ch.), Elie to St Monans (2 m. 7ch.), and St Monans to Anstruther Junction (2 m. 5 ch.), Anstruther Junction to Anstruther Station (0 m. 89 ch.).

There were signal boxes at Thornton Station, Thornton North, Cameron Bridge, East Fife Central Junction, Leven, Methil East, Largo, Kilconquhar, Elie, St Monance, Anstruther Junction and Anstruther Station. Kilconquhar and Pittenweem never had signal boxes but were provided with ground frames housed in small sheds rather reminiscent of wardrobes, while Lundin Links had an open ground frame. In 1919 the signal boxes at Thornton North, Cameron Bridge, Methil East and East Fife Central Junction were open continuously on weekdays and from 5.00 am to midnight on Sundays, whereas the remainder of the boxes were open on weekdays from 6.00 am (or in some cases 6.15 or 6.30) to 8.00 pm; at that time all signal boxes were closed on Sundays although after the war Sunday trains were run along the L&EoFR line as far as Crail.

The following sections of secondary line in East Fife were worked by train staff in 1901: Durie Pit branch (section: Leven and Durie Pit) – train staff No. 4; Leven Dock (Leven Dock and fouling point between Leven Dock branch and Shunting siding,

The signalman exchanges the tablet at Kilconquhar West with the driver of the 12.52 pm Crail-Thornton Junction service headed by No. 62478. *J.L. Stevenson*

The station ground frame at Kilconquhar, 4th July, 1964. *C.C. Thornburn*

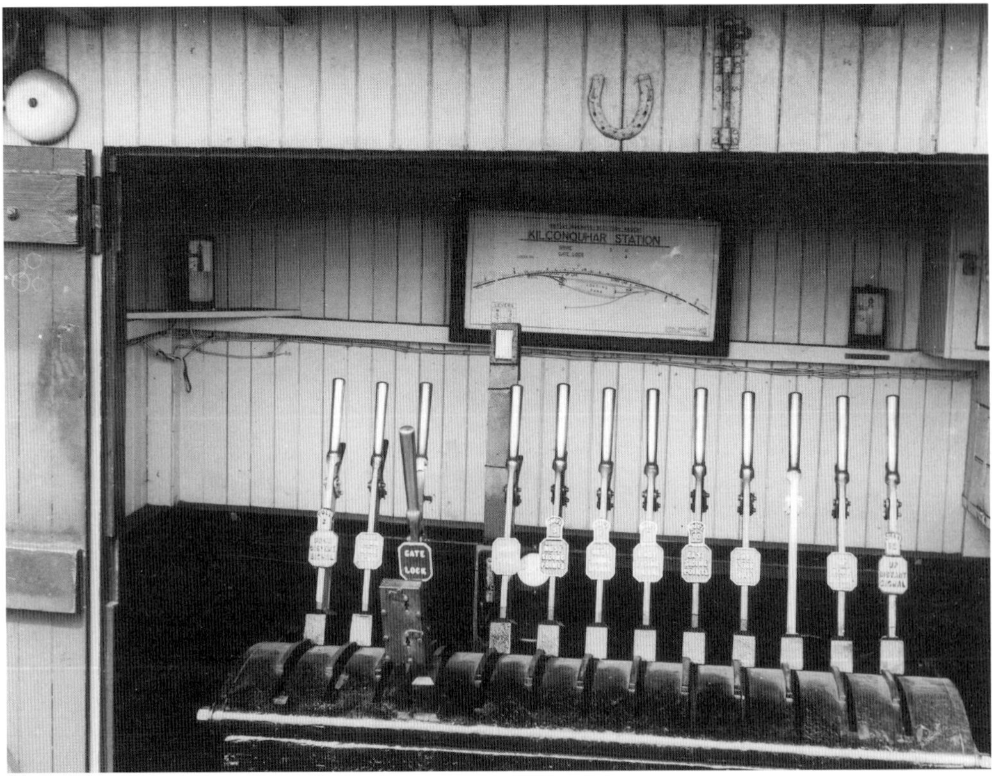

The 2.35 pm Crail-Thornton train exchanges the token at Elie on 3rd April, 1965. *J.L. Stevenson*

St Monance signal box, and signalman, 1962. *Authors' Collection*

Kirkland home signal and the Sawmill or Iron bridge. *Alan Goodwillie*

Fog marker at St Monance on 10th August, 1963. *C.C. Thornburn*

Leven station) train staff No. 1; Muiredge branch (Cameron Bridge and Cameron Pit sidings) train staff No. 2; East Fife Central Railway (East Fife Central Junction and terminus at Lochty) train staff No. 1.

The following sidings were listed as being controlled by the Electric Train Tablet or Electric Train Staff in 1901: Drumcaldie Distillery siding, Silverburn siding, Lundin Links station siding and Pittenweem station siding and in 1922 the following sidings were listed as being worked by Tablet Lock: Leven Brickworks siding, Silverburn siding, Lundin Links siding and Pittenweem siding.

On the Leven Dock line Balfour Bridge hut had signals which,

> ... were worked from a ground frame [and] stand normally in the 'clear' position. Before shunting movements are commenced which will foul the ingoing or outgoing lines near to the mill siding at the east end of Kirkland Yard, the signals must be put to danger by Guards, Shunters or oithers concerned.

The Muiredge branch was, from 1922, worked in an unusual fashion:

> From a point 35 yards east of Cameron Bridge Storage Sidings: Worked by 'one engine in steam' (No. 2 train staff). At a point 35 yards east of the sidings a board is erected, one side of which indicates to trains going to Cameron Pit Junction the point at which train staff working begins. The other side indicates to trains from Cameron Bridge Junction the point at which yard working begins ... Pirnie Pits and Cameron Pit Junction are worked by Annett Key affixed to the train staff. The Muiredge Branch terminates at Cameron Pit Sidings. Catch points have been laid about 30 feet north of Cameron Pit Sidings Points and drivers must be careful to shunt their trains clear of these points until signalled by the guard to pass over them. The catch points are secured by Annett lock, the key of which is attached to the train staff for the branch.

LNER and BR Period

No major changes in signalling were made although North British signals and signalling apparatus was replaced in some cases by LNER-pattern equipment. However distant signals were repainted in the now familiar and distinctive yellow (rather than red) and black chevron scheme, and a yellow light (rather than red) was displayed at night, on the East Fife lines with effect from 24th March, 1932. The electric tablet/electric token block system remained in use over the single track sections of the line but the signal boxes at Stravithie and Anstruther Station were abolished. On 25th October, 1932 Kilconquhar West signal box became part-time, i.e. capable of being switched out when not required:

> The tablet instrument and locking frame at Kilconquhar West Signal Box have been altered so as to admit of long section working between Largo and Elie when Kilconquhar West signal box is switched "out of circuit". When long section working is in operation, the down loop line will form the running line for up and down trains, all down line signals will stand in the clear position, the new up home signal for long section working and the up distant signal will stand in the clear position and the up home and up starting signals applicable to the up loop line will stand in the danger position.

Kilconquhar West signal box and loop were closed in 1962. Signals remained largely of LNER pattern or BR replacements but some original North British Stevens-pattern lower quadrant signals remained, particularly at Kirkland Yard and Methil

Exchanging tokens at Anstruther Junction on the last day of passenger services, 4th September 1965. *Norman Turnbull*

An Edinburgh-bound dmu passes the 1894 signal box at East Fife Central Junction. *W.A.C. Smith*

Docks. In 1962 Anstruther was resignalled using upper quadrant signals. Tablet exchange was done manually and no automatic tablet exchange apparatus was ever fitted. Towards the end of the line's existence, and after the withdrawal of passenger services, 'one engine in steam' working was in operation between Crail and Leven.

Level Crossings

On the Thornton to Anstruther line there were a number of public level crossings, many of which being operated by crossing keepers who were often the wives or family members of surfacemen who worked on the line and who occupied the crossing cottages rent-free in exchange for carrying out their gate duties. Kilconquhar was worked by the station staff who cycled along the platform. Level crossings were normally protected by signals but on the coastal line the crossings at Viewforth and Serpentine, which were normally open only for foot traffic, could be opened for vehicular traffic provided that the station-master at Largo was given prior warning so that the line could be specially protected. On the Muiredge line the train staff operated the gates.

Staff

In total over 100 persons were employed either directly on, or in consequence of, the Leven & East of Fife railways, and this number excluded those employed in coal mining. In the hierarchy of employees, the locomotive driver came first and although some trains were crewed by Haymarket or Dundee men, the large shed at Thornton (one of the largest on the North British system) and the small sub-shed at Anstruther covered the rest. Next came the station masters (originally referred to as station agents) whose salaries and duties depended on the status of their stations, and the number of porters, clerks, shunters and other staff under their control which varied from two at smaller stations such as Lundin Links to 20 or more at Leven and Anstruther. In connection with goods traffic there were carriers and, later, lorry drivers who delivered goods to consignees and in connection with passenger trains porters and local children would deliver and collect luggage and parcels. Wages were normally higher than those of local agricultural workers and the fringe benefits, such as coal and free family travel, added to the attraction of such employment. However, although it was not uncommon to begin one's railway career at a station close to home, in order to gain promotion it was usually necessary to move to pastures new and the local newspapers were full of reports of dinners and presentations to railway staff who were being transferred to other locations on the North British. Employees originally worked a 12 hour single shift but with the introduction of the 8 hour day in 1919, railwaymen eventually worked an 8 hour shift, frequently with regular overtime. A small number of canvassers and agents for other railway companies were also employed in the area, principally in connection with the fish traffic, and at Anstruther the Midland Railway had a permanent agent. In 1911 the Midland man, David McGill, left the town to travel via Siberia to China, where he had 'been appointed to a good position under the Imperial Railways' there. In the previous year Daniel McGregor, a former employee at Anstruther station was appointed first class senior station master at Natal in South Africa.

Usually relations between the public and railway staff were cordial and the North British were at pains to point out to their employees that they were the public face of the company and they encouraged them to take an interest in local affairs and to

An NBR class 'D' 0-6-0 at Leven complete with local railwaymen *circa* 1890. *Authors' Collection*

The Anstruther station staff pose on the up platform in 1956 with (*back row, left to right*) R. Milne (clerk), T. Millet (clerk), W. Stewart (goods porter) and A. Bogie (lorryman), (*front row left to right*) unknown (train guard), Mr Fraser (station maser), Tom Dunsire (porter) and Leo Dzigiewicz (porter) and a station dog (name unknown but believed to be Mr Fraser's) - in the background is, of course, the main building of Waid Academy. *Wince Stewart Collection*

be vigilant in seeking trade. The station master's lot was not always an easy one and at a railwaymen's dinner held in Anstruther Town Hall in 1899 it was said that,

> The close observation of little things is the secret of success in business and in every pursuit in life. Human knowledge is but an accumulation of small facts. It requires a fund of patience and good humour not readily met with in human beings to be a successful railway official. Some people fancy that when they have purchased a ticket that they have subsidised the entire railway system of the United Kingdom. Of course there are exceptions but what I wish to convey, that it is becoming more and more difficult every day to understand the wants and requirements of the travelling public.

A sentiment, no doubt, echoed by present-day railway officials! When Edward Fenton, the Elie station master, was promoted in 1915 it was said that he had,

> ... earned the respect of every person who had to deal with him for his assiduous and constant attention to duty, and for the good temper and courtesy with which he has always met the dozens and hundreds of angry people who had had things broken on the railway. He did not know of anything that could not be broken on the railway.

Sometimes the problems were of an internal nature – for example in 1873 the Anstruther station master, J.C. Gray, tendered his resignation because of a break-down in communication with some of the Leven & East of Fife officials that had become 'of so unpleasant a nature that he felt that he could not with any self-respect or satisfaction continue to hold the appointment' despite the fact that he 'gained for himself the respect and confidence of all with whom he has come in contact'.

Before World War I there were a handful of female ticket clerks and book-keepers employed at local stations and, due to the shortage of men in World War I, women were employed as carriage cleaners, booking clerks, porters and engine cleaners. In World War II there were female porters and signalwomen at local stations and a few of these continued to serve after the war, in a couple of cases right up to the closure of the line. Other women were employed in the refreshment rooms at Thornton and Leuchars and in the bookstalls at Leven, Elie, Anstruther and St Andrews. Sometimes employment on the railway could be a hazardous one, especially in the early days when shunting and other operations could be haphazard and potentially dangerous and the local newspapers are full of accounts of gruesome injuries, mutilations and death while in service.

The railwaymen, however, tended to socialize with each other and dinners and smoking concerts were organized in various locations such as Leven and St Andrews while the annual Railwaymen's Dance at Anstruther was a noted local event from its inception in 1897 right up until the 1960s. Presentations on the marriage, promotion and retirement of local men were avidly reported and the gifts presented included wallets of treasury notes, silver jelly dishes, marble clocks, Gladstone bags, silver-tipped walking sticks and other desirable contemporary items; contributions towards such gifts were made not only by fellow employees but also by local passengers, traders and other well-wishers. Other railwaymen's activities included local railway ambulance classes organized by the St Andrew Ambulance Association. Unions became organized on a local basis after the 1919 strike when branches of the National Union of Railwaymen were opened at Thornton, Anstruther and St Andrews.

Notable local railwaymen included James Brown, the first station master at Kilconquhar, who was a native of Anstruther and was originally employed as the local agent of the Anstruther & Leith Steamship Co. Retiring to farm in 1871 he later became a local government officer and died, aged 65, in 1893. Another original employee at Kilconquhar station was James McMillan, a native of Freshwick near Wick; at the age of 20 he was promoted to the post of station master at St Monance and later to that of station master at Cameron Bridge, a post he occupied for 30 years and was described as 'a general favourite with all classes of the travelling public'. On retirement he became a baillie and died in 1938, aged 95. Another vintage railwayman was 'Auld Will' otherwise known as James Brown who began his service at Anstruther in 1863; previously he was the agent for the 'Forth' steamer service and, as a writer in the *East Fife Observer* in 1927, the year of his death, wrote 'I suppose that the railway company by appointing him [thought that] they would capture the steamer's trade'. John Ross began his railway career at Leven on 4th July, 1858 and spent 3½ years in the audit office there before being appointed as the passenger and goods clerk there until 1864, afterwards being promoted to station master at Pittenweem until 1866 and St Monance until 1868. After a spell in America he worked for the East Coast railways as a goods agent, serving in Anstruther and elsewhere to seek to canvass the fish trade before being appointed in the same capacity at Kirkcaldy from where he retired in 1906. James Young, station master at Largo in the 1920s and 1930s was well known for the landscaping works that he carried out there and in particular for the shell decorations including a model of the 'Flying Scotsman', covered in shells. As a result of his efforts the station won the LNER 'best-kept' award for a station in its category for 1924 and 1925. In 1955 James Raeburn, the crossing keeper at Burnmill Crossing, retired after 35 years – typical of the long and faithful service given by East Fifers to their railway.

INTERESTING PRESENTATION CEREMONY AT ELIE.

A TESTIMONIAL TO THE STATION AGENT.

On Monday evening, a large and representative assembly of the residenters of Elie and Earlsferry and also the visitors, met in the general waiting room of the new station, to witness the presentation to Mr Affleck, the respected station agent, of a handsome timepiece and purse of sovereigns, and a cake basket to his wife, on the completion of his semi-jubilee at Elie station. On the motion of Mr Bethune of Blebo, Bailie Shepherd was called to the chair, and among those present were Rev. Mr and Mr Dunlop, Rev. Mr and Mrs Miller, Mrs and the Misses Duff; Mrs and Mr Andrew Russell; Dr and Mrs Borrowman; Dr and Mrs Smith; Mr Mr W. R. Ketchen, Largo; Mr and Mrs H. M. Ketchen, and Miss Paterson; Mr and Miss M'Gavin; Mrs Kirkwood, Mrs Wood, Mr Sandford, Mrs Shepherd, Miss Bethune, Miss Gray, Bailie Don, Messrs Jamieson, Foggo, Berwick, Braid, Bowman, J. and A. Morris, Smith, Crombie, O'Shaughessey, Rodger, Mr and Miss Milligan, &c. The gifts to be presented were laid out on a table, and the time piece and cake-basket were very much admired.

Mr Affleck is honoured in the *East of Fife Record* in 1902 .

Chapter Nineteen

Living with the Railway: A trainspotter's paradise

This chapter was written by Alan Goodwillie of the North British Railway Study Group in response to an appeal for information from the authors; having read it we have little hesitation in including it here as it captures the essence of a vanished era of train-spotters, school trippers and passing engines at Leven as well as describing the station and the men who worked there.

As a young boy brought up in Leven in the 1950s and 1960s, fascinated by the railway and the industries it served, I had ample time to observe the railway scene with my friends. These were more relaxed times when children could roam freely and, if they were well enough mannered and polite, would be welcomed into areas of adult life, now much restricted.

Leven station had quite a grand, if a little austere looking, main station building, built on the up platform where trains would arrive from the coast line and set off for Thornton Junction on their way to Edinburgh or Glasgow. The main station building had the station master's house on the upper level and bookstall, ticket office, ladies' waiting room (with a ladies' toilet), porter's room/parcels office and gentlemen's toilet at the far end with a drinking fountain outside on the platform. Drinking from the chained iron cup provided left a distinctive metallic taste to the mouth. It is surprising how many people passed through the station to have a quick drink and buy something from the John Menzies bookstall. The up platform also had the signal box and a couple of ancient four-wheeled coach bodies used as storage for garden implements, etc. for the station platforms and gardens. The Post Office van and the railway delivery Scammell tractor (a three-wheeled vehicle and trailer) entered from the station road onto the station's up platform to make deliveries and pick-ups directly from the trains. Unfortunately this facility was not available on the other platform and every parcel or postal bag had to be manhandled across the track on sleepered walkways by the staff. The postal sorting office was not far away on Commercial Road. You could also enter the station from the east end of the platform where there was a gated walkway across the line, which enabled access to the other platform as well as a throughway for the public to cross the line. At this end of the station there was a garage for British Road Services lorries in their green livery. Road transport was another arm of the railway at this time. Nearby there was the town laundry, which also dealt with railway deliveries.

Crossing to the down platform, which served as the platform for arrivals from Thornton and for trains going around the coast to Dundee, there was a second station building. This building had waiting rooms similar to the main building, a small store to the east end for parcels and at the west end a gentlemen's toilet; again watering facilities were provided as much as for watering the gardens as for use by the public. The sound of golf clubs being made in the building behind the station on this side could be heard all day long; many of these were sent by passenger train to find themselves exported all over the world. The main garden, which was always well-tended, was on the down side towards the west end. Several rustic cast-iron and wood benches were provided for travellers on the platform. The garden and benches formed a real suntrap and it was very pleasant to sit on a summer's day between trains and listen to the rails 'crunk' as they expanded in their chairs. The heat would also bring out the smell of creosoted sleepers to the nostrils, mixed with

No. 62418 *The Pirate* with the 12.08 pm to Crail at Thornton on 22nd April, 1957.
NBRSG, Hennigan Collection

Thornton Junction on 25th July, 1959 with the Leven and East of Fife service awaiting the connection with a down train. *NBRSG, Hennigan Collection*

the scent of geraniums and other flowers from the station gardens. During the spring and summer season hundreds of boxes of flowers would arrive from the Scilly Isles, sometimes in an ex-GWR Siphon van, and be unloaded onto the station platform, adding to the scent of this area of the station.

At the west end of the station there was a footbridge to allow passengers to cross from one platform to the other in safety. On the opposite platform the benches were often used by train crew who were glad to get a break from the stifling heat of the steam locomotive cab while parcels and newspapers were dealt with. From this footbridge you could look up the double-track line towards Thornton and have a clear view of trains approaching from some distance away as they passed first Kirkland Yard and then the old station site, which was used as a goods yard by this time. There was great competition by the local 'spotters' to recognize particular locomotives by their rear end view if the train's locomotive was travelling in reverse; the corridor connections of Gresley 'A4s' being the most welcome as they hove into view under the Glenlyon Road bridge. Looking the other way, trains could be seen approaching from the coast line which was a single-track line, although it appeared to be double due to the fact that there was a long excursion siding which went some way beyond the Scoonie Road bridge. Engine men often closed the throttle just before the bridge prior to any braking. Many of the passenger trains on the coast line were in the hands of 'Scotts' or 'Glens' which gave a distinct bustling appearance as they appeared under the bridge with a 'Tifa-Tisa' sound coming from the small valve just behind the chimney; this sound was quite characteristic of these engines running at speed. Brakes were only often applied as the train reached the east end of the platform and the characteristic 'crunk' as the brakes in the locomotives finally locked up and the locomotive came to a stand just past the footbridge. Starting away the locomotive would give a 'Tockhh' from the valve as the regulator opened and the engine moved off with a gentler 'ffuf – ffuf' typical of the older North British Railway locomotives quite unlike the sharper 'bark' of the more modern, higher-pressured, locomotives.

The station buildings dated from the improving and updating of the line during the North British regime and there was now no trace of the original station building although the site was still used as a goods yard. One of Thornton's Hunslet diesel locomotives was often to be seen there shunting wagons for the paper and textile mills, which had road access only to the yard. Constantly throughout the day could be heard the sound of material being tipped into wagons from the loading dock. There was little shelter for men working in this small yard as all the small bothies no longer seem to have been in use by this time. The yard did have a connection to the station in the form of a long loop, but this was seldom used for freight traffic, except for permanent way trains and excursion traffic which also used an additional siding which ran along the back of Harris's repair garage. The upper part of the main station building had become fairly uninhabitable during the 1950s due to leaks in the roof; the station master and his wife had taken to living further along the coast. The station ticket office smacked of everything North British with no concessions to the modern period at all, but at least it was bright and airy compared to the rather gloomy interior of the waiting rooms which had hard wooden fixed benches around the walls as well as a large heavy central table with equally heavy wooden chairs around it. From the tops of the benches to eye level there were vertical panels of wood, cream coloured, as were the walls above them. The benches, furniture and the doors were dark brown. Brown ship's linoleum was the main floor covering, although I believe a carpet was laid on the floor of the ladies' waiting room.

The broad canopy over the platform added to the darkness. As evening would come on, one of the porters would go around and light the station gas lamps inside and out.

No. 64790 leaving Elie with the 12.52 pm Crail to Thornton Junction train on 3rd October, 1959.
Roy Hamilton

No. 62475 stands in the platform as the mail is loaded at Leven in 1960. *M.B. Smith*

The hiss and smell of the lamps added to the atmosphere of the waiting room and during the winter the fire would be lit in its black iron surround, lighted coals being brought along the platform for the purpose. The smoky fug did little for the decor, which was gradually turning brown also due, in part, to the heavy smoking habits of many of the passengers. The most interesting part of the decor, by far, were the printed boards depicting paintings commissioned by the LNER to brighten up their waiting rooms. One of these was 'Grain Ships on the Orwell' which depicted two ships in evening light painted, I think, by Sam Brangwyn in the 1920s. Others were a Tyneside shipyard and more pastoral scenes although most had been graffitied, mainly in pencil although the Bic pen had made an appearance by this time. The station staff tried to keep graffiti to a minimum and were proud of their station which they tried to keep clean and tidy, despite its undisputedly Victorian period feel. Between trains, windows and stone platforms would be washed, handles and any other brass polished, interiors cleaned as well as the toilets and the brass and copper piping in the Gentlemen's toilet cleaned, even though they were open to the elements. The ash areas of the platform extensions would be regularly raked to free them of weeds, to keep them well drained and the garden maintained. The station master helped the porters at special times when inspectors were due and station garden competitions were being held. The station always looked well and it was a credit to the men who worked there, but it did not have the 'cute' feel of many of the smaller coastal stations. It was not unknown for small boys to be roped in to help with the chores and Margaret, the kind plump lady who ran the bookstall, would sometimes hand me what was left of the previous day's papers to burn in the engine's firebox on the mid-afternoon train. Most days the locomotive of this train would be a 'Glen' (mostly *Glenfinnan*, *Beasdale* or *Quoich*) or my favourite, *The Pirate*, which was one of the 'D30' 'Scott' class. The drivers were used to seeing me and most times I would end up in the cab. The papers were ceremonially taken and put aside to be burnt on the way up to Thornton.

If I had been caught in the rain, my short trousers and jersey would start to steam in the heat of the cab and my knees started to roast as the fireman worked on his fire for the journey. Looking around the cab, things were fairly spartan for both driver and fireman, there being two small folding wooden seats for the crew, the driver's one being above the screw reverser with its large wheel; mostly the crew stood to work the engine. The Reid cab with its single window on either side was fairly protective if the weather was bad when running forward, but really poor in reverse. This was even more true of the 'J35', 'J36' and 'J37' freight locomotives with their lower tenders, which could be particularly 'Baltic' when running in reverse. They would channel rain or snow or a cold east wind coming in off the North Sea into the wintery cab. Some protection could be relied on by rolling down a canvas which would be dropped down from the rear of the cab roof. This caused difficulties, for the poor driver trying to see while running in reverse. Most of the branch freight workings allowed for the engines to be turned at Anstruther, but locomotives working down to Kirkland Yard or Methil from Thornton came down in reverse, there being no turntable in either location. The coastal line was also restricted, the largest locomotive normally being the 'B1s', but I have also seen photographic evidence of a 'WD' 2-8-0 at Lundin Links station on a freight. Most times Kirkland Yard was as far as these locomotives would travel down from Thornton. I also had a friend who filmed a Deltic on the early morning paper train at Leven; needless to say the train terminated at Leven.

When you start to tell people just what was possible to see on some of the workings they are often surprised. The line down to Leven had the same restriction as the main line going through Thornton. As an enthusiast, I discovered that the

The crew of 'B1' class 4-6-0 No. 61343 pose at Largo on 4th July, 1964. *C.C. Thornburn*

Alan Goodwillie in the cab of Gresley 'V2' class 2-6-2 No. 60957 on the 8.40 pm Leven to Edinburgh service. *Alan Goodwillie Collection*

Alan Goodwillie in the cab of 'B1' class 4-6-0 No. 61344 in 1965. This locomotive-hauled the last steam train from Anstruther to Thornton. *Alan Goodwillie Collection*

most interesting train of the day had to be the lunchtime train to Edinburgh. This happened to coincide with the lunch hour at Parkhill Primary School. I had two friends, Derek Cumming (whose father worked at Thornton shed in the repair shop) and Ken Christie, who lived almost on the station as his house was next to the British Road Services depot. We would rush to meet the 12.47 which would arrive as empty coaching stock, locomotive running in reverse at the down platform. There were three regular sets of crews on a three week cycle. I always got the impression that they were Haymarket crews, who maybe liked the relatively unusual job of coming down to Leven. One crew would never allow us on board, the second crew allowed us on board but the third were the by far the most popular as they let us up, and under supervision, allowed us to take turns at driving! To add to this delight this was a Haymarket running-in turn, so it was not unusual to get a Pacific locomotive straight from the works in immaculate condition. I remember thinking how apt the name of *Hornet's Beauty* was a she rolled in gleaming in the midday sun. Being a running-in turn all number of locomotives would turn up, including 'A1s', 'A2s', 'A3s' and 'A4s', 'V2s', 'B1s', 'D49s', 'K3s', 'Clans' as well as some of the 'V1'/'V3' tanks, a return from Edinburgh to Leven being the limit they were allowed to travel. Many of the locomotives were also from sheds in the North East of England including Gateshead, Leeds and Heaton, to name a few. Sadly locomotives from York were never included – it seems that Haymarket would often use locomotives if they were stopping over for a few hours between other duties.

Ken Christie discovered that the 8.43 pm on a Saturday night was a similar duty and this would also draw us down to the station on a Saturday night, before the delights of discovering girls and the local Troxy and Regent cinemas. Unfortunately, this train was one of the first to be dieselized when one of the Swindon-built Edinburgh to Glasgow sets was used. My local knowledge of this train came in handy one Saturday night when our family became stranded at Thornton, having missed the previous branch connection. The Thornton station master explained to my father that there were no trains going down to Leven at this time of night, but I drew his attention to the fact that the Swindon set would be worked down from Edinburgh as empty coaching stock and said, 'Could we not get on that?' To my father's delight and astonishment he was told that if the train stopped in the station then some arrangement would be made with the guard so that we could travel down from Thornton on the empty train, which is exactly what happened. The guard spent much time allowing me to sit in his cab while he explained the workings of the secondary half-cab situated some way down the train. This was, as far as I am aware, a unique arrangement as far as Scottish multiple-units were concerned for it allowed the division of larger sets. They also had a buffet carriage as part of the formation. I have often wondered how often this half-cab option was used outside the maintenance depot. I do not think I have ever seen a photograph of one being worked in this way.

My father did on two occasions come to the station to photograph both the 12.47 and the 8.43 – much to my disgust at the time neither train boasted a Pacific, the 12.43 having a 'V2' and the 8.43 a 'K3'. My father was not too pleased as I had spent the whole Saturday evening pestering him as we were visiting my spinster aunts Mabel and Daisy, who lived next to the Waggon Road level crossing and whose house shook with the passing of every train. Most of the other trains which worked through Leven used locomotives based on Thornton Junction shed, but sometimes the odd Dundee or Perth engines would appear. One exception was the 'Fife Coast Express' which used stock from the LNER 'Silver Jubilee' set which was very plush. The fairings had been stripped off and the stock painted red but the chrome window surrounds were left to

'B1' class 4-6-0 No. 61146 crosses the viaduct at Largo prior to stopping at the station with the 9.08 am Glasgow (Buchanan Street) to Dundee (Tay Bridge) service on 27th July, 1963. Note the interesting mixture of stock. *Roy Hamilton*

'B1' class No. 61133 enters St Monance with a Thornton train on 10th August, 1963. *C.C. Thornburn*

sparkle and the fact that the stock was articulated gave an extra feeling of prestige to the main business train of the day. The train picked up at all stations around the coast but would run to express timings on the main line. An early start made for a good arrival time in the city with the train returning in the early evening. During the winter the service was worked by a Thornton locomotive, a 'D11' or in later years a 'B1'. The summer months saw the trains being worked through by a Perth 'Black Five', the only regular class '5' working around the coast. 'Black Five' locomotives would sometimes appear on the land cruises and on the TV train (excursions which ran using open excursion vehicles and a pair of class '5s').

The more usual diet of locomotives on the branch trains going down the coast included the 'Scotts', 'Glens', the 'D11s' which would also work the breakdown train on occasions, 'J39s' which on rare occasions would share the branch pick-up goods with the 'J35' and 'J37' classes. Once the branch had been passed to take 'B1s' they increased in regularity and eventully ousted all the older classes except for the 'J37s'. One day Jim, one of the two signalmen who worked the box, called me over to say that a brand new class of locomotive was about to appear on the branch train. Within a few minutes the locomotive arrived light engine from Thornton, to do a clearance check. It was one of three brand-new BR class '4MT' tender 2-6-0 engines delivered to Thornton that week and numbered 76111. All the station staff came out to admire the new baby which looked very smart in its freshly lined-out back livery. I personally liked the modern high stepping look of the high running plate, but some of the others were not at all convinced. The locomotive had a nice clean sharp exhaust, which was a joy to hear. I did travel behind it on a few occasions and it did accelerate well and could have a good turn of speed. It often ran on workers trains from Thornton to Rosyth, a duty it shared with 'J37s' when it was not working on the branch.

The station at Leven showed frantic activity during the summer months, when many extra trains were run and hordes of visitors from Glasgow came to stay during Fair Fortnight. Many of the trains ran non-stop from Glasgow to Leven and either terminated there or would continue round the coast. Many were worked by Eastfield locomotives but Carlisle Canal 'K3s' were temporarily drafted to Eastfield for that fortnight. They were not allowed beyond Leven. Thornton was given an additional headache when Eastfield had to use one or two of its brand-new English Electric type '1' diesels (class '20') which were not passed for the Leven line and had to be swapped at the junction. They were then parked in sidings as the crews reached the end of their shifts and went back to Glasgow that night 'on the cushions' leaving the new locomotives stranded for three days. Thornton lacked crews trained on these new locomotives. These were the days before the masses used cars and the exotic pleasures of fly-away holidays had not come to pass. Leven was well geared up for summer visitors, with many forms of entertainment. During the Fair Week a British Transport policeman was stationed at Leven to help expedite matters. The masses of people would often arrive and local children would be sent down to the station with their 'bogies' to make a bit of money carting bags etc. to the local hotels.

The policemen decided one year that they were more trouble than they were worth and banned them and, as it turned out, us from the station precincts. My friends and I were most concerned as we were going to lose out on some of our rarer locomotives. I decided on another approach, which was to go and buy a platform ticket from our friend at the booking office clerk, knowing that there was no such thing. The clerk was at first puzzled, but once he had heard the story was most sympathetic, had a word with John the station master, who immediately told the policeman that we were part of the station family as it were, and within a short time

In clouds of steam 'J37' class No. 64618 leaves Elie on a westbound service while a diesel service for Dundee (Tay Bridge) prepares to leave. *W.J.V. Anderson*

'B1' class 4-6-0 No. 61103 stands at Cameron Bridge. *Brian J. Dickson*

Derek, Ken and I were back on the platform again. - much to the chagrin of the other boys who had to make do with Station Road. The three porters, all of whom answered to the title 'Jock', had more tips, however! Later that same week we copped, a term meaning 'saw for the first time', a complete class of locomotives all in one day. The class was known as the 'K4s' and they had all been drafted through to Thornton away from the West Highland line which they had served for many years. The shed master had obviously decided to try them out on the branch that day just to help out. They did not become common on the branch, however, and only made occasional appearances despite being handsome and compact locomotives.

Three porters, one young and built like a drain pipe, a second with dark eyebrows and matching disposition and the other an old gentleman close to retirement, all had different duties to perform. The young man often drove the Scammell delivery truck and the old gentleman worked the level crossing gates at Waggon Road between certain hours, which probably coincided with the hours that the horse-drawn Co-operative delivery vans and coal lorries made their deliveries. Most vehicular traffic took the detour over the Scoonie bridge. It was not unknown for some of the delivery men to blow their whistles from some distance up the road to make sure that Jock would have the gates open in plenty of time for them to charge through. When a train was approaching the 'train due' indicator in the little cabin controlled by the signal box gave Jock ample warning. The middle porter was in charge of the station at all times. Of the two signalmen, Jim was the only one who, on occasions, would invite us all up to his box. All the equipment was gleaming and kept in excellent order and my house-proud grandmother would have been impressed. The best times to visit the box were when the station master had not yet arrived in the morning or if he was away on business. At these times would sit Jim and tell tales of derring do, of his exploits driving the 'Scotsman' and other unlikely stories. I was very pleased when one day he gave me a badge of *Walter K. Whigham* for helping to collect tickets at a very busy time. Jim would often have to cross the line to the other platform to pass the single line token to the driver, having already set the signals. He would remain at the end of the platform to collect tickets from the passengers disembarking and leaving that end of the station. Jim was a kindly man and, like many of the other men who worked at the station, a good Christian. Which comment brings us to the Sunday School Trip trains.

Scoonie Kirk had a large congregation and Sunday School and every June a trip was organized. This required a train to take us from Leven to our destination. We would be lined up with our Sunday School teachers on the platform to await our train which was sitting in the excursion siding. At the appropriate moment the locomotive, normally a 'Scott' or a 'Glen', would be signalled forward and would move slowly into the platform. With the Sunday School Superintendent shouting orders, we would be channelled into the Gresley or Thompson suburban stock, and told to sit on our springy seats and not to be tempted to jump on them. An end compartment in the Thompson stock had some prestige for spotters as it had an extra window seat. The station staff would come along and lock the compartment doors with big brass keys. A coveted door position meant that you could sit or stand by the window and throw brightly coloured streamers you as you travelled along and the train would be completely festooned by the end of the journey. As boys our favourite destination was Ladybank where the engine and stock would be taken over to the shed. We would slip away from the races for a little time to see the mid-afternoon express fish train from Aberdeen pass by. This was normally an 'A2' job and the train would come round the Ladybank curve at about 50 mph and open up as she entered the station, a stirring sight followed by a strong smell of fish. We always made it back to the field in time for

No. 64577 heads eastwards over the Dumbarnie links near Kilconquhar. *G. Fairlie*

'B1' class 4-6-0 No. 61261 beside the seaside at Largo as it crosses an eastbound dmu on the last day of passenger services. *Norman Turnbull*

our food bags. Other destinations included Kingskettle and Elie. The road followed the railway along the coast to the latter and those members of the congregation with cars would 'chase the train' and pile out onto the platform at Kilconquhar to wave and cheer our as our train rushed through.

There was always plenty of railway interest in the Levenmouth area. Freight and coal heading for Methil docks came through Cameron Bridge and Kirkland Yard behind 'B1s', 'WDs', 'J37s' and 'J38s' and Kirkland Yard had a specific purpose to sort the coal from various collieries into trainloads of the correct mix for power stations down south. This coal would be taken on to the coal hoists at Methil docks for onward shipment. Bunkering coal for the ships themselves was also important. Smaller locomotives of the 'N15' class transferred the coal round to the docks with class 'J88' and 'J83' engines used for shunting within the dock area itself. My father would often make a detour down to Methil on a winter's night, going to see my grandmother in Buckhaven. The car would bounce on the wet cobbles as I would try to see through the wet window the locomotives lined up on the ash pit that passed for Methil shed. The power station provided electricity for the town and the docks but the dim dock lights had an unusual colouration which added to the atmosphere. The railway had put in the electric lighting at Methil during the third dock extension and even the lower quadrant signals were electrically lit. A number of the 'N15s' were misfits in that they had odd chimneys and domes fitted and each was a 'character'. A newly-built 'J72' was used in the Leven coal yard and this engine also worked Donaldson's sawmill, the foundry sidings and Leven goods yard from time to time. All of these shunting and trip locomotives were withdrawn in the late 'fifties and their duties were taken over by BR 350 hp diesel shunters and a bunch of Hunslet shunters which were sent up in a cavalcade to Thornton shed on a Saturday morning for refuelling and maintenance.

I cycled down to Kirkland Yard one frosty Saturday morning, having observed the lifting gang using a crane to relay a crossover in the yard the previous week. Hoping the work was continuing, I had brought my camera to take a few photographs and I asked the yardman permission to be there but the relaying had been completed amid a great deal of blue language – an education in itself as swearing in public was not common in those days. I took several shots of 'J37' No. 64616 as it brought a long train of coal down to the yard and shunted its train. 'B1' No. 61133 also picked up a set of empties to return to the Junction. The yard was quite full of wagons and I was careful when walking as the hoar-frost was thick on the sleepers. A clear sky reflected on the locomotives which were both in good, clean condition. After the morning cavalcade of shunters sauntered past, No. 64616 passed the yard exit and points on to the National Steel Foundry on its way up to Thornton Yard with another load of empties. Unfortunately there were no 'WDs' in the yard that morning. Late at night I used to lie listening to the last train of empties being worked up the line from the yard which was about half-a-mile away. This train was normally worked by a 'WD' and 'J37', the rather mournful hooter of the 'WD' contrasting with the brighter and sharper NBR whistle as the train crews exchanged signals to each other. On a clear night the sound of the long train could be heard working its way up to Cameron Bridge.

As the yard quietened down the yard master called me over and suggested that I could come and warm myself by the bothy fire. Talking railways with the yard shunters, one of them suggested that if I was interested in engine numbers then I should take a look at the yard logs which were kept in a wooden trunk. I was amazed to discover that every locomotive had been recorded there including the fairly rare wartime workings. I wished I had asked to keep one of those logs! A similarly pleasurable frosty morning was spent at Cameron Bridge and I rode on the DS88 Ruston shunter as it tripped grain wagons into the distillery. The vapours surrounding the plant along with the soot from engines combined to give a very gloomy appearance to the buildings. Accidents could happen from time to time and on one occasion I remember a man falling from a multiple unit just beyond the platform at Cameron Bridge. He stood up right after his fall but the train continued on to Leven with the offending door wide open. Another time I was on a train that hit a sheep between Cameron Bridge and Thornton and the driver had to clear off the remains and then walk across a field to tell the farmer what had happened.

Jim, our friendly signalman at Leven, was instrumental in us 'discovering' Thornton Junction and after many tales from him we went to Thornton in a friend's father's car. Imagine our surprise in seeing an 'A4' shunting stock for the run down to Leven and eventually the 8.43 from there to Edinburgh. The locomotive looked impressive in the golden sunlight of a late summer's evening as we watched from the footbridge. We were unable to go onto the platform as there was a ticket collector's kiosk at the foot of the bridge. On seeing Jim the following week he suggested that we go by train to spot but with half-a-crown weekly pocket money and the train fare being 1*s.* 6*d.* it was clear that we could not afford many such trips. However, Jim met the train as we arrived each day and returned the ticket to us and, as long as we didn't leave the confines of Thornton station, we could reuse our tickets for the whole of their three day validity. On the third day we would leave the station and go up to the loco shed to wander among the lines of engines and see Derek's father working in the wheel lathe shop, where locomotive wheels were turned at high speed. Imagine having access to that under today's safety rules and regulations.

Trips along the coast were much rarer but included one of the last 'J37' workings on a passenger train organized by the St Andrews University Railway Society. I travelled to Dundee and met up with No. 64602 at the shed. The locomotive was looking very spick and span and various items of its anatomy were picked out in white including the buffers, number plates and door hinges - this 'bulling up' was typical of Dundee shed at that time with its diminishing number of locomotives. The engine performed well over the Tay Bridge and around the coast, St Andrews station looking very attractive with its flower baskets. Each of the coast stations was well looked after, their gardens colourful in the sunshine. Trains were passed at Crail, Anstruther and Elie with many passengers taking photographs at these stops. We returned via Ladybank and the 'J37' could still hold its own with a passenger train. We came to rest at the West station in Dundee for the final time as that station was due to close permanently later that evening. The final train on the East of Fife was a dmu and Sandy Harrison and I decided that we would travel instead on the last steam-hauled service to Anstruther and back. The locomotive was turned at Anstruther shed where we were able briefly to 'cab' it before it was placed on the train. We were the only passengers on that train but the official last train the next day, the dmu, was packed with folk but by then we had already said our sad goodbye.

Life on the East of Fife was for the most part quiet and leisurely and, being some distance from the central control, less bound by rules. The signalman at one station, I have been told, did haircuts in his box and it is said that the local coal man at another station ran off with the station master's wife. With the railway long gone I have, with a number of friends, built models of Largo, Kilconquhar, Leven and Cameron Bridge stations at different periods and gained much pleasure researching and building these projects.

Appendix One

A Brief Chronology

In compiling the following lists the authors have wherever possible included the actual (as opposed to official) dates of opening and closures, which failing they have made educated guesses based on the information available.

Sections of line

Thornton Junction to Leven – opened (P&G) 07.08.1854; doubled 19.06.1910; closed (P) 06.10.1969; (singled) 12.1970.

Leven to Kilconquhar – opened (G) to Lundin Mill 01.02.1857, open throughout (P&G) 11.08.1857, closed (P) 06.09.1965, (G) 18.07.1966, out of use 18.12.1966.

Kilconquhar to Anstruther (Old) – opened (P&G) 01.09.1863; closed (P) 06.09.1965; (G) 18.07.1966, all traffic 18.12.1966.

Anstruther Junction to Anstruther (New) – opened (P&G) 01.09.1863, closed (P) 27.12.1883 all traffic 18.12.1966.

Cameron Bridge to Muiredge – opened (G) 01.11.1868; closed Cameron Bridge to Plunks 10.1936 and Plunks to Buckhaven 3.1938.

Leven to Leven Dock – opened (G) 01.03.1880, doubled 19.06.1910, closed Methil East to Methil Docks 1991, rest of line disused from 2000.

Passenger stations

	opened	*closed*	*Note*
Anstruther (1)	01.09.1863	27.12.1883	a
Anstruther (2)	01.09.1883	06.09.1965	b
Cameron Bridge	07.08.1854	06.10.1969	
Elie	09.01.1863	06.09.1965	
Kilconquhar	11.08.1857	06.09.1965	c
Leven (1)	07.08.1854	10.08.1857	d
Leven (2)	11.08.1857	06.10.1969	
Largo	11.08.1857	06.09.1965	
Lundin Links	11.08.1857	06.09.1965	
Pittenweem	01.09.1863	01.01.1917	e
	01.02.1919	06.09.1965	
St Monance	01.09.1863	06.09.1965	f
Thornton	04.09.1848	06.10.1969	g

Notes: (a) closed when NBR services diverted to new station; (b) opened when A&StAR services commenced Pittenweem to Boarhills, station re-named 'Anstruther for Cellardyke' 31.12.1933; (c) 'Kilconquhar for Elie' from 11.08.1857 to 31.08.1863; (d) replaced by new station on different site, (e) temporary wartime closure; (f) 'St Monans' between 10.1875 and 2.1936; (g) known as 'Thornton Junction' in public and working timetables from *c*.1860 but officially renamed 01.07.1923.

Goods facilities

	opened	*closed*	Note
Anstruther Goods	01.08.1863	01.04.1966	
Burnmill Siding	*c*.1955	*c*.1962	
Cameron Bridge Goods	07.08.1854	11.09.1967	
Cameron Bridge Distillery Sidings	07.08.1854	–	a
Creosote Works (Bruce & Co.) Siding	1899	*c*.1968	
Cyanide Works Siding	1896	1905	
Donaldson & Co. Siding	1890	1959	b
Drumcaldie Distillery Siding	1897	1903	
Durie Siding	1906	*c*.1958	c
Durie Colliery Siding	04.1888	12.1906	
Durie Foundry Siding	03.1880	*c*.1968	
Earlseat Siding	22.08.2012	–	
Elie Goods	09.01.1863	06.09.1965	d
Haughmill Siding	07.08.1854	*c*.1897	
Kilconquhar Goods	11.08.1857	29.01.1965	
Kirkland Works Branch	01.01.1858	*c*.1885	
Kirkland Yard	19.06.1910	0.09.1977	
Largo Goods	11.08.1857	18.07.1965	
Leven Brickworks Siding	1859	*c*.1940	
Leven Council Siding	1920	1926	
Leven Dock Siding	01.03.1880	01.05.1986	e
Leven Goods	07.08.1854	20.01.1965	
Leven Oilcake Mills Siding	06.1910	1955	f
Lundin Links Goods	11.08.1857	06.09.1965	g
Methil Power Station	08.1965	11.2001	
Muiredge Goods	01.11.1868	01.12.1900	h
National Steel Foundry Sidings	1910	*c*.1968	
Pittenweem Goods	01.09.1863	18.07.1966	i
St Monance Goods	01.09.1863	18.07.1966	j
Silverburn Siding (1)	1857	*c*.1880	g
Silverburn Siding (2)	12.06.1888	05.10.1964	
Strathairly Siding	06.1908	1912	k
Thornton Goods	20.09.1847	26.04.1965	

Notes: Private sidings are notoriously difficult to date and closure dates relate to when they were last known to be in use, however intermittently. (a) Temporary wartime closure 1941 to 1948; still extant but little used since 2002. Also known as DCL sidings; (b) also known as Wemyss Saw and Planing Mills sidings, (c) southern section of Durie Colliery siding; (d) open for seed potato traffic until 12.1966; (e) also known as Leven Shorehead sidings; (f) also known as John Balfour Mills siding; (g) assumed opening date but possibly as late as 1859; (h) renamed Buckhaven (Old) 05.05.1887; (i)remained open for limited goods service 01.01.1917 until full service resumed 02.1919; (j) St Monans between 10.1875 and 02.1936; (k) temporarily reopened 1920.

Signal boxes

	opened	*closed*	Note
Anstruther Junction	09.09.1883	05.10.1965	a
Anstruther Station	20.12.1883	02.09.1926	
Cameron Bridge (1)	*c*.11.1868	29.05.1910	
Cameron Bridge (2)	29.05.1910	18.03.1970	b
East Fife Central Junction	21.08.1898	03.03.1970	
Elie	06.11.1898	18.12.1966	c
Kilconquhar West	28.07.1907	07.02.1962	d
Largo	29.06.1894	05.10.1965	
Leven	12.12.1885	12.10.1969	
St Monance	21.10.1900	18.12.1966	e
Thornton Central	28.04.1878	25.03.1973	f
Thornton North	03.07.1910	16.06.1980	
Thornton Station (1)	1884	03.07.1910	g
Thornton Station (2)	13.07.1910	16.06.1980	

Notes: (a) Renamed 'Anstruther' 21.06.1926; (b) Replaced by ground frame 03.1970; (c) Reduced to ground frame 05.10.1965; (d) Summer only from 25.10.1925 (e) 'St Monans' until 2.1936 (f) opened as 'Thornton Station' and renamed *c*.1884, (g) originally 'Thornton North' and renamed 13.07.1902.

Trains crossing at Kilconquhar West signal box on 18th July, 1959. *J.L. Stevenson*

Appendix Two

Locomotives working on the line, 1950 and 1965

The following locomotives were known to have been used on trains on the LEoFR coastal (main) line in 1950: Thornton (62A) locomotives are shown with the suffix (t), Dundee Tay Bridge locomotives with (d), Glasgow Eastfield locomotives with (g).

'B1' class 4-6-0s

61064 (g) 61072 (t) 61101 (d) 61102 (d) 61103 (t) 61116 (g) 61118 (t) 61146(t) 61147 (d) 61148 (t) 61243 (g)* 61260 (g) 61261 (g) 61262 (t) 61263 (t) 61278 (d) 61292 (d) 61293 (d) 61340 (g) 61342 (g) 61344 (g) 61402 (d) 61403 (d)

* - *Sir Harold Mitchell*

'D11' class 4-4-0s

62671 (g) *Bailie MacWheeble*
62672 (g) *Baron of Bradwardine*
62473 (g) *Evan Dhu*
62674 (g) *Flora McIvor*
62675 (g) *Colonel Gardiner*
62676 (g) *Jonathan Oldbuck*
62680 (g) *Lucy Ashton*
62861 (g) *Captain Craigengelt*
62682 (g) *Haystoun of Bucklaw*
62684 (g) *Wizard of the Moor*
62686 (g) *The Fiery Cross*
62687 (g) *Lord James of Douglas*
62688 (g) *Ellen Douglas*
62689 (g) *Maid of Lorn*

'D29' 'Scott' class 4-4-0s

62410 (t) *Ivanhoe*
62411 (t) *Lady of Avenel*

'D30' 'Scott' class 4-4-0s

62418 (t) *The Pirate*
62419 (d) *Meg Dodds*
62427 (d) *Dumbiedykes*
62429 (t) *The Abbot*
62434 (d) *Kettledrummle*
62436 (d) *Lord Glenvarloch*
62438 (d) *Peter Poundtext*
62439 (t) *Jingling Geordie*
62431 (d) *Kenilworth*
62442 (d) *Simon Glover*

'D33' class 4-4-0s

62460 (g) 62462 (g)

'D34' 'Glen' class 4-4-0s

62467 (t) *Glenfinnan*
62668 (t) *Glen Orchy*
62469 (g) *Glen Douglas*
62470 (g) *Glen Roy*
62472 (g) *Glen Nevis*
62474 (g) *Glen Croe*
62475 (t) *Glen Beasdale*
62477 (g) *Glen Dochart*
62478 (t) *Glen Quoich*
62779 (g) *Glen Sheil*
62480 (g) *Glen Fruin*
62482 (g) *Glen Mamie*
62485 (d) *Glen Murran*
62489 (t) *Glen Dessary*
62492 (t) *Glen Garvin*
62493 (g) *Glen Gloy*
64296 (g) *Glen Loy*
62497 (g) *Glen Mallie*
62498 (g) *Glen Moidart*

'D49' 'Shire' class 4-4-0s

62704 (t) *Stirlingshire*
62708 (t) *Argyllshire*
62713 (d) *Aberdeenshire*
62717 (t) *Banffshire*
62718 (d) *Kinross-shire*
62728 (d) *Cheshire*
62729 (t) *Rutlandshire*

'J35' class 0-6-0s

64464 (t) 64466 (t) 64474 (t) 64477 (t) 64482 (d) 64488 (t) 64485 (d) 64495 (t) 64500 (t) 64514 (t) 64516 (t) 64521 (t) 64522 (t) 64530 (d)

'J36' class 0-6-0s

65218 (t) 65291 (t) 65309 (d) 65330 (d) 65333 (d) 65345 (t)

'J37' class 0-6-0s

64530 (d) 64546 (t) 64549 (t) 64550 (t) 64564 (t) 64565 (t) 64575 (d) 64587 (d) 64596 (t)
64597 (t) 64598 (d) 64600 (t) 64602 (t) 64612 (t) 64618 (t) 64629 (t) 64635 (t)

'J38' class 0-6-0s

65901 (t) 65902 (t) 65903 (t) 65904 (t) 65907 (t) 65908 (t) 65910 (t) 65911 (t) 65913(t)
65921 (t) 65931 (t) 65932 (t)

'J39' class 0-6-0s

64786 (d) 64790 (d) 64792 (d) 64822 (d) 64892 (d) 64950 (d)

'V4' class 2-6-2s

61700 (g) *Bantam Cock* 61701 (g)

'K2' class 2-6-0s

61764 (g) *Loch Arkaig* 61774 (g) *Loch Garry* 61775 (g) *Loch Treig*
61776 (g) 61779 (g) 61781 (g) *Loch Morar*
61784 (g) 61785 (g) 61786 (g)
61792 (g) 61793(g) 61794 (g) *Loch Oich*

'K1'/'K4' class 2-6-0s

61993 (g) *Loch Long* 61994 (g) *The Great Marquess* 61997 (g) *MacCailin Mor*
61998 (g) *MacLeod of MacLeod*

'WD' 2-8-0s

90017 (d) 90071 (d) 90077 (d) 90198 (d) 90444 (d) 90463 (d) 90515 (d) 90600 (d) 90727 (d)

By 1959 the following LMS and BR standard locomotives were also seen on the line:

40054 (d) 42691 (d) 42692 (d) 43135 (g) 43136 (g) 43137 (g) 44702 (g) 44707 (g) 44787 (g)
44908 (g) 44954 (d) 44956 (g) 44557 (g) 44967 (g) 44970 (g) 44996 (g) 45164 (d) 45384 (d)
45486 (d) 44964 (d) 45164 (d) 45384 (d) 45486 (d) 46463 (d) 46464 (d) 76109 (t) 76110 (t)
76111 (t) 80123 (d) 80124 (d)

By 1965 the number of steam locomotives had greatly reduced but the following locomotives were still apparently at work on the line:

46464 (d) 61008 (g)* 61102 (d) 61103 (t) 61116 (g) 61132 (t) 61133 (t) 61140 (g) 61147 (d)
61148 (t) 61172 (d) 61180 (d) 61261 (g) 61261 (t) 61262 (d) 61262 (d) 61263 (d) 61278 (d)
61292 (d) 61293 (d) 61330 (t) 61340 (d) 61343 (t) 61403 (d) 65319 (d) 65345 (t) 64547 (d)
64558 (d) 64576 (d) 64570 (t) 64577 (d) 65488 (t) 64598 (t) 64597(d) 64602 (d) 64606 (t)
64608 (d) 64618 (t) 64620 (d) 65624 (d) 64547 (d) 64558 (d) 65602 (d) 64624 (d) 65901 (t)
65905 (t) 65907 (t) 65909 (t) 65910 (t) 65911 (t) 65914 (t) 65915 (t) 65916 (t) 65922 (t)
65925 (t) 65932 (t) 80124 (d) 90020 (t) 90117 (t) 90168 (t) 90350 (t) 90441 (t) 90444 (t)
90468 (t) 90628 (t) 90727 (t)

* - *Kudu.*

Acknowledgements

This book could not have been written and so well illustrated without the help of the following to whom the authors give their sincere thanks: Alan Brotchie, Euan Cameron, Donald Cattanach, Brian J. Dickson, George Fairlie, Brian Malaws, Graham Meacher, Alan Goodwillie, John Hurst, R.M. Casserley, Bill Lynn, Jim Page, Douglas Paul, Alan Rodgers, Mike Smith, Wince Stewart, Hamish Stevenson, Jim Stormonth, C.C. Thornburn, Norman Turnbull, Nicholas Walker, Pete Westwater and Douglas Yuill; the librarians and staff of the Advocates Library, Anstruther Public Library, the Scottish Fisheries Museum, Anstruther (which the authors highly recommend a visit to) and the National Library of Scotland and its Map Room; and especially to those railway enthusiasts of the past who are no longer with us: Ian Addison, W.J.V. Anderson (with thanks to his son Keith Verden Anderson and Brian Stephenson for permission to reproduce some of his magnificent Fife pictures), J. Boyd, H.C. Casserley, J.J. Cunningham KC, A.G. Ellis, Roy Hamilton, Willie Hennigan, L.A.C. Horne, G.A. Lyall, W.A.C. Smith, J.L. Stevenson and T.G. Hepburn and to the early photographers whose names are no longer known and to any more recent ones whose work we have failed to recognize and to whom we offer our apologies. Sincere thanks are also given to Ian Kennedy of Oakwood Press who has managed to turn all of our haphazard efforts into such a handsome and attractive book. Finally, to all of those who are seriously interested in the North British Railway and its successors up to the present day the authors would recommend contacting the North British Railway Study Group of whom they are members and full details can be found at www.nbrstudygroup.co.uk. We would welcome all comments, corrections, additions or correspondence through our publishers and we look forward to meeting our readers again in the fourth and final of our East Fife railway ramblings: *The East of Fife Central Railway* (The Lochty Branch) which will appear ere long.

The lion over the wheel - a remnant of Largo station rockery, 1976. *Brian Malaws*

Index